The so-called 'Antioch Incident' – the confrontation between the apostles Peter and Paul in Galatians 2.11–21 – continues to be a source of controversy in both scholarly and popular estimations of the emergence of the early church and the development of Pauline theology.

Paul and the Crucified Christ in Antioch offers an innovative interpretation of Paul's account of and response to this event, creatively combining historical reconstruction, detailed exegesis and theological reflection. S. A. Cummins argues that the nature and significance of the central issue at stake in Antioch – whether the Torah or Jesus Christ determines who are the people of God – gain great clarity and force when viewed in relation to a Maccabean martyr model of Judaism as now christologically reconfigured and redeployed in the life and ministry of the apostle Paul.

S. A. CUMMINS is Associate Professor of New Testament at Canadian Theological Seminary, Regina, Saskatchewan. He has taught both in Canada and the UK, and has published in academic journals.

SOCIETY FOR NEW TESTAMENT STUDIES
MONOGRAPH SERIES
General Editor: Richard Bauckham

114

PAUL AND THE CRUCIFIED CHRIST IN ANTIOCH

Paul and the Crucified Christ in Antioch

Maccabean Martyrdom and Galatians 1 and 2

STEPHEN ANTHONY CUMMINS
Canadian Theological Seminary

PUBLISHED BY THE PRESS SYNDICATE OF THE UNIVERSITY OF CAMBRIDGE
The Pitt Building, Trumpington Street, Cambridge, United Kingdom

CAMBRIDGE UNIVERSITY PRESS
The Edinburgh Building, Cambridge CB2 2RU, UK
40 West 20th Street, New York NY 10011-4211, USA
477 Williamstown Road, Port Melbourne, VIC 3207, Australia
Ruiz de Alarcón 13, 28014 Madrid, Spain
Dock House, The Waterfront, Cape Town 8001, South Africa
http://www.cambridge.org

© S. A. Cummins 2001

This book is in copyright. Subject to statutory exception
and to the provisions of relevant collective licensing agreements,
no reproduction of any part may take place without
the written permission of Cambridge University Press.

First published 2001

Printed in the United Kingdom at the University Press, Cambridge

Typeset in Times New Roman and New Hellenic Greek [AO]

A catalogue record for this book is available from the British Library

Library of Congress cataloguing in publication data

Cummins, Stephen Anthony, 1958–
 Paul and the crucified Christ in Antioch: Maccabean martyrdom and
Galatians 1 and 2 / Stephen Anthony Cummins.
   p. cm.
 Includes bibliographical references and indexes.
 ISBN 0 521 66201 X (hardback)
 1. Bible. N.T. Galatians I–II – Theology. 2. Martyrdom (Judaism).
3. Maccabees. I. Title.
BS2685.52.C86 2001
227'406–dc21   2001035585 CIP

ISBN 0 521 66201 X hardback

For Jayne,
and Leah, Hannah and Jared

CONTENTS

Preface	*page* xiii
List of abbreviations	xv
Introduction	1

PART ONE MACCABEAN MARTYRDOM

1. **Maccabean martyrdom: formative texts and traditions** 19
   1. The Maccabean revolt and the emerging Hasmonean dynasty: a historical overview 20
   2. The suffering and vindication of the people of God: a theological analysis of constitutive Maccabean texts 26
   3. Daniel's 'one like a son of man' and emerging messianic expectations 38
   4. Conclusion: the Maccabees, the Messiah and Galatians 1–2 52

2. **Maccabean martyrdom in first-century Judaism and Paul** 54
   1. Maccabean martyrdom and first-century Jewish nationalist aspirations 55
   2. Maccabean martyrdom in first-century Jewish texts and traditions 72
      An excursus: the Maccabean martyr cult in Antioch 83
   3. Maccabean martyrdom and Paul: Romans 3.21–6 and its Maccabean tradition-history 86
   4. Conclusion 90

PART TWO PAUL AND THE CRUCIED CHRIST IN ANTIOCH

3. **Paul as a paradigm of conformity to Christ: the Galatian context, conceptual framework and autobiography** 93
   1. The context. Conflict and persecution in Galatia: Paul and the Galatian church, then and now 95
   2. The conceptual framework. Messiah Jesus as eschatological redeemer: the origin and nature of Paul's gospel and mission 106
   3. Conformity to Christ. Paul's autobiography as paradigm: from Jewish zealot to Christian martyr figure (Gal. 1.13–2.10) 114
   4. Conclusion 135

4. **Jews and Christians in Antioch** 138
   1. The history and self-identity of the Jewish community in Antioch 138
   2. The messianic community in Antioch 145
   3. Conclusion 160

5. **Paul and the crucified Christ in Antioch: Galatians 2.11–14** 161
   1. The narrative substructure of Galatians 2.11–21 162
   2. Peter's table-fellowship with the Antiochene Christians and the delegation from James (Gal. 2.12a) 164
   3. Peter's withdrawal: its nature and significance (Gal. 2.11, 12–13) 173
   4. Paul's response: a defence of the truth of the gospel (Gal. 2.14) 179
   5. Conclusion 188

6. **Paul and the crucified Christ in Antioch: Galatians 2.15–21** 189
   1. Paul's remonstration: an ironical use of intra-Jewish polemic (Gal. 2.15) 190
   2. Paul's remonstration. The vindication of the righteous: the 'works of the law' versus the faithfulness of the Messiah (Gal. 2.16) 193
   3. An objection and its denial: servant(s) of sin versus servant(s) of God (Gal. 2.17) 206

4. Paul's counter-claim: Israel-in-Adam as a servant of sin (Gal. 2.18)	212
5. Paul's positive explanation: Israel-in-Adam and Israel-in-Christ (Gal. 2.19–20)	216
An excursus: the Messiah's deliverance of Israel-in-Adam (Rom. 7.1–8.11)	219
6. Paul's concluding statement: the grace of God in the death of the Messiah (Gal. 2.21)	228
7. Conclusion	229
Conclusion	**231**
Bibliography	233
Index of passages	260
Select index of Greek words and phrases	279
Index of modern authors	281
Select index of names and subjects	285

PREFACE

This monograph is an abbreviated version of a doctoral dissertation accepted by the University of Oxford in 1995, further revised in various respects while interacting with more recent significant studies. At every stage of this project I have benefited greatly from the wisdom and support of many scholars, colleagues, friends and institutions, and with appreciation here acknowledge their considerable contribution.

Above all I am indebted to my supervisor, Canon Revd Dr N. T. Wright, whose exemplary commitment to both church and academia continues to evoke fidelity to the task at hand. The Revd Dr Andrew Goddard, a soul mate in matters Pauline, was a constant and enduring source of insight and inspiration. Others who contributed in ways they may not know include Professor Christopher Rowland, the Revd Robert Morgan, Dr Jan Willem van Henten, and the examiners, Dr John Barclay and Dr William Horbury. Additionally, aspects of my research in progress were presented in the form of papers read at the annual meetings of the Canadian Society of Biblical Studies, the Society of Biblical Literature and the British New Testament Conference; and I learned much from the responses of various participants.

Concurrent with writing the dissertation I enjoyed the empathetic environment provided by students and colleagues in the Department of Religious Studies, Cheltenham & Gloucester College of Higher Education, and at Wycliffe Hall, Oxford. I am also most grateful to the Revd Dr Roger Beckwith and Mrs Mary Oxford at Latimer House who provided a quiet and congenial context within which to work. Throughout I was encouraged and assisted by a theological support group, variously comprising Sabina Elkire, Andrew Goddard, Paula Gooder, Kendall Harmon, Bruce Hindmarsh, Moyer Hubbard, Sylvia Keesmaat, Rick Simpson and Nick Townsend.

Companionship and comic relief were also provided by Norman Klassen.

Gratefully acknowledged is the considerable financial assistance provided during the period of my doctoral research by the following bodies: the Social Sciences and Humanities Research Council of Canada for successive doctoral fellowships; the Committee of Vice-Chancellors and Principals of the Universities of the United Kingdom for an Overseas Research Student Award; and Oxford University Faculty of Theology for a Hensley Henson Award.

In revising the dissertation I have enjoyed the congenial context of Canadian Theological Seminary, not least the warmth and support of successive students and colleagues. Considerable technical expertise was deployed by Mr Gerry Hall and Dr Andy Reimer. I am especially thankful for the assistance and wisdom of my colleague and friend, Dr Mabiala Kenzo. Additional thanks to Dr Robert Webb for his sound judgement and grace. Finally, I express appreciation to Professor Richard Bauckham for his careful consideration of the manuscript; to Mr Kevin Taylor, Publishing Director (Humanities and Social Sciences), for his patience and kindness; and to Jan Chapman for her remarkable attention to detail.

My vocation in biblical studies would not have taken place without the formative influence of my parents. This monograph would have been neither undertaken nor completed without the faithfulness of my wife Jayne and, *in media res*, the joy that is our three children Leah, Hannah and Jared. To them it is dedicated with love.

ABBREVIATIONS

Publications

AB	Anchor Bible
ABD	*Anchor Bible Dictionary*
ABRL	Anchor Bible Reference Library
AGJU	Arbeiten zur Geschichte des antiken Judentums und des Urchristentums
ANRW	*Aufstieg und Niedergang der römischen Welt*
ARw	*Archiv für Religionswissenschaft*
ATR	*Anglican Theological Review*
BA	*Biblical Archaeologist*
BAGD	Bauer, Arndt, Gingrich and Danker, *A Greek–English Lexicon*
BAR	*Biblical Archaeologist Reader*
BBB	Bonner biblische Beiträge
BBR	*Bulletin for Biblical Research*
BECNT	Baker Exegetical Commentary on the New Testament
BETL	Bibliotheca ephemeridum theologicarum lovaniensium
BFCT	Beiträge zur Förderung christlicher Theologie
Bib	*Biblica*
BJRL	*Bulletin of the John Rylands University Library of Manchester*
BN	*Biblische Notizen*
BNTC	Black's New Testament Commentaries
BR	*Biblical Research*
BRS	Biblical Resource Series
BTS	*Bible et terre sainte*
BU	Biblische Untersuchungen
BZ	*Biblische Zeitschrift*
BZNW	Beihefte zur ZNW
CAH	*Cambridge Ancient History*
CBQ	*Catholic Biblical Quarterly*
CBQMS	Catholic Biblical Quarterly Monograph Series
CNT	Commentaire du Nouveau Testament
CRINT	Compendia rerum iudaicarum ad novum testamentum
CTM	*Concordia Theological Monthly*
DSD	*Dead Sea Discoveries*
ETL	*Ephemerides theologicae lovanienses*
EvK	Evangelische Kommentare

EvT	Evangelische Theologie
ExpT	Expository Times
FRLANT	Forschungen zur Religion und Literatur des Alten und Neuen Testaments
FrRu	Freiburger Rundbrief
HDR	Harvard Dissertations in Religion
HeyJ	Heythrop Journal
HKNT	Handkommentar zum Neuen Testament
HNT	Handbuch zum Neuen Testament
HTKNT	Herders theologischer Kommentar zum Neuen Testament
HTR	Harvard Theological Review
HTS	Harvard Theological Studies
HUCA	Hebrew Union College Annual
ICC	International Critical Commentary
JBL	Journal of Biblical Literature
JJS	Journal of Jewish Studies
JQR	Jewish Quarterly Review
JR	Journal of Religion
JRH	Journal of Religious History
JSHRZ	Jüdische Schriften aus hellenistisch-römischer Zeit
JSJ	Journal for the Study of Judaism in the Persian, Hellenistic and Roman Periods
JSNT	Journal for the Study of the New Testament
JSNTSup	Journal for the Study of the New Testament Supplement Series
JSOT	Journal for the Study of the Old Testament
JSOTSup	Journal for the Study of the Old Testament Supplement Series
JSPSup	Journal for the Study of the Pseudepigrapha Supplement Series
JTS	Journal of Theological Studies
KEK	Kritisch-exegetischer Kommentar über das Neue Testament (Meyer)
LCL	Loeb Classical Library
LD	Lectio divina
LXX	Septuagint
LumVie	Lumière et Vie
MBT	Münster Beiträge zur Theologie
MGWJ	Monatsschrift für Geschichte und Wissenschaft des Judentums
MNTC	Moffatt NT Commentary
MT	Masoretic Text
NICNT	New International Commentary on the New Testament
NIGTC	New International Greek Testament Commentary
NovT	Novum Testamentum
NovTSup	Novum Testamentum Supplement Series
NTD	Das Neue Testament Deutsch
NTS	New Testament Studies
OTL	Old Testament Library
OTS	Oudtestamentische Studiën
PAPS	Proceedings of the American Philosophical Society
PG	J. Migne, Patrologia graeca
PL	J. Migne, Patrologia latina

PVTG	Pseudepigrapha Veteris Testamenti graece
RB	*Revue biblique*
REJ	*Revue des études juives*
RelSRev	*Religious Studies Review*
RevQ	*Revue de Qumran*
RevScRel	*Revue des sciences religieuses*
RHPR	*Revue d'histoire et de philosophie religieuses*
RMP	Rheinisches Museum für Philologie
RNT	Regensburger Neues Testament
RSR	*Recherches de science religieuse*
RSV	Revised Standard Version
SB	Sources bibliques
SBFLA	*Studii biblici franciscani liber annuus*
SBL	Society of Biblical Literature
SBLDS	SBL Dissertation Series
SBLEJL	SBL Early Judaism and Its Literature
SBLSBS	SBL Sources for Biblical Study
SBLSCS	SBL Septuagint and Cognate Studies
SBLSP	*SBL Seminar Papers*
SBS	Stuttgarter Bibelstudien
SBT	Studies in Biblical Theology
SJSJ	Supplements to the Journal for the Study of Judaism
SJT	*Scottish Journal of Theology*
SNTSMS	Society for New Testament Studies Monograph Series
SNTU	*Studien zum Neuen Testament und seiner Umwelt*
SR	*Studies in Religion/Sciences religieuses*
ST	*Studia Theologica*
STANT	Studien zum Alten und Neuen Testaments
SUNT	Studien zur Umwelt des Neuen Testaments
SVTP	Studia in Veteris Testamenti pseudepigrapha
TAPA	*Transactions of the American Philological Association*
TBei	*Theologische Beiträge*
TDNT	Kittel and Friedrich (eds.), *Theological Dictionary of the New Testament*
TextS	Texts and Studies
TGl	*Theologie und Glaube*
Th.	Theodotion
ThBl	*Theologische Blätter*
THKNT	*Theologischer Handkommentar zum Neuen Testament*
TLZ	*Theologische Literaturzeitung*
TQ	*Theologische Quartalschrift*
TRE	*Theologische Realenzyklopädie*
TSAJ	Texte und Studien zum antiken Judentum
TZT	*Tübinger Zeitschrift für Theologie*
USQR	*Union Seminary Quarterly Review*
VC	*Vigiliae christianae*
WBC	Word Biblical Commentary
WMANT	Wissenschaftliche Monographien zum Alten und Neuen Testament

WUNT	Wissenschaftliche Untersuchungen zum Neuen Testament
ZAW	*Zeitschrift für die alttestamentliche Wissenschaft*
ZBK	Züricher Bibelkommentar
ZKT	*Zeitschrift für katholische Theologie*
ZNW	*Zeitschrift für die neutestamentliche Wissenschaft*
ZST	*Zeitschrift für systematische Theologie*
ZTK	*Zeitschrift für Theologie und Kirche*

Bibliographical

ed.	editor, edited by, edition
eds.	editors, edited by
ET	English Translation
intro.	introduced by
no.	number
rev. edn	revised edition
trans.	translator, translation, translated by
vol(s).	volume(s)

INTRODUCTION

By common critical consent Paul's account of, and theological reflection upon, the so-called 'Antioch incident' (Galatians 2.11–21) remains a *crux interpretum* in New Testament studies. The various interrelated problems which it presents are complicated and wide-ranging, not least concerning the reconstruction of both Pauline theology and the development of the early church. Given that this monograph proposes a markedly new approach to this much debated subject, certain preliminary considerations are necessary and will be addressed in this introduction. First, by way of an orientation to the current scholarly state of play, I shall offer a brief outline of certain prominent antecedent evaluations of the Antioch incident, with particular reference to recent developments arising out of the so-called 'new perspective' upon Paul as exemplified in the analysis of James D. G. Dunn. In observing various deficiencies and lacunae in these estimations, I also begin to set forth the nature of this enterprise and the manner of its undertaking.

This leads to a second introductory consideration, that of method. Here an attempt is made to explicate and justify what will prove to be a range of new angles on this long-standing issue, some of which are themselves a departure from the current consensus. Foremost among these is the intention to view the Antioch incident within the framework of Maccabean martyrdom. Hence, it will be helpful to observe briefly the (albeit limited) work in this specific area – a significant subject in its own right – noting especially the recent contributions of J. W. van Henten. In so doing I shall also account for the particular reconstruction of Maccabean martyrdom offered here, and for its subsequent use in relation to a detailed analysis of Galatians 1 and 2. It will be argued throughout that the Antioch incident is the more clearly understood by reference to a Maccabean model of Judaism now christologically reconfigured and redeployed in the life and (Antiochene) ministry of Paul.

The Antioch incident: problems and proposed solutions from the patristic period to the present day

From the patristic period to the present day, the Antioch incident has been the subject of much confusion and controversy, not least because of its pivotal role in any consideration of Pauline theology and New Testament ecclesiology. It is neither possible nor necessary to replicate the detailed and comprehensive histories of interpretation already on offer.[1] Rather, the more modest aim is to provide a thumbnail sketch of certain older and influential lines of approach, and then to focus particularly upon the more recent contribution of the 'new perspective' on Paul, especially that of James D. G. Dunn. This will allow me to highlight certain significant shortcomings and oversights, and to set forth what remain as the most pressing issues demanding further inquiry and the manner in which they may be addressed.

The Antioch confrontation fuelled the cause of various unorthodox elements during the early period of the church: Marcion (d. c. AD 160) deployed it in service of his antagonism towards Judaism; the Pseudo-Clementines (early third century AD) drew upon it in a thinly veiled attack upon Paul; and Porphyry (c. 232–303) cited it in castigating Christianity itself. Indeed, in responding to such elements, and then also to one another, the Church Fathers found the Antioch incident to be a source of much consternation and controversy. Thus, for example, Irenaeus (c. 130–200), in combatting certain gnostic advocates of Paul, attempted to cast Peter in a more positive light by arguing that Paul readily submitted to the Jerusalem apostles' authority; in so doing, Irenaeus resorted to some dubious exegesis in claiming that Paul had earlier acceded to the request to circumcise Titus (see Gal. 2.5). Tertullian (c. 160–220), reacting against Marcion, also engaged in exegetical expediency. Maintaining that the two apostles shared the same basic gospel, Tertullian argued that Paul – with the zeal of a new convert – had reproached Peter because of his behaviour and not because of his preaching. While this concerted attempt both to rehabilitate Peter and to comprehend Paul upheld a long-standing tradition of them

---

[1] On what follows, and for detailed references to both primary and secondary sources, see especially Kieffer, *Foi et justification à Antioche*, pp. 81–132; and Wechsler, *Geschichtsbild und Apostelstreit*, pp. 30–295; more briefly, Mußner, *Der Galaterbrief*, pp. 146–67.

as the two great apostles (see *1 Clem*. 5-6), clearly it did so by erring on the side of Peter and at the expense of New Testament exegesis.[2]

Two even more remarkable attempts to deal with the confrontation were apparently initiated by Clement of Alexandria and Origen respectively. According to Eusebius, Clement (*c*. 150-215) simply maintained that the Peter of Galatians was not the apostle Peter, but rather another of the seventy disciples bearing the same name (see Luke 10.1).[3] Even more imaginative was the theory which seems to have begun with Origen (*c*. 185-254), to the effect that Peter and Paul were only pretending to dispute with one another. That is, though actually of common mind on the issue at hand, they devised a scene which would enable Paul to condemn more effectively the Judaizers, this being in virtue of Peter's humble acknowledgement of admonishment which would then serve as an example of the submission required of them. Although such a theory only served to impugn the integrity of *both* apostles, it was taken up and embellished by no less a figure than Chrysostom (*c*. 354-407), who afforded Peter an even more active role in the ruse.[4] It was also strongly advocated by Jerome (*c*. 342-420), and became the subject of his heated exchange of correspondence (*c*. 395-405) with Augustine (354-430). The latter sought to disabuse Jerome of a view which he regarded as undermining the truth of the gospel and the authority of scripture.[5]

Augustine's view on the matter was influential throughout the Middle Ages, with Aquinas' commentary on Galatians offering a notable and representative case in point. Aquinas (1225-74) followed Augustine in viewing Paul's public rebuke of Peter as a necessary response to an action which was an unacceptable renunciation of the truth. Nonetheless, inasmuch as it was an act of human frailty by one otherwise in receipt of the Holy Spirit, Aquinas argued that it thus constituted a venial rather than a mortal sin. How-

---

[2] See Kieffer, *Foi et justification à Antioche*, pp. 83-7, 90-4, who also notes that whereas certain Latin Fathers (e.g., Cyprian and Jerome) attempted to exculpate Peter, others emphasizing the importance of Pauline theology (e.g., Victorinus, Augustine) felt less need to exonerate him. Kieffer stresses, however, that neither side sought to discredit one or other protagonist in the forceful manner of the Pseudo-Clementines or Marcion.

[3] For a modern and scholarly, if ultimately unpersuasive, attempt to argue for a Cephas/Peter differentiation, see Ehrman, 'Cephas and Peter'.

[4] See Kieffer, *Foi et justification à Antioche*, pp. 88-9.

[5] See the discussions in Auvray, 'Saint Jérôme et Saint Augustin'; Kieffer, *Foi et justification à Antioche*, pp. 95-9.

ever, it was precisely in this respect that Luther (1483–1546) was to differ, and in so doing give expression to an immensely influential interpretation of the event.

Luther's view of the Antioch incident emerged over the course of his three commentaries on Galatians. He clearly differentiated himself from both Jerome and Aquinas: the conflict was no mere pretence, nor was Peter's action but a venial sin. Rather it was a desertion of the truth of the gospel. Luther's understanding of what precisely this meant is strongly coloured by his own struggle in relation to the ecclesiastical authorities of his day. The veneration of the saints (even of the leading apostles), the significance of papal decisions, the value of works of satisfaction, and so on, are all, for Luther, relativized in relation to the truth of a gospel whose central tenet becomes justification by grace through faith, *not* through 'works of the law' (Gal. 2.16). The Antioch incident furnished Luther with both a model of behaviour and a central doctrine by which to live. His estimation of the event has governed its interpretation – and that of Pauline theology as a whole – from his own time to the present day. Indeed, only of late has the dominant Lutheran interpretation come under strenuous re-evaluation. However, before considering this critique, one further influential approach to the Antioch incident may be noted.

F. C. Baur, founder of the so-called Tübingen school, made Galatians 2.11ff. (together with 1 Cor. 1.12ff.) a key element in his reconstruction of the historical development of the early church.[6] For Baur, the churches in Jerusalem (led by James) and Antioch (led by Paul) represented the outworking of a division between two Christian 'parties': the conservative 'Hebrews' and the more liberal 'Hellenists' (see Acts 6.1–8.4). The Antioch confrontation between Peter and Paul attested to this emergent theological divide, as the conservative faction moved towards a more retrenched Jewish legalism and the Pauline liberal faction became increasingly universal in its outlook. Baur's view has been a dominant force in nineteenth- and twentieth-century interpretations of the Antioch incident – notably in German scholarship – and it too has only recently been subjected to a concerted critique.[7]

---

[6] Baur, 'Die Christuspartei'.
[7] By Craig C. Hill, *Hellenists and Hebrews*, who argues for a much more complex and fluid estimation of the nascent church.

Introduction 5

Indeed, the combined effect of the interpretations of Luther and Baur, together with the attendant emergence of the historical-critical method, has proved to be the major impediment in more recent attempts to arrive at what might be termed an 'ecumenical' approach to the Antioch incident. Clearly the event has become the thin end of a very large theological wedge. Now at stake are such fundamental and wide-ranging issues as justification by faith, and the role of exegetical method in relation to matters of theology, dogma and praxis. Certain conciliatory efforts have been made, but the Antioch incident remains as much of a divide today as it did in its own context of origin.[8]

At this point it will be helpful to itemize certain interrelated observations arising out of this brief review of older interpretations. First, assessment of the Antioch incident has often been governed by vigorous apologetical interests. Indeed, like the protagonists in the event itself, these have often stood in direct antithesis to one another: the various attempts of certain Church Fathers to rehabilitate Peter in defence of ecclesiastical authority; conversely, Luther's appropriation of Paul in service of his critique of such authority, this also being an impetus towards his stress upon justification by faith as the essential aspect of both gospel and church. While, as modern hermeneutics has rightly stressed, the reader's own horizons cannot (or need not) be dispensed with, clearly a more circumspect approach to this most pivotal of texts was required.

Second, apologetic interest has often been at the expense of the exegesis of Galatians 2.11ff. and its context. This certainly applies to the more specious and ingenious estimations of certain Fathers, but also (as will be seen) to that of Luther. And, although the rise of the historical-critical method has in some measure addressed this matter, this critical approach has itself been constrained by its alliance to particular interpretative frameworks – whether (frequently) that of Luther or, in the case of Baur, another prevailing ideology (Hegel). Thus an exegetical rigour, informed by a clearer understanding of the wider historical and theological considerations which properly bear upon the text in question, must be taken as fundamental in any attempt to comprehend the nature and significance of the Antioch incident.

Third, the apologetical and exegetical considerations have obviously been determinative in estimations of what was at stake in the

[8] See Wechsler, *Geschichtsbild und Apostelstreit*, especially pp. 4–14.

confrontation between Peter and Paul. Augustine and Luther rightly recognized that for Paul the issue of church unity and authority was subsumed under the more fundamental question of the truth of the gospel. Luther also saw that the truth of the gospel involved a certain antithesis between 'works of the law' and the outworking of God's grace in Jesus Christ. However, as noted, his understanding of this antithesis was in considerable measure a retrojection of his own opposition to the ecclesiastical excesses of his day. This issued in a stark contrast between a legalistic Judaism preoccupied with 'works of the law' as a way of meriting salvation, and faith in Jesus Christ as that which constituted the essence of the truth of the gospel. It is precisely this estimation of the truth of the gospel – and thus of what was at stake in Antioch – which has come under considerable fire in recent years.

Finally, though Marcion was woefully misguided, and Baur's reconstruction simplistically schematic, each in their own way at least recognized that the Antioch incident had to be viewed in relation to the larger question of the nascent church's emergence from its parent body, Judaism. Their horizons constrained by apologetical considerations, older interpreters of Galatians 2.11ff. had failed to see that its theological and ecclesiological concerns – not least as these devolved upon 'the truth of the gospel' – were the more properly perceived when viewed within this historical context. This too has been taken up in more recent analyses of the Antioch incident, the most significant of which will now be considered.

In recent years a reassessment of the very nature of first-century Judaism has lead to a 'new perspective' upon Paul and, in turn, to a new evaluation of the Antioch incident in particular. Countering the traditional (Lutheran) estimation of Judaism as a legalistic religion of 'works righteousness', E. P. Sanders has argued on the basis of a massive treatment of the relevant documentation that Jewish self-understanding was essentially that of Israel as the covenant people of God. Properly understood, Torah-obedience was not about entering the covenant or earning salvation, but all about maintaining the covenant relationship with God: indeed, 'righteousness in Judaism is a term which implies the *maintenance of status* among the group of the elect'.[9] Sanders argues that, viewed from the standpoint of this 'covenantal nomism', Paul's wholesale rejection of the law was not on grounds of its legalism, but rather due to his post-

---

[9] E. P. Sanders, *Paul and Palestinian Judaism*, p. 544.

conversion perspective that '*it is not Christianity*' (earlier citing Gal. 2.21 as a notable example of this logic).[10] Furthermore, Paul's polemic against 'works of the law' (in Galatians) is not a refutation of self-righteousness, but rather a rejection of Torah-obedience as 'the condition on which Gentiles enter the people of God'.[11]

James D. G. Dunn is among a growing number of scholars who has welcomed Sanders' work as '"breaking the mould" of [modern] Pauline studies' and allowing 'a new perspective on Paul'.[12] Pursuant to Sanders, Dunn likewise stresses that 'covenantal nomism' had to do with being the people of God: it was 'what the devout Jew did to express his Jewishness, that which distinguished him from the other nations'. From this standpoint, Paul's critique of the 'works of the law' did not concern 'legalism' traditionally understood, but rather Jewish 'covenant markers' (circumcision, food laws, sabbath, and the like) which he viewed as expressing a narrow, nationalistic and ethnic conception of the people of God.[13]

It is this which governs Dunn's significant contributions to the interpretation of the Antioch incident.[14] He observes that the particular controversy over mixed table-fellowship was a function of the wider debate concerning the 'works of the law' (versus Jesus Christ) as that which demarcated the people of God. Dunn argues that although this table-fellowship was basically Torah-observant, the men from James viewed it as altogether insufficient and as a virtual abandonment of the Torah. Part of the impetus for their position was the increasingly difficult wider historical context, as

---

[10] Ibid., pp. 443, 552. Paul's logic, claims Sanders, now functions from solution (God's righteousness available in Christ) to plight (an Israel whose Torah simply does not effect righteousness); see especially pp. 442–7. See Thielman, *From Plight to Solution*, for a judicious estimation of this position.

[11] E. P. Sanders, *Paul, the Law, and the Jewish People*, p. 18.

[12] Dunn, *Jesus, Paul and the Law*, p. 184. For further favourable accounts of this paradigm shift, see Watson, *Paul, Judaism and the Gentiles*, pp. 1–22; Barclay, *Obeying the Truth*, pp. 3–6; among more recent and wide-ranging estimations, see Boyarin, *A Radical Jew*, pp. 39–56; Donaldson, *Paul and the Gentiles*, pp. 3–27. Contrast the detailed analyses of Westerholm, *Israel's Law and the Church's Faith*; Schreiner, *The Law and Its Fulfillment*; and Kruse, *Paul, the Law, and Justification*.

[13] Foremost among many publications by Dunn on this matter: *Jesus, Paul and the Law*, pp. 183–214, 215–41; *The Partings of the Ways*, pp. 117–39; 'Yet Once More – "the Works of the Law": A Response'; 'Paul and Justification by Faith'; '4QMMT and Galatians'; *The Theology of Paul the Apostle*, pp. 354ff.; together with his commentaries, *Romans* and *Galatians*. The citation is from *The Partings of the Ways*, p. 130.

[14] In addition to the aforementioned publications, see Dunn, *Jesus, Paul and the Law*, pp. 108–28, and especially 129–82.

mounting Jewish nationalism constrained the Jerusalem Jewish-Christian community to be all the more Torah-observant. Indeed, there is some evidence that the local Antiochene Jewish community – always vigilant with respect to its own identity and rights – would also have applied similar pressure.

Paul, says Dunn, would no doubt have recognized both the logic of covenantal nomism and the constraints of the broader religio-political environment. However, Paul followed the logic of faith: life within the covenant people was not tied to Torah regulations such as those governing food laws and table-fellowship; rather '*it should depend solely on faith* (2.16)'.[15] Indeed, Galatians 2.16 looms large in Dunn's estimation of Paul's response to the Antioch crisis. Here Paul starts out on common ground with Peter, and with the accepted view amongst those Jewish Christians to whom he is appealing: covenantal nomism is not called into question by, but rather more precisely defined in relation to, Jesus as Messiah (so Gal. 2.16a). That is, as the Antiochene Torah-observant table-fellowship readily indicated, belief in Jesus as Messiah did not require Jewish Christians to set aside that which traditionally characterized their response to covenant grace, nor to forsake their Jewishness. However, Paul, compelled by the view that God's verdict upon a person was contingent only upon grace through faith, then moved from qualification to an outright antithesis (in Gal. 2.16b–d):

> Perhaps, then, for the first time, in this verse faith in Jesus Messiah begins to emerge not simply as a *narrower* definition of the elect of God, but as an *alternative* definition of the elect of God ... Jesus as Christ becomes the primary identity marker which renders the others superfluous.[16]

Thus, says Dunn, we have a transition from 'a form of Jewish Messianism to a faith which sooner or later must break away from Judaism to exist in its own terms'.[17]

It is Dunn's significant new interpretation of the Antioch incident which provides the most appropriate point from which to set forth our own considerations. It may readily be agreed that the ensuing confrontation between Peter and Paul is one of competing claims about what it meant to be the people of God – a concern which

---

[15] Dunn, *The Partings of the Ways*, p. 133.
[16] Dunn, *Jesus, Paul and the Law*, p. 196.
[17] Ibid., p. 198.

embraced entrance, maintenance of status, and vindication (both present and future) as such. Furthermore, Dunn correctly points to the wider historical context within which this must be viewed, noting especially both the Maccabean period as one in which covenant markers such as food laws and circumcision were massively reinforced,[18] and to first-century Jewish nationalism as a factor in the demands for greater Torah-obedience in Antioch. These are extremely important observations. However, in a manner to be set forth momentarily, they may be given even greater weight than Dunn has allowed.

Less satisfying, however, is Dunn's evaluation of Paul's response to the confrontation, which is deficient in at least two fundamental respects. First, while it may be granted that Paul was concerned that 'works of the law' belie a narrow, nationalistic perspective, Dunn does not press with sufficient weight the question as to *why* this is the case. That is, we need to get at what Paul deemed to be the root cause of this state of affairs, in order to have a proper understanding as to why Paul rejected covenantal nomism as a legitimate and viable way of being the people of God. This matter is inextricably related to a second deficiency: Dunn's estimation of Paul's response in terms of 'the logic of faith'.

It is not at all clear that Dunn's exceptive and 'two-stage' reading of Galatians 2.16 is warranted. Certainly it is difficult to find anything comparable elsewhere in Paul. This immediately casts doubt on his claim that Jewish Christians – including Paul, at least until the Antioch incident – commonly held that belief in Jesus as Messiah simply gave greater precision to, rather than called into question, their Jewish way of life. Indeed, this raises what is in fact *the* most fundamental issue at stake in Antioch: the role of Jesus the Messiah in the outworking of divine grace. Dunn, having asked on behalf of the Antiochene Jewish Christians 'Why should a Jewish belief in a Jewish Messiah make any difference to ... Jewish distinctives', argues that Paul's response was to invoke the logic of justification by grace through faith.[19] But this only begs a series of key interrelated questions. How does Paul understand 'faith'?[20]

---

[18] See for example, Dunn, *The Partings of the Ways*, pp. 28–31.
[19] Dunn, *Jesus, Paul and the Law*, p. 196; cf. the wider discussion in *The Theology of Paul the Apostle*, pp. 371–9.
[20] Here, of course, the much debated question as to whether πίστις 'Ιησοῦ Χριστοῦ (Gal. 2.16) is to be taken as an objective genitive (so Dunn and others) or a subjective genitive (so other commentators) comes into play.

What is its relationship to the manner in which God has manifested his grace in Messiah Jesus? And, perhaps, most fundamentally, what does this have to do with Paul's remark that 'I' – in virtue of crucifixion with the Messiah – 'through the law died to the law'? Such considerations suggest that Paul's antithesis between 'works of the law' and πίστις Ἰησοῦ Χριστοῦ as the means of demarcating the people of God was a much more long-standing, constitutive and contentious aspect of his life and ministry than Dunn seems to allow. Indeed, it may be argued that it is these interrelated *Messiah*-focused considerations which were the focal point of his defence of the truth of the gospel at Antioch.

Thus this study will pursue the insights of commentators such as Dunn, while also addressing many of the remaining deficiencies and lacunae. So, for example, by way of giving greater focus and force to the important observations that (i) covenant markers such as food laws and circumcision loomed large during the Maccabean period, and (ii) Jewish nationalism may have impinged upon the Antioch confrontation, here I shall offer a two-stage reconstruction of Maccabean martyrdom as an illuminating framework against which to interpret Galatians 1–2 and its climactic Antioch incident. This will first involve an estimation of two notable interrelated aspects of the Maccabean period itself: (a) the broadly based theme of the suffering and vindication of the people of God, not least as devolved upon those willing to die for Torah, and (b) that Daniel's 'one like a son of man' figure (Dan. 7.13–14) became an important backward reference point for ongoing and widespread Jewish expectations that God would act through his Messiah to rescue, restore and rule Israel (chapter one). Both features will prove to be central elements in the later attempt to address more fully the significance of Paul's view of Jesus as Messiah and Son of God, and of the afflictions attending those conformed to him. The second stage of this enterprise will demonstrate the currency of Maccabean martyrdom within the Judaism known to Paul, both in terms of the nationalist socio-political climate and the living traditions well represented in certain texts of first-century provenance. Here I shall also offer a brief excursus on the intriguing (albeit disputed) possibility of a Maccabean martyr cult in Antioch itself (chapter two).

Despite the manifestly contentious aspects of the Antioch incident, and the force of such salient themes as coercion to Judaize and crucifixion with Christ, virtually all commentators have failed to discern its underlying theme of suffering and persecution. Alerted by the Maccabean framework, and by locating the incident within its more immediate historical and literary contexts, I shall begin to redress this oversight. First, by considering in turn Paul's past and present relations with Galatia, the conceptual framework within which he responded to the Galatian crisis, and especially his autobiographical reflections leading up to the Antioch dispute (Gal. 1.13–2.10), I shall indicate how Paul's view of his life and apostolic ministry involved an ironic reworking of the two central features outlined earlier in connection with the Maccabean background. That is, for the Paul who here offers himself as a paradigm for others, the suffering and vindicated people of God are those who remain conformed to the one in whom they believed – the martyred but now exalted Messiah Jesus – even in the face of the competing claims of their Jewish(-Christian) opponents.[21] It is from this most determinative of standpoints that Paul's relations with the Jerusalem apostles – and Peter in particular – may be properly understood (chapter three). Second, the evaluation of the Antioch incident itself will be prefaced by consideration of the external information concerning the Jewish and Christian communities in Antioch. Here particular attention is paid to evidence which suggests that their relations would have focused upon competing and often contentious claims concerning what it meant to be the faithful (and afflicted) people of God (chapter four).

Finally, I shall bring to bear the various converging lines of evidence summoned to date – not least the Maccabean framework – in attempting to offer a persuasive new analysis of Paul's account of the Antioch incident (chapter five) and his theological reflections thereon (chapter six). At this point I take up issues such as the nature of the table-fellowship, the significance of Peter's withdrawal, and Paul's defence of the truth of the gospel, and also attempt to trace his highly compressed and complex line of argumentation in Galatians 2.15–21. The governing consideration throughout is to demonstrate how Paul's claims for the outworking of God's grace in the form of the martyred and exalted Messiah (and his people), represented a dramatic and ironic reworking of the position of his Jewish(-Christian) opponents who stood in the tradition of their Maccabean forebears.

[21] The designation 'Jewish(-Christian)' is employed as a succinct way of acknowledging Paul's engagement with a broad and fluid spectrum of Jews whose understanding of and commitment to Jesus Christ differed in various respects (not least vis-à-vis Torah) from that of his own.

Questions of method, with particular reference to Maccabean martyrdom

Inasmuch as this thesis brings to bear a range of new perspectives upon the Antioch incident – a number of which are themselves somewhat contentious – it will be helpful to offer some preliminary comments concerning method. Here attention focuses upon two interrelated considerations. First, after briefly noting antecedent estimations of Jewish martyrology, I outline the intent, rationale, method and focus of the particular reconstruction of Maccabean martyrdom offered in part one. Second, this leads to various observations concerning the manner in which this reconstruction is subsequently appropriated in the detailed examination of Galatians 1 and 2 in part two.

It may be acknowledged at the outset that there are comparatively few studies on Jewish martyrology in general and Maccabean martyrdom in particular. To my knowledge, the most significant recent contributions in this area have been those of J. W. van Henten.[22] Van Henten has noted certain deficiencies in method in the course of his succinct but comprehensive review of the limited and often disparate treatments of Jewish martyrology.[23] He observes that although there have been some welcome detailed analyses of particular texts, most works have drawn upon Jewish martyrology only insofar as this has facilitated particular analyses of martyrdom in early Christian sources. Unfortunately, this has often lead to a one-sided and distorted perspective upon Jewish martyrology, such as the unwarranted retrojection of the Christian view of the martyr as 'witness [μάρτυς]' into the interpretation of antecedent Jewish texts,[24] or the debatable claim that the New Testament passion narratives (and even the gospels as a whole) are modelled upon an already extant and readily identifiable genre in the Jewish martyr literature.[25] In fact, it has even been claimed that 'Die Idee des Martyriums und die Vorstellung des Märtyrers sind christlichen

---

[22] Among several studies, note van Henten, 'Einige Prolegomena'; 'De Joodse martelaren'; 'Das jüdische Selbstverständnis'; and, especially, *The Maccabean Martyrs*; see also Heard, 'Maccabean Martyr Theology'.
[23] Notably in van Henten et al. (eds.), *Die Entstehung der jüdischen Martyrologie*, pp. 5–15.
[24] Lohmeyer, 'Die Idee des Martyriums'; Michel, 'Prophet und Märtyrer'.
[25] For example, Surkau, *Martyrien in jüdischer und frühchristlicher Zeit*, pp. 82–103.

Ursprungs.'[26] More constructive evaluations have come from Frend and Baumeister, though these too have been significantly shaped by the ultimate end in view, namely, Christian martyrdom.[27] Other more Jewish-specific studies have focused upon the disputed relationship between the Old Testament prophets and the intertestamental martyr figures,[28] or the correlation (if any) between the wider Jewish motif of the suffering righteous and the martyr.[29] But this has only served to stress further the need to try to comprehend the origin and character of Jewish martyrology on its own terms.

Towards this end van Henten has begun to forge a more critical and cogent way forward. Jewish martyr texts are to be examined in their own right, with due recognition of both the breadth of the period covered (c. 2 BC to early rabbinic literature) and the variety in form and content. The clearest points of departure are texts such as Daniel 3 and 6, and 2 Maccabees 6–7, even if they represent the outworking of earlier traditio-historical developments. Indeed, Jewish martyrology is to be approached as an essentially literary rather than historical phenomenon, while still being attentive to the relevant socio-cultural contexts. The martyr narratives must be carefully located within their wider literary framework in order that their nature and function may be more accurately discerned. The narratives themselves exhibit certain common features which focus upon the martyr's refusal to forsake the Jewish way of life, even in the face of prolonged suffering and a horrible death at the hands of his Gentile overseer.[30] From this and other considerations, van Henten rightly notes that the martyr narrative attests to important aspects of Jewish religio-cultural self-understanding. The martyr was a key representative figure whose selfless example encouraged the Jewish nation to live as the faithful people of God. Finally, as to attempts to trace lines of continuity between Jewish and Christian martyrology, van Henten urges caution in the use of correspondent motifs, affinities in literary form(s), quotations and allusions, and

---

[26] Von Campenhausen, *Die Idee des Martyriums in der alten Kirche*, p. 1.

[27] Frend, *Martyrdom and Persecution in the Early Church*; Baumeister, *Die Anfänge der Theologie des Martyriums*; see also Williams, *Jesus' Death as Saving Event*; Pobee, *Persécution and Martyrdom*.

[28] Contrast, for example, Fischel, 'Martyr and Prophet'; and Steck, *Israel und das gewaltsame Geschick der Propheten,* pp. 162–4, 252–4.

[29] Ruppert, *Der leidende Gerechte*; Kleinknecht, *Der leidende Gerechtfertigte*.

[30] Cf. the typologies in van Henten et al. (eds.), *Die Entstehung der jüdischen Martyrologie*, pp. 16, 130; van Henten, *The Maccabean Martyrs*, p. 8.

common martyrological concepts.[31] Analogies need not necessarily presuppose interdependency, and thus a linear development from Jewish to Christian martyrology cannot be taken for granted.

Generally speaking, van Henten's circumspect approach is admirable, and I have endeavoured to keep it in view throughout this undertaking. However, the nature and demands of my interests are such that I have adopted the following line of inquiry. First, the intent is not to attempt to detail the origin, trajectory and character of Jewish martyrology in general, but rather to offer a cogent (albeit circumscribed) reconstruction of Maccabean martyrdom in particular, both in terms of its context of origin and its first-century currency. Second, the rationale for this specific focus arises out of various considerations, but primarily (a) that the Maccabean crisis was an epic and symbolic event in Jewish history, and we can be confident of its influence upon certain strands of the first-century Judaism known to Paul; and (b) that, as we shall see, the Galatian crisis, and especially the issues involved in the Antioch incident (notably Torah-obedience and conformity to the crucified Christ), can be the more readily perceived when measured against that event and the traditions related thereto.

Third, hence the approach is not to restrict the inquiry to a (typological) treatment of certain martyr texts as a literary phenomenon, but to offer a more broadly based reconstruction which summons various interrelated historical, theological and literary considerations. Specifically, with respect to both the Maccabean period and its first-century influence, I attend to the wider religio-political context and also give careful consideration to a range of constitutive texts, which together attest to the vibrancy of the Maccabean model of Judaism and its martyr traditions. Fourth, the focus is deliberately upon two important interrelated themes: the suffering and vindication of the people of God and, emerging from this context, certain messianic expectations concerning an eschatological redeemer who would rescue afflicted Israel. The former is fundamentally constitutive of the evidence under review. The latter, arising in relation to Daniel 7.13–14, is a more contentious element, and it does take us beyond the Maccabean framework. However, it represents a significant lacuna in estimations of our subject and, together with the suffering and vindication theme, will prove to be of great significance in the later analysis of Galatians 1 and 2.

---

[31] See van Henten, 'The Martyrs as Heroes of the Christian people'.

This brings us to the use of the Maccabean framework in relation to Paul and the Antioch incident, about which two further interrelated points may be made. First, as already intimated, having made the case in part one, I shall then presuppose throughout part two that Maccabean traditions were very much alive, available and known to Paul. Indeed, as will be seen from the evaluation of Galatians 1 and 2, they would have been formative in Paul's life as a zealous Jew, and a factor in his interaction with Jewish(-Christian) detractors in his later vocation as a Christian apostle. Wherever and whenever Paul engaged fellow Jews – and, indeed, sought to explicate the outworking of God's design for humanity through Messiah Jesus – the Maccabean crisis and its model of Judaism could and would have informed the discussion.

Second, the degree to which these (christologically reworked) Maccabean traditions actually did influence and illuminate Paul's understanding of the Antioch incident is, ultimately, borne out by a detailed evaluation of this matter. This involves offering a series of new arguments concerning the following:

(i) the Galatian context, with particular reference to Paul's past and present Galatian ministry;
(ii) the conceptual framework governing Paul's response to the Galatian conflict;
(iii) the fundamental nature of Paul's autobiographical recollections at Galatians 1.13–2.10;
(iv) the external evidence regarding Jewish and Christian relations in Antioch;
(v) Paul's account of his Antioch confrontation with Peter at Galatians 2.11–14;
(vi) Paul's theological reflections on this dispute at Galatians 2.15–21.

At every stage I highlight how both in broad outline (the scenario in view, the schema presupposed, the narrative or argumentative sequence set forth) and in various details (themes, issues, terms) the nature and significance of each of these interrelated factors is the more clearly discerned when measured against the Maccabean framework. Thus it is not a matter of itemizing otherwise isolated verbal 'parallels' of variable merit. Rather, in essence, by examining converging lines of evidence – involving both historical reconstruction and theological argument – I present a cogent and cumulative argument in support of the case being made.

With a brief review of antecedent interpretations now in place, and some preliminary consideration given to questions of method, I may now state as succinctly as possible the basic thesis of this study: the historical and theological significance of the Antioch incident (Galatians 2.11–21) gains great clarity and weight when viewed in relation to a Maccabean martyr model of Judaism as now christologically reconfigured and redeployed in the life and (Antiochene) ministry of the apostle Paul.

PART ONE

Maccabean martyrdom

1

MACCABEAN MARTYRDOM: FORMATIVE TEXTS AND TRADITIONS

The Maccabean revolt was an epic event in Jewish history and was to loom large in the nation's collective memory as a central symbol of God's rescue and restoration of his afflicted people. In reconstructing something of the substance and significance of this event, I shall focus upon two salient and interrelated features which will also provide the fundamental frame of reference for the later examination of Galatians 1–2. First, after an introductory historical overview of both the revolt and the emerging Hasmonean dynasty, I consider certain key texts which reflect the broadly based Jewish theological perspective upon this period in terms of the suffering and vindication of the people of God. Here particular attention is paid to the crucial role of Israel's faithful representatives as portrayed by the Danielic heroes, the military leaders of the revolt and the Maccabean martyrs.

The second consideration is the more contentious claim that arising out of the wider context of the nation's longing for vindication, there emerged speculation concerning an eschatological redeemer figure who would rescue and vindicate beleaguered Israel. Specifically, it will be argued that there are certain indications that Daniel's 'one like a son of man' (Dan. 7.13–14) became an important backward reference point for ongoing and widespread expectations that God would act through his Messiah to redeem, restore and rule the nation. This correlation between the Maccabean period, the Danielic 'one like a son of man', and messianic expectation will be of some significance in the later estimation of Paul's christologically governed autobiography at Galatians 1–2.

20   Maccabean martyrdom

1. The Maccabean revolt and the emerging Hasmonean dynasty: a historical overview

In virtue of its modest but highly strategic domain, post-exilic Israel constantly struggled to forge and maintain its national identity under a series of superpower overseers: the Babylonians, the Persians and then the Greeks. Indeed, in the wake of Alexander the Great's conquests (336–323 BC), and the infighting of his successors (the Diadochi, 323–281), Israel found herself pressed between two powerful and antagonistic dynasties – the Seleucids in Syria and the Ptolemies in Egypt – each vying for control of Coele-Syria.[1] For much of the third century BC Israel was under Ptolemaic rule. However, when Antiochus III defeated Ptolemy V in 200 BC to regain control of Syro-Palestine, the Jews actively welcomed Seleucid jurisdiction. Antiochus III reciprocated by decreeing that Israel should be allowed to live according to her ancestral laws (Josephus, *Ant.* 12.138–46).[2] And it would appear that such an arrangement continued relatively unhindered during the ensuing reign of Antiochus' son, Seleucus IV Philopator (187–175) (2 Macc. 3.1–3).

All this changed dramatically with the succession of Antiochus IV (175–164), who was to take the ominous titles 'God Manifest' (Θεὸς Ἐπιφανής) and 'Victorious' (Νικηφόρος). The ongoing assimilation of Greek culture had by now been an aspect of life within Israel for many generations, and was inevitably a source of continued tension between its Jewish advocates and opponents.[3] However, it was as a result of Antiochus IV Epiphanes' vigorous Hellenization campaign that such tensions rapidly escalated into what has become known as the 'Maccabean crisis' or the 'Maccabean revolt': zealous Jews actively resisted what they deemed to be a perilous assault upon the Jewish way of life.

It may be acknowledged at the outset that the degree to which Antiochus and his Jewish sympathizers saw themselves as engaged

---

[1] Coele-Syria comprised that whole area from Egypt to the Euphrates, thus encompassing Palestine.

[2] On these decrees, see Tcherikover, *Hellenistic Civilization and the Jews*, pp. 82–9; Fischer, *Seleukiden und Makkabäer*, pp. 1–10.

[3] Jewish Hellenization in this period is classically documented in Hengel, *Judaism and Hellenism* (though see Millar, 'The Background of the Maccabean Revolution'), with a judicious summary estimation in Grabbe, *Judaism from Cyrus to Hadrian*, pp. 147–70. See also Schürer, *The History of the Jewish People*, vol. II, pp. 29–80; Feldman, *Jew and Gentile in the Ancient World*, especially pp. 3–31; and Rajak, 'The Hasmoneans and the Uses of Hellenism'.

in a political policy or religious persecution – a programme or a pogrom – continues to be the subject of considerable deliberation.[4] As we shall see, the interpretation of events which prevailed within the early Jewish tradition was decidedly theological: the crisis was the outworking of divine discipline upon an errant Israel through its Gentile enemies (Dan. 9; 2 Macc. 5.17–21; 6.12–16). Ancient Roman sources intimate that others regarded it as the attempt of a megalomaniac Antiochus to enforce enlightenment upon a parochial and exclusivistic Judaism (Polybius 26.1; Livy 41.20.1–4; Tacitus, *Hist*. 5.8).[5] Modern commentators have offered a range of more nuanced explanations. The crisis was largely:

(i) a civil war between Jewish reformers and traditionalists, later recalled as a struggle with the Seleucids;[6]
(ii) a class struggle between the pro-Hellenist aristocratic families in Jerusalem and the Hasidean-led common people, which precipitated intervention by Antiochus;[7]
(iii) Antiochus' emulation of the Roman practice of suppressing potentially subversive elements by taking control of foreign cultic practices – in this case, the Jerusalem Temple cult;[8]
(iv) Antiochus' attempt to control Jerusalem while at the same time to 'reform' Jewish ancestral customs by 'rationalizing' the Temple cult along Hellenistic lines;[9]
(v) Antiochus' all too pragmatic policy of trying to consolidate political power and finance his expansionist plans;[10]
(vi) Antiochus' attempt to restore his reputation after Rome had forced him to abandon his Egyptian campaign, by crushing all vestiges of civil strife within the lesser power Israel.[11]

---

[4] See Grabbe, *Judaism from Cyrus to Hadrian*, pp. 247–56; Gruen, 'Hellenism and Persecution: Antiochus IV and the Jews', pp. 250–64.

[5] Cf. 1 Macc. 1.41–3; 2 Macc. 6.9; 11.24. For a more moderate variation on this theme, see Schürer, *The History of the Jewish People*, vol. I, pp. 147–8. Other modern historians have, however, countered such negative estimations of Antiochus, arguing that he was an able enough ruler, if ill informed about internal Jewish affairs; so Mørkholm, *Antiochus IV of Syria*, pp. 181–91; Habicht, 'The Seleucids and Their Rivals', pp. 341–3.

[6] Bickerman(n), *The God of the Maccabees*; Hengel, *Judaism and Hellenism*, vol. II, pp. 277–303; see especially Dan. 11.30; 1 Macc. 1.11; 2 Macc. 13.3–8; *Ant*. 12.385.

[7] Tcherikover, *Hellenistic Civilization and the Jews*, pp. 186–203.

[8] Goldstein, *I Maccabees*, pp. 104–60; with modifications in *II Maccabees*, pp. 104–12.

[9] Scurlock, '167 BCE: Hellenism or Reform'.

[10] Bringmann, *Hellenistische Reform und Religionsverfolgung in Judäa*; more succinctly, 'Die Verfolgung der jüdischen Religion durch Antiochos IV'.

[11] Gruen, 'Hellenism and Persecution: Antiochus IV and the Jews', pp. 261–4.

The enormity of the crisis itself cautions against too narrow an explanation. No doubt a complex and fluid permutation of religious, political and socio-economic factors obtained. Whatever the motivations at work, a broad outline of the major protagonists, issues and events involved in the Maccabean crisis and the ensuing ascendency of the Hasmonean dynasty (c. 175–135 BC) is discernible from our principal sources, 1 and 2 Maccabees (whose theological distinctives will be examined separately below).[12]

Evidence of internal division within the Jewish leadership even prior to Antiochus IV Epiphanes' assumption of power is attested by a dispute between the High Priest Onias III and his disaffected Temple captain, Simon. The latter's appeal to Seleucid arbitration precipitated an unsuccessful assault on the Temple treasury by the Seleucid minister Heliodorus (2 Macc. 3). However, civil strife continued. In 175 BC Antiochus IV Epiphanes became king. Persuaded by financial and political considerations, Antiochus transferred the High Priesthood from Onias III ('a zealot for the laws', 2 Macc. 4.2)[13] to his brother Jason who then undertook to 'Hellenize' Jerusalem. That is, through such measures as the establishment of Greek institutions (a gymnasium and ephebate), he began to rival the city's Torah-based way of life (πολιτεία) by forming an 'Antiochia in Jerusalem'.[14] In effect, he was moving the city towards a Greek way of life (2 Macc. 4.9–17).[15]

Jason was himself usurped as High Priest only three years later by a certain Menelaus who, like his predecessor, made Antiochus

---

[12] Questions of introduction concerning 1 Maccabees (c. 135–104) and 2 Maccabees (c. late 1 BC) are succinctly reviewed in Sievers, *The Hasmoneans and Their Supporters*, pp. 1–10. Josephus' account (*J.W.* 1.31–158; *Ant.* 12.237–14.79) is largely dependent upon 1 Maccabees. Notable historical surveys/syntheses are to be found in Schürer, *The History of the Jewish People*, vol. I, pp. 125–242; Goldstein, 'The Hasmonean Revolt and the Hasmonean Dynasty'; and Grabbe, *Judaism from Cyrus to Hadrian*, pp. 269–311.

[13] Translations of the Bible and Apocrypha either follow the RSV (as here) or are the author's own.

[14] The precise significance of this is disputed. Bickerman(n), *The God of the Maccabees*, pp. 59–65, has argued that this involved the establishment of a self-governing body/community of Hellenized Jews within Jerusalem. Others argue that what is envisaged is the complete conversion of Jerusalem into a Greek *polis* (so Tcherikover, *Hellenistic Civilization and the Jews*, pp. 161–9; Bringmann, *Hellenistische Reform und Religionsverfolgung in Judäa*, pp. 84–92). See the discussion of πολιτεία (and πολίτευμα) in reference to the Antiochene Jewish community in chapter four.

[15] Grabbe, *Judaism from Cyrus to Hadrian*, p. 278, counters the general impression given by 2 Maccabees by suggesting that the paucity of evidence against Jason's actions (viz., 2 Macc. 4.14, 18–20; cf. 1 Macc. 1.15) suggests that they had considerable popular support.

a lucrative offer which the king could not refuse. Menelaus' early tenure was marked by a series of actions which exacerbated civil unrest, including complicity in the murder of Onias III in Daphne, near Antioch (2 Macc. 4.33–5).[16] Also during this period Antiochus caused much consternation by plundering the Jerusalem Temple in order to defray the costs of his first Egyptian campaign (1 Macc. 1.16–28; Dan. 11.28). Matters worsened with a disturbance in Jerusalem arising out of Jason's failed (and fatal) attempt to regain the priesthood (2 Macc. 5.5–10). Having just been compelled to withdraw from his second Egyptian campaign, Antiochus now learned that 'Judaea was in revolt' (2 Macc. 5.11). Returning to Jerusalem in 168 BC he massacred thousands of its inhabitants, sold many others into slavery and installed officials to bolster Menelaus' regime (cf. Dan. 11.29–30; 2 Macc. 5.11–14, 22–3).[17] Further drastic measures ensued two years later when Antiochus dispatched Apollonius, a commander of mercenary forces, to carry out further massacres and enslavement (cf. 2 Macc. 5.24–6; 1 Macc. 1.29–32). Additionally a fortress was erected (the Akra), and would remain a symbol of Seleucid domination until 141 BC. Over this period its constituency probably included not only the occupying forces but also foreign settlers, both captive and renegade Jews, and those 'Antiochenes' drawn together around Jason.[18]

Whether or not Antiochus' climactic assault against the Jews was enacted under the auspices of a kingdom-wide edict demanding an end to native customs (1 Macc. 1.41–3),[19] there can be little doubt that throughout Judaea in 167 BC a series of repressive decrees were targeted specifically at key Jewish customs. On pain of death for those who resisted, the Temple cult was modified in the direction of pagan practice; the sabbath and sacred festivals were profaned; circumcision was forbidden; copies of the holy Torah were burned; and various activities repugnant to Jewish sensibilities were instituted (1 Macc. 1.44–64; 2 Macc. 6.1–11; *Ant.* 12.251–4). The ultimate act of desecration was the introduction of a pagan altar into a Jerusalem Temple now rededicated to 'Zeus Olympios' (Ζεὺς

---

[16] Whether Menelaus' general conduct warrants the ascription 'extreme Hellenizer' (so Tcherikover, *Hellenistic Civilization and the Jews*, pp. 170–1) is disputed by Grabbe, *Judaism from Cyrus to Hadrian*, p. 280 (noting Bringmann, *Hellenistische Reform und Religionsverfolgung in Judäa*, pp. 93–4). But see *Ant.* 12.240.

[17] It is possible that he also once again plundered the Temple, though 2 Macc. 5.15–21 might refer to his antecedent expropriation.

[18] Cf. 1 Macc. 1.33–40; Dan. 11.39; *Ant.* 12.252.

[19] Grabbe, *Judaism from Cyrus to Hadrian*, p. 249, rejects any such idea as lacking credibility and corroboration.

'Ολύμπιος) – Daniel's 'desolating rebellion' (הפשע שמם, ἡ ἁμαρτία ἐρημώσεως) or 'desolating abomination' (שקוץ[ים] שמ[ם]), τὸ βδέλυγμα τῆς ἐρημώσεως).[20]
Apparently, early Jewish resistance was precipitated by the Phineas-like Mattathias of Modein. He killed an apostate Jew about to offer a pagan sacrifice and also the Seleucid officer who had issued the command; he then fled with his five sons into the wilderness.[21] There they, together with other dissident Jews – including certain 'Hasidim' – began a guerilla warfare initially directed against apostate Jews (1 Macc. 2.42–8).[22] Judas Maccabeus succeeded his deceased father as leader, and was able to repel the early and modest efforts made by the local Seleucid commanders Apollonius and Seron to stamp out this nascent Jewish resistance movement (1 Macc. 3.10–26). Meanwhile Antiochus, preoccupied with more important matters in the eastern provinces, appointed his friend Lysias as guardian of his son Antiochus V and vice-regent over domestic affairs (1 Macc. 3.27–37). Lysias directed Ptolemy, the military commander of Syria and Phoenicia, to dispatch the commanders Nicanor and Gorgias to deal with the revolt.[23] However, when they too were turned back, Lysias himself advanced the next year (165 BC) with an invasion force. Whether Lysias was likewise defeated (so 1 Macc. 4.26–35) or simply withdrew following negotiations (see 2 Macc. 11.6–15) is not certain. In any event, Judas was now able to retake, purify and rededicate the Temple. This epic event was thereafter annually commemorated by Hanukkah or the Festival of Lights (1 Macc. 4.36–59; 2 Macc. 10.1–8; *Ant.* 12.316–25).

With Judas attacking his Gentile neighbours (1 Macc. 5) and besieging the Akra (1 Macc. 6.18–27), Lysias undertook a second campaign against the Jews in 163 BC. After an early setback, Judas'

[20] Cf. 1 Macc. 1.54; 2 Macc. 6.2; Dan.MT/LXX 9.13, 27; 11.31; 12.11; *Ant.* 12.253. See Grabbe, *Judaism from Cyrus to Hadrian*, pp. 258–9, for a summary estimation of the disputed nature of the cult.

[21] The whole narrative concerning Mattathias is conspicuously absent from 2 Maccabees (but see 2 Macc. 5.27), and while it may be credible (Bar-Kochva, *Judas Maccabaeus*, pp. 196–9) it does pose difficulties (Sievers, *The Hasmoneans and Their Supporters*, pp. 29–37).

[22] We may posit a complex and fluid mix of factions. Attempts to discern and delineate particular groupings – whether the circles which produced Daniel, Taxo and his sons (*As. Mos.* 9), or the Hasidim (on whom see Kampen, *The Hasideans and the Origin of Pharisaism*) – have often issued in uncritical conflations and generalizations.

[23] The principal figure varies according to the sources, whether Gorgias (1 Macc. 3.38–4.25) or Nicanor (2 Macc. 8.8–36).

complete defeat seemed imminent. However, following Antiochus' death (1 Macc. 6.1–17; 2 Macc. 9), an attempted coup forced Lysias to settle terms – agreeing 'to let [the Jews] live by their laws' – and return to Antioch (1 Macc. 6.55–63; 2 Macc. 13.23–4). At this point, perhaps to placate Judas, he also executed Menelaus (*Ant.* 12.383–5), and Alcimus was appointed as the new High Priest. However, Lysias and his charge Antiochus V were themselves executed by the latter's cousin Demetrius I (1 Macc. 7.1–4; 2 Macc. 14.1–2).[24] After being confirmed in office by the new king, Alcimus persuaded him to dispatch his deputy Bacchides to deal with Judas. The fact that Alcimus had considerable Jewish backing, whereas Judas' support may have been on the wane, might be inferred from a number of the Hasidim now seeking peaceful terms from Bacchides.[25] Nonetheless, these Hasidim were summarily executed (so 1 Macc. 7.12–16) and Judas continued to be a thorn in Alcimus' side, which suggests that the revolt had by no means died out. Indeed, Nicanor, the governor of Judaea, was now sent to address the problem. After negotiations, and possibly a truce, the inevitable confrontation ensued, in which Nicanor was defeated and killed. Judas commemorated this remarkable victory by declaring another annual celebration, Nicanor's Day (1 Macc. 7.26–50; 2 Macc. 14.12–15.36). While 2 Maccabees ends on this high note, Judas had to seek an alliance with Rome and later suffered defeat and death at the hands of an avenging Seleucid army commanded by Bacchides (so 1 Macc. 8.1–9.22), suggesting that the Maccabees still fell far short of their ultimate goal of Jewish independence.

However, considerable strides in this direction were made under Judas' successor, his brother Jonathan. He was able to evade Bacchides' initial advances, gain some respite from the power vacuum created by the death of Alcimus, and was thus able to withstand the commander's later attack long enough to force a long-term withdrawal (1 Macc. 9). Later he managed to exploit to his own advantage the competing claims to the Seleucid throne of Demetrius I and Alexander Balas,[26] gaining from the latter (the eventual winner) the title of High Priest in 153 BC and governorship of Judaea a few years later (1 Macc. 10.18–20, 59–66). Such privileges were

---

[24] Demetrius had recently escaped from fourteen years in Roman custody, and now assumed the kingship earlier denied him by his uncle Antiochus IV Epiphanes.
[25] So Grabbe, *Judaism from Cyrus to Hadrian*, p. 290.
[26] The latter posing as a son of Antiochus IV Epiphanes.

confirmed and augmented by subsequent Seleucid kings likewise indebted to Jonathan's assistance: Demetrius II and Antiochus VI (1 Macc. 11).[27] Confirmation of the treaty with Rome and a new alliance with Sparta suggest that Jonathan may have been planning to declare Jewish independence (1 Macc. 12.1–23). However, the general Tryphon, with designs on the Seleucid kingship, orchestrated a ruse to entrap and eventually execute Jonathan (1 Macc. 12.39–53; 13.23).

Simon, the last Maccabee, now had widespread popular support, and shrewdly negotiated further major concessions from Demetrius II who still hoped to regain the throne. These concessions were tantamount to political autonomy, such that it could now be declared that 'In the one hundred and seventieth year [143–142 BC] the yoke of the Gentiles was removed from Israel ...' (1 Macc. 13.41). A stela which was erected and inscribed with the deeds of the Maccabean brothers confirmed Simon's status as High Priest (1 Macc. 14.27–47).[28] Amongst the achievements accredited to Simon are the removal of the occupying forces from the Akra and a renewal of the treaties with Rome and Sparta.[29] However, peace and prosperity were always under threat, both from without and within. Demetrius II's successor, Antiochus VII Sidetes, had to be repelled by Simon's sons, John and Judah; and Simon himself was murdered by his own brother-in-law, the Jewish general Ptolemy. Yet there can be little doubt that by now much had been achieved through the remarkable exploits of the Maccabean brothers. Certainly the author of 1 Maccabees is happy to leave his readers with the impression that the Hasmonean dynasty would now continue from strength to strength under the worthy succession of John Hyrcanus (1 Macc. 16.23–4).

2. The suffering and vindication of the people of God: a theological analysis of constitutive Maccabean texts

With a sense of the main historical events and figures involved in the Maccabean revolt in place, we now turn to a necessarily brief theo-

---

[27] The latter, the young son of Alexander Balas, displaced Demetrius II through the military assistance of his father's general Tryphon.

[28] That his powers required official Jewish authorization may intimate that some Jews were reluctant to grant them and that negotiations were required (see Sievers, *The Hasmoneans and Their Supporters*, pp. 119–27).

[29] 1 Macc. 13.51–2; 14.16–24; 15.15–24.

logical analysis of certain texts widely regarded as constitutive of the Jewish response to the Maccabean crisis: the Danielic stories (Daniel 1–6), and 1 and 2 Maccabees.[30] The focus throughout will be upon the fundamental and common theme of the suffering and vindication of Israel, this coming to sharpest expression in the key role of her representative figures: the Torah-obedience of the wise and servant-like Danielic heroes; the military exploits of the Maccabean 'saviours'; and the efficacious self-sacrifice of the Maccabean martyrs. While the Maccabean crisis was no doubt a more complex phenomenon than such texts allow, they nevertheless bear witness to its impact upon the hearts and minds of the Jewish nation: Israel's God had mercifully acted in and through his faithful representatives to rescue and restore his covenant people to himself.

Israel and the pagan nations: stories of contest and conflict in Daniel 1–6[31]

The overarching theme of the compositionally bipartite Daniel is God's dramatic deliverance and vindication of his suffering people Israel (and/or their representatives) from the oppressive Gentile enemy. The origin and development of the stories (Dan. 1–6) is traceable to the early post-exilic eastern Diaspora. However, their final redaction and combining with the visions (Dan. 7–12) took place in Palestine (probably Jerusalem) during the early phase of the Maccabean crisis (c. 165–155 BC) – perhaps within the circles of the משכילים, 'the wise' (Dan. 11.33–5; 12.3).[32] Thus the narratives, bound up with Daniel as a whole, were thereafter inevitably associated with the Maccabean period, just as their protagonists were seen as prototypical martyr figures.[33] The individual narratives may

---

[30] Pobee, *Persecution and Martyrdom*, pp. 14–19, offers a helpful summary review of a wide range of texts bearing upon Jewish martyr theology throughout the Second Temple period and beyond. Here comment is confined to those sources proximate to the Maccabean crisis; chapter two briefly considers additional pertinent texts and traditions in some proximity to Paul's first-century context.

[31] Notable among the many commentaries: Montgomery, *A Critical and Exegetical Commentary on the Book of Daniel* (1927); Plöger, *Das Buch Daniel* (1965); Porteous, *Daniel: A Commentary* (1965); Delcor, *Le livre de Daniel* (1971); Hartman and Di Lella, *The Book of Daniel* (1978); Goldingay, *Daniel* (1989); and Collins, *A Commentary on the Book of Daniel* (1993).

[32] So Collins, *The Apocalyptic Vision of the Book of Daniel*, pp. 54–9.

[33] Cf. Goldingay, *Daniel*, pp. xxxvi–xxx; Pobee, *Persecution and Martyrdom*, p. 14; and Agus, *The Binding of Isaac and Messiah*, pp. 41–3, on later traditions concerning Daniel and its martyr-heroes.

be considered collectively under the following convenient schema: an introductory story, and stories of contest (Dan. 2, 4, 5) and conflict (Dan. 3, 6).[34]

The programmatic opening story (Dan. 1) sets the scene and introduces the protagonists, and is notable in two key respects. First, as throughout Daniel 1–6, Daniel and his companions are characterized by their wisdom and beauty (Dan. 1.4, 17–20). This might signify that they represent the brutalized remnant of Israel now coming through the destruction and exile to fulfil and give expression to the fourth Servant Song of Isaiah (Isa. 52.13–14; 53.2–3).[35] Second, they demonstrate their exemplary character and conduct by refusing to eat the king's rich food and drink his wine. In the story's original context, this may have had less to do with strict conformity to Jewish food laws as such and more with the broader question of Gentile association and assimilation.[36] In any event, from a (post-) Maccabean standpoint it had everything to do with the willingness to suffer and die for the Torah dietary regulations so fundamental to the Jewish way of life. That Daniel and his companions were all the stronger for their ordeal attested to the power of Israel's God and the vindication of his faithful representatives.

Daniel's wisdom figures prominently in the contest stories (Dan. 2, 4, 5). In the first of these he witnesses to God's sovereignty by being the only one able to 'make known' and interpret Nebuchadnezzar's dream. Again, whatever the original significance of the four successive empires to be overthrown by a 'stone ... cut out by no human hand' (Dan. 2.34–5),[37] in the wake of the Maccabean crisis this would have been taken as the movement towards the climactic destruction of Antiochus IV Epiphanes and the ensuing inauguration of a messianic kingdom.[38] The basic message is clear. Israel's faithful God does not dwell 'with flesh' (Dan. 2.11) as if constrained by mere humanity. Rather he reveals 'mysteries' concerning what is to come: he 'will set up a kingdom which shall never

---

[34] See Humphreys, 'A Life-style for Diaspora: A Study of the Tales of Esther and Daniel'.

[35] So Efron, *Studies on the Hasmonean Period*, p. 107.

[36] So Philip R. Davies, *Daniel*, pp. 89–90; cf. Goldingay, *Daniel*, pp. 13, 18–19.

[37] Note Philip R. Davies, *Daniel*, p. 96, cautions against an uncritical correlation of Dan. 2 and 7.

[38] Collins, *The Apocalyptic Vision of the Book of Daniel*, p. 44. While the symbolic stone may well have evoked a range of associations, the inference that a messianic interpretation was operative in Josephus' day seems reasonable from his oblique handling of Dan. 2 in *Ant.* 10.203–10.

be destroyed, nor shall its sovereignty be left to another people ... and it shall stand for ever' (Dan. 2.44). A similar theme is played out in the following contests (Dan. 4, 5). Only the wise prophet-seer Daniel can 'make known' because God's spirit dwells in him (Dan. 4.6[8]; 5.13–16). Whether the fatal flaw is the Gentile king's failure to heed Daniel and 'practise righteousness' by showing mercy to the needy (Dan. 4.24[27]), or his arrogance in defiling the sacred Jerusalem Temple vessels by their usage in a pagan celebration (Dan. 5.1–4), the outcome is the same. Any such king, not least Antiochus IV Epiphanes, will be humiliated, compelled to acknowledge Israel's God, and/or suffer divine destruction (cf. Dan. 4.28–34[31–7]; 5.20–1).

A particularly sharp edge is given to the motif of the suffering and vindication of God's people by the conflict stories (Dan. 3, 6) which were especially formative in the later development of martyr narratives. The Jewish heroes are characterized by their fear of God (so the Three),[39] or by a peerless servant of God filled with the spirit and faith and thus found to be without fault (Daniel).[40] They willingly hand themselves over to affliction rather than worship another (false) god. In this way the matter is taken completely out of their adversary's hands. However the king views the ordeal, it is in fact to be seen as God's testing of the faithful. The king is defeated whether the victims do (as here) or do not (as, for example, in 2 Macc. 7) escape martyrdom, because it is precisely in and through (not from) the fiery furnace or the lion's den that their vindication is effected.[41] That is, the crucial factor is their willingness to remain faithful and, if necessary, suffer on behalf of God and his people. Of course, in this instance vindication is dramatically experienced here and now through divine deliverance in the form of a heavenly being.[42]

In sum, in the context of the Maccabean crisis, the Danielic stories – with their wise and spirit-filled protagonists – issued a clarion call to remain obedient to the Jewish way of life in the midst of affliction. Israel's faithful were to be assured that they, like their repre-

[39] Dan. 3.12, 17 (the LXX employs φοβέομαι). Antiochus IV Epiphanes is, like Nebuchadnezzar but unlike Daniel, noted for his arrogance and failure to fear God (Dan. 3.13–15; 10.12, 19; 11.12).
[40] Dan. 6.21–4[20–3]. Cf. the description of Daniel in the Greek translations: ὁ δοῦλος τοῦ θεοῦ (Dan.Th. 6.21[20]); δικαιοσύνη ἐν ἐμοὶ εὑρέθη (Dan.LXX 6.23); and ἐπίστευσεν ἐν τῷ θεῷ αὐτοῦ (Dan.Th. 6.24[23]).
[41] See Goldingay, *Daniel*, pp. 73–4.
[42] Dan. 3.25; 6.23[22]. On the former, cf. Dan.LXX 3.92 (ὁμοίωμα ἀγγέλου θεοῦ) and Dan.Th. 3.92 (ὁμοία υἱῷ θεοῦ).

sentative heroes would, even in and through their suffering, be delivered and vindicated by their sovereign God.

Israel and her conquering heroes: the saviours of the people of Israel in 1 Maccabees[43]

I have already drawn extensively from 1 Maccabees in providing a historical reconstruction of the Maccabean crisis. In what follows our attention is restricted to a brief estimation of the latent theological perspective of what is otherwise an *apologia* for the Hasmonean dynasty (see 1 Macc. 5.62).[44] Once again the emerging unifying theme is that of the suffering but ultimate vindication of the people of God. This may be illustrated by reference to various aspects of the character and conduct of the Jewish protagonists and their enemies, the nature of the struggle in which they are engaged, and the dramatic final outcome of their efforts to rescue and restore the nation.

Israel's enemy was both without and within. Certainly she had to contend with her Gentile adversaries. At best, they were devious overseers with vested interests whose policies could never be trusted. At worst, typically in Antiochus IV Epiphanes, they were tyrants whose will was enacted with brutal oppression. However, in all this they were aided by certain 'lawless men' who 'abandoned the holy covenant ... and sold themselves to do evil' (1 Macc. 1.11–16). Designated 'those troubling the people [οἱ ταράσσοντες τὸν λαὸν]', these apostate Jews were responsible for much evil 'among the sons of Israel' – with Alcimus' complicity in the deception and murder of the worthy Hasidim just one notable case in point (1 Macc. 3.5; 7.12–23).

In brief, what was at stake was the Jewish way of life; the repressive measures of the enemy, climaxing in the persecution and suffering under Antiochus IV Epiphanes, were designed to replace Israel's central symbols – Temple, Torah, circumcision, and so forth – with various Hellenistic distinctives. Given the nature of the

---

[43] On 1 Maccabees in general, see, for example, Abel, *Les livres des Maccabées* (1949); Schunck, *Die Quellen des 1. und 11. Makkabäerbuches* (1954); Goldstein, *I Maccabees* (1976); Schürer, *The History of the Jewish People*, vol. III (1986), pp. 180–5; Bar-Kochva, *Judas Maccabaeus* (1989), pp. 151–70; Sievers, *The Hasmoneans and Their Supporters* (1990), pp. 1–4; and Bartlett, *1 Maccabees* (1998).

[44] A view pressed hard by Goldstein, *I Maccabees*, pp. 4–26, 64–78.

conflict, many faithful Jews were prepared to undergo martyrdom rather than violate Torah (1 Macc. 1.57, 60–3).[45] Others, while also willing to give up their lives, decided to resort to armed resistance, galvanized under the leadership of the Maccabees.

The Maccabees are characterized throughout by their zeal: the devout Mattathias (1 Macc. 2.23–6); Judas and his 'body of faithful men [ἐκκλησίαν πιστῶν]' (1 Macc. 3.13, 45, 58–9); Jonathan, ready to imitate his martyred brother Judas (1 Macc. 9.23); and, finally, Simon, likewise willing to emulate his brothers and die for Torah, Temple and Israel (1 Macc. 13.3–6).[46] Their zeal is directed at Gentile and Jewish apostates alike. Initially this takes the form of guerilla resistance, and includes such counter-measures as tearing down pagan altars and enforcing circumcision of uncircumcised Jewish boys (1 Macc. 2.45–6). Later they are able to take vengeance upon the Gentile victimizers of their Jewish brethren (1 Macc. 5). As an emerging force, they are in a position to compel the Seleucids to settle terms – literally, 'give the right hand [διδόναι δεξιάν]' (1 Macc. 6.58) – and to allow them to live according to Torah. And under Jonathan they become power-brokers, advancing their own cause by means of treaties with the superpower Rome (1 Macc. 12.1–23).[47]

This advance towards national independence is taken as the outworking of God's covenant purposes for the nation Israel through the exemplary endeavours of her representatives, the Maccabees. They are inspired by Israel's heroes of the past (1 Macc. 4.9, 30) in whose tradition they stand (1 Macc. 2.49–60).[48] They are guided by Torah (1 Macc. 3.48, 56), and enabled by the 'strength [that]

---

[45] Martyrdom does not play the pivotal role in 1 Maccabees that (as we shall see) it clearly does in 2 Maccabees. This need not be construed as a tacit disparagement of its merits; rather, it may simply reflect the particular aim of 1 Maccabees to chart the successes of the Maccabean resistance.

[46] Cf. *Ant.* 13.198–9, including Simon's declaration to his supporters that 'you are not without a leader [ἡγεμόνος] who is able to suffer and do the greatest things on your behalf [ὑπὲρ ὑμῶν]'.

[47] Official letters figure prominently in these negotiations. A notable feature of this correspondence is a certain ambivalence: while repeated reference is made to the Gentile allies as 'brethren' (see 1 Macc. 12.6, 7, 11) – perhaps attesting to the earnestness with which the alliance is sought – there are also various disclaimers to the effect that those having Torah and God on their side have no need of such treaties (1 Macc. 12.9, 15).

[48] Cf. *Ant.* 12.290–2, referring to the exemplary forefathers 'who because of their righteousness' won many battles against much larger forces.

comes from heaven'.[49] Indeed, they are the defenders and saviours of Israel, their removal of 'those who troubled the people [οἱ ταράσσοντες τὸν λαόν]' acclaimed as that which 'turned away wrath from Israel' (1 Macc. 3.5, 8; cf. 1.64).[50] Upon their self-sacrificial deaths, they are mourned, entombed, and – like the festivals commemorating their victories (Hannukah, Nicanor's Day) – are thereafter remembered throughout the nation (1 Macc. 2.70; 9.19–21; 12.25–30).[51] The outcome of their remarkable exploits climaxes with the removal of the Gentile yoke and the inauguration of what is tantamount to a new age/order under Simon. Lauded for his 'faithfulness' and 'justice and loyalty [δικαιοσύνη καὶ πίστις]' to the nation (1 Macc. 14.35), Simon is invested with sweeping powers:

> And the Jews and their priests decided that Simon should be their leader and high priest for ever, until a trustworthy prophet should arise ... and that he should be clothed in purple and wear gold. And none of the people or priests shall be permitted to nullify any of these decisions or to oppose what he says ... Whoever acts contrary to these decisions or nullifies them shall be liable to punishment. (1 Macc. 14.41–5)

Through the divinely inspired and zealous leadership of the Maccabees, Israel's Torah-obedient Jewish way of life had been upheld. Indeed, the nation's 'saviours' had defeated the enemy – both the Gentiles and Jewish apostates – and thereby vindicated the nation and her God. Israel now enjoyed a religio-political autonomy not seen since King David. Such an achievement would live long in the memories of subsequent generations, not least amongst those first-century Jews disaffected with Roman rule, and who were thus looking for a trustworthy leader who would regain the glory of the Maccabees.

---

[49] 1 Macc. 3.19; cf. 4.10, 24. This is the familiar motif of the holy war (cf. Exod. 15.15–16; 23.27–8; etc.) which, as is the more clearly seen in 2 Maccabees and especially Daniel 7–12, presupposes the synergism of God's heavenly host with the Maccabees' earthly army.

[50] This makes explicit what is otherwise implicit in 1 Maccabees, namely, that Israel's afflictions are a function of God's anger at her covenant transgression.

[51] Cf. *Ant.* 13.212, which follows 1 Macc. 12.30 in suggesting that the seven pyramids purportedly built in connection with Jonathan's tomb 'have been preserved to this day'.

Dying and rising with Israel: the Maccabean martyrs and the rescue and restoration of Judaism in 2 Maccabees[52]

The abridgement of a five-volume work, no longer extant, by an otherwise unknown Jason of Cyrene, 2 Maccabees offers itself as a 'historical narrative' (2 Macc. 2.23–32) covering the early period of the Maccabean crisis (175–161 BC). Though complementing the information provided in 1 Maccabees 1–7, in virtue of certain distinctives it warrants examination in its own right. Here I shall briefly trace the outworking of its stated theme: the rescue and restoration of Israel via the divine grace 'from heaven to those who strove zealously on behalf of Judaism [ὑπὲρ τοῦ Ἰουδαϊσμοῦ]' (2 Macc. 2.19–22). In the course of this, particular attention will be paid to the pivotal role of the Maccabean martyrs in precipitating the climactic vindication of the afflicted people of God.

By way of an overture to the work as a whole, the introductory episode involving Heliodorus' attempt to plunder the Temple (2 Macc. 3) graphically illustrates the substance of the problem (the Gentile assault on Judaism due to Israel's sin) and foreshadows the nature of the solution (the penitent invocation of help from heaven).[53] However, once again the enemy comprises not only Gentiles – principally, the arrogant Antiochus IV Epiphanes and his dissembling emissaries – but also Jewish apostates. Foremost among the latter are the High Priests Jason and Menelaus, complicit in the nation's regression from Judaism towards Hellenism (2 Macc. 4).[54] Likewise the nadir of the Jewish suffering is reached when they are compelled to forsake the Torah and their Temple is desecrated. Such was the situation that 'a man could ... [not] so much as confess himself to be a Jew' (2 Macc. 6.6).[55] Furthermore, Israel was

---

[52] See Abel, *Les livres des Maccabées* (1949); Habicht, *2 Makkabäerbuch* (1976); Doran, *Temple Propaganda* (1981); Goldstein, *II Maccabees* (1983); Bar-Kochva, *Judas Maccabaeus* (1989), pp. 170–85; Sievers, *The Hasmoneans and Their Supporters* (1990), pp. 4–10 (who suggests that 2 Maccabees may be of Pharisaic provenance); and van Henten, *The Maccabean Martyrs* (1997), especially pp. 17–57.

[53] The designation of God as 'the Sovereign of Spirits' is otherwise absent from the LXX; however it, and the comparable 'Lord of the Spirits' (*1 Enoch* 38.2, 4, 6) seems to imply that Israel's God is ruler over all creation, both heaven and earth.

[54] Cf. Judaism (Ἰουδαϊσμός) and Hellenism (Ἑλληνισμός) (2 Macc. 2.21; 4.13), the latter the earliest known instance of the term with the extended meaning 'Greek culture'.

[55] This observation is unparalleled in the pertinent Jewish literature (so Goldstein, *II Maccabees*, p. 276).

caught up not only in a struggle to retain her national identity, but in an assault of cosmic proportion directed at the Creator God upon whom her very existence depended.[56]

What is latent in 1 Maccabees is made quite explicit by our present author: the ultimate cause of Israel's 'misery' (2 Macc. 6.9b) is that its apostasy has provoked God's wrath (2 Macc. 4.16–17; 5.17–20). However, there is yet hope of future reconciliation (2 Macc. 5.20b). Israel's present suffering is the merciful outworking of divine discipline through its Gentile enemies. It is designed both to bring Israel to repentance (thereby averting further wrath) and to increase the sins of its tormentors (thereby leading them to final destruction). In this way God will vindicate his oppressed people and uphold his own name (2 Macc. 6.12–17).

Crucial to Israel's repentance and eventual restoration is the role of the Maccabean martyrs. Just as the conflict stories in Daniel 3 and 6 indicated that deliverance could be effected in and through suffering, so in 2 Maccabees the torment and death of the martyrs is the means whereby Judas and his army receive the divine help needed to rescue and renew the nation. The first of two central martyr narratives concerns the aged scribe Eleazar (2 Macc. 6.18–31).[57] The worthy Eleazar resisted all attempts to 'compel [ἀναγκάζω]' him to violate Torah food laws by eating pork. He is 'privately [κατ' ἰδίαν]' urged by long-standing – though now apostate – acquaintances to save his life by simply 'pretending' to eat idol meat.[58] However, he refuses on the grounds that such pretence would be unworthy of his long and exemplary 'way of life [ἀναστροφή]' and could mislead Jewish youths who might assume he had indeed gone over to an alien religion. He fears God rather than his Gentile tormentors, and is confident that his self-sacrifice is known to the Lord.[59] Thus, he goes 'at once [εὐθέως]' (2 Macc. 6.28) to torture and martyrdom, leaving the nation with 'an example of nobility and a memorial of courage' (2 Macc. 6.28b–31).

---

[56] An early indication of this cosmic dimension is the heavenly warfare above Jerusalem which foreshadowed Antiochus' desecration of the Temple (2 Macc. 5.2–4; cf. 3.25–6; 10.29–30; 11.8; 12.22; 15.27).

[57] While there is little doubt that martyrdoms did occur during the Maccabean crisis (and that a work such as Daniel would have inspired such resolve), it is self-evident that these exemplary and highly thematic stories are comprised of traditional elements.

[58] Cf. ὑποκρίνομαι at 2 Macc. 6.21, 24; and ὑπόκρισις at 6.24.

[59] And confident that the nature of his self-sacrifice 'is clear to the Lord in his holy knowledge' (2 Macc. 6.30).

Eleazar's self-sacrifice is an immediate source of inspiration: seven young brothers and their admirable mother likewise defy all efforts to compel them to eat swine flesh, preferring to 'give up [προ-δίδωμι]' their lives rather than 'transgress [παραβαίνω]' the laws of their fathers (2 Macc. 7.1–42).[60] Not even promises of riches and prestige can induce them to 'turn away [μετατίθημι]' from the way of their forefathers, nor can their mother be convinced to 'persuade [πείθω]' them to forbear their resolve. The distinctive emphases of the narrative are readily discernible. (i) The martyrs are ready to suffer and die for Torah, Israel and God.[61] (ii) This is understood to be the outworking of divine discipline for sin, both theirs and that of the nation as a whole.[62] (iii) The hope which sustains them throughout is the punishment of their wicked enemies,[63] and their own reconciliation and resurrection[64] – the latter consonant with, and an eternal expression of, the covenant life to which they have been faithful (2 Macc. 7.36).

Whether these martyrdoms are to be viewed as examples of vicarious atonement or simply as efficacious is a matter which continues to be debated.[65] In any event, our author is in no doubt as to their outcome, as a select reference to the ensuing sequence of events readily illustrates. At once we learn that the early success of Judas' men – who now 'secretly entered [παρεισπορευόμενοι] the villages' and 'enlisted those who had continued in the Jewish faith [ἐν τῷ Ιουδαϊσμῷ]' – is attributable to the fact that the martyrs' sacrifice had redirected God's wrath away from Israel and towards its enemies (2 Macc. 8.1–5, 28, 30). Thus, Judas' forces now have a keener perspective upon the task at hand, always 'keeping before their eyes' the Gentiles' attempt at 'the overthrow of their ancestral way of life

---

[60] Goldstein, *II Maccabees*, pp. 296ff, discusses the vexed question of the location(s) which this narrative presupposes, positing that there may have been three versions of the story with the locus of the martyrs' place(s) of origin, arrest and death varying between Jerusalem and Antioch.

[61] 2 Macc. 7.2, 6, 9, 16, 23, 28.

[62] 2 Macc. 7.18–19, 32–3; the references to 'we' probably include Israel as a whole.

[63] 2 Macc. 7.17, 19, 31, 34–5, 37.

[64] 2 Macc. 7.9 (cf. Dan. 12.2), 11, 14, 23, 29, 33. See Kellermann, *Auferstanden in den Himmel*, pp. 38–40, 54–9.

[65] The former is rejected by many, including Kellermann, ibid., pp. 12, 78; Goldstein, *II Maccabees*, p. 337. However, the martyrs' representative role and the stated desire that their willing deaths bring about divine mercy (2 Macc. 7.37–8) might argue in its favour. See the discussion by van Henten, *The Maccabean Martyrs*, pp. 140ff., who suggests that 'the idea of a vicarious death is conveyed in 2 Macc. 7', p. 141.

[τὴν τῆς προγονικῆς πολιτείας κατάλυσιν]'. In this they are also conscious of the heavenly power at work in and through their willingness 'to die for their laws and their country' as participants in divine reconciliation (2 Macc. 8.12–29). Indeed, they are deemed invulnerable because of their zeal for the laws of their Defender God (2 Macc. 8.36).

Thus, the great reversal now quickly approaches its climax. In a dramatic juxtaposition, the arrogant Antiochus IV Epiphanes – who had presumed to 'touch the stars of heaven' – suffers an ignominious demise, whereas Judas is able to restore the Temple cult (2 Macc. 10.1–8).[66] While all the trappings of the human dimension of the ongoing warfare are always in near view, it is evident throughout that Judas' angelically assisted victories represent the outworking of God's mercy upon Israel.[67] In essence, 'the Hebrews' are invincible.[68] Thus after negotiations and a truce between Judas and Nicanor have been undermined,[69] the outcome of the ensuing final battle is never in doubt. Indeed, two events foreshadow its outcome. First, the priests implore God to defend the Temple (2 Macc. 14.34–6). Second, the author interposes another martyr narrative involving a certain Razi, revered as 'father of the Jews' and one who 'had been accused of Judaism [Ιουδαϊσμοῦ], and for Judaism [ὑπὲρ τοῦ Ιουδαϊσμοῦ] ... with all zeal risked body and life' (2 Macc. 14.37–8). Rather than suffer the ignominy of Gentile arrest and injury, Razi dies nobly by taking his own life, confident that 'the Lord of Life and spirit' would restore his body to him (2 Macc. 14.46).

With this, Judas' victory – and the realization of our author's theme – is assured. In rallying his men for the final conflict Judas urges confidence in their 'help from heaven', exhorts them from the law and the prophets, and recalls former victories (2 Macc. 15.7–9). Finally he relates a dream or waking vision in which the noble (martyred?) Onias III appeared to him together with the prophet Jeremiah. The great prophet is said to intercede in heaven on behalf of the people and their city, and furnishes Judas with a holy sword

[66] 2 Macc. 9.1–10.9; cf. Isa. 14.12–19; Dan. 8.9–12.
[67] See 2 Macc. 10.14–11.15 (especially 10.29–30, 38; 11.6, 8–9).
[68] 2 Macc. 11.13; cf. the reference to 'the Hebrews' at 2 Macc. 7.31, attesting to the common cause of both tortured and battle-fallen martyrs.
[69] Nicanor and Judas first 'exchange pledges of friendship [δοῦναι καὶ λαβεῖν δεξιάς]' and meet 'privately [κατ' ἰδίαν]' to agree terms, with mutual admiration ensuing (so 2 Macc. 14.19–25).

with which to strike down his adversaries (2 Macc. 15.12–16).[70] Thus, just as in Hezekiah's miraculous victory over Sennacherib (2 Kings 18.13–19.36), so now God manifests his righteousness in Judas' triumphant conquest of Nicanor (2 Macc. 15.20–7).

Clearly 2 Maccabees' central concern is consonant with that of the Danielic stories and 1 Maccabees: God's vindication of his afflicted faithful. More in view is the crucial role played by the exemplary Maccabean martyrs, who repudiate all efforts to compel them to transgress Torah and turn away from Judaism. Divine discipline is devolved upon their suffering and deaths on behalf of errant Israel; and it is precisely in virtue of this that God's wrath now gives way to mercy. The great reversal which reconciled Israel to God is immediately worked out in national life. The nation is rescued and restored through the divine grace manifest in the 'strength from heaven' which empowered Judas' zealous army to one miraculous victory after another. And the longevity of that achievement is attested in the fact that even in the author's own day Jerusalem still remained in the possession of the 'Hebrews' (2 Macc. 15.37).[71]

It need not be disputed that our extant (Jewish) sources have oversimplified and overdrawn various aspects of the Maccabean revolt. Its origin and outworking must have been highly complex. As already noted, the precipitous persecutions of Antiochus IV Epiphanes might well be attributed to a volatile mixture of various social and religio-political factors. Certainly the starkly portrayed dichotomy between the protagonists – Gentiles and apostate Hellenizers versus Torah-obedient Israel – masks what was no doubt a much more fluid spectrum of positions. Furthermore, the path towards eventual liberation from Seleucid rule cannot have been a rapid or effortless one. Hard-fought victories would have been accompanied by notable setbacks, and enduring success attained largely through the all too pragmatic means of military and political manoeuvring.

Nonetheless, it remains remarkable that what started out as no more than a guerrilla warfare aimed at the restoration of the desecrated Temple ended up with Israel's political independence under the Hasmonean dynasty. Thus it is not surprising that in those

---

[70] Cf. *1 Enoch* 90.19, 34.
[71] That is, those pious Jews who gave of themselves in the Jewish cause (cf. 2 Macc. 7.31; 11.13), perhaps an implied critique of those falling short of their example (such as the later Hasmoneans).

Jewish literary witnesses proximate to the period, and (as we shall see) in the memory of later generations of Jews, the Maccabean revolt was of enormous significance. Through the eyes of religio-political fervour, God had mercifully acted in and through the efficacious blood of the martyrs and the zeal of his holy army to ensure the survival of Judaism and the (re)establishment of a people covenanted to himself. However, what may already be implicit at certain junctures in a text such as 2 Maccabees, becomes all the more apparent under the deficiencies of the Hasmonean dynasty and its eventual capitulation to Roman rule in 63 BC: ever-sinful Israel continued to experience affliction from which it still required divine deliverance.

3. Daniel's 'one like a son of man' and emerging messianic expectations

In what now follows I seek to outline and trace certain aspects of a notable development which arose out of the Maccabean context in relation to Israel's continued desire for deliverance and vindication, namely, the prominent role of the Danielic 'one like a son of man' within ongoing messianic expectations concerning a redeemer and ruler figure who would rescue and restore Gentile-oppressed Israel. It may be acknowledged at the outset that the complex and disparate nature of the pertinent sources renders them open to a certain range of reconstructions.[72] Thus critics rightly resist any tendency towards a simplistic and synthesized concept of the Messiah, and similarly any monolithic estimation of the 'one like a son of man'. Nonetheless, with due caution and some indebtedness to recent illuminating studies, it may be suggested that there is evidence for the development of a prevalent and coherent Jewish messianic expectation by the time of Jesus and Paul, and that an important aspect of this entailed the messianic associations of Daniel's 'one like a son of man'. In this way the traditions and hopes of the Maccabean period continued to be a source of inspiration for an Israel whose deliverance from Seleucid oppression was superseded by subser-

---

[72] As is immediately evident when comparing even a selection of recent studies: for example, Neusner et al. (eds.), *Judaisms and Their Messiahs* (1987); Charlesworth (ed.), *The Messiah* (1992); Collins, *The Scepter and the Star* (1995); Pomykala, *The Davidic Dynasty Tradition in Early Judaism* (1995); Cohn-Sherbok, *The Jewish Messiah* (1997); Oegema, *The Anointed and His People* (1998).

vience under Roman rule. Moreover, as we shall see, this correlation between the Maccabean period, the Danielic 'one like a son of man', and messianic expectation bears upon our subsequent assessment of Paul's christologically governed remarks in Galatians 1–2.

The development of Jewish messianic expectations

The case for a widespread and coherent Jewish messianism has recently been made with some force in William Horbury's notable monograph.[73] Here messianism is broadly understood as the expectation of a pre-eminent divinely approved ruler, and is deemed traceable from its Old Testament origins to the Second Temple period and beyond. Although the extensive evidence analysed and correlated is wide-ranging, and thus at points susceptible to alternative estimations, overall Horbury's largely exegetical argument is impressive and its essential elements and conclusions worthy of careful consideration.

From at least the second century BC onwards the Old Testament designation of Israel's king as 'the Lord's Anointed' (1 Sam. 24.7[6], etc.) had often become abbreviated to '(the) Anointed' in reference to a divinely appointed ruler, and regularly used in a manner which suggested that this reference was readily and widely understood. First-century linguistic evidence of this is found in the use of μεσσίας (messias) in the Greek New Testament (at John 1.42; 4.25), which is a transliteration of the Aramaic משיחא (meshiha), corresponding to the Hebrew מָשִׁיחַ[ה] ((ha-)mashiah). This indicates that by this time the term משיחא ('the Anointed') was quite current in the Jewish vernacular; that it had a technical sense such that it required transliteration into Greek;[74] and that it corresponded to a readily recognized idea that required no further clarification. Horbury is able to show that the idiomatic and vernacular use of 'Messiah' without additional explanation is attested in a wide range of Jewish literature from at least Daniel 9.25–6 onwards.[75] From all this he concludes that the limited literary instances of the term need not be interpreted as a lack of interest in the Messiah; that consistent usage questions the common claim that messianism was divergent and

---

[73] Horbury, *Jewish Messianism*.
[74] Although, of course, the term was also translated into Greek as χριστός (christos).
[75] Horbury, *Jewish Messianism*, pp. 9–11.

variable; that messianic expectation is marked by quite detailed accounts of the Messiah's 'advent, wars, and reign'; and that Old Testament vocabulary and contexts provide the origins of the term 'Messiah' and the essential aspects of all that it subsequently evoked.[76]

Indeed, Horbury goes on to argue that the manner in which the Old Testament was edited, collected and shaped in the post-exilic period reflects a vibrant ongoing messianic hope. Here an important contributing factor was the wider political context within which this process took place. The prominent role and influence of monarchical governments during wide-ranging conflicts of the Persian and Greek period, reinforced by non-Israelite oracles conveying nationalist hopes and fears, clearly influenced Israel's own concept of kingship and nationalism. The impact of this is especially evident in the growth of the Old Testament, not least in the way in which the Pentateuch, Prophets and Psalms taken together 'offer a single striking series of oracles expressing national aspiration in the form of hopes for a coming king'.[77] Moreover, within the Old Testament itself one may discern certain 'messianic prototypes' which also collectively contribute to broadly based developments in Jewish messianic expectation: Moses; David; the servant of Isaiah 53; the smitten shepherd of Zechariah 13.7; and the 'Son of man' in Daniel 7.[78] In sum, the Old Testament offers ample evidence of a deep-rooted, cohesive and influential Jewish messianic expectation at the beginning of the Second Temple period.

That being the case, it is not surprising that Horbury finds reasons to challenge the claim that there was a 'messianological vacuum' between the fifth and second centuries.[79] In addition to the evidence in connection with the formation of the Old Testament, Horbury discusses in some detail a number of important elements.[80] He notes an intense focus in the biblical literature of the Persian period upon both God as king and the kingdom of God (albeit without explicit reference to a Messiah figure). There is also a developed range of

---

[76] Ibid., p. 12.
[77] Ibid., pp. 26–7, with various pertinent references at pp. 27–9. This would lead to later developments as other oracles were interpreted messianically, and with greater precision concerning the anticipated profile of the expected ruler, as is evident from the second-century LXX (at Num. 24.7; Hab. 2.3) and Qumran's 4Q285, so pp. 29–30.
[78] Ibid., pp. 31–4.
[79] So especially Collins, *The Scepter and the Star*, pp. 31–8, 40.
[80] Horbury, *Jewish Messianism*, pp. 36–63.

messianic interpretations in the period after Alexander the Great, involving a sequence of exegetical interconnections, which are built into the LXX Pentateuch. Moreover, Horbury argues that the absence of explicit reference to messianic hope in most of the largely second-century texts of the Apocrypha is mitigated by the Davidic expectation evident in Sirach and 1 Maccabees. Additionally, a lively and expanding messianism during this period is nonetheless readily apparent in the roughly contemporary Qumran texts, a development further attested in the apocalypses from the end of the Herodian period (e.g., 4 Ezra and *2 Baruch*). The cumulative weight of the available data causes Horbury to conclude that messianic expectation was more persistent and active throughout the Second Temple period than has normally been recognized.

Yet given the sheer range of the evidence in question, can it also be claimed that this Jewish messianism was coherent and concentrated upon the expectation of a divinely approved king? Horbury considers two factors which together suggest an affirmative answer. In biblical and post-biblical passages the hoped-for Messiah is closely connected with the sequence of Jewish kings and rulers, a continual association which provided a certain cohesion to messianic expectation. Additionally, the messianic interpretation of Jewish rule can also be seen in certain significant respects as a counterpart to prevailing conceptions of the Gentile ruler-cult, this being a further important factor in coalescing and shaping Jewish messianic expectations and rhetoric during this period.[81]

Horbury then complements his positive case for coherence by countering the common claim that there are at least three aspects of Jewish messianism which seem to confound attempts to argue for coherence. First, he dismisses the idea that an emphasis upon a sovereign God's own deliverance of Israel necessarily implied a considerably diminished or even absent messianic expectation. The supposed near silence of certain sources on messianism is often questionable and, even when apparent, its significance can be accounted for in ways that are not incompatible with a concomitant messianic hope. Second, also to be rejected is the idea that angelic figures envisaged as heaven-sent deliverers necessarily precluded the

---

[81] Horbury, ibid., pp. 68–77, considers three especially pertinent aspects of the ruler-cult: 'its capacity for integration with ancestral religion, its characteristically exuberant form of praise and prayer, and the variegated pattern of Jewish reaction to it, through participation as well as opposition', p. 69.

role of an earthly messianic ruler. On the contrary, a biblical pattern variously traceable from the Exodus narratives onwards, strongly suggests that the two were often closely coordinated. (Further observations on this matter will be made in connection with our ensuing discussion of Daniel's 'one like a son of man'). Thirdly, in similar fashion one may also disallow the contention that in cases where the Messiah is characterized by angelic and superhuman traits,[82] this constrasts significantly with the usual Jewish perception of the Messiah as a human figure. There is sufficient biblical precedent to suggest that the Messiah could be viewed as the earthly embodiment of an angel-like spirit.[83] In sum, the case for a pervasive and coherent Jewish messianism would seem to be more compelling than has often been allowed.

The Maccabean period, messianic expectations and the Danielic 'one like a son of man'

Within the wider framework of the broadly based Jewish messianism outlined above, particular attention may now be directed towards the significant role of Daniel's 'one like a son of man' in relation to ongoing messianic expectations. Initially, I revisit and reject claims of a 'messianological vacuum' with particular reference to the Maccabean period. The focus then turns to a consideration of the much controverted matter of the identity of the 'one like a son of man' figure within the context of Daniel itself. Finally there follows a survey of the evidence for a decidedly messianic interpretation of this figure in a range of pertinent texts in the Second Temple period.

It has already been observed that the use of the Hebrew המשיח[ה] ((ha-)mashiah) at Daniel 9.25–6 (a text of Maccabean provenance) with very little explanation is an early extant instance of the overall evidence for the widespread currency of the term 'Messiah'.[84] Yet it has often been argued that 'there is no evidence of messianism at the time of the Maccabean revolt', as throughout the Second Temple

---

[82] As, for example, in 4 Ezra, also considered further below.

[83] The background lies in the LXX's estimation of God as the lord of angels and spirits, and in the spiritual and superhuman portrayals which arise out of the exalted features of various messianic texts in the Hebrew Scriptures, and which are amply attested post-LXX Pentateuch biblical interpretation; so Horbury, *Jewish Messianism*, pp. 86–7, with evidence on this and related themes in a wide range of literature at pp. 87–108.

[84] In Dan. 9.25 the term probably designates as 'anointed' either Zerubbabel (as the legitimate ruler) or Joshua (as the ruling high priest), and at Dan. 9.26 possibly Onias III (cf. 2 Macc. 4.34; Dan. 11.22).

period.⁸⁵ As noted above, the latter and wider claim has been countered by Horbury; but his various arguments may be drawn upon further with particular reference to the Maccabean period. Of immediate note are Qumran documents, most of which are roughly contemporary with texts such as 1 and 2 Maccabees, and a number of which variously attest to an active messianism throughout the Hasmonean period. We might also recall the broad influence of the Gentile ruler-cult upon Jewish conceptions of kingship (noted above),⁸⁶ which was sharply and negatively felt with Antiochus IV Epiphanes' imposition of pagan worship upon the Jerusalem Temple cult, evoking the nationalist response reviewed earlier from 1 and 2 Maccabees. In such a climate one might expect some traces of messianic aspirations in the Maccabean literature.

Consideration of any evidence in this direction may begin by noting the fact that narratives such as 1 and 2 Maccabees, with their martyr-like heroes, express strong hopes for national redemption through themes such as divine consolation, ingathering to Zion and vengeance upon Israel's enemies (so, for example, 2 Macc. 1.24–9; 2.17–18), themes which can readily evoke a messianic ingathering.⁸⁷ Indeed, the Maccabean books indicate something of an overlap between kingship and messianism, with their lofty portrayals of kings and high priests which 'surround contemporary rulers with a messianic atmosphere'.⁸⁸ Yet, although the Maccabees are hailed as the saviours of Israel, and the kingdom and priesthood have been restored to the nation under the Hasmoneans, complete divine deliverance in the form of a messianic ingathering has yet to take place. Nonetheless, that this may at least be in view could be inferred from the dying words of Mattathias, who holds up King David as an exemplar for his sons – a David who, 'because he was merciful, inherited the throne of the kingdom for ever' (1 Macc. 2.57). Thus, 'a specifically Davidic messianic element should not therefore be excluded from the Maccabean future hopes ...'⁸⁹

Much more controversial is the claim that there is also a messianic aspect to the 'one like a son of man' figure in Daniel 7, a text

---

⁸⁵ So Collins, 'Jesus and the Messiahs of Israel', p. 288.
⁸⁶ Not least during the second-century conflicts between the Seleucids and the Ptolemies which gave rise to the vision of wars between 'the king of the north' and 'the king of the south' in Dan. 11, and also found expression in the nationalist oracles of the four kingdoms in Daniel.
⁸⁷ See *Pss. Sol.* 17.26, 42–4; 4 Ezra 13.39–40.
⁸⁸ Horbury, *Jewish Messianism*, p. 56.
⁸⁹ Ibid., p. 57.

likewise of Maccabean provenance.[90] A range of often highly nuanced and occasionally overlapping interpretative options concerning the precise identity and significance of this human-like figure may be conveniently considered under three main categories.[91]

(1) *A collective symbol for victorious (faithful) Israel.* This view, infrequent in earlier interpretations, has been advocated by many modern commentators.[92] It is argued that inasmuch as the 'four beasts' represent four kings/kingdoms (Dan. 7.17), the parallel human-like figure most naturally denotes Israel, a claim strengthened if an implied identification with the 'saints' (Dan. 7.18) – understood as Israel – is allowed. Against this it has been contended the identification with the 'saints',[93] and perhaps also of the 'saints' with the Jewish people, is by no means certain.[94]

(2) *A heavenly being: an exalted angel and/or a manifestation of God himself.* Although absent in traditional exegesis, a more recent and increasingly popular view argues that the 'one like a son of man' is an exalted angelic deliverer (probably Michael)[95] and/or a

---

[90] Certain historical allusions indicate that Daniel 7–12 was completed during the early stages of the Maccabean crisis, prior to the death of Antiochus IV Epiphanes and the rededication of the Temple (c. 165–164 BC). Thus, for example, readily discernible are thinly veiled references to Antiochus' initial injurious decrees (Dan. 7.25); Jewish complicity in his actions (Dan. 9.27; 11.30); and the desecration of the Temple cult (Dan. 8.9–12, 22–5; 9.24–7). Particularly noteworthy is the extended *ex eventu* prophecy of known historical events leading up to and climaxing with Antiochus' persecutions (Dan. 11.2–39), followed by an actual but imprecise prediction of his death (Dan. 11.40–5).

[91] Among the many surveys, see Casey, *The Son of Man*, pp. 24–40; Goldingay, *Daniel*, pp. 169–72; Collins, *A Commentary on the Book of Daniel*, pp. 306–10; Slater, 'One Like a Son of Man in First-Century CE Judaism'.

[92] For example, Porteous, *Daniel: A Commentary*, p. 192; Hartman and Di Lella, *The Book of Daniel*, pp. 85–102. Notable, if minority, emphases include the claim that the figure is Israel in both its suffering and glorification (Hooker, *The Son of Man in Mark*, pp. 11–30; Moule, *The Origin of Christology*, pp. 11ff.); a pure symbol to which no experience of suffering can be attached (Casey, *The Son of Man*, pp. 7–50); and the apotheosis of Israel at the eschaton (M. Black, 'Die Apotheose Israels'; cf. option (2) below).

[93] Rowland, *The Open Heaven*, p. 180, is among those who note that an explicit one-to-one identification – such as that between 'the beasts' and the Gentile kings/kingdoms – is conspicuous by its absence.

[94] So Collins, *A Commentary on the Book of Daniel*, p. 309, in the course of arguing for option (2) below.

[95] Gabriel (Dan. 8.16–26; 9.21–7), the 'man clothed in linen' (Dan. 10.5ff.), or some otherwise unidentified angel, have all been proposed. However, the preferred candidate is Michael (Dan. 10.13, 21; 12.1), a position first argued by N. Schmidt, 'Was *bar nash* a Messianic Title?' and 'The "Son of Man" in The Book of Daniel', and now especially advocated by Collins, *The Apocalyptic Vision of the Book of Daniel*, pp. 123–52; *A Commentary on the Book of Daniel*, p. 310; *The Apocalyptic Imagination*, pp. 101–4; cf. Rowland, *The Open Heaven*, pp. 178–83.

manifestation of God.[96] The scenario at Daniel 7.9–14 may be seen as standing in a long tradition of Old Testament throne theophanies,[97] and as envisaging no mere symbol but a real figure entering God's heavenly throne-room.[98] Furthermore, in Old Testament visionary texts divine beings (whether angels or God) revealed to a seer are regularly perceived and described analogously as having the 'appearance', 'form' or 'likeness' of a man.[99] Commentators stressing either the angelic or divine aspect can also invoke correspondence with the 'saints' (understood as denoting the angelic host)[100] or the use of cloud imagery (signalling divine presence) respectively.[101] However, this interpretation is not without its difficulties. The claim that we are dealing with an angelic being (probably Michael), raises the question why this is nowhere specified.[102] The claim that we have some manifestation of God himself must be tempered by the differences and deference inherent in the respective roles of the Ancient (as host, giver) and the 'one like a son of man' (as presentee, recipient).[103]

(3) *Israel's Messiah, one fulfilling the Davidic promises.* This view is prominent within the earliest Jewish interpretations (on which

---

[96] Whether a manifestation of his glory or a hypostatization of his self-revelation: cf. Procksch, 'Der Menschensohn als Gottessohn'; Feuillet, 'Le fils de l'homme de Daniel'; Rowland, *The Open Heaven*, pp. 97–8; Kim, *'The "Son of Man"' as the Son of God*, pp. 16–19; Bittner, 'Gott-Menschensohn-Davidsohn', p. 371; Caragounis, *The Son of Man*, p. 80. Here we may also recall M. Black, 'Die Apotheose Israels', who argues for the divinization of Israel.

[97] See 1 Kings 22.19–22; Isa. 6.1–8, Ezek. 1.26–8; 2.1ff.; cf. 8.1–?; 10.1–4; also *1 Enoch* 14.18; 60.2; 90.20, and contexts. See M. Black, 'The Throne-Theophany Prophetic Commission and the "Son of Man": A Study in Tradition-History'; Rowland, 'The Visions of God in Apocalyptic Literature'.

[98] So Rowland, *The Open Heaven*, p. 181.

[99] Cf. Gen. 18.2; 19.1; Josh. 5.13; Judg. 13.6, 8, 16. The most significant instances include: Ezek. 1.26–8 (God); 8.2 (God, so Rowland, *The Open Heaven*, pp. 95ff.; an angel, so Collins, *A Commentary on the Book of Daniel*, p. 306); 9.11 ('a man clothed in linen' = an angel; Dan. 8.15; 9.21 (Gabriel); 10.5; 12.5–7 ('men clothed in linen' = angels). On the wider correspondences between Ezekiel and Daniel, see Rowland, *The Open Heaven*, pp. 94–102; Kim, *The Origin of Paul's Gospel*, pp. 204–17; and Slater, 'One Like a Son of Man in First-Century CE Judaism', pp. 191–2.

[100] So Collins, *A Commentary on the Book of Daniel*, p. 310, pressing Michael's candidacy as the pre-eminent champion of the heavenly host.

[101] Among many references, cf. Deut. 33.26; Pss. 68.5[4]; 104.3. On clouds in the Old Testament as accompanying a theophany (rather than angelophany), see Feuillet, 'Le fils de l'homme de Daniel', pp. 187ff.; cf. Emerton, 'The Origins of the Son of Man Imagery', pp. 231ff.; R.B.Y. Scott, 'Behold He Cometh with Clouds'.

[102] For example at Dan. 7.14, or perhaps at 7.18, 22, 27.

[103] The attempt of Bittner, 'Gott-Menschensohn-Davidsohn', pp. 351–2, to overcome objections to the complete identification of the two falls short of addressing these concerns.

see below), and also in Christian scholarship until the close of the twentieth century.[104] However, it has had a limited number of modern advocates offering relatively modest support,[105] with the notable exception of the contribution of Horbury.[106] This position argues for an individualistic and representative interpretation of evidence summoned in favour of option (1): just as the 'four beasts' in Daniel 7 denote the earthly Gentile kings who represent their kingdoms – and not the angelic princes who oppose Israel's angelic patron (Dan. 10.13, 20–1) – so the human-like figure denotes the Jewish King-Messiah who represents Israel. Moreover, an enthroned figure in receipt of what could be construed as a messianic kingdom (Dan. 7.14, 25), does have Old Testament precedent in certain royal psalms (Pss. 2; 20–1; 45; 72; 110) which extol Yahweh's rule over the rebellious nations through Israel's anointed king and God's adopted Son.[107] Consistent with the wider evidence of coordination between human and angelic leaders (noted above), a messianic interpretation can be seen as quite compatible with due recognition to the exalted role afforded Michael in Daniel 12.[108] Finally, as we shall now see, Daniel's 'one like a son of man' was recognized as the messianic king in subsequent Jewish interpretation, possibly in 4Q246 and most prominently in the *Parables of Enoch* and 4 Ezra. It would thus appear to be difficult to maintain that Daniel evinces little interest in a human Messiah.[109] Indeed, the foregoing observations concerning Daniel's 'one like a son of man' correlate well with the broader evidence for the widespread messianic expectations noted earlier, and a further important element in the latter is the strong evidence for the messianic interpretation of the Danielic 'one like a son of man' in the texts which we now briefly consider.

[104] See Koch, *Das Buch Daniel*, pp. 217–18.
[105] See Beasley-Murray, 'The Interpretation of Daniel 7'; Witherington, *The Christology of Jesus*, pp. 240–1.
[106] Horbury, *Jewish Messianism*, pp. 33–5; 83–6, and especially 'The Messianic Associations of "The Son of Man"'.
[107] An ancillary argument offered by Horbury is that the designation 'Son of Man' bears close comparison to various words for 'man' in certain pre-Danielic messianic oracles such as Num. 24.17; 2 Sam. 23.1; Ps. 80.18[17]; and Zech. 6.12. See Horbury, *Jewish Messianism*, p. 34; and his more extended argument in 'The Messianic Associations of "The Son of Man"', pp. 48–52.
[108] So Horbury, *Jewish Messianism*, pp. 83–6. Moreover, the exalted character of 'the one like a son of man' is also in keeping with the elevated portrayal of a spiritual messiah likewise discussed by Horbury, pp. 86ff.
[109] So Collins, *A Commentary on the Book of Daniel*, p. 309.

Messianic interpretations of the Danielic 'one like a son of man'

Recent commentators have eschewed any notion that the 'one like a son of man' in Daniel 7.13–14 gave rise to a fixed and recognizable Jewish title, concept or doctrine, messianic or otherwise.[110] Certainly one must guard against the later retrojection of uncritical composite readings, Jewish or Christian. Nevertheless, there are a number of notable sources – principally 4Q246, *1 Enoch* 37–71, and 4 Ezra 11–13 – which variously attest to what appears to have been an early and extended messianic interpretation of the 'one like a son of man', this being a subset of a broadly based Jewish messianism during the Second Temple period. In this way Daniel 7, and thus the Maccabean crisis and its outworking, continued to be an important backward reference point for Jewish aspirations of a deliverer who would represent, redeem and vindicate afflicted Israel.[111]

What are the indications of the pre-Christian currency of a messianic interpretation of the Danielic 'one like a son of man'? The Qumran text 4Q246, with its enigmatic reference to a central figure entitled 'son of God ... son of the Most High', offers an early, intriguing, but perhaps ultimately uncertain possibility.[112] Despite the fragmentary and ambiguous nature of this text, certain parallels with Daniel seem likely.[113] What is less clear is whether the unfolding apocalyptic drama envisaged:

---

[110] See the secondary literature cited in Kim, '*The "Son of Man"' as the Son of God*, p. 19 n. 23; and Collins, 'The Son of Man in First Century Judaism', pp. 448–9. Earlier studies accepting 'the Son of Man' as a recognized messianic title in Jewish apocalyptic literature include Cullmann, *The Christology of the New Testament*, p. 150; and Tödt, *The Son of Man in the Synoptic Tradition*, p. 22.

[111] Consideration of another pertinent text, the *Assumption of Moses*, is deferred to chapter two because of its wider (first-century) witness to the Maccabean crisis as a whole.

[112] Formerly designated 4Q243 and also 4QpsDnAa; dated c. 25 BC, the published text is in Puech, 'Fragment d'une apocalypse en Araméen' (cf. his 'Notes sur le fragment d'apocalypse 4Q246'). Recent notable discussions include Cook, '4Q246'; Flusser, 'The Hubris of the Antichrist'; García Martínez, 'The Eschatological Figure of 4Q246'; Milik, 'Les modèles araméens', pp. 383–4; Collins, 'The Son of God Text from Qumran', *The Scepter and the Star*, pp. 154–72, and 'The Background of the "Son of God" Text'; Fitzmyer, '4Q246: The "Son of God" Document from Qumran'; Knibb, 'Messianism in the Pseudepigrapha', pp. 174–7.

[113] Compare 1.1–4 ('distress upon the earth') and Dan. 5.6, 12.1; 2.1 ('son of the Most High') and Dan. 7.22, 25, 27; 2.2–3 ('they' who will rule the earth and 'trample' people and provinces) and Dan. 7.23; 2.4 ('the people of God arises') and Dan. 7.18, 22, 27; 2.5 (inauguration of an 'everlasting kingdom') and Dan. 3.33[4.3], 4.31[34], 7.27; 2.7a (a kingdom receiving worldwide homage) and Dan. 7.14, 27; and 2.7b (God ensuring the kingdom's universal dominion) and Dan. 3.33[4.3], 4.31[34], 7.14.

(a) depicts the escalation of an oppressive, transitory kingdom (1.4–2.3) – then superseded by the kingdom of God's people (2.4–9) – within which the reference to the 'son of God' is the more likely to denote an evil figure, whether historical (Alexander Balas, or Antiochus IV Epiphanes?),[114] apocalyptic (an Antichrist?),[115] or both; or

(b) depicts scenes oscillating between eschatological distress (1.4–6; 2.2–3) and the announcement – perhaps in an (earthly) throne-room (1.2) – of divine intervention and the rule of the people of God (1.7–2.1; 2.4–9), within which the reference to 'son of God' is the more likely to denote a highly esteemed figure, whether corporate Israel,[116] a Davidic ruler[117] or Messiah,[118] or a heavenly being.[119]

The current critical trend seems to lean away from category (a) and towards category (b), with Collins in particular pressing hard the claim that 4Q246 provides what may well be the earliest extant messianic interpretation of the Danielic 'one like a son of man'.[120] It is indeed notable that a King-Messiah figure is the individual most frequently designated in terms of divine sonship in the Old Testament (cf. 2 Sam. 7.14; Pss. 2.7; 89.27–8[26–7]), and is variously attested at Qumran (4QFlor; cf. 1QSa and 4Q369). Notable, albeit later, references to a messianic 'son of God' include 4 Ezra 13 (see below), and the striking parallel designations 'son of the Most High' and 'son of God' ascribed to Jesus in Luke 1.32, 35.

However, there is also reason to consider carefully category (a),

---

[114] Alexander Balas is suggested by Milik, 'Les modèles araméens', p. 383; and Antiochus IV Epiphanes by Cook, '4Q246'.

[115] So Flusser, 'The Hubris of the Antichrist'.

[116] Hengel, *The Cross and the Son of God*, pp. 42–3, allows for 'a collective interpretation in terms of the Jewish people'.

[117] Fitzmyer, '4Q246: The "Son of God" Document from Qumran', pp. 173–4, positing a member of the Hasmonean dynasty, but resisting any attempts to view such a figure as messianic.

[118] Collins, 'The Son of God Text from Qumran', pp. 76–82; *The Scepter and the Star*, pp. 154–72; 'Jesus and the Messiahs of Israel', pp. 293–6; 'The Background of the "Son of God" Text'. This also appears to be the preferred interpretation of Puech, 'Fragment d'une apocalypse en Araméen', pp. 122–31; 'Notes sur le fragment d'apocalypse 4Q246', pp. 553–6.

[119] García Martínez, 'The Eschatological Figure of 4Q246', p. 178, proposes identification with the one variously designated in Qumran texts as Michael, Melchizedek, or Prince of Light.

[120] See especially Collins, 'The Son of God Text from Qumran', pp. 69–73; *The Scepter and the Star*, pp. 154–72; and 'The Background of the "Son of God" Text'.

and wonder whether the 'son of God' might not in fact be an evil figure. It is noteworthy that 4Q246 only says that 'he will be *called* son of God ... they will *call* him son of the Most High' (2.1);[121] and, furthermore, that 'they' are immediately denoted as those whose temporary rule will 'trample' upon the earth (2.1–3; cf. Dan. 7.23). From this it might be inferred that the 'son of God' is more likely to be an oppressive Gentile ruler, whose subjects address him in a manner which indicates his delusions of grandeur as one having a place in the heavenly council. This might echo elements of Psalm 82.6–7, and also offer another instance of Jewish opposition to (and appropriation of) aspects of the Gentile ruler-cult.[122]

For our purposes it may not be necessary to settle this matter with precision. With some probability, it can be affirmed that we have a Qumran text, from the early Hasmonean period, with allusions to Daniel 7, which envisages a figure with the elevated ascription 'son of God ... son of the Most High'. Whether this figure denotes a divine deliverer or evil oppressor of Israel, in either instance it may well have evoked, in association with Daniel and its 'one like a son of man', messianic expectations.[123]

The conjunction of Daniel's 'one like a son of man' and a Messiah figure is, however, the more evident in the *Parables* (or *Similitudes*) *of Enoch*. Part of the composite *1 Enoch*, this text comprises three mutually complementary revelatory discourses (*1 Enoch* 38–44, 47–57, 58–69) focusing upon a series of heavenly tableaux depicting the outworking of the final judgement of the righteous and their persecutors.[124] The ultimate end of the righteous will be their glorious eschatological existence with their deliverer: 'they shall eat

[121] Alternatively, 'designate himself' as such; Flusser, 'The Hubris of the Antichrist', p. 33, notes that both readings are possible.
[122] See Horbury, 'The Messianic Associations of "the Son of Man"', p. 42; and *Jewish Messianism*, p. 74.
[123] Horbury, 'The Messianic Associations of "the Son of Man"', pp. 42–3, cautiously notes that both the Qumran text 11QMelch and *Ezekiel the Tragedian* offer some additional evidence of the early messianic exegesis of Dan. 7.
[124] The current consensus is that the *Parables* is a Jewish work to be dated at some point (probably early) within a 1 BC–AD 1 time frame. Nickelsburg, *Jewish Literature*, pp. 222–3, rightly maintains that it is unlikely that a Christian author would have identified Enoch with the Son of Man (so *1 Enoch* 70–1) and, conversely, that a Jewish author would have used the designation Son of Man after it had been appropriated as a title for Jesus. He also argues that at least the traditions embodied in the *Parables* were extant at about the turn of the era. See further Greenfield and Stone, 'The Enochic Pentateuch' (1977); Suter, 'Weighed in the Balance' (1981); Coppens, *La relève apocalyptique du messianisme royal* (1983); VanderKam, *Enoch: A Man for all Generations* (1995), pp. 132–42; Collins, *The Apocalyptic Imagination*, pp. 177–93.

and rest and rise with that Son of Man for ever and ever' (*1 Enoch* 62.14). The term 'Son of Man' is, in fact, one of four designations applied to the *Parables'* redeemer figure, the others being 'Righteous One', 'Elect One' and, most significant for our purposes, 'Anointed One'.[125]

Strictly speaking, the frequent designation 'this/that Son of Man' refers back to the figure first introduced at *1 Enoch* 46.1.[126] However, from the allusions to Daniel 7.9, 13 at *1 Enoch* 46.1–3 – and also Daniel 7.9–10 at *1 Enoch* 47.3 – it is quite evident that the 'Son of Man' presupposes throughout an association with the Danielic 'one like a son of man'. It is therefore all the more significant that the *Parables'* 'Son of Man' is the same figure as is also depicted as Messiah. It is in the context of the figure's commissioning and role as judge that the language and imagery of the Davidic King-Messiah is employed.[127] Thus, the humiliation of 'the kings of the earth' due to their denial of 'the Lord of the Spirits and his Messiah' at *1 Enoch* 48.8–10 bears close comparison to Psalm 2.[128] Additionally, reference to his 'spirit of righteousness' and 'the word of his mouth' deployed in judging the kings, echoes the messianic strand of the servant tradition (Isa. 11.1–5; *1 Enoch* 62.2; cf. 49.2–4). It might be said (with Collins) that 'the assimilation of the Son of Man to the Davidic messiah in the Similitudes is quite limited';[129] but it is all the more remarkable then that the identification between the two seems to be taken for granted.[130] In any event, we have an unambiguous instance of the Danielic 'one like a son of man' interpreted in terms of a messianic redeemer.

[125] See VanderKam, 'Righteous One, Messiah, Chosen One, and Son of Man in 1 Enoch', for a succinct analysis of the occurrences and inextricable interrelationship of these four terms.

[126] Collins, *A Commentary on the Book of Daniel*, p. 80 n. 56 (citing Casey, *The Son of Man*, p. 100) notes that while the Ethiopic demonstrative could be a rendering of the definite article in an earlier Greek version, it is conspicuously absent in relation to the title 'Elect One'.

[127] See especially Theisöhn, *Der auserwählte Richter*, pp. 114–26.

[128] Cf. also the second instance of the term 'Anointed One/Messiah' at *1 Enoch* 52.4, employed in informing the seer that all the events disclosed to him occur 'by the authority of [God's] Messiah so that he may give orders and be praised upon the earth'.

[129] Collins, 'Jesus and the Messiahs of Israel', p. 292.

[130] On possible solutions to the vexed matter of the identification of the seer Enoch and the Son of Man in *1 Enoch* 70–1, cf. VanderKam, 'Righteous One, Messiah, Chosen One, and Son of Man in 1 Enoch', pp. 182–5; M. Black, 'The Messianism of the Parables of Enoch', pp. 165–68; Collins, 'The Son of Man in First Century Judaism', pp. 453–59; *The Scepter and the Star*, pp. 178–81; Knibb, 'Messianism in the Pseudepigrapha', pp. 177–80.

Fourth Ezra was composed in the wake of the destruction of Jerusalem, probably in Palestine, and comprises seven visions which respond to the traumatic situation facing an Israel now 'devoured' by its Roman overseers (4 Ezra 6.55–9).[131] In the fifth vision and its interpretation (4 Ezra 11.1–12.51), a lion-like figure, symbolizing Judahite descent (cf. Gen. 49.9–10), destroys an eagle-like entity said to represent the fourth kingdom which appeared to Daniel (4 Ezra 12.11). This lion is then interpreted explicitly as 'the messiah whom the Most High has kept until the end of days, who will arise from the posterity of David' (4 Ezra 12.32), and he is said to bring joy to his own during a four-hundred-year messianic kingdom, but then die before the last judgement (4 Ezra 12.34; cf. 7.33).

The complementary sixth vision and its interpretation (4 Ezra 13.1–56) is likewise indebted to Daniel 7.[132] It concerns a 'figure of a man come up out of the heart of the sea', who 'flew with the clouds of heaven' and, upon a mountain top, destroys his enemies and receives a peaceable multitude (4 Ezra 13.1–13). The 'man' is identified, in Latin and Syriac versions, as 'my son' (4 Ezra 13.37, 52) and thus with the Messiah who is called 'my son' at 4 Ezra 7.28.[133] The influence of Isaiah 11.4 can be seen in the account of the man's fiery breath which repels the onslaught of the multitude (4 Ezra 13.10–11). Additionally, the Zion setting and depiction of the Gentile assault at 4 Ezra 13.33–8 is reminiscent of Psalm 2.[134] One might also note that the motif of the ingathering of the people (4 Ezra 13.12–13) is connected with the Messiah in *Psalms of Solomon* 17.26.

It may be concluded that in the above instances there is clear evidence of a messianic understanding of Daniel's 'one like a son

---

[131] On matters of provenance, see Stone, *A Commentary on Fourth Ezra*, pp. 10–11; cf. the discussion in Schürer, *The History of the Jewish People*, vol. III, pp. 294–307.

[132] Stone, *A Commentary on Fourth Ezra*, pp. 398–400, argues that while the fifth vision drew directly from Daniel 7, the sixth has drawn upon another source itself dependent upon Daniel 7.

[133] Stone, *Features of the Eschatology of 4 Ezra*, pp. 71–5; and *A Commentary on Fourth Ezra*, pp. 207–8, may be correct in arguing that in the (non-extant) antecedent Greek text the Latin term *filius* would have been rendered by παῖς (not υἱός), reflecting an original Hebrew עבד (rather than בן), and would thus echo the Isaianic servant. However, given the interchangeable use of παῖς and υἱός in Wis. 2.13, 16, it may be that *filius* instead denotes sonship. In any event, the Davidic King-Messiah tradition is also otherwise clearly evident in what follows.

[134] Likewise the contemporaneous *2 Apoc. Bar.* 36–40, in a climactic Zion-focused scenario comparable to that of 4 Ezra 13, seems to presuppose a messianic and judicial interpretation of the Danielic 'one like a son of man'.

of man'. While, in their final form, the latest of these texts may be dated towards the end of the first century, the trajectory of Jewish exegesis to which they attest is likely to have spanned the period from the Maccabean crisis to the fall of Jerusalem and beyond.[135] Moreover, this trajectory is itself to be seen as one strand within the wider Jewish messianism of the period. Hence, such exegetical associations would have been available to a first-century Jew such as Jesus. Indeed, while this complex matter can not be pursued here, the New Testament gospel traditions concerning Jesus have reasonably been adduced as further evidence of the phenomena under consideration.[136] However, it is also in virtue of early Jewish-*Christian* estimations of Jesus' life, death and resurrection, that Jewish expectations of a messianic redeemer also became subject to a radical reconfiguration.

4. Conclusion: the Maccabees, the Messiah and Galatians 1–2

The Maccabean period – comprising crisis, revolt and the emerging Hasmonean dynasty – was a memorable era in Jewish history. The burden of the argument throughout has been that its key constitutive texts and traditions bear witness to two arresting and interrelated features. First, readily apparent is the broadly based theme of the suffering and vindication of the people of God, particularly as focused upon Israel's leading martyr-heroes, such as Eleazar and the seven brothers, whose deaths are clearly regarded as precipitating Israel's divine deliverance. Second, as we have just seen, emanating from the Maccabean period is a prominent role afforded the Danielic 'one like a son of man' within widespread messianic expectations concerning a redeemer and ruler who would represent and rescue Israel's faithful from their continued affliction under Gentile rule.

Whether or not Jesus himself consciously engaged such Jewish

---

[135] On the additional later evidence along similar lines provided by the *Sibylline Oracles*, Book Five (e.g., 5.108–9, 414–33), the interpretation of Daniel 7.9 attributed to Akiba (*b. Hag.* 14a, *b. Sanh.* 38b), Justin Martyr's *Dialogue with Trypho* (32.1), and other sources, see Horbury, 'The Messianic Associations of "The Son of Man"', pp. 40–1, 44–6; and Head, *Christology and the Synoptic Problem*, p. 222.

[136] For example, the combination of Daniel 7.13 and Psalm 110.1 at Mark 14.62, and John 1.45 and 12.34, variously attesting to Jewish messianic expectations in association with Daniel's 'one like a son of man'. See Nickelsburg, 'Son of Man', pp. 142–7; Collins, *A Commentary on the Book of Daniel*, pp. 90–105; Head, *Christology and the Synoptic Problem*, pp. 223–4.

hopes (as would seem likely), his followers became convinced that he was indeed Israel's Messiah, though in a manner which entailed a radical reworking of Jewish expectations: as one martyred, risen and exalted. As we shall see, it was recognition of this astonishing fact – through his own encounter with the risen Christ – which transformed Paul from a zealous Pharisee into Paul the apostle of Christ. Furthermore, it is this transformed understanding which is determinative of Paul's response to the Galatian crisis, including his opening autobiographical remarks in Galatians 1–2, and not least the climactic account of the Antioch incident at Galatians 2.11–21. Here, in the midst of Jewish and Christian conflict over what it meant to be the people of God, Paul's governing concern was that the Antiochene Christians must remain faithful to their exemplar and eschatological redeemer, Jesus, the Messiah and Son of God.

However, before this particular matter can be pursued, there is a second important step to be taken in our reconstruction of the Maccabean framework: to indicate all the more fully its currency within the wider first-century Jewish context known to Paul.

2

MACCABEAN MARTYRDOM IN FIRST-CENTURY JUDAISM AND PAUL

Given the traumatic nature of Antiochus IV Epiphanes' assault upon the Jewish way of life, and the dramatic deliverance brought about by the Maccabean revolt, it should occasion little surprise that such events lived on in the memories of later generations. Indeed, the analysis in chapter one has already intimated as much. However, the significance of this fact has not always received the consideration it deserves. Thus, while recognizing the multifarious nature of Second Temple Judaism, the intent of this chapter is to establish that the Maccabean period – and not least the pivotal role of its martyr figures – was current as an inspirational living tradition readily at hand to a first-century Jew such as Paul.

This task will be undertaken by summoning three complementary classes of evidence. First, by reference to the work of Farmer, Hengel and Wright, it will be argued that there is a discernible religio-political continuity between the Maccabean movement and first-century Jewish nationalist aspirations, and that at least some members of the Pharisaic movement (including Paul) may be located in close proximity thereto. A sharp focus upon this wider context will also be provided by means of an examination of the Jewish response to the Caligula Temple edict. This incident evoked painful memories of the Maccabean crisis and its impact may also be traceable in the early Jewish Christian community. Second, I shall then examine a range of additional texts and traditions which variously attest to the significance of the Maccabean period in the minds of Jewish authors spanning the first century and beyond. This section will also include an excursus on the possibility of a Maccabean martyr cult in Antioch. Third, with the later analysis of Galatians 1 and 2 *sub judice*, I shall provide one significant piece of evidence that this living tradition was not only available to, but also actually appropriated by, the apostle Paul. This will involve consideration of a recent claim that Romans 3.21–6, so constitutive of Paul's atonement theology, has a traditio-historical background in certain key Maccabean texts. With this final element in place, we shall be in a position to undertake a detailed examination of Galatians 1 and 2.

1. Maccabean martyrdom and first-century Jewish nationalist aspirations

That first-century Palestinian and Diaspora Judaism was a complex and diverse entity has been well documented in recent scholarship.[1] Thus not surprisingly the same may be said of the resistance movements which gave expression to widespread Jewish nationalist aspirations, and which climaxed in the ill-fated revolt against Rome in AD 66–70. In what follows, such a complexity will be presupposed throughout. However, our interest and argument may be more narrowly defined and advanced as follows. (i) There is a broad correspondence between the character and conduct of the Maccabean movement and first-century Jewish resistance against Rome. (ii) Included within the latter were at least some Pharisees, ready to complement their zeal for Torah (in matters such as food laws) with involvement in the religio-political concerns of nation Israel. (iii) Later it will be argued that one such Pharisee was Saul/Paul, whose own account of his former zeal for Judaism (Gal. 1.13–14) is depicted in terms which are also evocative of the Maccabean aspirations. In an ancillary argument, we shall also examine the Jewish response to Caligula's traumatic action against the Temple in 39–40 as an especially evocative instance of Maccabean-inspired zeal. This incident may well have impinged upon the nascent Christian community, not least in terms of its ever-precarious relations with its parent Jewish body. Together the ensuing analysis will serve to indicate something of the nature and significance of the Maccabees upon the wider social and religio-political environment within which Paul lived as both Jew and Jewish Christian convert.

---

[1] Among the ever expanding studies, see, for example, Safrai and Stern (eds.), *The Jewish People in the First Century*, vols. I and II (1974, 1976); Schürer, *The History of the Jewish People*, vols. I–III (1973–87); E. P. Sanders, *Judaism: Practice and Belief, 63 BCE–66 CE* (1992); Grabbe, *Judaism from Cyrus to Hadrian*, vol. II (1992); N. T. Wright, *The New Testament and the People of God* (1992), pp. 145–338; Feldman, *Jew and Gentile in the Ancient World* (1993); Hayes and Mandell, *The Jewish People in Classical Antiquity* (1996); Barclay, *Jews in the Mediterranean Diaspora* (1996); Collins, *Between Athens and Jerusalem* (2000).

Correspondence and continuity: Farmer and Hengel

The case for religio-political continuity between the Maccabees and first-century Jewish nationalist aspirations was first systematically set forth by William Farmer, and has since been complemented by the wide-ranging study of Martin Hengel.[2] Before considering their contribution, it may be acknowledged at the outset that Hengel's more comprehensive estimation of first-century movements of revolt is but one of at least three interpretations currently on offer.[3] Hengel himself claims a broadly based and generally cohesive resistance movement. This embraced its inception by Judas the Galilean in AD 6, development under the leadership of various members of his family, and eventual disintegration as a result of the Roman victory in AD 70.[4] However, Richard Horsley is representative of those who have argued that our principal source, Josephus, attests to a much more variegated scenario involving diverse groups with different socio-economic and political concerns.[5] In particular, he draws a distinction between ordinary brigands (λησταί), the 'Sicarii' as rebels whose origins are traceable to a scribal milieu, and the 'Zealots' as a particular body which only emerged at the onset of the Jewish War in AD 66. A third reconstruction is that of Martin Goodman who has contended that the initiative and direction of the otherwise popular movement was derived from the Jewish aristocracy.[6]

It is neither possible nor necessary here to argue for a nuanced reconstruction of the emergent first-century Jewish resistance movements. Rather, it will suffice to enumerate our basic working presuppositions by reference to the three positions just outlined. First, it may be granted (with Horsley) that this opposition to Rome was a complex phenomenon, and that the climactic revolt of 66–70 represented the convergence of various factions with a range of (albeit interrelated) agendas at work. Second, that this attracted the self-serving involvement of the aristocracy (so Goodman) need not be

---

[2] Farmer, *Maccabees, Zealots and Josephus*; Hengel, *The Zealots*.
[3] Conveniently summarized and critiqued in N. T. Wright, *The New Testament and the People of God*, pp. 177–81, prefaced by his own itemization of certain evidence at pp. 170–7. See also Mendels, *The Rise and Fall of Jewish Nationalism*, pp. 191–383.
[4] See especially Hengel, *The Zealots*, pp. 76–145; 313–76.
[5] Notable among many publications: R. A. Horsley, 'The Sicarii'; 'Ancient Jewish Banditry'; 'The Zealots'; '"Messianic" Figures and Movements'; *Galilee: History, Politics, People*; and Horsley and Hanson, *Bandits, Prophets and Messiahs*.
[6] Goodman, *The Ruling Class of Judaea*.

doubted, but it is unlikely that much more than this can be attributed to them. Third, the term 'Zealot' was indeed the specific self-designation of a particular faction which emerged during the war. Nevertheless, it may still be claimed (to modify Hengel) that this group was but one amongst a number of elements which together comprised an ongoing, broadly based, and variously manifest religio-political 'zeal' directed against Rome. Indeed, the title 'Zealot' could have been readily ascribed to many Jews who regarded themselves as standing in the tradition of their Maccabean forebears. With such considerations in view, we may now turn to a summary and critique of the evidence summoned by Farmer and Hengel.

In essence, Farmer is able to demonstrate both (a) the common character and cause of the Maccabean and first-century resistance movements, and (b) that the latter actively commemorated the achievements of their Maccabean forebears.[7] His evidence for (a) is drawn largely from Josephus who, though certain apologetical, theological and personal motivations caused him to obscure the connection, nevertheless remained 'too honest an historian' to erase entirely its extensive nature and significance.[8] Farmer collates the extensive data in terms of a shared commitment to the Torah and to the Jerusalem Temple. The former may be briefly set forth as follows.

A common commitment to the Torah[9]
(i) Distress at the burning of the sacred Torah Scrolls.
(ii) Resistance to the enforced consumption of swine's flesh.
(iii) Opposition to cultural Hellenization in Palestine (e.g., building projects according to Greek custom) seen as antipathetic to Torah.[10]
(iv) Zeal in the armed defence of the Torah.
(v) A concomitant willingness to suffer and die for the Torah.
(vi) Religious suicide rather than capitulation to the enemy.
(vii) Circumcision (even by force) as fundamental to covenant identity and blessing.

---

[7] Here I focus upon the former, taking up the latter within the broader context of a subsequent analysis of first-century texts and traditions pertaining to the Maccabean martyrs.

[8] See Farmer, *Maccabees, Zealots and Josephus*, pp. 11–23; citation from p. 22.

[9] Ibid., pp. 47–83, providing various references to the pertinent sources, principally 1 and 2 Maccabees and Josephus.

[10] These included Herod's building projects in Antioch (*J.W.* 1.425; *Ant.* 16.149).

(viii) Strict sabbath observance, with expediency in order to do battle in time of warfare.

The Maccabees and first-century nationalists likewise exhibited a similar Torah-based devotion to the Jerusalem Temple.[11] As the central institutional symbol of Jewish national life, the Temple was the obvious target of attempts by both the Seleucids and the Romans to attain and maintain control over Israel. In both periods it was despoiled, whether by the forced entrance of a Gentile ruler, the plundering of its treasury and/or sacred furnishings, or its (actual or threatened) transformation into a pagan cult. And in both periods, drawing inspiration from the biblical story of God's defence of Jerusalem against the Assyrian king Sennacherib (2 Kings 18.13–19.36), zealous Jews resisted the Gentile enemy, whether by taking up arms or through non-violent protest.[12] Indeed, Antiochus IV Epiphanes' traumatic desecration of the Temple in 168–165 BC has its first-century counterpart in the cataclysmic Roman destruction of the Temple in AD 70. The resultant cessation of the sacrificial cult ended all hope for the city and nation, and the Romans' blasphemous sacrifices to their emperor constituted the final ignominious 'desolating sacrilege'.[13]

In the course of noting such correspondences Farmer reaches certain important conclusions which may be itemized as follows. (i) The Maccabees and the first-century Jewish nationalists were motivated by the same Torah-grounded and Temple-focused covenant theology. (ii) As such the Maccabees constituted the nearest historical counterparts (if not prototypes) to those who later resisted Rome. (iii) In fact, it could be said that the period from Antiochus IV Epiphanes to Titus comprised a single narrative concerning the rise and decline of Jewish nationalism.

It may be granted that, generally speaking, Farmer's evidence secures points (i) and (ii). Any reservations in this respect arise largely out of our earlier observations regarding the complexity of the first-century resistance movements. It is this concern, applying

---

[11] Farmer, *Maccabees, Zealots and Josephus*, pp. 84–124, again with appropriate references from 1 and 2 Maccabees and Josephus.

[12] Farmer, ibid., pp. 93–7, draws a notable parallel between Jewish passive resistance to the Temple assaults of Heliodorus and Petronius (under Caligula's edict), both purportedly successful due to divine intervention (cf. 2 Macc. 3.7–21; *J.W.* 2.184–98; *Ant.* 18.263–72).

[13] *J.W.* 6.316. Eusebius, *HE* 3.5.4, regarded the event as the fulfilment of Dan. 9.27; cf. Matt. 24.15; Mark 13.14.

equally to the Maccabean movement and the emergent Hasmonean dynasty, which perhaps demands a modification of his third point. That is, under the more secular aspect of the later Hasmoneans – engendering, for example, Pharisaic opposition towards Alexander Jannaeus – Jewish nationalism seems to have diminished somewhat. It then appears to resurface with the emergence of Roman rule and the Herodian puppet government. Thus, one might speak of the 'rise, decline, and rise of Jewish nationalism'. In any event, for our particular purposes it is enough to observe the broad correspondence in the common character and cause of the two movements.

It is primarily through Hengel's extensive discussions of the concept of zeal and of the eschatological aspects of the 'Zealot movement' that breadth and depth has been given to Farmer's earlier analysis.[14] With respect to the former, Hengel rightly notes that the Maccabees and the 'Zealots' exhibited common features in their conception and enactment of religious zeal;[15] for example, they both:

(i) adopted Phineas as a key model;
(ii) regarded foreign domination as a sign of divine wrath to be overcome by zealous action;
(iii) renounced their possessions, fled into the desert and initiated resistance in the form of a holy war;
(iv) executed judgement upon Torah transgressors;
(v) were convinced that they constituted the true Israel and thus the bearers of divine promise;
(vi) in virtue of their tradition of zeal for God, upheld the right to rule (so the Hasmonean family) or made certain messianic claims (so the family of Judas the Galilean).

Hengel also itemizes certain differences between the two movements, though it could be argued that these are not as great as he would have us think.[16] Thus, for example, he claims that Antiochus IV Epiphanes' persecutions threatened the very foundation of Israel's faith, whereas Roman rule sought to guarantee religious freedom. However, this may overdraw the true nature of Antiochus' intent,[17]

---

[14] Given the earlier provisos concerning Hengel's estimation of the first-century nationalism, 'Zealot' and 'Zealot movement' (his terminology) will here be qualified by inverted commas.
[15] Hengel, *The Zealots*, especially pp. 171–2.
[16] Ibid., pp. 172–3.
[17] Which, though cataclysmic in Jewish estimation, may have been designed to ensure political control rather than religio-political eradication.

and probably underestimates the limits of Roman tolerance.[18] In a similar vein, Hengel suggests that the original religious impetus of the Maccabees later declined to the level of political infighting, whereas any such compromise would have been unacceptable to the 'Zealots'. But this is too facile an estimation of the complexities attending the rise and later decline of Maccabean/Hasmonean rule, and likewise too purist and – given that they never ruled – too hypothetical an assessment of the 'Zealot' motivations.[19] Finally, Hengel argues that the 'Zealots' exhibited a remarkable degree of eschatological intensification conspicuous by its absence from 1 Maccabees. Yet this is to sell short the wide-ranging evidence (not least Daniel 7–12) which readily indicates that at least a significant element during the Maccabean crisis were just as preoccupied with inaugurating the kingdom of God as were the later 'Zealots'.[20] In sum, without denying differences in detail, it may still be claimed that there is a considerable correlation between the Maccabees and the 'Zealots' in terms of their common commitment to and expression of religious zeal – this being basically understood, with Hengel, as 'an eschatological intensification of the Torah'.[21]

In portraying the eschatological aspects of the 'Zealot' movement Hengel discusses a number of further motifs evocative of the Maccabean period.[22] So, for example, just as the Maccabees viewed Antiochus' persecutions as a climactic 'time of trouble' and testing which precipitated the inauguration of God's kingdom (Dan. 12.1), so the 'Zealots' identified Roman rule as a period of eschatological distress to be foreshortened and overcome by confronting and conquering their oppressors. Towards this end, like the Maccabees they were prepared to offer themselves as martyrs in what they understood to be a holy war. Moreover, not surprisingly, emerging out of this context were various prophetic figures and messianic pretenders,

---

[18] Hengel, *The Zealots*, p. 173 n. 142, himself notes Caligula's action against the Temple; and surely Roman response during the Jewish War readily indicates that they (like the Seleucids) delimited the extent to which Israel could be allowed to give concrete expression to its religio-political aspirations.

[19] That even the early Maccabees were prepared to negotiate with the Seleucid enemy is self-evident from 1 and 2 Maccabees. Josephus' own defection to the Roman cause itself indicates that Jewish nationalists comprised a spectrum of interests whose threshold varied according to what was no doubt a highly complex and fluid situation.

[20] Hengel appears to have a flat and overly quietistic estimation of the Hasidim, many of whom may well have been involved in the early Maccabean revolt.

[21] Hengel, *The Zealots*, p. 224.

[22] Ibid., pp. 229–312.

who together galvanized popular expectation of the imminent redemption of Israel and the final rule of God. Indeed, further to Hengel, those Maccabean-inspired freedom fighters with messianic pretentions – such as Simon, Anthronges, Menahem, and Simon ben Giora – are especially noteworthy.[23] It is possible that they bear witness to a concrete socio-political manifestation of Jewish messianic hopes based in part upon certain texts having Daniel 7.13–14 (and thus the Maccabean crisis) as an important backward reference point.[24]

In any event, this brief estimation of Hengel's analysis corroborates and strengthens the basic case set forth by Farmer. There is indeed a close correspondence between the fundamental distinctives and disposition of the Maccabean and first-century resistance movements. Their common zeal for Torah and Temple, Israel and its God, was no doubt known to and (in varying degrees) shared by a broad cross-section of the Jewish people. That this was true of at least some of those involved in the Pharisaic movement seems probable on *prima facie* grounds alone, and may be substantiated by the considerations which now follow.

Jewish nationalism and the Pharisees: Wright

The complex matters concerning the origin, development, self-designation and character of the Pharisaic movement cannot be taken up in any detail here.[25] Nevertheless, for our purposes it is

---

[23] *J.W.* 2.57–98 (*Ant.* 17.273–84); 2.433–49; 5–6 *passim*; 7.25–36, 153–4. R. A. Horsley, '"Messianic" Figures and Movements', pp. 276–95, is unnecessarily dismissive of the role of Davidic royal ideology; and Mendels, *The Rise and Fall of Jewish Nationalism*, pp. 267–8, is more cautious about attributing messianic aspects to these figures.

[24] As noted in chapter one, Daniel appears to have been particularly prominent in fostering such aspirations. Josephus (*Ant.* 10.203–10) deliberately alters Daniel 2.1–45 in such a way as to imply that the 'stone' was being taken as a symbol of the messianic kingdom which would overcome Rome. Daniel may also be a/the source of the 'ambiguous oracle' which Josephus applies to Titus even as he observes that pious Jews applied it to a (Jewish) leader, a great king (*J.W.* 6.312–15).

[25] The secondary literature is vast: see, for example, Neusner, *The Rabbinic Traditions* (1971) and his many subsequent works; Alon, *Jews, Judaism and the Classical World* (1977), pp. 18–47; Schürer, *The History of the Jewish People*, vol. II, pp. 381–403; Saldarini, *Pharisees, Scribes and Sadducees* (1988); E. P. Sanders, *Jewish Law from Jesus to the Mishnah* (1990), and *Judaism: Practice and Belief, 63 BCE–66 CE* (1992), on which contrast Hengel and Deines, 'E. P. Sanders' "Common Judaism", Jesus, and the Pharisees' (1995); Mason, *Flavius Josephus on the Pharisees* (1991); Schäfer, 'Der vorrabinische Pharisäismus' (1991); Stemberger, *Jewish Contemporaries*

desirable to press the case – made with some force by Wright – that at least a segment of the Pharisees were actively involved in those religio-political concerns so fundamental to the common cause of the Maccabees and the first-century nationalists.[26] At the outset, we may note Wright's summary estimation of the agenda and influence of the Pharisees, set forth in relation to three prominent current accounts of the evidence. It may be claimed: '(i) (with Sanders) that the Pharisees, though never a Jewish "thought-police" in the first or any other century, did concern themselves with matters wider than private or ritual purity; (ii) (against Sanders) that these concerns often embraced political and revolutionary action, such that the idea of a self-contained Jerusalem-based group with little influence, and not much interest in who was doing what elsewhere, is out of the question; (iii) (between Neusner and Sanders) that the purity codes were a vital part of pre-70 Pharisaism, functioning in close symbolic relationship to the wider political agenda.'[27] This case is argued with respect to four historical periods, the first two of which – the Hasmonean (164–63 BC) and Roman rule until the fall of Jerusalem (63 BC–AD 70) – are most directly applicable to our interests.

It would appear that the Pharisees first emerged as a religio-political pressure group in *some* proximity to the Maccabean revolt. Certainly they attained considerable *de facto* influence over subsequent Hasmonean rulers, notably in upholding Israel's Torah-based traditions in the face of the ever-present threat of pagan assimilation. Certain evidence for this may be briefly detailed as follows.

(i) With its stress upon both purity laws and resurrection, it is possible that 2 Maccabees is of Pharisaic provenance.[28]
(ii) Josephus attributes to Jonathan Maccabeus (161–143 BC) the recognition that his remarkable victories were due to 'God's providence in all his affairs' (*Ant.* 13.163). This

---

of Jesus (1995). The 'minimalist' estimation of the influence of first-century Pharisaism is represented by Neusner, reflected in Goodblatt, 'The Place of the Pharisees', and critiqued by Mason (cf. also his 'Josephus and Nicolaus on the Pharisees Reconsidered').

[26] On what follows, see N. T. Wright, *The New Testament and the People of God*, pp. 181–203, here supplemented at various junctures by additional considerations. Wright seeks to substantiate and further the suggestions of Hengel, *The Zealots*, pp. 228, 334; Rhoads, *Israel in Revolution 6–74 C.E.*, pp. 38ff.; Saldarini, *Pharisees, Scribes and Sadducees*, pp. 285–7; E. P. Sanders, *Jewish Law from Jesus to the Mishnah*, pp. 242–5, and *Judaism: Practice and Belief, 63 BCE–66 CE*, pp. 380–451.

[27] N. T. Wright, *The New Testament and the People of God*, pp. 186–7.

[28] See especially Sievers, *The Hasmoneans and Their Supporters*, pp. 7–8.

suggests some sort of alignment with the Pharisaic view of providence. Indeed, Josephus goes on to interpose into his (1 Maccabees-based) account of Jonathan's exploits a brief discussion of three Jewish schools of thought, with the Pharisees described in terms closest to Jonathan's sentiments (*Ant.* 13.171–3).[29]

(iii) The Pharisees' otherwise close relationship with John Hyrcanus (135–104) – who sought to please them by emulating their righteousness – came to an abrupt end over a noteworthy incident. The king was angered by the Pharisees' failure to recommend a sufficently severe punishment for one of their number – an aptly named Eleazar – who had insulted him by demanding that he forfeit the High Priesthood because his mother had been a captive under Antiochus IV Epiphanes, and thus defiled (*Ant.* 13.288–98).

(iv) Pharisees were probably involved in the riots against the oppressive Alexander Jannaeus, 103–76 BC (*J.W.* 1.88–9; *Ant.* 13.372–3). Jannaeus' death-bed advice to his wife – that she 'yield a certain amount of power to the [influential] Pharisees' – suggests as much (*Ant.* 13.399–404).

(v) The Pharisees wielded considerable influence during the reign of Alexandra Salome (76–67). The Queen restored those Pharisaic regulations in accord 'with the traditions of their fathers' which had been lost under Alexander Janneus. Indeed, in Josephus' (perhaps hyperbolic) estimation, the Pharisees were 'the real administrators of the state' (cf. *J.W.* 1.110–14; *Ant.* 13.408–18).

(vi) Certain Pharisees advised the Jerusalem populace to admit Herod into the city. This was clearly not a pro-Herod act, but an expression of their disaffection with what they now deemed to be a corrupt Hasmonean dynasty (cf. *Ant.* 14.172–6; 15.1–4).

The foregoing provides sufficient cause to posit significant Pharisaic religio-political involvement during the Hasmonean period. While this was no doubt a complex matter, at its most altruistic it was an attempt to uphold the same vital Jewish traditions for which the Maccabees had fought and died. Furthermore, their character-

---

[29] Note also similar views expressed by the first-century Pharisee and rebel Ananias (Josephus, *Life* 197, 290; *J.W.* 2.451).

istic concern to intensify biblical purity regulations need not be taken as at variance with this. Rather, when located within the wider cultural concerns of national life, and correlated with the Maccabean martyrs' readiness to die rather than transgress Torah food laws, it may be seen as representing the 'individual analogue of the national fear of, and/or resistance to, contamination from, or oppression by, Gentiles'.[30]

While the advent of Roman rule (63 BC–) necessarily curtailed the extent of their influence, the Pharisees remained at the forefront of those committed to a Torah-based, theocratic national life. This included a continued critique of the corrupt Jerusalem Temple establishment, and a concomitant perception of themselves as offering a purer alternative. Most significantly, it appears that their zealous commitment to nation Israel could be expressed in one of two complementary ways: active involvement with the Jewish freedom fighters or an even greater Torah devotion in study and praxis. Divergence of opinion on the most appropriate course of action may well have engendered (periodic) division within the movement.[31] Indeed, despite Josephus' desire to exculpate the Pharisees from complicity in the resistance against Rome, Wright is able to assemble considerable evidence of Pharisaic participation, representative of which is the following.[32]

(i) Pharisees opposed allegiance to Herod and, later, Caesar (*Ant.* 15.370; 17.41–5; *J.W.* 1.571–3).
(ii) Pharisaic teachers were involved in the removal of the Roman golden-eagle insignia from the Jerusalem Temple in 4 BC (*J.W.* 1.648–55; *Ant.* 17.149–67).[33]
(iii) A Pharisee, Zaddok, was a leading figure in the 'Fourth Philosophy' rebellion in AD 6; and Judas the Galilean's

---

[30] N. T. Wright, *The New Testament and the People of God*, p. 188, referring to Goodman, *The Ruling Class of Judaea*, pp. 99ff.; cf. Saldarini, *Pharisees, Scribes and Sadducees*, p. 286.

[31] This division is perhaps reflected in the later rabbinic debates which, in the light of two catastrophic revolts, depoliticized the issue into disputes over degrees of adherence to Torah purity codes. See Goodman, *The Ruling Class of Judaea*, pp. 107ff., 209ff.

[32] N. T. Wright, *The New Testament and the People of God*, pp. 190–3.

[33] This is apparent from the description of the leaders as 'unrivalled interpreters of the ancestral laws' (*Ant.* 17.149) and their designation as 'σοφισταί [sages]' (*Ant.* 17.152). Note that it is characteristic of Torah-obedient Daniel that he is able to reveal the divine mysteries that are hidden from the Gentile σοφισταί (Dan. 2).

designation as a σοφιστής perhaps also brings him within
the ambit of Pharisaic piety (*J.W.* 2.118, 433; *Ant.* 18.4–
10).[34]

(iv) The Pharisee Simon denounced king Herod Agrippa (37–
44) as unclean and unworthy to enter the Temple (*Ant.*
19.332–4).

(v) Those protesting to Agrippa II concerning the killing of
James in AD 62 were in all probability Pharisees (*Ant.*
20.200–2).

(vi) The Pharisee Simon ben Gamaliel was a close associate of
one of the key popular leaders during the Jewish War, John
of Gischala (*J.W.* 4.159; *Life* 189–98).[35]

(vii) It is possible that the *Megillath Taanith*, a Maccabean-
inspired first-century nationalist document, is of Pharisaic
provenance.

(viii) The excavations at Masada have indicated that the *mikvaot*
(ritual bathing pools) were built according to Pharisaic
specifications.

In sum, when such evidence is viewed in relation to post-AD 70
rabbinic accounts of division within pre-AD 70 Pharisees, it may be
suggested that the new situation under Herodian and Roman rule
engendered a complex and fluid range of Pharisaic responses. Some
may have focused upon Torah-devotion within the framework of
Roman rule (e.g., Hillel, Gamaliel and, later, Johanan ben Zakkai).[36]
Others endorsed active involvement in the attempt to resist and
overthrow Roman rule (e.g., Shammai and his house).[37] Nevertheless, in a manner analogous to the twin Pharisaic foci upon purity
and politics during the Hasmonean period, such responses could
be viewed as variant expressions of the same zeal for Torah/Israel/
God which was so constitutive of the Maccabees and first-century
nationalists.

---

[34] See Schürer, *The History of the Jewish People*, vol. II, p. 603 n. 36.

[35] Simon's antagonism towards the 'Zealots' was probably directed against certain aspects of this particular faction and not the resistance movement as such.

[36] Note also Mendels, *The Rise and Fall of Jewish Nationalism*, pp. 263–6. He suggests that Pseudo-Philo's *Biblical Antiquities* (*c.* AD 70), which may have originated amongst pre-AD 70 Pharisees or moderate Zealots, attests to those opposed to extreme Jewish nationalism.

[37] See Gafni, 'The Historical Background', p. 11, who cites *m. Shab.* 1.4; *b. Shab.* 13b; *y. Shab.* 1,3c; *t. Shab.* 1.16–20.

Saul the Pharisee

One first-century Pharisee who may well have stood in close proximity to the more religio-political active element of the Pharisees was Saul/Paul, later to become a Christian apostle. Granted, our primary information concerning Paul's pre-Christian life is unfortunately limited to retrospective glimpses from the standpoint of his later Christian ministry, supplemented by certain details in Acts.[38] Nonetheless, Hengel (for one) has offered a viable reconstruction of this period, not least concerning his strict Jewish upbringing in Tarsus in a 'family of Pharisaic stamp', and subsequent adolescent training as a Pharisee in Jerusalem.[39]

Given our limited information, and presupposing a breadth to first-century Pharisaism, we need not press too hard the question whether Paul had been a Hillelite or a Shammaite.[40] Nonetheless, that as a Pharisee Paul was *'zealous* for the law' and prepared to employ force in upholding Judaism seems to locate him among its more radical element. Thus he is more likely to have been sympathetic to the Maccabean-inspired theocratic aims of the first-century Jewish nationalists. Indeed, the invocation of his heritage as a 'Hebrew born of Hebrews' (Phil. 3.5; cf. 2 Cor. 11.22), invites comparison with the somewhat polemical use of the designation 'Hebrew' in 2 Maccabees, there in reference to those devout Jews faithful to the point of martyrdom on behalf of the Jewish way of life.[41] The bearing of Paul's former zeal for Judaism – not least its Maccabean background – upon his argument in Galatians 1 and 2 will be pursued further in chapter three.

The Caligula Temple episode: Jewish and Christian evocations of Antiochus IV Epiphanes

Complementing the earlier claims for the emergence of traditions based on Daniel 7.13–14 (and thus Maccabean-based) concerning a Jewish messianic redeemer, it has been argued that there is a dis-

---

[38] Principally, Rom. 9.3–5; 11.1; 2 Cor. 11.21b–22; Gal. 1.13–14, 23; Phil. 3.4–6; and Acts 8.1–3; 9.1–2; 21.37–22.5; 23.6; 26.4–11.

[39] Hengel, *The Pre-Christian Paul*, citation from p. 39; cf. Murphy-O'Connor, *Paul: A Critical Life*, pp. 32–70.

[40] The alternative positions represented by Jeremias, 'Paulus als Hillelit', and Haacker, 'Die Berufung des Verfolgers', respectively.

[41] 2 Macc. 7.31; 11.13; 15.37; cf. 4 Macc. 12.7; 16.15.

cernible common character and cause to the Maccabean and first-century Jewish resistance movements, and also noted in passing that the latter found particular expression in periodic prophetic and/or messianic actions against Rome. I shall now seek to give greater clarity to, and further appreciate the complexity of, this broad scenario, by adopting as a 'case study' one very instructive and traumatic incident: Gaius Caligula's attempt to erect an image of himself within the Jerusalem Temple (AD 39–40), an event evocative of Antiochus IV Epiphanes' archetypal desecration of the Temple in 165 BC. The focus of immediate interest will be upon the Jewish response to this crisis, and to the admittedly more contentious evidence for its reception within the early Christian community (including Paul). Towards this end, in turn, I shall briefly outline certain salient aspects of the incident; consider the claim that its impact may be discerned in certain traditions embedded within the Marcan apocalyptic discourse; and conclude with the observation that elements of this discourse, and also of the Caligula episode, may well have been known to Paul.

The administration of Rome's Syrian governor Vitellius (AD 35–9) had been overshadowed by the constant threat of Parthian expansionism, the need to intervene in the war between Herod Antipas and the Nabatean king Aretas IV, and increased unrest in Palestine. Such tensions continued under his successor Petronius (39–42), the period in which the Caligula episode occurred. While the precise nature of this episode remains somewhat uncertain, due to the problematic aspects of our otherwise notable sources, the broad outlines are relatively clear.[42] It was instigated by a potent mix of factors: the Jewish–pagan conflict in Alexandria and the ensuing Jewish embassy to Rome, together incurring the emperor's wrath;[43] anti-Jewish sentiment engendered by the Jews' destruction of an imperial altar in Jamnia;[44] and Caligula's self-apotheosis which was

---

[42] Philo, *Leg.* 197–227; *J.W.* 2.184–203; *Ant.* 18.256–309; cf. Tacitus, *Hist.* 5.9; and the *Megillath Taanith* (on which see below). See Balsdon, *The Emperor Gaius (Caligula)*, pp. 111–45; Smallwood, *The Jews Under Roman Rule*, pp. 174–80; Schürer, *The History of the Jewish People*, vol. I, pp. 394–8; Bilde, 'The Roman Emperor Gaius', pp. 68–9; Theissen, *The Gospels in Context*, pp. 125–65, especially his synoptic overview at pp. 142–4; and N. H. Taylor, 'Palestinian Christianity and the Caligula Crisis', parts I and II, 'Popular Opposition', and 'Caligula'.

[43] See Philo, *Flacc.* and *Leg. passim*; *Ant.* 19.278–91.

[44] Exacerbated by the malign advice of Caligula's anti-Jewish advisors (*Leg.* 199–205).

of course especially offensive to the Jews.⁴⁵ However, it is likely that the Jamnia incident was the crucial variable. It was a politically subversive 'Zealotic attack',⁴⁶ reminiscent of Mattathias' destruction of the pagan altar in Modein which had precipitated the Maccabean revolt (1 Macc. 2.15ff.).⁴⁷ Indeed, the analogy with the Maccabean crisis suggests that Caligula's counteraction was (like that of Antiochus IV Epiphanes) designed to forestall any Jewish insurgence and to enforce loyalty to his rule, by transforming the Temple into an imperial cult for worship of himself under the name of Ζεύς ('Επιφανής Νέος Γαΐος) (*Leg.* 188, 346).⁴⁸

In so doing he would have been well aware of the possibility of armed Jewish resistance. Hence Petronius was dispatched from Antioch with an army of some considerable force,⁴⁹ and with orders to execute and enslave any who opposed him (so *J.W.* 2.185). While the collective witness of our sources may be somewhat ambiguous, consonant with the depiction of Jewish nationalism in general offered earlier, it is more than likely that the Jewish response to this action was religio-political in motivation and (at the very least) threatened to be military in expression.⁵⁰ Certainly those Jews whom Petronius confronted in Phoenicia (and/or Antioch?) and subsequently in Tiberias,⁵¹ demonstrated a readiness to emulate their Maccabean forebears by suffering and dying on behalf of Torah, Temple and nation.⁵² That the episode was resolved without recourse to warfare

---

⁴⁵ *J.W.* 2.184; *Ant.* 18.256ff.; *Leg.* 198. Bilde, 'The Roman Emperor Gaius', pp. 71–3, suggests that Philo's particularly negative estimation of Caligula is more of a literary construct than a historical reconstruction.

⁴⁶ So Bilde, 'The Roman Emperor Gaius', pp. 74–5.

⁴⁷ Rightly Theissen, *The Gospels in Context*, p. 146 n. 44, who also (as Bilde, 'The Roman Emperor', p. 74) sees a parallel with the later cessation of Temple sacrifices on behalf of the emperor which, says Josephus, 'laid the foundation of the war with the Romans' (*J.W.* 2.409–10).

⁴⁸ So Bilde, 'The Roman Emperor Gaius', p. 75. Similarly Daniel R. Schwartz, *Studies in the Jewish Background of Christianity*, p. 82.

⁴⁹ Cf. the variable estimations in *Ant.* 18.262; *J.W.* 2.186; *Leg.* 207.

⁵⁰ Bilde, 'The Roman Emperor Gaius', detects an ambiguous mix of pacifist and non-pacifist elements, arguing that the former is redactional and the latter more representative of the actual historical situation. Cf. *J.W.* 1.185–7; *Ant.* 18.287, 302; and Tacitus, *Hist.* 5.9 ('they [the Jews] chose rather to resort to arms ...').

⁵¹ While it is unclear (from Philo's account in *Leg.*) whether or not the first encounter was with Antiochene Jews, it remains *prima facie* likely that Petronius would have met Jewish opposition in Antioch; see N. H. Taylor, 'Caligula', pp. 4ff.

⁵² The socio-political upheaval, and its affinity to the Maccabean martyr tradition, is also noted by N. H. Taylor, 'Palestinian Christianity and the Caligula Crisis', part I, pp. 104–13, who estimates that 'the protests were essentially a peasant movement, mobilized but non-violent, and determined to resist to the point of death: a phenomenon Crossan has aptly described as "mass unresisting martyrdom"', p. 106; see Crossan, *The Historical Jesus*, p. 131; cf. also Taylor's 'Popular Opposition'.

was probably due mainly to the diplomatic efforts of King Agrippa rather than to the traditional claim that disaster was averted only by Caligula's (miraculous) death in AD 41.[53]

Given that such a shocking incident, so evocative of the traumatic Maccabean crisis, took place in 39–40, it would appear *prima facie* probable that it was known to and had an impact upon the nascent Jewish Christian community. Indeed, Gerd Theissen, now followed by N. H. Taylor, has recently revived the claim that aspects of the incident have left traces in the apocalyptic (or eschatological) discourse of Mark 13.[54] Theissen's meticulous argument focuses upon Mark 13.7–8 and 13.14–16. With respect to the former, he enumerates various considerations which suggest that the envisaged 'birthpangs' – namely, wars, earthquakes and famines – can readily be derived from the circumstances which attended the Nabatean war in 36–7. Thus, for example, the following may be noted.

(i) The war between Herod Antipas and King Aretas IV – fought against the backdrop of the Parthian threat to Rome – demanded the intervention of Vitellius in order to avert further conflict (hence 'wars and rumours of wars').[55]

(ii) While Vitellius was in Jerusalem preparing for his campaign he would have received news of the catastrophic earthquake which took place in Antioch at that time.[56]

(iii) While direct evidence of famine is lacking, there is at least an indication of problems with the food supply and thus perhaps a food shortage (*Ant.* 18.90; 15.365). Later the Jews threatened not to work the land unless Petronius petitioned Caligula on their behalf (*J.W.* 2.201).

Theissen then argues that the situation in view at Mark 13.14–16 may be explained by reference to the immediately ensuing events of 39–40.[57] The distinctive expression 'desolating sacrilege' is clearly

---

[53] The latter claim is analogous to the prominent role attributed to divine intervention in the death of Antiochus IV Epiphanes (2 Macc. 9).

[54] Theissen, *The Gospels in Context*, pp. 125–65; N. H. Taylor, 'Palestinian Christianity and the Caligula Crisis', part II; see the earlier argument of Hölscher, 'Der Ursprung der Apokalypse Mk 13'.

[55] Cf. *Ant.* 18.111–12. It may be that the Nabatean war was a significant backdrop to Paul's early ministry; cf. 2 Cor. 11.32–3; Gal. 1.17.

[56] The earthquake (7 April, AD 37) is reported in Malalas (Dindorf (ed.), *Ioannis Malalae Chronographia*, 43.10).

[57] Though Theissen, *The Gospels in Context*, pp. 156–7, thinks that the intervening Mark 13.9–13 may have been added at a later date, he does allow that parts of it (e.g., verse 12) might have had a *Sitz im Leben* in Jerusalem's afflicted Hellenistic Christian community of the thirties AD.

evocative of Antiochus IV Epiphanes' Temple desecration, and thus it is likely that a comparable event is in view. That the Caligula episode is the most obvious candidate is probable on various counts.

(i) Given the lack of any indication elsewhere of an imminent 'desolating sacrilege',[58] combined with the recurrence of this resonant term in Mark 13.7, it is likely to have been precipitated not simply by a preformed topos but by an intervening specific and dramatic event.

(ii) As already noted, the Caligula episode was largely provoked by an incident analogous to that which was formative in the Maccabean resistance to Antiochus' actions: Mattathias' destruction of the pagan altar in Modein (1 Macc. 2.15ff.).

(iii) There are peculiar aspects to the key expressions employed. 'Sacrilege [βδέλυγμα]' connotes idolatry against God, as would have clearly been the case had the statue been erected.[59] While the neuter βδέλυγμα suggests a lifeless object, the masculine participle ἑστηκότα ('standing'), implies a person. The emperor's statue is both: a lifeless representation of Caligula himself.

(iv) It was the precise location – and not mere existence – of Caligula's statue which was so offensive; this correlates well with the pointed reference to 'the desolating sacrilege set up where it ought not to be' (Mark 13.14).

Although not everyone will concur with Theissen's argument in all of its details, the overall force of his careful case merits attention. Certain additional considerations may lend it some support and also provide an even broader perspective upon what may well have been a very complex situation engaging both Jews and Jewish Christians. First, it has long been recognized that the Marcan apocalypse is a large unit of material significantly indebted to Danielic tradition.[60] This in itself evinces the Maccabean crisis which, as seen in our antecedent historical reconstruction, was also an important reference point for the Jewish response to the Caligula incident. It might thus

---

[58] Theissen, ibid., pp. 158–9, deems the expectation of some religio-political persecution affecting the Temple in *As. Mos.* 8.1–5 (*c.* 4 BC–AD 30) as falling short of that envisaged by 'desolating sacrilege'.

[59] As distinct from, for example, the actual destruction of the Temple in AD 70.

[60] Classically in Hartman, *Prophecy Interpreted*, pp. 145–77, with particular reference to Dan. 7.8–27; 8.9–26; 9.24–7; 11.21–12.13.

be inferred that these apocalyptic discourse traditions – in the course of their transmission within the early church – could, within a wider and ongoing context of tension between Christians and Jews, have been given further polemical force by reference to both the Maccabean crisis and its most recent notable analogue, Caligula's traumatic action against the Temple.[61]

Second, given the argument in chapter one concerning Jewish messianic speculation based on Daniel 7.13–14, the focal point of any tension between Jews and Jewish Christians, exacerbated by the Caligula episode, could well have been the claim that deliverance from this (and any other affliction) was only to be found in Messiah Jesus (cf. Mark 13.21–2, 26, 32 et par.). Third, inasmuch as first-century Jewish nationalism could take the form of prophetic or messianic actions against Rome, and the Caligula episode may have provoked just such a response (perhaps in relation to those known to have been willing to martyr themselves before Petronius for the Jewish cause), then of note is the discourse's reference to 'false Christs and false prophets' who will lead astray (Mark 13.6, 21–2). Fourth, the fact that the traditions comprising the discourse were extant very early on and known (in some form) to Paul appears likely on the basis of various such elements to be found in 1 Thessalonians 4–5.[62] Complementing this, and pressing the case for Jewish–Christian engagement with the Caligula incident, is the scenario in view at 2 Thessalonians 2.1–12, 'described in terms which may well have gained significance from the attempt of Caligula ... only some ten years earlier, to do just what is here predicted'.[63]

In sum, it is likely that Caligula's proposed assault on the Jerusalem Temple served as a something of a 'flashpoint' for the more broadly

---

[61] On this and our ensuing considerations, cf. the similar but even more wide-ranging arguments of N. H. Taylor, 'Palestinian Christianity and the Caligula Crisis', parts I and II, who suggests that Jewish Christians in Palestine would have seen Caligula's action as fulfilling Jesus' prophecy of the Temple's destruction and the prelude to his return, and thus did not attempt to impede it. In this way they incurred alienation and opposition from their fellow Jews, not least from those zealously resisting Rome (who would also have strenuously rejected Christian claims concerning Jesus).

[62] Wenham, 'Paul and the Synoptic Apocalypse'; Nickelsburg, 'Son of Man', pp. 147–8.

[63] So Moule, *The Birth of the New Testament*, p. 171; see Bruce, *1 & 2 Thessalonians*, pp. 180–1, who recognizes that the 'man of lawlessness' figure in 2 Thess. 2.1–12 is particularly evocative of Antiochus IV Epiphanes (cf. 2 Thess. 2.4; Dan. 11.36). See references in N. H. Taylor, 'Palestinian Christianity and the Caligula Crisis', part I, p. 104 n. 15; cf. his 'Caligula', pp. 10–12.

based Maccabean-inspired Jewish nationalism outlined earlier. Emulating the response of their forebears to Antiochus IV Epiphanes, the Jews of Paul's own day – probably including some of those in Antioch[64] – zealously resisted the implementation of the emperor's edict, many of them ready to undergo martyrdom in order to defend the Jewish cause. Furthermore, while the evidence is more contentious, there is reason to think that divergent Jewish and Christian interpretations of this traumatic incident – not least in conjunction with provocative Christian claims for the martyred and exalted Jesus as Israel's messianic redeemer – would have further fuelled Jewish–Christian conflict.

The foregoing has provided both a broad and a more narrowly focused perspective upon the significant influence of the Maccabean period on the religio-political environment of first-century Judaism. There can be little doubt that the memory of the Maccabees fuelled the nationalist aspirations of those Jews – such as Saul the Pharisee – who remained zealous for the cause of an Israel still under the domination of a foreign power. In an attempt to give even greater breadth to this reconstruction, I shall now also examine certain additional information which also attests to how the Maccabees lived on in the minds of the Jewish people.

2. Maccabean martyrdom in first-century Jewish texts and traditions

Having already examined those sources widely regarded as pertaining directly to the Maccabean crisis itself, it will also prove to be fruitful to note certain disparate texts and traditions, largely of first-century provenance, which together also bear witness to the living tradition of the Maccabees. Thus, in turn, I shall examine the *Assumption of Moses*, the *Megillath Taanith* and, especially, 4 Maccabees. Here, once again, there may be discerned a broadly based concern with the suffering and vindication of Israel and, emerging from within this, the pivotal role accorded the Maccabean martyr figures. Finally, in the form of an excursus, I take up the problematic but intriguing matter of a possible Maccabean martyr cult in Antioch.

---

[64] On the Caligula episode as a possible backdrop to uneasy Jewish and Christian relations in Antioch, note N. H. Taylor, 'Caligula'; and see chapter four.

The *Assumption of Moses*

The *Assumption of Moses* is a farewell discourse in which the prophet Moses purportedly offers a prospective overview of Israel's history from its entrance into the promised land to the inauguration of the eschatological kingdom of God.[65] For our purposes, most notable amongst its features is that it clearly indicates that the vicissitudes of early first-century Judaism were being interpreted by reference to the Maccabean crisis, and indeed responded to by means of a martyr-focused suffering and vindication schema consonant with that discerned in the earlier analysis of formative Maccabean texts. This may be illustrated by initially noting certain disputed introductory considerations, and then by providing a brief analysis of chapters 5–10 which have the greatest bearing upon our particular interests.

It is generally agreed that while the *Assumption of Moses* is probably of Palestinian provenance, lack of unambiguous information cautions against any attempts to locate it more precisely within a specific sectarian context. More contentious, and of some importance in any estimation of the text's precise nature and significance, are the interrelated questions of its date and literary integrity. There are two main proposals on offer: first, that it is a Maccabean document *c*. 168–165 BC (see *As. Mos.* 8.1–9.7), though updated in the early first century through the interpolation of *As. Mos.* 6.1–7.10 (which, by common consensus, clearly refers to King Herod's reign);[66] second, it has been argued that it is a wholly first-century document, probably composed during the first three decades.[67] On either view it remains true that a comparison of chapters 6–7 and 8–9 alone readily attests that early first-century Jews were viewing their own arduous circumstances in relation to the earlier Maccabean crisis. On balance, however, the arguments in favour of the second option are most convincing,[68] and the ensuing discussion of key aspects of chapters 5–10 will proceed on that basis.

---

[65] See Tromp, *The Assumption of Moses*, for text, translation, introduction, commentary and a comprehensive bibliography.

[66] So Nickelsburg, *Resurrection, Immortality and Eternal Life*, pp. 28–31, 43–5; and Nickelsburg (ed.), *Studies on the Testament of Moses*, pp. 33–7; following Licht, 'Taxo, or the Apocalyptic Doctrine of Vengeance'.

[67] See Charles, *The Assumption of Moses*, pp. lv–lviii; Priest, 'Testament of Moses', pp. 920–1; and Tromp, *The Assumption of Moses*, pp. 116–17.

[68] See especially the summary and critique of Nickelsburg by Tromp, *The Assumption of Moses*, pp. 110–11, 120–1.

The situation depicted in chapter 5 reflects upon the transgressions of the later Hasmoneans who through their misrule – not least in defiling the Temple cult – forsook the 'truth of God'.[69] Indeed, their actions bear comparison to those of the apostate Jewish leaders complicit in the Maccabean crisis when 'truth was cast down to the ground' (Dan. 8.12). An immediate consequence of their conduct is that they then suffer at the hands of their equally evil successor, the 'petulant' King Herod (*As. Mos.* 6.2). This is followed by further punishment of sin when, in turn, Herod is superseded by direct Roman intervention into Palestinian affairs (*As. Mos.* 6.8–9). At this point, the author's own day, the scene is one of unsurpassed sin which signals the onset of the eschaton (*As. Mos.* 7; cf. Dan. 12.1).

The climactic chapters 8–10 probably do not depict the Maccabean crisis itself – so the first option above – but rather the manner in which the author envisages the eschatological scenario now under way. Nonetheless this situation is clearly portrayed in terms which draw upon traditions underlying the various accounts of the Maccabean crisis found in 1 and 2 Maccabees (and also *Ant.* 12). Thus, for example, the divine wrath upon Israel's sin which now ensues (cf. 1 Macc. 1.64; 3.8) is enacted through 'the king of the kings of the earth' who is clearly modelled on Antiochus IV Epiphanes.[70] His terrible actions comprise imprisonment, torture and execution. In particular, this includes hanging (or crucifixion) of those who confess their circumcision (= Judaism); enslavement to temple prostitution; enforced epispasm; and compulsion to blaspheme the Torah and Temple cult (*As. Mos.* 8).

In the midst of all this, one exemplary Jew remains steadfast: a Levite named Taxo admonishes his seven sons to be faithful and ready to die rather than transgress Israel's ancestral laws and religion, assured that God will avenge them (*As. Mos.* 9; cf. 2 Macc. 7, etc.).[71] It is their concord with the covenant faithfulness of their Torah-obedient ancestors which empowers them to face suffering

---

[69] A critique of the later Hasmoneans may also be detectable in certain allusions in 4Q169 and 4QpHab; note the implied critique in the reference to אנשי האמת ('men of truth') who *do* keep Torah at 4QpHab 7.10.

[70] Detailed cross-references to the Maccabean literature are provided in Tromp, *The Assumption of Moses*, pp. 214–22.

[71] Collins, *The Apocalyptic Vision of the Book of Daniel*, pp. 198–210, rightly compares this martyr disposition with that in Daniel (see 11.31–5), though whether *As. Mos.* may thus be said to emanate from similar circles (which may have been opposed to active resistance) is less clear.

and possible martyrdom. That their self-sacrifice has an atoning effect is apparent from what then ensues: God intervenes to rescue his people and inaugurate his kingdom (*As. Mos.* 10).

In this climactic episode Satan is expelled and Taxo and his sons are vindicated by an exalted priestly 'messenger [*nuntius*]' – a term indicating a mediatorial role and the judicial power to avenge (*As. Mos.* 10.2). While most commentators suggest that this 'messenger' is the archangel Michael (cf. Dan. 10.13, 21; 12.1), Tromp has argued that it is more likely to be Taxo himself.[72] In any event, following a metaphor-laden account of nature's response to this theophany (*As. Mos.* 10.3–6), the Israel-specific outcome of Taxo's action is finally portrayed: like its leading representative, Israel will be highly exalted – fixed 'firmly in the heaven of the stars' (*As. Mos.* 10.8–10; cf. Dan. 12.3).

In sum, it may be said that the *Assumption of Moses* testifies to the early first-century currency of those aspirations so central to Israel during the Maccabean period. It is designed to encourage greater Torah-obedience and covenant faithfulness as the only antidote to sin-engendered affliction. Indeed, it invites Israel's faithful to give of themselves even to the point of martyrdom, confident that in this way God will likewise be faithful and deliver, vindicate and exalt his people.

Megillath Taanith ('Scroll of Fasts')

Brief notice may be given here to the first-century document entitled the 'Scroll of Fasts' (*Megillath Taanith*, מגלת תענית) – and to certain annual Jewish celebrations closely associated therewith – because together they further indicate the esteem of the Maccabees amongst first-century Jewish nationalists.[73] The 'Scroll' comprises a list of days, arranged according to the Jewish calendar, on which fasting was prohibited and memorable events in Israel's history celebrated.[74] While certainty concerning its provenance is impossible, it

---

[72] Tromp, *The Assumption of Moses*, pp. 229–31, noting that the unprecedented introduction of an angel is less likely than the exalted priestly ordination of one who is of Levitical descent (*As. Mos.* 9.1).

[73] Text, translations and secondary sources are listed in Schürer, *The History of the Jewish People*, vol. I, p. 114, to which add K. Beyer (ed.), *Die Aramäischen Texte vom Toten Meer*, pp. 354–8. Notable studies include Zeitlin, *Megillat Taanit*; Lichtenstein, 'Die Fastenrolle'; cf. Mantel, 'Fastenrolle'.

[74] This is accompanied by a Hebrew scholia (commentary) widely regarded as later (Talmudic) and secondary.

is likely that it received final redaction prior to AD 70,[75] and emanated from those circles deeply committed to the Jewish nationalist cause against Rome. Indeed, rabbinic tradition associates it with Hananiah ben Hezekiah ben Garon in whose house the 'Eighteen Halakoth' were said to have been formulated by the more strict wing of the Pharisaic movement.[76]

On intrinsic evidence, one of its major effects (if not deliberate aims) would have been the furtherance of the nationalist cause against Rome by drawing inspiration from past Jewish victories. While some entries are unclear, readily identifiable are references to the institution of Hanukkah, Nicanor's Day, and the final evacuation of the Akra in Jerusalem.[77] Additionally, scholars have variously identified between six to eleven other entries with events recorded in 1 and 2 Maccabees. In view of our earlier claim that Caligula's Temple edict would have recalled the Maccabean crisis, it is also noteworthy that alongside references to various Maccabean events is a reference to the report of Caligula's death as ending his threat to the Temple.[78]

Finally, a related matter which may be reinforced at this point is the ongoing celebration of Hanukkah (the 'Feast of Dedication') and probably also of Nicanor's Day.[79] Hanukkah annually celebrated the Maccabees' victories and the rededication of the Temple (1 Macc. 4.36–59; 2 Macc. 1.1–2.18), surviving throughout the first century and beyond.[80] Additionally, although Nicanor's Day (1 Macc. 7.39–50; 2 Macc. 14.31–3; 15.6–11, 22–36) appears not to have enjoyed the longevity of Hanukkah, Josephus witnesses to the fact that it was still observed in his own day (*Ant.* 12.412).

---

[75] So Lichtenstein, 'Die Fastenrolle', p. 264; cf. the discussion in Farmer, *Maccabees, Zealots and Josephus*, pp. 205–9.

[76] *b. Shab.* 13b; the scholion attributes it to his son, Eleazar. Efron, *Studies on the Hasmonean Period*, deems the document to be 'conclusive evidence of Pharisee identification with national aims', p. xii.

[77] Entered under the 25th of Kislev (cf. 1 Macc. 4.59; 2 Macc. 10.8), 13th of Adar (cf. 1 Macc. 7.49; 2 Macc. 15.36), and 23rd of Iyyar (cf. 1 Macc. 13.51) respectively.

[78] Entered under the 22nd of Shebat.

[79] See discussions in Zeitlin, 'Hanukkah. Its Origin and Its Significance'; Stein, 'The Liturgy of Hanukkah'; Farmer, *Maccabees, Zealots and Josephus*, pp. 132–51; and Alon, 'Did the Nation and Its People Cause the Hasmoneans to be Forgotten?', pp. 10–14.

[80] Cf., for example, John 10.33; *Ant.* 12.319, 324–5; and the *Mishnah* (*m. Bik.* 1.6; *m. Rosh HaSh.* 1.3; *m. Taan.* 2.10; *m. Meg.* 3.4, 6; *m. Moed Q.* 3.9; *m. B. Qam.* 6.6).

The Maccabees as exemplars for first-century Diaspora Judaism: 4 Maccabees

The anonymous 4 Maccabees[81] is a rhetorical and philosophical Jewish composition based upon the proposition that devout reason is superior to human passion, and this is primarily illustrated through what is ostensibly a graphic expansion of the martyr narratives concerning Eleazar and the seven Jewish brothers found in 2 Maccabees 6.18–7.40.[82] Our interest in this text is essentially threefold: first, in addressing basic questions of introduction, to observe that 4 Maccabees attests to a living Maccabean martyr tradition readily available to Paul, this being all the more likely if (as is possible) 4 Maccabees emanated from Antioch; second, by reference to its opening philosophical discourse, to note the basic apologetical claim made for Torah with a view to our later analysis of Paul's estimation of Torah in relation to Christ (see chapter six); third, by delineating common characteristic features of the martyr narratives, to set forth (as in chapter one in relation to 1 and 2 Maccabees) a nexus of important issues, themes and terminology – together focusing upon the suffering, atoning significance and vindication of the martyr – which is of significance for the later Antioch-focused exegesis of Galatians 1 and 2.[83]

The provenance and purpose of 4 Maccabees

It would appear that Bickerman(n)'s influential study arguing for a date *c.* 20–54 for 4 Maccabees has now been superseded by an emerging consensus in favour of a later date *c.* 90–100.[84] However,

---

[81] For bibliography, see Klauck, *4. Makkabäerbuch*, pp. 680–5; deSilva, *4 Maccabees*, pp. 158–63; and especially van Henten, *The Maccabean Martyrs*, pp. 305–34.

[82] So van Henten, *The Maccabean Martyrs*, pp. 70–3. Surkau, *Martyrien in jüdischer und frühchristlicher Zeit*, p. 29, argued for independent use by 2 and 4 Maccabees of an older common tradition. See the discussion in Klauck, *4. Makkabäerbuch*, pp. 654–7.

[83] At this point it may be worth reiterating and particularizing certain of the earlier introductory comments concerning method. The warrant for and viability of correlating 4 Maccabees and Galatians 1 and 2 does not depend on Paul having had access to a text whose precise proximity must remain uncertain. Rather 4 Maccabees is but one further (albeit important) indication of an ongoing and widespread living tradition which, via various converging lines of evidence, I argue is available to, and known and appropriated by Paul.

[84] See especially van Henten, 'Datierung und Herkunft des vierten Makkabäerbuches' and, most recently, *The Maccabean Martyrs*, pp. 73–81. In the course of

given that 4 Maccabees clearly depends upon and develops the much earlier 2 Maccabees 6–7, it may still be allowed that it offers an important indication of the currency of traditions associated with the Maccabean martyrs during the first century. Of further significance is that its provenance, though not certain, might be assigned to Antioch (or, possibly, a city in Asia Minor).[85] Less clear is its purpose and immediate setting. References to 'the present occasion' (cf. 4 Macc. 1.10; 3.19; 14.9) and a Jewish epitaph (4 Macc. 17.8–10) have lead some to suggest that it was originally composed for oral delivery, whether as a synagogal sermon (perhaps delivered at Hanukkah), a homily given in commemoration of the Maccabean martyrs (perhaps at their burial site) or a festival speech on some other occasion.[86] However, it is more likely that 4 Maccabees was from the outset a literary work; that its various features bear close comparison to the philosophical diatribe and also epideictic speech;[87] but that this is in service of a document which is concerned with the threat of assimilation – and possible periodic persecution – in the Jewish Diaspora.[88] That is, while 4 Maccabees gives no indication of a crisis such as that which precipitated the Maccabean revolt, first-century Diaspora Jews regularly experienced various socio-economic and cultural pressures – these on occasion escalating to violent persecution – which could engender abandonment of their ancestral way of life. In any event, it will suffice to note that, at the very least, Maccabean martyr traditions are here being invoked in order to undergird and explicate the ever-threatened identity and praxis of Diaspora Judaism, this being in some tem-

---

his examination of the evidence, van Henten rejects the early/mid first-century dating (of Bickerman(n), 'The Date of Fourth Maccabees', until recently followed by many), and also certain arguments for a second-century dating (variously proposed by Dupont-Sommer, *Le quatrième livre des Machabées*, p. 75; Breitenstein, *Beobachtungen*, pp. 173–5; and Campbell, *The Rhetoric of Righteousness*, pp. 219–28). Instead, van Henten cautiously concludes that 'a date in the last decades of the first century C.E. or further in the second century cannot be excluded', p. 78. Cf. Barclay, *Jews in the Mediterranean Diaspora*, pp. 369–80, 448–9, favouring 'a date around the end of the first century', p. 449.

[85] See van Henten, 'Datierung und Herkunft des vierten Makkabäerbuches' (followed by Klauck, *4. Makkabäerbuch*, pp. 666–7), and *The Maccabean Martyrs*, pp. 78–81.

[86] These options are reviewed and rejected by van Henten, *The Maccabean Martyrs*, pp. 58–62.

[87] So van Henten, ibid., pp. 62–7.

[88] Barclay, *Jews in the Mediterranean Diaspora* (following Klauck, *4. Makkabäerbuch*, pp. 664–5), holds that 'the work is designed to counter the temptations to assimilation among acculturated Jews', pp. 378–9.

poral and perhaps geographic proximity to the life and ministry of Paul.

The philosophical discourse

Conforming to the rules of classical rhetoric, the opening exordium (4 Macc. 1.1–12) sets forth both the thesis – 'whether devout reason [ὁ εὐσεβὴς λογισμός] is sovereign over the emotions' (4 Macc. 1.1a) – and the bipartite method to be used in its demonstration: (a) a brief theoretical discourse (4 Macc. 1.13–3.18) and (b) a lengthy narrative demonstration focused upon the Maccabean martyrs (4 Macc. 3.19–18.24).[89] Given our concerns, the discourse is significant in at least three respects. First, here it is most evident that our highly acculturated author is recasting popular Stoic ideals within his firmly Jewish frame of reference in a sophisticated attempt to persuade his audience – whether Jew or Gentile – that the wisest way of life (philosophy) is that governed by a godly way of thinking (devout reason) whose ultimate basis and sufficiency is Torah-obedience, even to the point of death.[90] Second, in so doing, a Daniel-like outlook is readily discernible: a Torah-obedient upbringing and lifestyle – not least abstinence from prohibited foods (4 Macc. 1.33–5) – effects the wisdom which is able to discern the ways of God in the world. Indeed, as the example of the Patriarch Joseph readily attests, Torah-grounded reason can prevail over any kind of 'desire [ἐπιθυμία]':

> Thus the law says, 'You shall not covet your neighbour's wife ... or anything that is your neighbour's.' In fact, since the law has told us not to covet, I could prove to you all the more that reason is able to control desires. (4 Macc. 2.5–6b)

Thirdly, another Diaspora-based Jew likewise concerned to speak out of an essentially Jewish framework in a manner comprehensible to Jew and Gentile alike is the apostle Paul. However, as a Jewish *Christian*, he argues that sin's effect upon Torah within Judaism

---

[89] On the exordium, see Klauck, 'Hellenistische Rhetoric im Diasporajudentum'; on the rhetorical aspect of 4 Maccabees as a whole, see Klauck *4. Makkabäerbuch*, pp. 659–62.

[90] On the philosophical aspect of 4 Maccabees, see Renehan, 'The Greek Philosophic Background'; Weber, 'Eusebeia und Logismos'; and van Henten, *The Maccabean Martyrs*, pp. 270–94.

renders it incapable of achieving what is being claimed for it here in 4 Maccabees. Indeed, the Torah-obedience which God requires (even unto martyrdom) is only made possible by life conformed to the martyred (and risen) Messiah Jesus.[91]

The martyr narratives

The author introduces the 'narrative demonstration' of his thesis with a thumbnail historical preface which often inaccurately recapitulates and enhances details found in 2 Maccabees (4 Macc. 3.20–4.26).[92] Of particular note here is that the synopsis of Antiochus IV Epiphanes' persecution is depicted by employing a collocation of stock themes and terms which, as will be seen, are likewise prominent at key junctures throughout Galatians 1 and 2. Thus, for example, Antiochus 'plunders [πορθέω]' Jerusalem; is resisted by those braving death by refusing to 'abolish [καταλύω]' Torah-observance; and therefore tries 'to compel [ἀναγκάζω]' the nation 'to eat defiling foods and to renounce Judaism [τὸν Ἰουδαϊσμόν]' (4 Macc. 4.22–6).

Thus the stage is set for three dramatic encounters between the devout representatives of Judaism – Eleazar, the seven brothers and their mother – and the archetypal Gentile antagonist Antiochus IV Epiphanes.[93] It is nothing less than a 'divine contest' whose outcome the whole world anxiously awaits (4 Macc. 17.11, 14). And it is one in which each of the protagonists will suffer, atone and vindicate Israel. Clearly these Daniel-like Jewish representatives are utterly devoted to Torah. Indeed, there is an inextricable interrelationship between their very createdness and their Torah-obedience to the point of death. Thus Eleazar can claim that Israel's Creator God has conformed Torah to the very nature (κατὰ φύσιν) of the Jewish people (4 Macc. 5.25b–26). Indeed, by means of an elaborate birth/nurture metaphor, the author correlates creation/covenant/Torah, in arguing that it is the fusion of the seven brothers' natural (fraternal) development and common Torah training within the nation Israel, which renders their 'brotherly love' the more ardent

---

[91] Cf. especially the excursus on Romans 7.1–8.11 in reference to Galatians 2.19 in chapter six.
[92] Stowers, '4 Maccabees', pp. 927–8, briefly itemizes the notable inaccuracies.
[93] Currently the most penetrating analysis of the religious and political significance of the faithful Maccabean martyrs, drawing upon both 2 and 4 Maccabees, is that of van Henten, *The Maccabean Martyrs*, especially pp. 125–269.

and thus their faithfulness in the face of torture and death the more enduring (4 Macc. 13.19–14.1; cf. 11.15). In this way they are able to contend fearlessly for what is understood to be (as in Daniel) a creation-wide battle for the truth (ἀλήθεια), namely, Torah, the Jewish way of life, and (ultimately) the holy name of Israel's God. They do so by defending Torah, principally through their steadfast refusal to transgress its food laws and thereby nullify its authority.[94] They also seek to advance its cause by various means at their disposal, principally mutual encouragement towards martyrdom, and the persuasion and admonishment of Antiochus – all this engendering the amazement of their persecutors (cf. 4 Macc 6.11; 8.5).

In fact, as already noted in the earlier analysis of texts in relation to the Maccabean crisis, it is precisely in and through the martyrs' suffering and death that they atone for Israel's sin, defeat the enemy and vindicate themselves and the nation.[95] Thus even in their terrible torment they remain upright (ὀρθός) and resolutely fixed upon the One who not only protects them from, but also transforms them out of, their trial to the point of death. In effect, they are 'running the course toward immortality' and will 'live to God' (4 Macc. 7.17–19; 9.8, 22; 14.5–6). In the midst of this they invoke divine mercy upon Israel: 'Be merciful to your people and let our punishment suffice for them. Make my blood their purification, and take my life in exchange for theirs' (4 Macc. 6.28–9). Here, in essence, Eleazar is imploring God to receive his faithfulness until death as a vicarious atonement on behalf of the sins of the Jewish people. The implication (made explicit elsewhere) is that this will bring about (a) victory over Antiochus' oppressive regime, and the tyrant's destruction and eternal punishment; and (b) a renewal of the Jewish way of life.[96] Indeed, further to the latter, the author concludes his encomium on the seven brothers by alluding to the profound impact their sufferings continue to have upon Jews in his own day (4 Macc. 14.7–10).

No doubt it is a function of the ancient understanding of gender that the most dramatic demonstration of the author's thesis is the

---

[94] Eleazar disdainfully rejects the opportunity to save himself by 'pretending [ὑποκρινόμενος]' to eat swine's flesh, as unworthy of one who had lived so long in accordance 'with the truth [πρὸς ἀλήθειαν]' (4 Macc. 6.15–18).

[95] On the effective death and vindication of the martyrs in 4 Maccabees, see van Henten, *The Maccabean Martyrs*, pp. 150–3, 182–4.

[96] 4 Macc. 1.11; 6.10; 9.24, 30–2; 11.20–7; 12.17–18; 17.20–2; 18.4.

third and climactic conflict in which Antiochus is amazingly overcome, not by mere age or youth, but by a woman and mother (4 Macc. 14.11–17.6).[97] Directing her innate maternal love so that her mind disdained all torment, the mother of the seven youths also proved to be 'of the same mind as Abraham' (4 Macc. 14.11–20; cf. 15.28). Her own travail (and virtue) had been to witness her sons' suffering, her devout reason 'unmoved' throughout 'because of [her] faith in God' (4 Macc. 15.24). Now, in virtue of her own self-martyrdom, she has likewise 'nullified' the tyrant and demonstrated her own faith, 'Nobly set like a roof on the pillars [ἐπὶ τοὺς στύλους] of [her] sons'.[98]

The concluding peroratio (4 Macc. 17.7–18.24) draws together and underscores many of the central themes. Thus, for example, an epitaph (whether authentic or a literary construct) stresses the 'political and patriotic' import of the martyrs as those who vindicated the nation over the tyrant who 'wished to destroy the way of life of the Hebrews [βίαν τὴν Εβραίων πολιτείαν καταλῦσαι θέλοντος]' (4 Macc. 17.9–10).[99] An extended athletic metaphor conveys the national and cosmic aspect of the contest (4 Macc. 17.11–16). Then the atoning significance of the death and exaltation of the martyrs is made all the more explicit:

> because of them our enemies did not rule over our nation, the tyrant was punished, and the homeland purified – they having become, as it were, a ransom for the sin of our nation. And through the blood of those devout ones and their death as an expiation [τοῦ ἱλαστηρίου τοῦ θανάτου αὐτῶν], divine Providence preserved Israel that previously had been afflicted. (4 Macc. 17.20c–22)

Finally, the author exhorts his audience – the 'offspring of the seed of Abraham'[100] – to obey the Torah so that they too may share in the divine inheritance accorded the martyrs (4 Macc. 18.1–4). From the concluding section it would appear that what is envisaged is instruction from the scriptures – not least concerning the zeal of Phineas and the blessedness of Daniel – with a view to effecting the (national) 'resurrection life' which they promise (4 Macc. 18.9–

---

[97] 2 Macc. 7.41 simply records the mother's death.
[98] On the depiction of the mother and sons at 4 Macc. 17.2–6, cf. Dan. 12.1–3.
[99] So van Henten, 'A Jewish Epitaph in a Literary Text', p. 69.
[100] Cf. 'sons of Abraham [οἱ δὲ Αβραμιαῖοι παῖδες]' (4 Macc. 18.23).

19).¹⁰¹ A benediction, found in variant forms in Paul's letters, is appended: ᾧ ἡ δόξα εἰς τοὺς αἰῶνας τῶν αἰώνων· αμην.¹⁰²

The reasons for devoting particular attention to 4 Maccabees will now be readily apparent. In a text of some temporal – and perhaps also geographic – proximity to the life and ministry of Paul in Antioch, we have a vibrant testimony to the ongoing influence of the Maccabean martyr traditions. Indeed, in the manner indicated at the outset of this analysis, there will be reason to draw upon various aspects of the issues, themes and terms attested to in 4 Maccabees in the later detailed analysis of Galatians 1 and 2. This will prove to be especially true of the dramatic Antioch incident, a scenario in which the contest between the Jewish (Maccabean martyr) versus Gentile (Antiochus IV Epiphanes) way of life is now radically redrawn in the form of a contest between a Christian (Paul) and a Jewish (Peter) pattern of existence. However, at this stage we may press the case concerning the currency of Maccabean texts and traditions one step further by noting the suggestion that some Jews may have venerated the Maccabean martyrs in Antioch.

An excursus: the Maccabean martyr cult in Antioch

That the exemplary steadfastness of the Maccabean martyrs had a significant influence upon the early church's cult of the saints has long been recognized.¹⁰³ Of particular interest for our purposes is the intriguing possibility that a Maccabean martyr cult existed in Antioch, with its origins traceable back to the first-century Jewish community there. By reference to disparate and late source materials – here given in reverse chronological order – the principal evidence for this somewhat contentious claim may be set forth as follows.¹⁰⁴

---

[101] Note the collocation of Ezek. 37.2–3 and Deut. 32.39; 30.20 at 4 Macc. 18.16–19, which seems to imply God's recreative activity upon both martyrs and nation as a whole in a manner which might be termed 'resurrection' (and which the author apparently does not view as inconsistent with his various other references to the martyrs' immortal life with God and to the nation's renewal).

[102] 4 Macc. 18.24; note Rom. 11.36; 16.27; Gal. 1.5; cf. 2 Tim. 4.18; see also Heb. 13.21.

[103] Significant studies on the Jewish roots of the Christian cult of martyrs and saints are noted by Horbury, 'The Cult of Christ and the Cult of the Saints', pp. 444–5, whose own significant contribution considers a wider range of evidence for the Jews' veneration of their saints from the Hasmonean period onwards.

[104] Especially Rampolla, 'Martyre et sepulture des Machabées'; Obermann, 'The Sepulchre of the Maccabean Martyrs'; E. Bammel, 'Zum jüdischen Märtyrercult'; Schatkin, 'The Maccabean Martyrs'; Williams, *Jesus' Death as Saving Event*, pp. 248–51.

(i) A medieval Judaeo-Arabic text, the *Farag-Book of Nissim Ibn Shahin of Kairowan*, incorporates rabbinic materials concerning the Maccabean martyrs. Embedded within it, though without rabbinic parallel, is the following: 'And there was built upon them [the martyred brothers and their mother] the synagogue of Hashmonith. The synagogue of Hashmonith was the first synagogue built after the Second Temple.'[105]

(ii) An Arabic topographical depiction of Antioch (*Codex Vaticanus Arabicus 286*), its content dating no later than the sixth century AD, attests to the existence of a Christian church in the western section of the city. Said to be called a 'house of prayer' by the Jews, this church was built on the grave site of the Maccabean martyrs, and named St Ashmunith in honour of the mother of the seven brothers.[106]

(iii) The sixth-century Byzantine chronographer Malalas records a local tradition that Demetrius I (162–150 BC) allowed Judas Maccabeus to bury those who had been martyred by Antiochus IV Epiphanes (outside Antioch) in a synagogue located in the Kerateion (southern) quarter of the city.[107]

(iv) A Syriac martyr calendar from Edessa (*c*. AD 412) includes a reference under 1 August to: 'those that were interred at Antioch, that is to say in Krtia, who were the sons of Shamuni, mentioned in (the book of) the Maccabees'.[108]

(v) In his *In solemnitate martyrum Machabaeorum* (Sermon 300), post-AD 391, Augustine refers to the Christian basilica in Antioch which revered the Maccabean martyrs, indi-

---

[105] The ET is that argued for by Obermann, 'The Sepulchre of the Maccabean Martyrs', pp. 255–9; text in Obermann, *The Arabic Original of Ibn Shahin's Book of Comfort*, pp. 25–8.

[106] ET in Schatkin, 'The Maccabean Martyrs', p. 101 (from the French translation of Rampolla, 'Martyre et sepulture des Machabées', p. 390); see also Stinespring, 'The Description of Antioch in Codex Vaticanus Arabicus 286'; Obermann, 'The Sepulchre of the Maccabean Martyrs', p. 252; Kraeling, 'The Jewish Community at Antioch', p. 140.

[107] Dindorf (ed.), *Ioannis Malalae Chronographia*, pp. 206ff. Bickerman(n), 'Les Maccabées de Malalas', p. 198, thinks that Malalas' version of the Maccabean crisis stems from a Seleucid account rather than 2 Maccabees. Rampolla, 'Martyre et sepulture des Machabées', pp. 384ff. argued that this synagogue (as also the Kerateion quarter) was built under Seleucus I Nicator (304–281 BC).

[108] Text and translation in W. Wright, 'An Ancient Syrian Martyrology'.

cating that it was built by the Christians themselves (*PL* 38.1379).[109]

(vi) Chrysostom's *In santos Maccabaeos homilia* 1,1 (*PG* 50.617) and *De sanctis martyribus sermo* 1 (*PG* 50.647), *c*. 386–98, attest that the tombs of the Maccabees were venerated in Antioch.

(vii) Gregory of Nazianzus, in his *In laudem Machabaeorum* (Oration 15) delivered in Cappadocia *c*. 365, defends the veneration of the Maccabean martyrs, though makes no mention of their relics (*PG* 35.911–34).

On the strength of the foregoing it is likely that no later than the mid to late fourth century AD Antiochene Christians were venerating the Maccabean martyrs. A related and reasonable claim is that this took place in a church which was a former synagogue taken over from the Antiochene Jews.[110] Whether this synagogue was one which had claimed to house the relics of the Maccabean martyrs is a more contentious matter.[111]

Even more uncertain are attempts to trace the cult back to a first-century Jewish community in Antioch. This claim rests largely on the late witness of Nissim Ibn Shahin to the effect that 'The synagogue of Hashmonith was the first synagogue built after the Second Temple.' His testimony may conflict with that of Malalas who seems to associate the burial site with an already existing synagogue. In any event, Nissim Ibn Shahin does not specify the city in which the synagogue to which he refers is located – though the correspondence between 'Hasmonith', 'St Ashmonith' (*Codex 286*) and 'Shamuni' (the Syriac martyr calendar) seem to favour Antioch.[112]

---

[109] Whether his remark 'Haec basilica a Christianis tenetur, a Christianis aedificata est [This basilica is occupied by Christians, it was built by Christians]' means the church was a 'repaired or remodeled' former synagogue (Williams, *Jesus' Death as Saving Event*, p. 250) is unclear.

[110] Schatkin, 'The Maccabean Martyrs', pp. 106–7, notes other instances of Christians seizing synagogues, and viably suggests that such an occurrence in Antioch may have been a reaction to the Judaizing problem so well attested in Chrysostom's *Adversus Judaeos* (*PG* 48.843–942).

[111] Jeremias, *Heiligengräber in Jesu Umwelt*, pp. 124ff.; and Bickerman(n), 'Les Maccabées de Malalas', pp. 201–4, both argue that this would have been possible without necessarily violating purity regulations.

[112] So E. Bammel, 'Zum jüdischen Märtyrercult', pp. 122–3; Schatkin, 'The Maccabean Martyrs', pp. 102–3; Williams, *Jesus' Death as Saving Event*, p. 251; contra Obermann, 'The Sepulchre of the Maccabean Martyrs', pp. 260–1, who argues for Jerusalem.

Some corroboration might be found in 4 Maccabees 17.7–10, if we could be confident that the proposed tomb of the martyrs mentioned there had some basis in fact and that 4 Maccabees had been composed in Antioch. Likewise, some support would be forthcoming if it could be shown that the Maccabean martyrs were indeed executed in Antioch, though the evidence cited in favour of this is not unambiguous.[113]

In sum, it is difficult to be assured one way or another on this matter. Some are confident that an Antioch-based Jewish Maccabean martyr-cult tradition goes back to the first century;[114] others allow for the possibility but remain cautious;[115] and still others are more dubious.[116] However, inasmuch as it is highly unlikely that the Antiochene Christians would have invented such a cult *de novo*, and given the various arguments we have summoned to date in support of the currency and significance of Maccabean martyr traditions in first-century Judaism, it must be deemed at least possible that a Jewish Maccabean martyr cult could have existed early on in Antioch.

3. Maccabean martyrdom and Paul: Romans 3.21–6 and its Maccabean tradition-history

A range of evidence has now been summoned in support of the claim that a living tradition concerning the Maccabees would have been readily available to a first-century Jew such as Paul. Indeed, at two particular junctures we had reason to press specifically in Paul's direction: (a) by arguing that he may well have been numbered amongst those Pharisees sympathetic to the Maccabean-inspired Jewish nationalism (a claim which will be substantiated in our later analysis of Galatians 1.13–14), and (b) by suggesting that echoes of the Caligula episode, with its evocations of Antiochus IV Epiphanes,

---

[113] Schatkin, 'The Maccabean Martyrs', pp. 98–9, points to: the setting and use of the Greek language in the dialogue of 2 Macc. 7 as both suggesting Antioch (v. Jerusalem); certain Jewish and Christian traditions concerning a 'third captivity' at Antioch under Antiochus (such as *y. Sanh.* 29c; *Lam. Rab.* 2.9; Chrysostom, *Adversus Judaeos* 5.4, 7; 6.2 [*PG* 48, 890]), confirmed by 4 Macc. 8.3; and the Syriac martyr calendar.

[114] E. Bammel, 'Zum jüdischen Märtyrercult'; Hadas, *The Third and Fourth Books of Maccabees*, p. 10; Hengel and Schwemer, *Paul Between Damascus and Antioch*, pp. 188–9.

[115] Horbury, 'The Cult of Christ and the Cult of the Saints', p. 452.

[116] For example, Klauck, *4. Makkabäerbuch*, pp. 675–77.

might be discernible in a text such as 2 Thessalonians 2. However, do we have any indication that Paul not only knew of, but actively engaged, the Maccabean traditions available to him? In this final section, with the ensuing detailed examination of Galatians 1–2 *sub judice*, I offer one notable piece of evidence that he did. This will take the form of a brief review of J. W. van Henten's argument that an important element of Romans 3.21–6 has a background in certain seminal Maccabean martyr texts.[117] Van Henten argues that the key constituent terms of the central phrase ἱλαστήριον διὰ τῆς πίστεως ἐν τῷ αὐτοῦ αἵματι (Rom. 3.25a) have a traditio-historical background in martyr-related ideas, notably the triad of faithfulness, effective (vicarious) death, and vindication (resurrection).[118] In a prefatory *status quaestionis* he sets forth the following ground-clearing observations: that Paul is drawing upon traditional imagery and terminology in Romans 3.24–6;[119] that it may be questioned whether its background is to be found exclusively in the Day of Atonement ritual (Lev. 16);[120] and that whether or not the contentious phrase διὰ [τῆς] πίστεως at Romans 3.25 constitutes a *Fremdkörper* in the traditional material cannot be assumed in advance. He concludes his introductory considerations by suggesting that this key phrase be taken as a staccato formulation explicating the atonement: 'an atonement – through faith – in (or: by the shedding of; or: at the cost of) his blood'.[121]

An extensive search for possible Jewish and pagan counterparts to various permutations of this phrase's constituent terms leads van Henten to explore in greater detail three possible parallels: DanielLXX 3.39–40; 2 Maccabees 7.37–8.5; and 4 Maccabees 6.28–9 and 17.2–24. The first of these involves the Prayer of Azariah (Dan.LXX/Th. 3.24–45) which is to be located against the immediate backdrop of Antiochus IV Epiphanes' persecutions

---

[117] Others who have argued, with varying degrees of cogency, for such a background to Rom. 3.21–6 include David Hill, *Greek Words and Hebrew Meanings*, pp. 41–7; Williams, *Jesus' Death as Saving Event*, pp. 38–41; and Heard, 'Maccabean Martyr Theology', pp. 461–517. See also Hengel and Schwemer, *Paul Between Damascus and Antioch*, pp. 191–6, for a broad consideration of possible points of contact between 4 Maccabees and the letters of Paul, including Romans.

[118] Van Henten, 'The Tradition-historical Background of Romans 3.25'.

[119] He adds that this need not necessarily involve the use of a pre-Pauline formula.

[120] Although the fact that the Day of Atonement is indeed *an* influence upon Rom. 3.24–6 is further confirmed by van Henten's word study; see, 'The Tradition-historical Background of Romans 3.25', pp. 106–7.

[121] Ibid., p. 106.

(Dan.LXX/Th. 3.28, 32). Consonant with the analysis offered in chapter one, it is noted that the focal concern is the suffering and vindication of Israel, this being in the form of a petition that God act to deliver his sinful people for his own name's sake.[122] A particular concern is that Israel currently lacks both a representative/ advocate (a 'prince, or prophet, or leader') and an operative Temple cult (Dan.LXX/Th. 3.38). Hence the three companions offer up their own suffering – namely, the prospective torment of the fiery furnace – in lieu thereof: 'may we be accepted ... such may our sacrifice be ... And now with all our heart we follow thee' (Dan.LXX/Th. 3.39–41). Furthermore, this is accompanied by an appeal for God to atone, ἐξιλάσαι.[123] The implication is clear: they are presenting themselves 'as an alternative sacrifice and ask [God] in this way for atonement, so that the sins of the people are being redeemed'.[124]

A second set of parallel terminology is to be found in 2 Maccabees 7.37–8.5. The martyrdom of the youngest brother climaxes with a tripartite prayer calling upon God to: act mercifully towards his people (ἵλεως ταχὺ τῷ ἔθνει γενέσθαι); compel Antiochus IV Epiphanes to acknowledge Israel's God; and through the lives of the brothers bring divine wrath upon the nation to an end (2 Macc. 7.37).[125] Thus it is that the youth dies pure, having completely entrusted (πεποιθώς) himself to God throughout his ordeal, with his martyrdom bringing about atonement.[126] Indeed, as noted in the earlier analysis of 2 Maccabees, the efficacy of the martyrs is immediately apparent in the successes of Judas' army, who duly acknowledges the youths' sacrificial 'blood [αἷμα]' (2 Macc. 8.1ff). All this leads van Henten to conclude that 'the phrases ἵλεως γενέσθαι (7.37), ἐπὶ τῷ κυρίῳ πεποιθώς (7.40) and αἵματα (8.4), form part of a coherent train of thought concerning the effective meaning of the death of the martyrs and their perfect obedience to the Lord'.[127]

Finally, 4 Maccabees offers two further instances of parallel ter-

---

[122] Dan.LXX/Th. 3.34–6; cf. Dan. 9.

[123] Dan.LXX 3.40b, this to be taken as the second singular aorist middle imperative of ἐξιλάσκομαι ('atone for', 'make atonement', 'propitiate').

[124] Van Henten, 'The Tradition-historical Background of Romans 3.25', p. 115.

[125] Note especially, ἐν ἐμοὶ δὲ καὶ τοῖς ἀδελφοῖς (2 Macc. 7.38). Van Henten, ibid., p. 118 n. 2, notes that ἐν indicates the location or mediation of the martyrs. Cf. the later analysis of ἐν ἐμοί at Gal. 1.16; 2.20.

[126] The effectiveness of his death is also implicit in the antecedent usage of καταλλάσσεσθαι at 2 Macc. 7.33 (cf. 1.5; 5.20; 8.29).

[127] Van Henten, 'The Tradition-historical Background of Romans 3.25', p. 121.

minology. In 4 Maccabees 6.28–9, Eleazar gives his life for Israel with a final intercession which employs the same formula used by the seventh son in 2 Maccabees 7.37–8: 'Be merciful to your people [ἵλεως γενοῦ τῷ ἔθνει σου] and let my (literally: our) punishment be a satisfaction on their behalf. Make my blood their purification and take my life instead of theirs [ἀντίψυχον αὐτῶν].'[128] In 4 Maccabees 17.20–4 (as noted earlier), the martyrs are honoured because their deaths were 'a ransom [ἀντίψυχον]' and their blood 'an expiation [ἱλαστήριον]' for errant Israel. Van Henten stresses the fact that διὰ τοῦ αἵματος ... καὶ τοῦ ἱλαστηρίου τοῦ θανάτου thus constitutes (as at Rom. 3.25) the use of traditional cultic terminology to express a non-cultic atonement through the death of a human being.[129]

Moreover, in addition to 4 Maccabees 17.20–2 exhibiting close parallels to two of the three key terms in Romans 3.25 (ἱλαστήριον, αἷμα), there are indications of a conception of 'faith' comparable to Paul's use of πίστις in Romans 3.25. A paramount concern of the martyrs is piety: 'Fight the sacred and noble fight for piety, through it may the just providence that protected our fathers become merciful to our people' (4 Macc. 9.24).[130] Here the combination of ἵλεως and διὰ + genitive phrase is suggestive of ἱλαστήριον διὰ τῆς πίστεως in Romans 3.25. Indeed, that εὐσέβεια in 4 Maccabees can be viewed as an alternative word for πίστις is suggested by two factors: (i) its regular use in instances where other authors would have readily employed πίστις (for example, in connection with the faith in God exhibited by Abraham and/or Isaac, Daniel);[131] and (ii) two occasions when πίστις or πίστεως are directly applied to the martyrs (4 Macc. 7.21; 17.2). From all this van Henten concludes that 'the triad of ἱλαστήριον, αἷμα and πίστις is traditional in a martyrological context, and that therefore πίστις probably refers to the faithfulness of the martyr until death'.[132]

I have followed van Henten's argument closely due to its technical nature and obvious bearing upon this study. In addition to the wide-ranging discussion above, it provides a strong *prima facie* case

---

[128] ET van Henten, ibid., p. 122; see 4 Macc. 9.24; 12.17. The interchangeability of 'blood' and 'life' might also be applied to Rom. 3.25, this pressing the idea that Jesus' blood is the climactic aspect of a faithful life.
[129] Ibid., p. 123.
[130] ET van Henten, ibid., p. 124.
[131] References, ibid., p. 125, n. 1; note especially 4 Macc. 16.22 where πίστις is actually used as a synonym for εὐσέβεια.
[132] Ibid., p. 126.

for Paul's engagement with Maccabean martyr traditions. Furthermore, it is all the more significant in that it involves one of the most central atonement texts in the Pauline corpus – one which, as will be seen, bears close comparison with Paul's argumentation at Galatians 2.15–21. Of course, as Romans 3.21–6 itself clearly attests, Paul's appropriation of these traditions involves their radical reconfiguration through his own experience and understanding of the rejected but now risen Jesus, the exalted martyr through whom God has now fully manifested his righteousness to Israel and the world. The nature and significance of this reconfiguration – and not least its bearing upon who constitute the faithful people of God – will comprise an important element of our ensuing consideration of Paul's argument in Galatians 1 and 2.

4. Conclusion

It has not been the intention of this chapter to argue for 'pan-Maccabeanism'. Rather, the more modest (and realistic) contention throughout has been that the Maccabean period continued to influence at least certain significant strands of the Jewish environment within which Paul lived as both zealous Jew and faithful Jewish Christian convert. Towards this end I have summoned various converging lines of evidence: the religio-political continuity between the Maccabees and first-century Jewish nationalism, embracing certain segments of the Pharisaic movement; the ardent Jewish response to the trauma of the Caligula Temple edict as a particular instance of this wider phenomenon; and certain variegated texts testifying to the living tradition of the Maccabean martyrs – not least, perhaps, in Antioch. Finally, albeit briefly, in Romans 3.21–6 I offered one notable piece of evidence that all this (and no doubt much more) was christologically reappropriated by Paul. That is, as will be seen, in virtue of his encounter with the risen Jesus, Paul had become persuaded that God's covenantal faithfulness was now being fulfilled through Israel's rejected, martyred, but now exalted Messiah, and in the Israel of God faithfully conformed to him.

PART TWO

Paul and the crucified Christ in Antioch

3

PAUL AS A PARADIGM OF CONFORMITY TO CHRIST: THE GALATIAN CONTEXT, CONCEPTUAL FRAMEWORK AND AUTOBIOGRAPHY

Paul's account of his confrontation with Peter in Antioch (Gal. 2.11–21) climaxes a select autobiographical narrative (Gal. 1.13–2.21) which is itself precipitated by the present crisis amongst his converts in Galatia. Thus, in order to reconstruct an illuminating frame of reference for the later detailed analysis of the Antioch incident, I shall provide here a tripartite examination of its wider context(s). First, I review and then go beyond the consensus position concerning the main features of the Galatian crisis, considering the much neglected but important role of conflict and persecution in Paul's past and present relations with his converts in Galatia. Particular attention is paid to the manner in which the Galatian situation, both in broad outline and in certain of its details, evinces aspects of the Maccabean crisis – though now as redrawn from Paul's standpoint as a zealous Jew who has become a follower of Jesus Christ.

Second, this leads to a consideration of the conceptual framework governing Paul's response to the Galatian crisis. At its most fundamental, it consists of a radical reworking of a Jewish apocalyptic schema – as exemplified by Daniel 7–12 and related texts – in the light of Christ and the Spirit. That is, Messiah Jesus is the long-awaited (but unexpected) Jewish eschatological redeemer, and the Spirit is the sign of the now inaugurated reign of God. An initial overview of this framework is set forth in terms of three interrelated levels (and dichotomies), which I designate the apocalyptic, anthropological, and ideological/sociological. Then, with a view to the pursuant analysis of the autobiographical section, further illustration of this is provided by particular reference to Paul's programmatic (and problematic) remarks concerning his gospel and mission at Galatians 1.10–12.

Finally, I undertake a detailed examination of Paul's autobiographical recollections at Galatians 1.13–2.10, commencing with a succinct assessment of the so-called 'apologetic' and 'paradigmatic' interpretations. Thereafter, consonant with the prior evaluation of the Galatian context as one of conflict and persecution, and of Paul's conceptual framework as primarily governed by Jesus Christ understood as Israel's (suffering) eschatological redeemer, I argue for a new 'paradigmatic' estimation of the (afflicted) apostle's autobiography. That is, Paul is offering himself as an example of one who, in the face of adversity due to the competing claims of various Jewish (-Christian) detractors,[1] remained completely conformed to the truth of the gospel, namely, the gracious outworking of God's covenant faithfulness through Messiah Jesus.

It is within this fundamentally paradigmatic reading that those aspects usually appealed to in support of the apologetic interpretation may be properly located and comprehended. From such a perspective it may be seen that the extent to which Paul can be said to distance himself from the Jerusalem apostles, and more particularly Peter, is due not merely to any purported charges of his dependence upon them. Rather they are best understood as arising in response to the degree to which, in Paul's estimation, Peter's recent conduct in Antioch falls short of his own self-sacrificial conformity to Christ, and is thereby in danger of misaligning himself with the Agitators whom Paul's autobiography is designed to counteract.

Again, of particular significance throughout this analysis is Paul's handling of certain themes, issues and even terminology resonant of the Maccabean crisis, which serves to underscore the complexity and contentiousness of what is at stake. In essence, Paul is recasting his former self and his current Jewish(-Christian) detractors as akin to those Jewish apostates who aligned themselves with Antiochus IV Epiphanes and his cause, and casting his present self as a faithful representative of the true Israel conformed to the martyred but now exalted redeemer, Jesus the Messiah and Son of God.

---

[1] It may be worth reiterating the earlier comment that the designation 'Jewish (-Christian)' is employed as a succinct way of acknowledging Paul's engagement with a broad and fluid spectrum of Jews whose understanding of and commitment to Jesus Christ differed in various respects (not least *vis-à-vis* Torah) from that of his own. A more nuanced appreciation of this complex phenomenon will emerge as the analysis proceeds. Among the many studies of the variegated nature of early Jewish Christianity, see R. E. Brown, 'Not Jewish Christianity and Gentile Christianity'; Craig C. Hill, *Hellenists and Hebrews*.

1. The context. Conflict and persecution in Galatia: Paul and the Galatian church, then and now

Paul's relationship with the Galatian churches provides the wider context for, and thus clearly bears upon, any evaluation of his autobiography and its climactic account of the Antioch incident. Hence, after noting the majority view concerning the essential features of the Galatian crisis, I shall be particularly concerned to delineate the little-noticed but very significant role played by conflict and persecution in Paul's past and present relations with the Galatians – not least in terms of its various evocations of the Maccabean situation. Thus, it will be shown that in recollecting his afflicted original ministry among the Galatians (Gal. 4.12–20), Paul emerges as an 'ironic Maccabean figure' in virtue of his costly conformity to Messiah Jesus,[2] and this is replicated in his receptive converts' ready identification with the apostle and his gospel. Subsequently, in setting forth the evidence for conflict and persecution as a major factor in the current situation, it will become evident that in both broad outline and certain of its central features, the Galatian scenario may be seen as a remarkable inversion of the Maccabean crisis.

The Galatian crisis

It is self-evident that Galatians is urgently responding to what Paul regards as an astonishing crisis amongst his Christian converts in Galatia: they are abandoning the gospel of God in Christ for a 'non-gospel' promoted by those whom he pejoratively labels 'Agitators' (Gal. 1.6–9). While the nature of our information is such that particular details will always remain disputed, it will be instructive to set forth briefly the consensus position *vis-à-vis* the identity of the Galatian brethren and the Agitators, the latter's activity and motivation, and Paul's wholly negative estimation thereof.[3]

First, notwithstanding the uncertainty concerning their precise

---

[2] Thus, by 'ironic Maccabean figure' I mean that Paul stands in the tradition of zeal as represented by the leading figures in the Maccabean revolt, but with a zeal which is now dramatically redeployed in service of his commitment to the martyred and risen Messiah Jesus.

[3] In addition to the standard commentaries and New Testament introductions, note the judicious analysis in Barclay, 'Mirror-Reading a Polemical Letter', pp. 86–90; *Obeying the Truth*, pp. 36–74; and Witherington, *Grace in Galatia*, pp. 21–5. Among many succinct surveys of scholarly opinion, see Mußner, *Der Galaterbrief*, pp. 14–24.

provenance, it is clear from references to their former idolatry (Gal. 4.8-9) and the fact that they were not originally circumcised (Gal. 6.12), that the Galatian believers were predominantly *Gentile* Christians.[4] Secondly, given the nature of their demands (see below), and Paul's estimation of these as constituting 'a different gospel, which is not another [gospel]' (Gal. 1.6), it is highly likely that the Agitators were *Jewish* Christians – even if the apostle himself would have denied them the appellation 'Christian'.[5] Moreover, these two factors, together with Paul's distinctive differentiation between the two parties,[6] suggests to most that the Agitators were a single group who came from outside the Galatian churches.[7] Whether they emanated from the Jerusalem church (via Antioch?) is less clear.[8] Paul is conspicuously imprecise about their identity (cf. Gal. 3.1; 5.10), and could have made much more of any such connection during his equivocal remarks concerning the Jerusalem apostles at Galatians 1.17–2.10. Nevertheless, the prominent role of Jerusalem

---

[4] On the oft-reviewed, interrelated and perhaps ultimately irresolvable issues concerning the dating and destination of Galatians, see the succinct assessments of Kümmel *Introduction*, pp. 296–8, and R. N. Longenecker, *Galatians*, pp. lxi–lxxxviii, who are representative proponents of the so-called 'North' and 'South' Galatian hypotheses respectively. From what follows, it will become evident that this case concerning Galatians 1–2, and the Antioch incident in particular, does not depend upon one option over the other.

[5] Also pertinent but problematic is the substantival present participle οἱ περιτεμνόμενοι (Gal. 6.13; cf. 5.3). (i) As a permissive middle referring to 'those who get themselves circumcised', it could denote judaizing Gentiles (so Munck, *Paul and the Salvation of Mankind*, pp. 87–90); but (ii) as either a causative middle referring to 'those who advocate circumcision' (so Lightfoot, *Saint Paul's Epistle to the Galatians*, pp. 222–3), or simply a loose designation referring to 'those who are circumcised' (Mußner, *Der Galaterbrief*, p. 412, n. 23; R. N. Longenecker, *Galatians*, p. 292), it could denote the Agitators. The latter is the majority view. But on these and other nuanced interpretations, see further Richardson, *Israel in the Apostolic Church*, pp. 84–9; and Howard, *Paul: Crisis in Galatia*, pp. 17–19.

[6] That is, his reference to the Galatians and the Agitators in the second and third person respectively throughout the letter – assuming, of course, that this is not simply a rhetorical ploy designed to create (rather than reflect) division (see Hansen, *Abraham in Galatians*, pp. 86–7).

[7] So, for example, Dunn, *Galatians*, pp. 10–11. Whether ὁ ταράσσων (Gal. 5.10) is a singular denoting a leading figure (so Barrett, *Freedom and Obligation*, pp. 14–15, 68), or simply generic with no such significance (so Betz, *Galatians*, p. 267) is unclear, though it is intrinsically probable that the 'Agitators' had their own leading representatives.

[8] R. N. Longenecker, *Galatians*, p. xcv, is representative of the many who advocate an origin in the Jerusalem Jewish Christian community, and Watson, *Paul, Judaism and the Gentiles*, pp. 59–61, of those who would also argue that the Agitators were the same 'men from James' who had precipitated the disturbance in Antioch.

throughout Galatians 1–2 and at Galatians 4.25–6, and the common use of 'compel [ἀναγκάζω]' (Gal. 2.3, 14; 6.12), may at least indicate that Paul sees some theological (if not historical) alignment between the actions of the Agitators, the Jewish Christians who troubled him in Jerusalem and Antioch (Gal. 2.3–5, 11–14).

In any event, thirdly, Barclay has rightly argued that the Agitators' involvement within the Galatian church centred upon a call for circumcision (Gal. 5.2–12; 6.12–13) and observance of Torah (Gal. 4.21; 5.3; cf. 4.10; 6.13a).[9] The rationale for the former would have been both theological (a scriptural appeal to Abraham's circumcision as a sign of the covenant) and sociological (an appeal to circumcision as a necessary demarcation of Jewish identity). Though less certain, the rationale for Torah-observance probably included an appeal to the fact that Abraham obeyed the Torah, and that the Torah and covenant were inextricably interrelated. It is possible that in support of their position they also argued that Paul the Jew had once practised circumcision (Gal. 5.11a), though perhaps less likely that they could have convincingly extended this to the claim that Paul the Jewish Christian, whether now or previously in his ministry, did so.[10]

Certainly, fourthly, *Paul's* own estimation of the Agitators' rationale was much more pointed and pejorative: they promoted circumcision and Torah-observance in order not to be persecuted for the cross of Christ (Gal. 5.7–12; 6.12–14). While it may be agreed that such polemic must be examined with due caution, it cannot be dismissed as pure rhetoric. Indeed, significantly, it is consonant with the essence of Paul's counter-argument throughout Galatians: the Abrahamic family is no longer defined according to circumcision and Torah, but in terms of those who (unlike the Agitators) are wholly identified with the crucified Christ (Gal. 6.12–14, 17; cf. 2.19–21; 5.11), and are sustained by the Spirit who inspires and empowers them in the midst of their afflictions (Gal. 3.1–5; 4.6, 29). It is this much neglected aspect of the Galatian crisis – the theme of suffering and persecution – which merits greater attention, and will now be

---

[9] Barclay, *Obeying the Truth*, pp. 45–74.

[10] That is, Paul clearly regarded 'preaching circumcision' and the preaching of the cross – to which he had been irrevocably committed since his encounter with Christ – as mutually exclusive (Gal. 5.11b), and no doubt this was well known to the Galatian believers amongst whom he had ministered (Gal. 1.8–9; 3.1; 4.19). That said, the Agitators could have used Paul's indifference (cf. 1 Cor. 7.18–19) and/or expediency (cf. Acts 16.1–3) *vis-à-vis* circumcision to their advantage.

considered in relation to both Paul's original and current ministry amongst his beleaguered converts.

Conflict and persecution as the context of Paul's original ministry in Galatia: Galatians 4.12–20

The primary source of information concerning Paul's original ministry in Galatia is found in his comments at Galatians 4.12–20.[11] Contrary to the prevailing view, this passage is not an erratic piece of paraenesis alluding to some unspecified illness, but a cogent argument arising from the apostle's recollection of the bodily affliction due to persecution which had attended his initial mission in Galatia.[12] For present purposes, the most pertinent aspects of this exhortation may be briefly outlined as follows.

Paul begins by urging the Galatian believers to continue in their conformity to his own paradigmatic example of faithfulness to Christ (Gal. 4.12a). That this appeal is made on the basis of their common and long-standing experience of conflict and suffering (Gal. 4.12b) becomes apparent from the ensuing account of the circumstances of Paul's early labour amongst them (Gal. 4.13–15). On that occasion Paul himself bore the marks of persecution, his 'weakness of the flesh [ἀσθένειαν τῆς σαρκός]' (Gal. 4.13). This vivid phrase invites comparison with the rhetorical question which climaxes the 'trial list' at 2 Corinthians 11.21b–29 – τίς ἀσθενεῖ, καὶ οὐκ ἀσθενῶ; τίς σκανδαλίζεται, καὶ οὐκ ἐγὼ πυροῦμαι; – whose own comparison with DanielTh. 11.33–5 suggests the afflicted apostle's condition may be seen as analogous to that of the martyred 'wise' during the Maccabean crisis, though now in the cause of Christ rather than Judaism.[13] For the Galatians, Paul's bodily affliction constituted a 'test/trial [πειρασμός]' as to whether or not they too would prove faithful in the face of comparable hardship (Gal. 4.14a).[14]

---

[11] It is less certain whether other remarks (e.g., Gal. 1.8–9; 3.1–5; and 5.7a) also bear on this matter, though they do merit consideration.

[12] For a detailed account of this position, here severely attenuated, see Goddard and Cummins, 'Ill or Ill-treated?'

[13] See further Goddard and Cummins, ibid., pp. 101–3, with particular reference to Barré, 'Paul as "Eschatologic Person"', p. 511.

[14] Cf. πειρασμός in reference to (i) Mattathias' recollection of Abraham's exemplary faithfulness under testing, 1 Macc. 2.52; and (ii) the persecution of Paul, Acts 15.26 (Western Text) and 20.19. On the phrase used to describe the locus of this test/trial – 'in my flesh [ἐν τῇ σαρκί μου]' – note the parallel and identical phrases at Gal. 6.17b and Col. 1.24 respectively, clearly employed in reference to suffering.

Their response at that time was not to 'despise [ἐξουθενεώ]' Paul, a disposition which would have replicated the disdain shown by the Gentile oppressors of the afflicted Maccabean faithful (2 Macc. 1.27; cf. *T. Levi* 16.2), and by the detractors of Jesus and his followers.[15] On the contrary, they received him 'as an angel, as Messiah Jesus [ὡς ἄγγελον θεοῦ ... ὡς Χριστὸν Ἰησοῦν]' (Gal. 4.14b,c). Such a comparison suggests that the Galatians received Paul (i) 'as an angel' because his faithfulness in the midst of persecution aligned him with those 'saints/sons of God' who had been martyred and exalted; and (ii) 'as Messiah Jesus' because in and through this experience he showed himself completely conformed to his eschatological redeemer, the martyred and exalted Christ.[16] Indeed, as a result of their reception of Paul and his gospel, they themselves experienced the 'blessedness [μακαρισμός]' that accompanies and demarcates the afflicted saints (Gal. 4.15a).[17] In fact, says Paul, they would have willingly plucked out their eyes and given them to him (Gal. 4.15) – a metaphor indicating the extent of their voluntary identification with and commitment to the persecuted apostle and his cause (cf. 1 Sam. 11.2; 4 Macc. 5.29–30).

Given the Galatians' former faithfulness in the midst of affliction, Paul is all the more astonished that they should now regard him (rather than the Agitators) as their enemy because he insists on upholding the truth of the gospel which they had once so readily accepted from him (Gal. 4.16), and which is now in danger of being cast down. Indeed, such is the extent of the Galatians' current receptivity to the Agitators that Paul despairs that he must once *again* be in travail until Christ be formed in them (Gal. 4.19).[18] That is, he must now replicate his earlier ministry amongst them by once more labouring so that they – not least by imitating himself – may be fully conformed to the crucified and risen Christ.[19]

---

[15] Cf. *T. Benj.* 9.3; Mark 9.12; Luke 23.11; Acts 4.11; 1 Cor. 1.28; 2 Cor. 10.10.
[16] See further Goddard and Cummins, 'Ill or Ill-treated?', pp. 107–10.
[17] On the use of μακαρισμός in relation to the early Christian tradition of blessedness in the face of suffering, see Baasland, 'Persecution', p. 146.
[18] For a recent variant analysis of Gal. 4.19 (and of 4.12–20 as a whole), see Bruce W. Longenecker, '"Until Christ is Formed in You"', especially pp. 99–108; Longenecker's brief objections (at p. 106 n. 36) to the extended argument on offer in Goddard and Cummins, 'Ill or Ill-treated?', require significant elaboration. Similarly Martin, 'Whose Flesh?', especially pp. 75–8, who rejects both the illness and persecution interpretation in favour of the 'weakness of the flesh' as a reference to 'the Galatians pre-gospel condition'.
[19] On the complex birth metaphor, note especially 4 Macc. 15.17 and context. The full significance of what Paul has in view at Gal. 4.19 will become the more apparent from the later discussions concerning Gal. 1.16 and 2.19–20.

Paul's exhortation at Galatians 4.12–20 indicates that suffering and persecution were constitutive elements in his original ministry in Galatia. In a manner ironically evoking central features of the Maccabean crisis, he recollects how his 'weakness of the flesh' was not depised by the Galatians. On the contrary, they withstood the trial presented in the form of the martyr-like apostle and, further, readily conformed their own lives to the crucified and risen Christ. Thus it is that Paul now urges them to recommit themselves to the truth of the gospel, even if this entails further affliction.

Conflict and persecution as the context of Paul's current ministry to the Galatians

Paul's remarks concerning his original ministry amongst the Galatians were clearly with a view to the current crisis. Indeed, they conclude with the language of animosity and zeal indicating that he regards the present situation as one of bitter conflict between two mutually exclusive and antagonistic groups: the Jewish(-Christian) Agitators together with the Gentile Christian Galatians who are responding to their zealous activity versus the Gentile Christian Galatians who remained faithful to the true witness of their apostle and to Christ (Gal. 4.16–20). In broad outline this represents a remarkable recasting of the archetypal Maccabean crisis, where the Gentile Seleucids and their Jewish sympathizers engaged in a Hellenizing campaign versus those zealous Jews who remained faithful to their covenant with Israel's God. Indeed, further correspondences in detail may be indicated as we now briefly consider the conflict and persecution aspect so integral to Paul's estimation of and response to the current Galatian crisis.

The fact that, to Paul's mind, there is a conflict which can be seen in terms of persecution and suffering is immediately suggested by the appearance of this theme at certain key junctures in his remarks.[20] Indeed, both the entire letter and the main body directly addressing the Galatians (viz., Gal. 3.1–6.18), are bracketed by references to it. Thus, early mention of the apostle's own rejection of his former life 'in Judaism' as a persecutor of the church (Gal. 1.13, 24) provides a framework against which to gauge the nature and significance of his

---

[20] Apart from Baasland, 'Persecution', the significance of this theme has virtually gone unnoticed. See Goddard and Cummins, 'Ill or Ill-treated?', pp. 118–20.

later intermittent remarks concerning the Agitators' activities and the response required from the Galatian faithful. At the close, when Paul eventually picks up the pen himself, it is to contrast starkly the Agitators' fearful coercion of the Galatians with his own fearless conformity to the crucified Christ, the latter underscored by a final appeal to his own disfigured body (Gal. 6.11–17).[21] In between, after completing his autobiographical remarks, Paul immediately reminds the errant Galatians of their initial commitment to the crucified Christ and the considerable suffering they had already endured (Gal. 3.1–5). And, towards the end of the argumentative section of the letter Paul draws a parallel between the persecution by Ishmael (= 'the flesh') of Isaac (= 'the Spirit') and the situation 'as it is now' (Gal. 4.29), here implying virtually normative and wide-ranging circumstances which included those concerning the Agitators and Galatians.[22] That all this cannot simply be dismissed as incidental evidence becomes the more apparent from a closer examination of the identity and activity of the respective protagonists.

Commentators have failed to note that Paul's polemical terminology for his Galatian opponents – 'those troubling [οἱ ταράσσοντες]' (Gal. 1.7b; cf. 5.10) and 'those agitating [οἱ ἀναστατοῦντες]' (Gal. 5.12) has its most notable antecedents in the Maccabean designations for those Gentile rulers (such as Antiochus IV Epiphanes) and/or Jewish apostates who were 'troubling' Israel's faithful.[23]

---

[21] On Gal. 6.17, parallels elsewhere in Paul render it highly likely that the combination of κόπος (cf. 2 Cor. 6.5; 11.23, 27) and τὰ στίγματα τοῦ Ἰησοῦ ἐν τῷ σώματί μου (cf. Gal. 4.14a; 2 Cor. 4.10; Col. 1.24) refer to the 'hardship, trouble' – even 'beatings' (see *TDNT* 3.827) – which left their marks upon the apostle's body. This is the consensus position; the alternatives are succinctly reviewed in Pobee, *Persecution and Martyrdom*, pp. 94–5; Mußner, *Der Galaterbrief*, pp. 418–20.

[22] There is some debate whether Paul here refers to (i) Jewish (synagogal) persecution of Christians in general (so most commentators), or (ii) the Agitators' conduct towards the Galatian believers in particular (so, for example, Mußner, *Der Galaterbrief*, p. 331). The breadth of both Paul's conceptual framework (cf. Gal. 5.17; see below) and his mission field encourages us to resolve the dichotomy in favour of both, even if the latter is here in near view (cf. Gal. 4.17, 30).

[23] A notable recent exception is Ciampa, *The Presence and Function of Scripture in Galatians 1 and 2*, pp. 79–82, who is alert to the use of ταράσσω in the Maccabean texts, while considering these against the wider backdrop of the Achan episode in Joshua 7 as an earlier antecedent for Paul's remarks. Particular attention should be drawn to the substantival use of ταράσσω at 1 Macc. 3.5; 7.22 (cf. Dan.LXX 11.12, 44; Dan.Th. 11.44) and of ἀναστατόω at Dan.LXX 7.23. Earlier Old Testament references to those 'troubling' Israel are found at Josh. 6.18; 7.25; Judg. 11.35; 1 Sam. 14.29, though only Judg.LXX 11.35A uses ταράσσω (non-substantively).

Additionally, that the Agitators' activity is said to include 'compelling' (ἀναγκάζω) the Galatians to be circumcised (Gal. 6.12b; cf. 2.3, 14) is especially reminiscent of Antiochus IV Epiphanes' efforts to compel (ἀναγκάζω) the Maccabean martyrs to forsake the fundamental expressions of their Torah-obedience (food laws, circumcision, etc.).[24] Ironically, from Paul's standpoint, the Agitators' compulsion towards circumcision (and Torah-obedience) was but a replication of the very persecution (for Christ) that it sought to avoid (Gal. 6.12c).[25]

As already noted, the Galatian brethren had originally fully identified themselves with Paul and his gospel. Indeed, the crucified Christ having been portrayed before them, they responded by 'hearing with faith'. In so doing, they were greatly empowered by the Spirit, such that they were able to suffer many things (Gal. 3.1–5). In essence, they willingly joined Paul as faithful members of the (afflicted) eschatological people of God, demarcated by Christ and the Spirit. This interpretation of Galatians 3.1–5 is somewhat different from (though not necessarily completely at variance with) the usual reading of these verses, taken as largely referring to miraculous experiences of the Spirit which accompanied the Galatians' reception of the gospel.[26] However, we may reiterate and develop the interrelated considerations in its favour.

(i) Paul 'portrayed Christ crucified' to the Galatians. The vivid and visual (rather than aural) language could indicate that Paul himself (not simply his preaching),[27] had represented the crucified Christ before the Galatians, not least in his afflicted person (cf. Gal. 6.17).[28]

(ii) The Galatians' 'hearing of faith' suggests that (in and through Paul) they recognized, responded to, and emulated

---

[24] 2 Macc. 6.1, 7, 18; 7.1; 4 Macc. 4.26; 5.2, 27; 18.5.

[25] Josephus could likewise view the enforced circumcision of Gentiles by Jews as persecution (*Life* 113, 149).

[26] So, notably, Betz, *Galatians*, pp. 134–6; more recently, Matera, *Galatians*, p. 156; Dunn, *Galatians*, pp. 156–8.

[27] That Paul here refers to his vivid preaching is the majority view; so, for example, Matera, *Galatians*, p. 112; Dunn, *Galatians*, p. 152; Martyn, *Galatians*, p. 283.

[28] Note also that Paul's sequence of thought invites some correlation between Gal. 2.19b–20 and 3.1, with *inter alia* their common use of the perfect passive in Χριστῷ συνεσταύρωμαι and Ἰησοῦς Χριστὸς προεγράφη ἐσταυρωμένος respectively – with the former clearly referring to Paul himself.

the crucified Christ who now empowered their own faithfulness.[29]

(iii) Concomitant with this was their receipt of the Spirit. Fundamentally, God's supply of the Spirit – the Spirit of his crucified but now exalted Son – is to inspire and empower those sharing sonship to bear witness to their Father (Gal. 4.6).[30] In this way the Galatians attested to the suffering, inheritance and ultimate vindication they now shared with Christ (cf. Rom. 8.14–18).[31]

(iv) The fact that suffering is indeed an aspect of their new life is indicated by the use of πάσχω, which in Paul – as throughout biblical Greek – denotes such an experience.[32]

(v) In this context, God's Spirit 'working wonders'[33] among the Galatians in virtue of their 'hearing of faith' (Gal. 3.5), may be seen as a demonstration of the eschatological outworking of divine rule over all that would oppose God and his (currently) afflicted people (2 Cor. 12.9–12; cf. Col. 1.29).

In this way, and not through adherence to 'works of the law', the Galatians demonstrate that they are the true heirs of Abraham (Gal. 3.6ff.; cf. Rom. 4.1–3), whose faith and righteousness under duress was legendary.[34] Apparently, Abraham was often a focal point of

---

[29] The debate whether ἐξ ἀκοῆς πίστεως denotes the Galatians 'believing what [they] heard' concerning Christ's faithfulness (R. N. Longenecker, *Galatians*, p. 103; cf. Hays, *The Faith of Jesus Christ*, pp. 143–9) or 'the hearing of faith' which activated the gospel in their own lives (Dunn, *Galatians*, pp. 154–5, following Williams, 'The Hearing of Faith', p. 90), might be resolved by embracing both elements within the wider framework of Paul's understanding of the outworking of divine grace. That is, while Paul may well have in near view the Galatians' own faithful receptivity to the gospel, this necessarily presupposes the prior faithfulness of God-in-Christ which effected and enabled this. See further the discussion of the equally contentious phrase πίστις 'Ιησοῦ Χριστοῦ in chapter six.

[30] On this role of the Spirit, see especially the discussion of the 'pneumatology of martyrdom' in Lampe, 'Martyrdom and Inspiration', pp. 122ff.

[31] Note also the role of the Spirit in relation to persecution and conflict at Gal. 4.29 and 5.17 respectively.

[32] 1 Cor. 12.26; 2 Cor. 1.6; Phil. 1.29; 1 Thess. 2.14. τοσαῦτα could refer to the extent ('so many things') and/or severity ('so great things') of the suffering.

[33] Cf. Rom. 15.19; 1 Cor. 12.10, 28.

[34] Cf. Gen. 15.6; 22; Sir. 44.20; 1 Macc. 2.52; *Jub.* 17.15–18; 21.2; *2 Apoc. Bar.* 57.1–2; and Pobee, *Persecution and Martyrdom*, pp. 25–6, noting rabbinic references (and the later theology of Abraham's martyrdom). On Abraham in Jewish tradition, see Hansen, *Abraham in Galatians*, pp. 167–215.

competing claims for true Israelite descent between Paul and other Jewish Christians.[35] In such instances, the apostle seems to have been ready to press his case by appealing to his own faithfulness in adversity[36] – just as he here invokes that formerly found among his Galatian converts. Indeed, in their recognition of Jesus Christ and in their ensuing Spirit-filled wisdom,[37] they patterned Stephen and Paul – themselves in the tradition of Daniel and the 'righteous ones' (cf. Wis. 1–6 and *1 Enoch* 37–71)[38] – in being conformed to their eschatological redeemer and becoming participants in the now inaugurated kingdom of God.

Now, however, all this was under threat. In the tradition of the athlete-martyr, the Galatians had been 'running well' (Gal. 5.7a). But through a 'persuasion [πεισμονή]' that was not of God, the Agitators had since 'cut in on' their progress, causing them to stumble and no longer obey the truth (Gal. 5.7b–8, 11c). Indeed, the Galatians were now 'turning away from [μετατίθημι ἀπό]' the gospel of Christ to that which was 'no gospel' at all (Gal. 1.6–7a).[39] Paul implies that the Agitators' action was tantamount to persecution, arising out of their own stumbling over the scandal of the cross (Gal. 5.11; cf. 6.12). In so doing, he evokes the Maccabean crisis not only in his designation of the Agitators themselves (Gal. 5.10b, 12), but also in the language and imagery used to express his fears concerning their pervasive and debilitating impact within the Galatian

---

[35] Recall our earlier estimation of the key role of Abraham in the Agitators' demands for circumcision and Torah-obedience; and cf. Rom. 9.7; 11.1.

[36] So 1 Cor. 11.22–9. Not surprisingly, Abrahamic descent figured prominently in the Maccabean martyr tradition (note, for example, 'O Israelite children, offspring of the seed of Abraham' at 4 Macc. 18.1). Thus it is all the more notable that Paul's argument at 1 Cor. 11.22–9 begins by counter-claiming his own status as a true Ἑβραῖος (cf. 2 Macc. 7.31; 11.13; 15.37) and climaxes with a reference to his 'weakness' which, as noted earlier in relation to Gal. 4.14, bears close comparison to Dan.Th. 11.33–5.

[37] The latter implied in Paul's contrasting estimation of them as presently 'foolish [ἀνόητος]' (Gal. 3.1, 3; cf. Luke 24.25–6).

[38] See further the discussion of the portrayal of Stephen and Paul in Acts in chapter four.

[39] The expression μετατίθημι ἀπό and the cognate μετάθεσις are found in the LXX only in reference to (i) the martyr Eleazar's *refusal* to forsake Judaism even in the face of affliction and apostasy (2 Macc. 7.24), and (ii) the assertion that 'the Jews do not consent to ... *change* to Greek customs, but prefer their own way of living ...' (2 Macc. 11.24).

churches: 'if you bite and devour one another take heed that you are not consumed by one another' (Gal. 5.15).[40]

If the Galatians were to avoid being completely cut off from God's grace in Christ (cf. Gal. 1.6; 4.17; 5.4), an immediate response was required. Paul's recommended course of action contained both defensive and offensive measures. The Galatians were to resist by refusing to resubmit to a (Jewish) yoke of slavery (Gal. 5.1).[41] Additionally, they had to cast out the cursed oppressors from their midst (Gal. 4.29–30; cf. 1.8–9).[42] In this way, with the Spirit empowering Christ-like faithfulness in the midst of suffering, they would ultimately attain the long-awaited (albeit now inaugurated) 'hope of righteousness' (Gal. 5.5; cf. 3.11). That is, while the Agitators face divine judgement (Gal. 5.10b; 6.7–8), the faithful Galatians will receive divine vindication and reign as God's true covenant people in his eternal kingdom (Gal. 6.8b, 15–16; cf. Rom. 8.18ff.).

Notwithstanding residual disputed details, there is something of a critical consensus concerning the essential aspects of the Galatian crisis. However, what has not been sufficiently delineated is the degree to which Galatians attests to conflict and persecution as a formative factor in Paul's past and present relations with his Galatian converts. In both broad outline and certain of its most salient features, this element is the more starkly seen when viewed as a christological reworking of the suffering and persecution so constitutive of the Maccabean crisis. For Paul, the former zealous Jew-become-Christian, the coercive Jewish(-Christian) Agitators have taken on the mantle of the Gentile and apostate Jewish oppressors of his

---

[40] Recall the depiction of the 'bestial' conduct of faithful Israel's oppressors in Dan. 7 and also in the *Animal Apocalypse* (*1 Enoch* 85–90). Cf. Ezek. 36.12–15. R. N. Longenecker, *Galatians*, p. 244, follows Burton, Schlier, Bruce (against Oepke, Mußner, Betz) in taking these remarks as Paul's view of what was transpiring amongst the Galatian brethren. See also Barclay, *Obeying the Truth*, p. 153, who speaks of 'a situation of discord in the Galatian churches'.

[41] That is, they were to avoid replicating their former slavery to Gentile idolatry (cf. Gal. 4.8–11). Recall that the Maccabean resistance was with a view to throwing off the 'yoke' of their Gentile oppressors (1 Macc. 13.41).

[42] Notably, the Maccabean crisis was viewed as the outworking of the Deuteronomic curse upon Israel's apostasy. Envisaged at its worst, it involved Israel's enemies (both Gentiles and Jewish apostates) seeking to eradicate all memory of Israel from the land by handing it over to alien residents (1 Macc. 3.34b–36; 12.53–13.6, 20). The required remedy was the destruction of the enemy, not least those from within (1 Macc. 3.1–9; 7.21–4), and a renewed covenant commitment by Israel.

Maccabean forebears, whereas those afflicted Galatians who remain faithful to Christ comprise the true Israel of God. As we shall now see, this startling perspective upon the Galatian context is but a function of a Jewish conceptual framework now reconfigured in the light of Paul's encounter with his eschatological redeemer, the martyred and exalted Messiah Jesus.

2. The conceptual framework. Messiah Jesus as eschatological redeemer: the origin and nature of Paul's gospel and mission

Paul located the Galatian crisis within a cosmic-wide conceptual frame of reference. In essence, this may be understood as a Jewish apocalyptic schema – such as that drawn upon by Daniel 7–12 in addressing the Maccabean crisis – but as now reworked in the light of God's dramatic new action in Jesus Christ and the Spirit. In what follows, I shall first draw together various otherwise disparate remarks by Paul in Galatians to offer a necessarily succinct estimation of this framework in terms of three interrelated levels: the apocalyptic, anthropological, and ideological/sociologial. Then, by way of a sharper focus upon this matter, and in preparation for the ensuing analysis of Paul's autobiography, I consider Paul's programmatic remarks at Galatians 1.10–12 concerning his gospel and mission as being not 'of man' but 'of God', that is, fundamentally determined by God's revelation of his eschatological redeemer, Messiah Jesus.

From the outset it is evident that Paul's conception of the Galatian scenario is governed by a christologically reworked Jewish apocalyptic schema: according to God's will, Jesus Christ 'gave himself for our sins to deliver us from the present evil age' (Gal. 1.4).[43] Here 'age' embraces both the temporal (past, present, future) and the spatial (heaven and earth), and the implied contrast is between two 'spheres', the one lying outside and the other within the rule of God respectively (cf. 1 Cor. 2.6–8; 2 Cor. 4.4). The old sphere is evil, transitory and in decline; the new sphere, now inaugurated by means of the deliverance brought about by Christ, is glorious,

---

[43] Among the many notable aspects of Martyn's *Galatians* is its recognition of the apocalyptic dimensions of this letter; see especially pp. 97–105. Also important is Bruce W. Longenecker, *The Triumph of Abraham's God*.

eternal and moving inexorably towards its full and final revelation. Either or both of these two mutually exclusive and conflicting spheres is variously discernible (or implied) at certain junctures throughout Paul's remarks; the following instances are of particular note.

(i) The enslaving 'elemental spirits of the universe [τὰ στοιχεῖα τοῦ κόσμου]' (Gal. 4.3, 9), that is, the demonic powers ('gods') 'which constitute and control' the present evil age, whether in Gentile or Jewish guise.[44]

(ii) The enslaved 'present Jerusalem' versus the free 'Jerusalem above' (Gal. 4.25bc–26).[45] The former signifies Jerusalem-specific manifestations of the 'present evil age', aligning together Jerusalem-centred Judaism, possibly the (Jerusalem-based?) Agitators and perhaps, even if at some remove, the Jerusalem Jewish Christian apostles (see below).[46] The latter evokes the new Jerusalem now already manifest amongst those made free through Christ and the Spirit, not least Paul's own Galatian converts.[47]

(iii) The 'world' (= creation apart from God) to which Paul has died in virtue of his crucifixion (and resurrection) with Christ, leaving behind circumcision (= Judaism), and entering a new creation (Gal. 6.12–15; cf. 2.19–20).[48]

(iv) Also of note is Paul's refusal to condone 'another gospel' contrary to his own, even if proclaimed by himself or an ἄγγελος ἐξ οὐρανοῦ/θεοῦ (Gal. 1.8; cf. 4.14). Such a remark

[44] On the much debated (range of) meaning of τὰ στοιχεῖα τοῦ κόσμου, see Burton, *Galatians*, pp. 510–18; *TDNT* 7.670–87; Mußner, *Der Galaterbrief*, pp. 293–304; Martyn, *Galatians*, pp. 394–5. Without denying its semantic range, or that Paul may here be exploiting certain aspects of this, we follow Betz, *Galatians*, p. 204, in the specific rendering offered here.

[45] This is, of course, only one of a series of parallel antitheses used by Paul in his complex and much disputed Sarah/Hagar allegory (Gal. 4.21–31), on which see Barrett, *Essays on Paul*, pp. 154–70; R. N. Longenecker, *Galatians*, pp. 199–206; Martyn, *Galatians*, pp. 431–57.

[46] Martyn, *Galatians*, pp. 457–66, imaginatively overplays the association between the Agitators – or Teachers (his term) – and the Jerusalem church and its apostles.

[47] Paul is clearly reappropriating rich Jewish traditions concerning the heavenly Jerusalem, on which see especially Lincoln, *Paradise Now and Not Yet*, pp. 9–32. Cf. Heb. 12.22; Rev. 3.12; 21.2, 10.

[48] See Martyn, 'Apocalyptic Antinomies', p. 412: Paul speaks 'of an old world, from which he has been painfully separated, by Christ's death, by the death of that world, and by his own death; and he speaks of a new world, which he grasps under the arresting expression, New Creation'; note also his *Galatians*, pp. 570–4.

seems to presuppose an interplay between the (afflicted) saints below (here, Paul) and the saints/angels above.[49]

In sum, Paul's response to his afflicted converts is predicated upon the fundamental conviction that through Christ and the Spirit they are participants in the now inaugurated reign of God, even if they must still do battle with the dying vestiges of the old age – a sphere which they have left behind and to which they must not return.

Interrelated with the apocalyptic aspect is, for want of a better term, an 'anthropological level', that is, not a body/soul dichotomy, but rather humanity apart from God versus humanity redefined by Christ and the Spirit.[50] Though rarely recognized as such, this is most clearly seen in Paul's pejorative and polemical use of ἄνθρωπος at Galatians 1.10–12, to be discussed in some detail below. However, it is also manifest via the 'flesh [σάρξ]' versus 'Spirit [πνεῦμα]' antithesis.[51] Though evident at various key points (Gal. 3.1–5; 4.29), this motif is most prominently displayed in Paul's paraenesis, coming to sharpest expression at Galatians 5.17: humanity, individually and/or collectively, is the locus of a struggle between the mutually exclusive and antagonistic ways of the flesh and Spirit. For Paul, this is all too apparent from the current conflict in Galatia, where 'flesh' is especially associated with the Jewish lifestyle promulgated by the Agitators (Gal. 3.3; 6.13).

At this point we overlap with a third level, an ideological/ sociological dualism, namely, idolatrous ways of life (whether pagan libertinism or Jewish nomism) versus the worshipping community demarcated by Christ and the Spirit. Consonant with the particular nature of the Galatian crisis, this is variously expressed as: Paul's gospel of Christ versus the Agitators' 'non-gospel' of circumcision and Torah-obedience (Gal. 1.6–7; cf. 5.11); a pattern of life marked by 'works of the law' versus the 'hearing of faith' (Gal. 3.1–5); exis-

---

[49] Note also Paul's later censure of the Corinthians' receptivity to those preaching 'another Jesus ... spirit ... gospel', who disguise themselves as 'servants of righteousness' when in fact they are aligned with 'Satan [who] disguises himself as an angel of light' (2 Cor. 11.4–15).

[50] That is, Paul the Jewish *Christian* now views Israel as equally given over to Adamic sin as her non-Jewish neighbours, and thus no longer conceives of humanity in terms of the Jewish people of God versus Gentile sinners. This issue is taken up in relation to Gal. 2.15–21 in chapter six.

[51] On which see especially Barclay, *Obeying the Truth*, pp. 178–215.

tence together 'under the [curse of] the law' versus 'the faith' (Gal. 3.23–5; 4.21).[52]

The pivotal (and paradoxical) role of Jesus Christ within Paul's conceptual framework comes especially into view in three highly compressed statements at Galatians 2.19–20; 3.13; and 4.4–6. The first of these will be discussed in some detail in chapter six. While the remaining two texts bristle with contentious aspects, here it suffices to note how they too reveal Paul's multi-levelled schema: at the appointed time, God's pre-existent Son entered creation (apocalyptic),[53] becoming a human being (anthropological), under the law (ideological/sociological). The Jewish-specific shape and universal outworking of this redemptive action are also equally evident: redeemed are those 'under the [curse of the] law' – namely, Israel-in-Adam bound but unable to obey Torah so that Israel comes under its curse rather than its blessing – and thus also the Gentiles who may join them in receiving divine sonship.[54] In sum, Jesus is the long-awaited (if unexpected) Jewish eschatological redeemer: the son of God who became a son of man so that the sons of men (Jew and Gentile) could become sons of God. Thus it is that Paul is adamant that his gospel and mission – unlike that of the Agitators – is not 'of man' but 'of God in Jesus Christ'.

Paul's gospel and mission: not 'of man' but 'of God in Jesus Christ' (Galatians 1.10–12)

Though crucial to any understanding of the immediately ensuing autobiography, Paul's programmatic remarks at Galatians 1.10–12 have been much misunderstood. By recourse to the 'mirror-reading' method, they are normally (and narrowly) taken as a succinct denial of the Agitators' charges that Paul was dependent upon the Jerusalem apostles for his gospel and apostolic office, with the subsequent

---

[52] 'The faith' would appear to be an elastic term embracing (the gospel of) God in Christ in the believing community (cf. also Gal. 1.23; 6.10).

[53] Amongst recent commentators, R. N. Longenecker, *Galatians*, p. 170; and Matera, *Galatians*, p. 151, deem it likely that pre-existence is here implied; Dunn, *Galatians*, p. 215, demurs. Cf. Rom. 8.3; 1 Cor. 8.6; Phil. 2.6–8; Col. 1.15–19.

[54] On this interpretation of Gal. 4.4–6 (and 3.13), see especially Donaldson, 'The "Curse of the Law"'. Our highly compressed interpretation of Israel 'under the [curse of the] law' is more fully discussed in relation to the interpretation of Gal. 2.15–21 offered in chapter six.

autobiography designed to substantiate this. Further notice of this 'apostolic defence' reading will preface the analysis of Paul's autobiography below. At this point, in keeping with the current contextual and conceptual estimation of Galatians as a whole, I shall argue that Paul's more fundamental and wide-ranging concern is to assert that his gospel and his mission are not 'of man' but 'of God in Jesus Christ'. That is, unlike the Agitators and any aligned therewith, the origin and nature of his gospel is consonant with God's disclosure of his eschatological redeemer, Jesus, the risen Messiah and Son of God (Gal. 1.10–12; 1.16); and thus his missionary activity is characterized by its (suffering) servant-like conformity thereto (Gal. 1.10). As will be seen, his ensuing select autobiography is concerned to illustrate the validity of this claim.

Fundamental to Paul's understanding of the origin, content and scope of the gospel which he lives and proclaims is that it is not κατὰ ἄνθρωπον but rather δι' ἀποκαλύψεως Ἰησοῦ Χριστοῦ (Gal. 1.11b, 12c). At its most fundamental, the expression κατὰ ἄνθρωπον is not generic ('according to the human person'), nor indefinite ('according to a man'), but *qualitative*: 'humanly, from a merely human standpoint'.[55] That is, it conveys the idea that Paul's gospel is not 'according to' (norm/nature) or 'in virtue of' (means/source) that sphere demarcated by the Adamic, fleshly, worldly and demonic. This is apparent from a comparison of the weight of κατὰ ἄνθρωπον elsewhere in Paul,[56] and it is consonant with the estimation of the overall conceptual framework presupposed throughout Galatians as set forth above.

That such breadth of vision is implicit in this phrase becomes the more evident by reference to its antithesis: δι' ἀποκαλύψεως Ἰησοῦ Χριστοῦ. Once again, this succinct statement is to be viewed in relation to Paul's christologically reconfigured Jewish apocalyptic framework, and refers to the dramatic divine disclosure of the martyred and now exalted redeemer, Jesus Christ.[57] On this reading δι' ἀποκαλύψεως Ἰησοῦ Χριστοῦ is taken as an indefinite objective genitive: 'through a [particular] revelation of [the person of] Jesus

---

[55] See the comparable analysis of Lategan, 'Is Paul Defending His Apostleship in Galatians?', pp. 419–21.

[56] Rom. 3.5; 1 Cor. 3.3; 15.32; cf. Col. 2.8; Eph. 4.20–4; 1 Pet. 4.1–2.

[57] This matter is briefly taken up again below in reference to Gal. 1.16, and more fully in relation to Gal. 2.20 in chapter six.

Christ [by God]'.⁵⁸ This inextricable interrelationship between God and Christ is of course variously expressed elsewhere in Paul, and indicates that it is not only God revealing Jesus Christ, but also Jesus Christ revealing the very character and conduct of God (Gal. 2.20).⁵⁹ In sum, just as κατὰ ἄνθρωπον conveys both norm and source, so δι' ἀποκαλύψεως Ἰησοῦ Χριστοῦ denotes not only the origin but also the intrinsic nature of Paul's gospel: it is both derived from and governed by his transformative encounter with Jesus Christ.

On account of the Galatia-specific aspect of Paul's immediately antecedent remarks at Galatians 1.6–9, the implied polemic of his almost parenthetical statement that he neither received nor was taught his gospel παρὰ ἀνθρώπου (Gal. 1.12a,b) is likely to have in near view the Agitators whose teaching has precipitated the Galatian crisis. Their 'non-gospel', with its demands for circumcision and Torah-observance, is 'of man' rather than God. Indeed, insofar as παρὰ marks ἄνθρωπος as both the immediate source and also the transmitter from a more ultimate origin,⁶⁰ then the Agitators – and any who follow their 'non-gospel' – are ultimately bound up with the evil age/sphere.

It would thus appear unlikely that, strictly speaking, Paul's opening remarks concerning his gospel at Galatians 1.11–12 constitute a direct response to charges of his dependence upon Jerusalem. Instead, they are more properly understood as a programmatic and polemical assertion that his gospel, unlike that of the Agitators – and any aligned therewith – is not 'of man' but 'of God in Jesus Christ', and further imply that Paul himself is a faithful recipient and servant of this gospel.⁶¹

Indeed, Paul's unswerving devotion to Christ's cause is made explicit in his antecedent comment at Galatians 1.10. Here, by means

---

⁵⁸ This does not preclude the distinct possibility that Paul viewed this initial and determinative revelation as being organically related to the totality of his ensuing lifelong experience of God-in-Christ.

⁵⁹ Hence the attraction of the subjective genitive reading of δι' ἀποκαλύψεως Ἰησοῦ Χριστοῦ.

⁶⁰ So Burton, *Galatians*, p. 39.

⁶¹ He is οὐκ ἀπ' ἀνθρώπων οὐδὲ δι' ἀνθρώπου (Gal. 1.1a); viz., he is not commissioned by, nor under the auspices of, anyone who is 'of man' – for example, the Agitators, the Jewish High Priest (cf. Acts 9.1). Rather, he is διὰ Ἰησοῦ Χριστοῦ καὶ θεοῦ πατρός (Gal. 1.1b); viz., ultimately under the authority of God in Christ.

of two rhetorical questions and a conditional statement, he succinctly and polemically contrasts the nature of his mission with that of the Agitators. That the Agitators are in view is immediately implied by the initial connective, γάρ. However, this, and the nature and significance of Paul's compressed comment, may be further substantiated by reference to three of its key features: the past–present contrast; the persuasion/pleasing motif; and Paul's self-designation as a 'slave of Christ'.

First, having just urged condemnation of the Agitators for their promulgation of a 'non-gospel', Paul answers his own rhetorical question as to whether he *now* (ἄρτι) seeks to persuade/please men or God by averring that if he *still* (ἔτι) did so he would not be a servant of Christ. This implies a 'now–then' contrast between Paul's present missionary approach and that which formerly obtained, the latter to be seen as analogous to the Agitators' current activities. On the basis of what is to follow at Galatians 1.13–16a, and Paul's parallel use of ἔτι in reference to his former preaching of circumcision at Galatians 5.11, it may be inferred that he is here contrasting his present slavery for Christ with his former enslavement to matters Jewish, and drawing an analogy between the latter and the Agitators' present promotion of circumcision and Torah-observance.[62] In essence, Paul is critiquing the Agitators and their Galatian sympathizers for pursuing a zealous Judaism – one, as we shall see, strongly evoking the Maccabean context – which he himself has left behind in order to serve Jesus the Messiah.

Second, this interpretation may be corroborated and given greater force by reference to Paul's disclaimer that he (unlike the Agitators) seeks to persuade/please men or God.[63] Four considerations may help us arrive at a more precise estimation of the much disputed πείθω.[64]

---

[62] It might also be inferred from a comparison with ἄρτι at Gal. 1.8, that a secondary and more narrowly circumscribed 'now–then' contrast is also in view, one which denies any shift between Paul's current and original ministry to the Galatians, while also implying that the same cannot be said of their response thereto (cf. Gal. 4.12–20). Much less viable is the merely 'argumentative' correlation of ἄρτι at Gal. 1.8 and 1.9 – 'now, in these utterances' (see Burton, *Galatians*, p. 29) – which does not do justice to the temporal aspects of Paul's remarks.

[63] For reasons that will become apparent, both instances of ἤ ('or') are taken as copulative, and the verbs 'persuade [πείθω]' and 'please [ἀρέσκω]' as semantically interrelated.

[64] In the active voice πείθω always denotes 'persuade, convince' rather than 'obey'; here it might be conative: '*trying to* persuade'.

(i) In 2 and 4 Maccabees πείθω is employed in reference to the Maccabean martyrs persuading one another to remain faithful in the face of their tormentors' efforts to persuade them otherwise – this being a means of convincing the latter of the superiority of the Jewish way of life.[65]
(ii) Similarly, Jews opposed to Caligula's Temple edict were willing to be martyred in order to persuade Petronius not to discharge his command (*Leg.* 233, 240, 242).
(iii) Paul, however, is convinced that the Agitators' demand for circumcision and Torah-observance is a 'persuasion [πεισμονή]' which does not come from the God who calls his Galatian converts to obey [πείθω] the truth (Gal. 5.7–8).
(iv) By contrast, as God himself knows, Paul seeks only to persuade men concerning divine justification and reconciliation effected by the death and resurrection of Christ (2 Cor. 5.9, 11).[66]

In essence, whereas the Agitators stand in the Maccabean tradition of persuading men and God of their zeal for the cause of Judaism, Paul's mission is devoted to persuading men and God of his commitment to the cause of Christ. Indeed, the wider context of Paul's only other active use of πείθω (at 2 Cor. 5.9, see above), suggests that underlying the variant missions of the apostle and the Agitators is an 'of man' (κατὰ σάρκα) versus 'of God' estimation of Christ (2 Cor. 5.16).

Third, consonant with the foregoing, is Paul's denial that he (unlike the Agitators) seeks to please men (and God), but rather is a servant of the Messiah. 'Pleasing' is an activity which Paul elsewhere rejects or encourages according to whether or not it undermines the true gospel by pandering to that which is 'of men', or furthers it by emulating the manner in which Christ self-sacrificially pleased God.[67] Here, by means of a polemical contrary to fact conditional clause, he both repudiates his own prior efforts as a zealous Jew to 'please men' (and God), and stresses that any such conduct is now precluded by a life that patterns the servanthood of

---

[65] 2 Macc. 7.26; 4 Macc. 2.6; 8.12; 9.18; 16.24 (active voice); 4 Macc. 5.16; 8.17, 26; 12.4–5; 18.1 (passive voice). Mutual persuasion was also an element in diplomatic negotiations between the Maccabean forces and their Gentile adversaries (2 Macc. 11.14).

[66] In the Corinthian situation, this being in marked contrast to others who are engaged in self-commendation and 'pleasing men'.

[67] For example, cf. Rom. 15.1–3; 1 Cor. 10.31–3; 1 Thess. 2.4 and context.

Christ.[68] His ensuing autobiography will further authenticate this claim.[69]

To conclude, Paul's reaction to the contentious Galatian scenario is governed by a Jewish apocalyptic conceptual schema – as typified by Daniel 7–12 and its response to the archetypal Maccabean crisis – but as now radically reworked through Christ and the Spirit; that is, those (afflicted) Galatians conformed to their eschatological redeemer, Messiah Jesus, and demarcated by the long-suffering Spirit comprise the people of God who even now participate in the inaugurated new creation. Conversely, those drawn to the Agitators and their coercive 'non-gospel' of circumcision and Torah-obedience are embracing a Jewish way of life no less bankrupt than their former Gentile idolatry, and so again become enslaved to the old sphere ('world', 'flesh', 'man').

It is all this which Paul has in view in his programmatic statement at Galatians 1.10–12. He is asserting that the origin and nature of his gospel and mission – unlike that of the Agitators – is not 'of man', but rather is unequivocally conformed to the revelation of God in the form of the martyred and exalted Jesus, Messiah and Son of God. Fundamentally, it is this which Paul's pursuant autobiography is designed to substantiate, thereby once again offering his own christologically reconfigured and exemplary way of life as a model for his beleaguered Galatian converts.

3. Conformity to Christ. Paul's autobiography as paradigm: from Jewish zealot to Christian martyr figure (Gal. 1.13–2.10)

This final section examines the select autobiographical recollections (Gal. 1.13–2.10) which lead up to Paul's climactic account of the Antioch incident (Gal. 2.11–21), detailed treatment of which is deferred to chapters five and six. After reviewing and critiquing both the so-called 'apologetic' and 'paradigmatic' interpretations, we offer our own new 'paradigmatic' reading of this passage. Consonant with the earlier contextual and conceptual evaluation of Galatians as a whole, it is argued that Paul's autobiography is fundamentally

---

[68] Ciampa, *The Presence and Function of Scripture in Galatians 1 and 2*, pp. 93–5, notes that it is likely that the idea of Paul as a 'faithful prophet-like apostle' underlies Gal. 1.10.

[69] See Dodd, 'Christ's Slave', for a comparable but broader 'paradigmatic' estimation of Gal. 1.10 in relation to Galatians 1–2.

designed to encourage his afflicted converts to remain faithful to
Christ by patterning his own commitment to the truth of the gospel
in the face of adversity, and that the full weight of this may be measured when seen as a christologically reworked Maccabean model of
Judaism. Additionally, it is within this essentially 'paradigmatic'
reading that Paul's purportedly 'apologetic' focus upon and ambivalence towards the Jerusalem apostles may be the more clearly
comprehended. In sum, I offer a more integrated account of the
nature and significance of Galatians 1.13–2.10, with Paul representing a radical reconfiguration of the tradition of the Maccabees in
that he offers himself as an exemplary martyr-like figure irrevocably
conformed to the crucified and risen Christ.

The 'apologetic' and 'paradigmatic' approaches to
Galatians 1–2: a review, critique and new proposal

The principal claims of the 'apologetic' interpretation of Paul's autobiography, found in various nuanced forms, have been conveniently
and concisely summarized by Lyons:

> (1) that [Paul] was dependent for his gospel and/or his
> apostolate on men in general and/or on the original apos-
> tles in particular – based on a 'mirror reading' of 1:1 and/
> or 11–12; or (2) that he was too independent, in that his
> was an incomplete or otherwise deficient compromise of the
> true gospel – based on a 'mirror reading' of 1:10.[70]

Additionally, these two views are often correlated: Paul's gospel was
derived from Jerusalem, but he subsequently compromised its rigour
to make it more appealing to the Gentiles.

Without discounting the judicious use of the 'mirror-reading'
method in relation to Galatians,[71] it must be said that such a reading of Galatians 1.1, 10–12 is wholly inferential. Indeed, an alternative reading of these programmatic verses has already been set
forth above, one much more consistent with Paul's antecedent

---

[70] Lyons, *Pauline Autobiography*, pp. 81–2, offers an extensive listing of various
proponents of one or both of these positions; see also that provided by Gaventa,
'Galatians 1 and 2', p. 310 n. 2.

[71] On which see especially Barclay, 'Mirror-Reading a Polemical Letter'. Lyons,
Pauline Autobiography, pp. 96–105, overstates his otherwise noteworthy strictures
against the 'mirror-reading' of Galatians.

remarks concerning the Galatian crisis (Gal. 1.6–9),[72] and with the conceptual framework of the letter as a whole. This is not to say that the Agitators could not have attempted to aid their cause by claiming that Paul was (or had been) dependent upon the Jerusalem apostles.[73] However, it is puzzling that we have no direct attestation of this elsewhere in Galatians.[74]

Indeed, the attempt to substantiate a strictly apologetic interpretation by reference to the autobiography proper (Gal. 1.13ff.) may well be undercut by key features of the passage itself. These render it unlikely that Paul's basic intent throughout is to offer a defence against the Agitators' purported charges of his dependence and/or (subsequent) independence upon the Jerusalem apostles.[75]

(i) Paul makes certain unguarded remarks and unnecessary concessions – for example, his fear that an unfavourable response from the Jerusalem apostles would undermine his mission (Gal. 2.2c).

(ii) He fails to take the opportunity to designate his own mission with the title 'apostolate', thereby underscoring its parallel standing with that of Peter's apostolic mission to 'the circumcision' (Gal. 2.8).

(iii) He readily acknowledges that the Jerusalem apostles, in spite of the demands of the 'false brethren' (Gal. 2.2–4), recognized and affirmed his gospel and ministry (Gal. 2.7–9).[76]

(iv) He openly states that he was eager to accede to the apostles' request that he remember the poor (Gal. 2.10).

In sum, if the primary concern of Paul's autobiography is to respond to an assault upon his apostolic authority and gospel, then his whole response is rather ill-conceived and badly executed.

To this we may add various other deficiencies with a strictly apologetic hypothesis in terms of its dubious and problematic im-

---

[72] And thus also the historical scenario which Gal. 1.6–9 envisages.

[73] Nor is it to exclude the possibility of some historical connection between the Agitators themselves and the Jerusalem apostles – though we earlier noted that it may be telling that Paul nowhere presses this point, and that in any event his fundamental concern resides in their uneasy *ideological* alignment.

[74] Gaventa, 'Galatians 1 and 2', p. 312, reasonably asks why Paul never explicitly states and directly addresses the supposed charges – as, for example, he does elsewhere (2 Cor. 10.10–11; cf. 11.5–6, 12–13). Note Josephus' enumeration of accusations in the course of recounting his autobiography (*Life* 132–5, 189–90, 424–6).

[75] See Lyons, *Pauline Autobiography*, pp. 83ff. on the following.

[76] Verseput, 'Paul's Gentile Mission', p. 37, rightly queries why Paul should appeal in such a way to the same source against whom he is supposedly trying to assert his independence.

plications and influences. (v) It implies that Paul was prepared to jeopardize the wider outworking of the gospel through the church at large (and also his relations with the Jerusalem apostles) in order to assert his own ministry. This is a reductionist estimation of his – and, if Galatians 2 and Acts 2–15 are any indication, the Jerusalem apostles' – usual selfless and costly commitment to the creation-wide cause of God's grace in the crucified Christ, *the* fundamentally *theological* issue at stake.[77] (vi) It has led to the erroneous view that Paul defended his position by appealing to the receipt of (pure) revelation over and against (derivative) tradition.[78] (vii) It has contributed to the long-standing and dominant view that Galatians 1–2 comprises personal narrative to be dissociated from the weightier theological argumentation of chapters 3–4, and the concluding ethical exhortations in chapters 5–6.[79]

In response to such concerns, an alternative 'paradigmatic' approach to Galatians 1–2 has emerged. It is argued that Paul uses his autobiography as a paradigm of the exclusive commitment to the gospel he seeks to evoke in his now wavering Galatian converts. Thus, for example, Gaventa has indicated how such an estimation makes much sense of various key features of Paul's remarks.[80]

(i) Paul's 'biography of reversal'[81] from Jewish to Christian zealot (Gal. 1.13–17) shows how the singular gospel demanded of him an extraordinary and unequivocal response.

---

[77] Variant but equally far-reaching reductionist estimations of Paul's motivations in Gal. 1–2 are represented by Watson, *Paul, Judaism and the Gentiles*, pp. 49–72; and Hall, 'Historical Interference and Rhetorical Effect'. Watson's laudable concern with matters historical and sociological is undermined by a distortion and depreciation of Paul's underlying Christ-shaped theology (cf. Barclay, *Obeying the Truth*, pp. 237–41). Hall's legitimate interest in pursuing a rhetorical approach results in the depreciation of even the historical element, arguing that persuasion was Paul's primary goal: plausibility was more important than matters of fact.

[78] The supposed incongruity between Gal. 1.11–12 and 1 Cor. 15.1–11 is often invoked in support of such a view (see especially Jack T. Sanders, 'Paul's "Autobiographical" Statements in Galatians 1–2'). However, such a revelation versus tradition antithesis is a false dichotomy: while Paul obviously regarded God's disclosure of Christ as the *sine qua non* of his life and ministry, he also clearly and happily drew upon early Christian traditions and teaching (e.g. 1 Cor. 11.2; 15.3; Gal. 6.16; Col. 2.6; 1 Thess. 4.1) – even as mediated via the the Jerusalem apostles (Gal. 1.18, on which see below) – insofar as these conformed to the gospel concerning Christ.

[79] This rather segmented estimation has been exacerbated by the tendency to isolate Gal. 1–2 as a locus for historical and sociological reconstruction – for example, of the Galatian crisis, Paul's background, Pauline and New Testament chronology in general – and to ignore its more immediate bearing within the letter as a whole.

[80] Gaventa, 'Galatians 1 and 2', pp. 313–19.

[81] The expression is that of Schütz, *Paul and the Anatomy of Apostolic Authority*, p. 133.

118   Paul and the crucified Christ in Antioch

(ii) This is subsequently epitomized in the apparently widely circulated report that Paul the persecutor of the Church had now turned proclaimer of the gospel (Gal. 1.22–3).

(iii) That Paul went to Jerusalem κατά ἀποκάλυψιν suggests the determinative role of the gospel in undertaking this journey (Gal. 2.2; cf. 1.12).

(iv) All this is consonant with the fact that the Jerusalem leaders – portrayed more positively than normally allowed – recognized in Paul's advocacy of the truth of the gospel that the grace of God was indeed operative (Gal. 2.7–9).

Additionally, Lyons, in also arguing for a paradigmatic reading, has astutely observed that the autobiography's focus upon Paul's interaction with the Jerusalem apostles could be more narrowly circumscribed in terms of his threefold encounter with Peter.[82] This serves to highlight that the 'fundamental parallelism' between them lies not in their apostolic authority, but in their common vocation and subordination to the gospel, with the Antioch incident clearly illustrating that the essential concern was always faithfulness to the truth of the gospel. Lyons thus concludes that the autobiography is not designed to establish Paul's independence from Jerusalem, nor his equality with Peter, but his 'ethos' as one who faithfully embodies the gospel of God's grace in Christ.

On balance, overall it would thus appear that the paradigmatic approach offers a better evaluation of the autobiographical data than a narrow apologetic interpretation. Nevertheless, in its current form(s), the paradigmatic reading is itself deficient in at least two (interrelated) respects. First, there may be residual concerns as to the degree to which it fully accounts for every aspect of Paul's Jerusalem-specific remarks.[83] Second, its case has not been set forth

---

[82] Lyons, *Pauline Autobiography*, especially pp. 89–91, 158–64.

[83] This concern, with particular reference to the analyses of Lyons and/or Gaventa, has been noted by Barclay, 'Mirror-Reading a Polemical Letter', p. 93 n. 44; *Obeying the Truth*, p. 41 n. 10; and Verseput, 'Paul's Gentile Mission', p. 37 n. 3. Verseput's own argument is that Paul (geographically) distances himself from the Jerusalem apostles because his 'gospel of salvation "outside" of the covenant security of Israel is shown to be true (i.e. οὐ κατά ἄνθρωπον) by the fact that the roots of his Gentile mission reach back to God himself independently of the Jewish Christian community...', p. 39. However, as our argument to date and to follow indicates, this is another reductionist reading (not least of κατά ἄνθρωπον at Gal. 1.11). Paul is not seeking to differentiate between God's purposes for Israel, the Jewish Christian community and his own Gentile mission; on the contrary, he is insisting that all equally conform to the (unexpected) outworking of God's grace in the gospel of Christ.

as strongly as it could be. For example, while both Lyons and Gaventa rightly argue that the *imitatio Pauli* motif at Galatians 4.12-20 lends support to a paradigmatic reading of Galatians 1–2,[84] they fail to observe that Galatians 4.12-20 also attests to the past and present conflict and persecution attending Paul's Galatian ministry.[85] Such an estimation allows an even closer correlation with Galatians 1–2 when the latter is likewise understood as essentially concerned to illustrate Paul's exemplary faithfulness in adversity throughout his long-standing labours for the gospel.[86] Additionally, though both Lyons and Gaventa also correctly emphasize the determinative role of faithfulness to the truth of the gospel in Galatians 1–2, by not discerning the potent and paradoxical Messiah Jesus shape of Paul's governing conceptual framework,[87] their paradigmatic evaluation of this lacks precision and force. That is, contra various conceptually reductionist estimations of Galatians 1–2, Paul's autobiography indicates that he and his mission have always remained fully conformed to the creation-wide outworking of God's covenant purposes (for Jew and Gentile alike) through Israel's crucified and risen Christ.

This brings us to the new paradigmatic reading of Galatians 1.13–2.10 to be pursued here. It has already been contended that the Galatian conflict may be perceived as an inversion of the Maccabean crisis, and that Paul's response to this scenario is governed by a conceptual framework to be understood as a Jewish apocalyptic (e.g., Danielic) schema, though now radically reconfigured through Jesus Christ, Israel's (unexpected) eschatological redeemer. It may now also be argued that the essentially paradigmatic aspect to Paul's autobiography is the more clearly and compellingly delineated when also viewed as a Maccabean model of Judaism radically reworked through Christ. In attending to the collocation of certain central themes, issues and terminology, it will become apparent that whereas both Paul's former self and his Jewish(-Christian)

---

[84] Lyons, *Pauline Autobiography*, pp. 164-8; Gaventa, 'Galatians 1 and 2', pp. 319-22.

[85] In Lyons' case, in attempting to redress the hermeneutical imbalance in favour of a rhetorical assessment of Galatians 1–2, he is unnecessarily negative about the accessibility and pertinence of any historical considerations.

[86] This goes some way to responding to the concern that a paradigmatic reading of the autobiography is of limited bearing upon the Galatians' situation (see Barclay, *Obeying the Truth*, p. 76 n. 1; Lategan, 'Is Paul Defending His Apostleship in Galatians?', pp. 423-4).

[87] Not least as measured against the Galatian conflict as reconstructed here.

detractors may be seen as occupying a role analogous to that of the Jewish apostates who aided the Seleucid cause, Paul the Jewish *Christian* emerges as an exemplary martyr figure but now as irrevocably conformed to the martyred and exalted Jesus, the Messiah and Son of God.

Furthermore, it is within this essentially paradigmatic approach that those features normally cited in support of the usual 'apologetic' interpretation may be recast, subsumed and more readily understood; that is, the extent to which Paul's autobiography attempts to distance him from the Jerusalem apostles (specifically, Peter) at certain junctures is not wholly (and therefore properly) accounted for as a defence against the Agitators' charges of his dependence upon his fellow apostles. Rather, such elements are more cogently understood as a function of the degree to which more latterly – the climactic Antioch incident being the most obvious case in point – the apostle Peter and those under his influence had (unlike Paul) fallen short in conformity to the crucified and risen Christ.[88] To this extent they were placing themselves in uneasy alignment with the way of life promulgated by the Agitators (who may have claimed them for their cause), and it is against this that Paul's autobiography now functions as a counter-offensive.

Paul and the tradition of the Maccabees: his transformation from zealous Jew to apostle of Christ (Galatians 1.13–17)

Paul's autobiographical section first responds to the Galatians' regression from Christ towards the Agitators' demands, by providing a counter-example of his own antithetical movement from Judaism to Christ (Gal. 1.13–17). This is not an attempt to argue for his independence from Jerusalem by showing that only a direct revelation

---

[88] This estimation of the key retrospective role of the Antioch incident *vis-à-vis* Paul's recollection of his antecedent interaction with the Jerusalem apostles is to be differentiated from that of Dunn (e.g., *Jesus, Paul and the Law*, pp. 108–264 *passim*) and N. H. Taylor, *Paul, Antioch and Jerusalem*. While both are commendably sensitive to a wide range of important historical and sociological considerations, their failure to recognize the profound, paradoxical and determinative role of God-in-Christ throughout Paul's ministry (in Jerusalem, Antioch, Galatia, etc.), issues in an inflated yet theologically reductionist evaluation of the Antioch incident. (See further the remarks on Dunn in the introduction and chapters five and six.) In Taylor's case, this is compounded by a highly schematic reconstruction which at various points is precariously grounded on little evidence and/or arguable interpretations of the evidence.

of God sufficed to turn him around (so the 'apologetic' reading). Rather, in remarks especially redolent of themes and even terminology evocative of the Maccabean crisis,[89] Paul informs his errant converts that he was once unparalleled in his pursuit of that now demanded by the Agitators, but that he is now completely conformed to the Son of God – and so implies that the same must be true of them too.

The Galatians heard of Paul's former way of life in Judaism (Gal. 1.13a). The emphatically positioned and aorist Ἠκούσατε suggests that they did so from Paul himself, possibly on the occasion of his original preaching amongst them.[90] Significantly the term ἀναστροφή is applied to the exemplary way of life of the martyr Eleazar (2 Macc. 6.23; cf. Tob. 4.14);[91] and Ἰουδαϊσμός is found in the LXX only in 2 and 4 Maccabees in reference to the martyrs' zeal and self-sacrifice on behalf of Judaism.[92] Indeed, the incorporative ἐν conveys the all-embracing commitment involved.[93] It may be taken as analogous to ἐν τῷ νόμῳ (Rom. 3.19; Phil. 3.6) and as standing in stark contrast to Paul's fundamental conception of his present life and that of all believers as ἐν Χριστῷ.[94]

Paul's brief depiction of his former life, comprising the correlative statements that he persecuted the church and advanced in Judaism (Gal. 1.13b–14), also employs a concentration of terminology whose meaning and significance is the more fully seen by reference to the Maccabean context. Thus, for example, that he 'pursued/persecuted [ἐδίωκον]' the 'church of God'[95] gains significance by comparison

---

[89] See now Ciampa, *The Presence and Function of Scripture in Galatians 1 and 2*, especially pp. 106ff, with particular reference to Niebuhr, *Heidenapostel aus Israel*.

[90] This is all the more likely if the conflict which attended it involved Jewish (-Christian) opposition.

[91] Cf. the alternative term ἀγωγή ('conduct, manner of life') at 2 Macc. 4.16; 6.8; 11.24. Usage of ἀναστροφή and the cognate verb ἀναστρέφω in the later New Testament literature attests to the emerging conception of an exemplary *Christian* 'way of life' (e.g., 1 Tim. 4.12; Heb. 13.7; 1 and 2 Pet. *passim*).

[92] 2 Macc. 2.21; 8.1; 14.38 (2x); 4 Macc. 4.26.

[93] On the Maccabean background of the important expression 'in Judaism', see Amir, 'The Term *Ioudaismos*'; Niebuhr, *Heidenapostel aus Israel*, especially pp. 21–35; Ciampa, *The Presence and Function of Scripture in Galatians 1 and 2*, pp. 106–8; Dunn, 'Who Did Paul Think He Was?', pp. 184–5.

[94] Gal. 1.22; 2.4, 17, etc. Cf. the discussion of Χριστός in chapter six.

[95] This expression, indebted to the Old Testament conception of the assembly (קהל) of Israel, is not localized (e.g., referring only to the Jerusalem *Urgemeinde*) but absolute: standing in opposition to 'Judaism' and denoting the messianic people of God as a whole (rightly Schlier, *Der Brief an die Galater*, p. 49). Of course, Paul's actions would have been focused upon particular communities – whether Jerusalem, Damascus or elsewhere.

with the Maccabees' relentless 'hunting down' of their Gentile oppressors and/or apostate Jews.[96] Likewise, that he 'ravaged/ destroyed [ἐπόρθουν]' the church has a notable analogy in Antiochus IV Epiphanes' 'plundering' Jerusalem and his 'destruction' of the martyrs.[97]

Similarly, Paul's status as one who 'was advancing [προέκοπτον]' in Judaism might be compared to the key role of the 'wise' during the Maccabean crisis, even though their commitment to the covenant and Torah-instruction meant that they 'stumbled [προσκόπτω/ ἀσθενέω]', that is, were martyred (Dan. 11.33; 12.3; cf. 2 Cor. 11.29).[98] Certainly Paul saw himself as one who outstripped his contemporaries in spearheading the cause of the Jewish nation. This was exemplified by his being zealous – literally, 'existing a zealot'[99] – for the traditions of his fathers. These traditions were probably Pharisee-specific while also (as the immediate context suggests) embracing the wider interests of Judaism in general.[100] As such, we may note the broadly based Jewish nationalist concerns conveyed by the cognate terms πατρῷος, πάτριος and πατρίς, all of which figure prominently – and, on occasion, interchangeably – in 2 and 4 Maccabees, often in reference to 'the ancestral laws, commandments, customs and country' for which the zealous Jew was prepared to live and die.[101] In sum, the collocation of the themes and terms deployed at Galatians 1.13–14 suggest that in his former life as a zealous Pharisee Paul stood firmly in the tradition of the Maccabees.[102]

---

[96] Rightly Dunn, *Galatians*, pp. 57–8; cf. 1 Macc. 2.47; 3.5, 24; 1 Cor. 15.9; Phil. 3.6; also Rom. 12.14; 1 Cor. 4.12; 2 Cor. 4.9; 1 Thess. 2.15.

[97] The only LXX occurrences of πορθέω are at 4 Macc. 4.23; 11.4; cf. Gal. 1.23; Acts 9.21. The verb is probably conative ('*tried to* destroy') and in this respect may bear comparison to πείθω and ἀρέσκω (Gal. 1.10).

[98] Cf. also the military 'advancement [προκοπή]' of Judas Maccabeus and his army – 'enlisted [from] those who had continued in the Jewish faith [ἐν τῷ Ἰουδαϊσμῷ]' – against their Gentile oppressors (2 Macc. 8.1, 8).

[99] Recall the discussion in chapter two concerning the correspondence between the Maccabees and first-century 'Zealot' activity, with particular reference to the studies of Farmer, Hengel and Wright. Note also Donaldson, 'Zealot and Convert'; *Paul and the Gentiles*, pp. 273–92; and Fairchild, 'Paul's Pre-Christian Zealot Associations'.

[100] For example, they would have included a commitment to both Torah and oral halakhah (cf. *Ant.* 13.297, 408; Acts 22.3; 23.6; 24.14; 28.17).

[101] See, for example, 2 Macc. 6.1; 7.2, 24, 37; 8.21; 13.21; 4 Macc. 4.23; 8.7; 9.1; 16.16.

[102] Indeed, it corroborates what was surmised from the discussion in chapter two: that the pre-Christian Paul would have been empathetic toward – if not involved in – the religio-political aspirations of the Maccabean-inspired first-century Jewish nationalists.

However, both Paul and his mission were dramatically transformed when God revealed his son 'in him' (Gal. 1.15–16a). This encounter may be seen as representing a radical reworking of the Jewish messianic expectations based on Daniel 7.13–14 with regard to a redeemer/ruler who would rescue and vindicate afflicted Israel, and inaugurate God's glorious rule. It was expected that Israel's vindication would include its now condemned enemies' astonished recognition that those whom they had formerly persecuted – not least as embodied in their righteous representative(s) – were in fact the now exalted saints/sons of God.[103] However, in God's disclosure of Jesus 'in Paul' this 'great reversal' is itself reversed. Here and now (not at the future judgement) it is Paul the exemplary zealous Jew who realizes that the one whom he had been persecuting – by means of his pursuit of Jesus' followers – was in fact Israel's (and the nations') Messiah and Son of God. The rejected and martyred Jesus now occupied an exalted role within the divine economy, and those conformed to him (whether Jew or Gentile) constituted the 'Israel of God' rescued from the evil age/sphere, who even now had a share in the glorious reign of their representative redeemer (cf. Gal. 1.4; 6.16).

Further indication of the nature and significance of this event may be discerned in Paul's highly compressed account of its immediate impact upon both his own life and mission (Gal. 1.16–17). With respect to the former, in terms which locate him in continuity with the covenantal context of Old Testament prophetic precedent (and also the Isaianic servant),[104] Paul remarks that God's gracious calling took the form of a disclosure of his Son *'in me* [ἐν ἐμοί]'.[105] Commentators have long puzzled over whether this is to be taken as a simple dative ('to me'), instrumentally ('through me'), or as denoting the profound inner reality – mystical or otherwise – of the experience ('within me').[106] However, it is more likely that Paul has in view that which underlies all such estimations, namely, the complete reconfiguration of his entire self ('in my person'); that is, the exalted Son of God is now constitutive of his entire life, an existence which Paul elsewhere describes as 'Christ in me' (see especially Gal. 2.20).[107] Indeed, given the argument offered thus far, and by com-

---

[103] Cf. Isa. 52–3; Wis. 4–5; *1 Enoch* 62–3.
[104] Cf. Isa. 42.6; 49.1–6 and Jer. 1.5.
[105] Cf. 1 Cor. 9.1; 15.8–10; possibly 2 Cor. 4.4–6.
[106] Discussions in Mußner, *Der Galaterbrief*, pp. 86–7.
[107] Note also Gal. 4.6: 'God has sent the Spirit of his Son into our hearts.'

parison with the phrase ἐν ἐμοί at 2 Maccabees 7.38, it may well be that Paul understands this to involve him in a martyr-like role as one whose faithfulness is a means of participating in divine redemption: God in Christ ... in him.[108]

This matter will be taken up in greater detail in a later discussion of Galatians 2.19–21 (in relation to Romans 7). However, at this juncture another observation may be added. In 4 Maccabees the Jewish martyrs' Torah-obedience even to the point of death rendered them 'reason' (read 'Torah') personified.[109] By comparison with such analogies it may be suggested (and will be pursued later) that Paul the representative Jew – formerly captive to sin's abuse of Torah 'in me [ἐν ἐμοί]' (cf. Rom. 7.13–25) – has now been reconfigured by the martyred and exalted Jesus who is the paradoxical fulfilment of Torah, and who now lives 'in him'. In essence, Paul is no longer the zealous Jew ready to die for Torah/Israel/God, but the faithful apostle ready to die for God in Christ in him.

A second and related aspect of Paul's transformation by the Son of God is his commission to proclaim 'him among the Gentiles' (Gal. 1.16b): the non-Jewish nations are now seen to be equally the object of divine redemption. Insofar as the Son of God is in Paul, and Paul is 'among the Gentiles', this phrase denotes not only the sphere of the apostle's ministry, but also that the Son of God (Christ) is himself among the Gentiles.[110] Given all this, Paul deemed it unnecessary to consult with 'flesh and blood' (Gal. 1.16c); nor did he go up to Jerusalem to those who were apostles before him (Gal. 1.17a). Care must be taken in interpreting these statements. Paul is not simply engaging in mere 'alibi-reasoning' to indicate limited contact with (and thus dependence upon) Jerusalem.[111] Nor is he attempting to dissociate himself completely from the Jerusalem apostles by dismissing them as merely human, in contrast to the

---

[108] This would evoke a past/present aspect reminiscent of that discerned in Gal. 4.12–20. Paul reminds his afflicted Philippian converts that they too are 'engaged in the same conflict which you saw in me [ἐν ἐμοί] and now hear [as being] in me [ἐν ἐμοί]' (Phil. 1.30). On the martyr motif in Philippians, see Lampe, 'Martyrdom and Inspiration', p. 132.

[109] 4 Macc. 14.2, this rendering them 'more royal than kings and freer than the free'.

[110] As was recognized by the Galatians when they received Paul 'as an angel of God, as Christ Jesus' (Gal. 4.14); note also Col. 1.21–4.

[111] So, for example, Holmberg, *Paul and Power*, p. 16; R. N. Longenecker, *Galatians*, p. 35.

divine revelation just received. Rather, consonant with Paul's governing conceptual framework, and as the 'not ... *not even* [οὐ ... οὐδέ]' sequence suggests, the reference to Jerusalem stands in both continuity and discontinuity with its antecedent. That is, it is in continuity only insofar as it might be inferred that the Jerusalem apostles could and occasionally did become misaligned with the 'merely human' (that which is κατὰ ἄνθρωπον/σάρκα), Peter's conduct in Antioch offering the most obvious case in point. It is in discontinuity insofar as the Jerusalem apostles were in fact worthily conformed to their otherwise legitimate status as true apostles of Christ. It is the fundamental 'of God in Christ' versus 'of man' distinction — and not simply the vicissitudes of certain purported charges or particular events — which provides the proper framework within which to understand Paul's statements here and the pursuant account of his interaction with the Jerusalem apostles.

At this point Paul adds only that he immediately went to Arabia and then returned again to Damascus (Gal. 1.17b,c), leaving commentators to speculate whether the interim period comprised preparation for, or constituted the first stage of, his Gentile mission. Internal evidence in support of the latter might be found in the force of the adverb 'immediately [εὐθέως]'.[112] Its significance cannot be reduced to the view that Paul is here simply saying he quickly got as far away from Jerusalem as possible. Rather, it is a temporal and volitional index of Paul's now redeployed missionary zeal.[113] As such it might be compared to the function of the adverb in 2 Maccabees, whether in reference to the immediate enactment of Gentile or Jewish policy/strategy,[114] or, most notably, to Eleazar's readiness to suffer martyrdom for Torah (2 Macc. 6.28). Indirect external support for such a reading may be found in the fact that while in Arabia Paul seems to have incurred the wrath of its King Aretas (2 Cor. 11.32–3). This is more likely to have been precipitated by disruption arising out of his conscientious but highly contentious missionary activity — especially if, as suggested in chapter two, it

---

[112] It governs both the negative and positive statements in Gal. 1.16b–17, but with its stress on the latter (so Burton, *Galatians*, pp. 53–4; contra Mußner, *Der Galaterbrief*, p. 89 n. 56).
[113] Cf. Acts 9.20: 'And in the synagogues immediately [Paul] proclaimed Jesus, saying, "He is the Son of God."' Contrast οὕτως ταχέως at Gal. 1.6.
[114] 2 Macc. 3.8; 4.10; 8.11; 14.12, 16.

took place against the wider backdrop of events leading up to the Caligula Temple edict.[115]

From his own account it is clear that in his former way of life as a zealous Jew – not least as expressed in his persecution of the church – Paul stood firmly in the tradition of the Maccabean model of Judaism. However, God's dramatic disclosure of Jesus as the Son of God had resulted in a radical reconfiguration of Paul's person and vocation: from latter-day Maccabean to a Christian apostle now completely conformed to the martyred and exalted Messiah Jesus. This transformation provided a stark counter-example for those of his Galatian converts now under the influence of Agitators' promulgation of matters Jewish, and was the fundamental standpoint from which Paul was prepared to critique even the apostle Peter whose recent conduct (in Antioch) also threatened to undermine conformity to Christ.

Jerusalem 1: Paul the persecutor turned proclaimer (Galatians 1.18–24)

That Paul's autobiographical account now involves the first of two visits to Jerusalem (Gal. 1.18–24; 2.1–10) need not in itself be construed as evidence that its primary intent is to defend the independence of his apostolate.[116] Indeed, the nature and significance of Paul's much disputed initial meeting with Peter is more clearly seen when it is realized that the overriding consideration throughout Galatians 1.18–24 is to demonstrate further Paul's dramatic transformation and example: the former persecutor of Christ and his people has become a faithful servant of both, and the Galatians and Jerusalem apostles must conduct themselves likewise.

The strenuous efforts of commentators to discern the precise nature of Paul's encounter with Peter have rightly focused upon the interpretation of the phrase ἱστορῆσαι Κηφᾶν (Gal. 1.18a), which

---

[115] Note the detailed accounts offered by Murphy-O'Connor, 'Paul in Arabia', and *Paul: A Critical Life*, pp. 81–5; and Hengel and Schwemer, *Paul Between Damascus and Antioch*, especially pp. 106–18, arguing cogently that Paul actively preached the gospel in Arabia (i.e., in the Nabatean kingdom), and that the volatile political situation was such that this no doubt precipitated life-threatening opposition.

[116] Both here and below, consideration of Paul's interaction with Jerusalem is confined to the evidence of Galatians, and does not press for a particular correlation with the external data provided in Acts. The various issues and options on this matter are well rehearsed in, for example, Fung, *Galatians*, pp. 9–28; Wenham, 'Acts and the Pauline Corpus II'.

could be rendered as either (i) 'inquire/acquire information from' or (ii) 'visit/get to know'.[117] Philological and other considerations have often been deployed in service of the majority 'apologetic' interpretation, which invariably has favoured (ii) over (i).[118] However, the lack of consensus on a precise interpretation, the verb's wide semantic range and the fifteen-day duration of the visit together suggest that Paul has in view the full scope of his contact with Peter; that is, it was a visit in which he became acquainted with the leading Jerusalem apostle, this necessarily involving a wide-ranging exchange of information, not least with respect to Jesus and the church's proclamation of the gospel.[119]

It is within the framework of their fundamental common commitment to God in Messiah Jesus – one which radically differentiated them from the vast majority of their fellow unbelieving Jews – that any differences between apostles are to be viewed, and the profound nature of Paul's concern the more readily understood. Thus Paul's claim that his initial contact with Jerusalem was restricted to Peter and James (Gal. 1.19) does not reflect an attempt to defend his own apostolic ministry over and against theirs *per se* (so the 'apologetic' interpretation). Rather it is likely to be an indication of the discretion required, given the ever-threatening circumstances under which the three apostles, equally committed to a contentious gospel, met and conferred.[120] Indeed, the oath which underscores Paul's assertion (invoking God as witness to his faithfulness),[121] and the pointed reference to the immediate resumption of his labour in Syria and Cilicia, both indicate that Paul's fundamental concern throughout is to stress his (costly) conformity to Christ and his people.

---

[117] See the discussion in Dunn, *Jesus, Paul and the Law*, pp. 110–13, 126–8 – in dialogue with Hofius, 'Gal.1.18: ἱστορῆσαι Κηφᾶν' and Walter, 'Paulus' – which judiciously settles on an amalgam of both (i) and (ii).

[118] For example, Betz, *Galatians*, p. 76 n. 196, can admit (i) is 'possible philologically' but rejects it because it 'runs counter to Paul's defense'. Others, while granting that Paul may well have received oral Jesus traditions from Peter, stop short of any suggestion that he was dependent upon him for instruction and/or authentication of his ministry (Fung, *Galatians*, pp. 73–5).

[119] See Hengel and Schwemer, *Paul Between Damascus and Antioch*, pp. 144–50, which, though too constrained to the 'apologetic' reading, nonetheless rightly stresses the extensive interaction between Peter and Paul.

[120] A point well made by Hengel and Schwemer, ibid., pp. 134ff.

[121] Gal. 1.20; cf. 2 Cor. 5.11b. Recall the almost axiomatic view of the Gentiles as violators of oaths (2 Macc. 15.10), and also Eleazar's refusal to 'transgress the sacred oaths of my ancestors concerning the keeping of the law' (4 Macc. 5.29).

This aspect comes into clear view with Paul's pursuant remark that though he had no wider contact with the Judaean believers, they nevertheless heard reports to the effect that 'He who once persecuted us is now preaching the faith he once tried to destroy' (Gal. 1.23). The imperfect periphrastic ἤμην δὲ ἀγνοούμενος τῷ προσώπῳ (at Gal. 1.22) indicates an ongoing situation which obtained during this early phase of Paul's Christian ministry. Thus, though he was personally unknown to the Judaean churches in his new capacity as apostle of Christ, this need not preclude the possibility that they had nevertheless known of him in his former role as persecutor of those Judaeans ἐν Χριστῷ.[122] While the precise transmission of these ongoing reports about Paul's dramatic reversal is uncertain, it is probable that they emanated from various sources, not least Antioch.[123] They would then have been received and disseminated within the Judaean churches themselves.

In any event, Paul's preaching of the faith he had once tried to destroy represented an astonishing turnaround from persecutor to proclaimer. Indeed, insofar as this would have inevitably led to his own affliction,[124] Paul the Jewish zealot and persecutor of the church had now become Paul the Christian martyr figure.[125] Such is the transformation that the Judaean believers ἐδόξαζον ἐν ἐμοὶ τὸν θεόν (Gal. 1.24). That is, in terms evocative of Isaiah 49.3, they recognized that Paul – in virtue of God revealing his Son 'in him' (recall ἐν ἐμοί at Gal. 1.16) – is now an exemplary (suffering) servant of the Messiah-conformed Israel in whom God is truly glorified. Such

---

[122] Indeed the otherwise redundant qualification of ταῖς ἐκκλησίαις with ἐν Χριστῷ might allude to the extensive overlap between Jewish and Jewish *Christian* assemblies, and imply something of the highly intramural aspect of Paul's persecuting activities at that time. That the Judaean church ἐν Χριστῷ 'Ιησοῦ had endured persecution is attested in 1 Thess. 2.14–16 – a text which Lampe, 'Martyrdom and Inspiration', p. 125, rightly locates in relation to early Christian reworkings of the Jewish prophet-martyr tradition.

[123] This would have been the likely base of his mission in Syria. This implies what is probable on *prima facie* grounds alone, viz., that the Antiochene Christians (and also Jews) were well apprised of the autobiographical details here recounted (with their evocations of the Maccabean background).

[124] R. N. Longenecker, *Galatians*, p. 40, reasonably suggests that some of the hardships cited in 2 Cor. 11.23–9, unattested in accounts of Paul's later missionary activities, may well have occurred during this earlier phase of his ministry.

[125] Thus, without accepting the more dubious aspects of his analysis, the basic insight of E. Bammel, 'Galater 1,23', that Gal. 1.23 is to be located within a Jewish martyr frame of reference, remains valid and more instructive than later commentators have allowed.

recognition from those amongst whom Paul had not even ministered clearly constitutes a thinly veiled polemic against his errant Galatian converts, who are now in danger of glorifying that which Paul has rejected in and through his conformity to the crucified Christ (Gal. 6.12–13).

Jerusalem 2: Paul's conformity to the truth of the gospel (Galatians 2.1–10)

At its most fundamental, the account of the second Jerusalem visit depicts neither a 'struggle for power' nor a 'delicate balancing act' between Paul and the Jerusalem apostles. Rather it is a further demonstration of the fact that Paul's life and ministry are completely governed by the truth of the gospel as disclosed in God's Son, Jesus the Messiah. The significance of this will become apparent as, in turn, consideration is given to the key constituent elements of the narrative: the nature and intent of the trip (Gal. 2.1–2); Paul's defence of the truth of the gospel (Gal. 2.3–5); and the complex scenario involving the apostolic agreement (Gal. 2.6–10). In the course of this examination I shall again have cause to note the reworking of certain Maccabean themes and issues. From this Paul emerges as a zealous defender of the truth of God in Christ under siege from certain Jewish(-Christian) opponents, and one whose endorsement by the Jerusalem apostles has more latterly been somewhat undermined by Peter's conduct in Antioch.

Accompanied by the respected Barnabas, and taking along the Gentile convert Titus as perhaps something of a 'test case', Paul's visit to Jerusalem was κατὰ ἀποκάλυψιν (Gal. 2.1–2a). This much disputed phrase denotes not – or at least not merely – a revelation specific to this event,[126] nor Paul's disclaimer of the Agitators' charge that he had been summoned to be reprimanded,[127] nor is it the first occasion on which Paul informed the Jerusalem apostles of his Damascus-road revelation concerning his circumcision-free

---

[126] Whether to Paul himself (Bruce, *Galatians*, p. 108), Agabus as recorded in Acts 11.28 (Duncan, *Galatians*, p. 38), or some otherwise unattested prophetic and/or charismatic disclosure within the Antiochene community in accordance with Acts 13.2; 1 Cor. 14.6, 26 (Catchpole, 'Paul, James and the Apostolic Decree', p. 433). While none of these historically particular events can be excluded (or confirmed) as of bearing upon Paul's visit, in themselves they cannot account for the essentially *qualitative* force of κατὰ ἀποκάλυψιν.
[127] Bring, *Galatians*, p. 59; Rohde, *Der Brief des Paulus an die Galater*, p. 76.

gospel to the Gentiles.[128] Rather, as the conceptual antithesis to κατὰ ἄνθρωπον at Galatians 1.11, and as analogous to that in view in Paul's use of ἀποκαλύψεως and ἀποκαλύψαι at Galatians 1.12c, 16a, κατὰ ἀποκάλυψιν indicates that the nature and intent of Paul's visit was 'in accordance with' the origin and subsequent apostolic outworking of God's disclosure of his Son in him. It was this which governed Paul's position in relation to all that transpired during this visit, not least any κατὰ ἄνθρωπον attempts to undermine the truth of the gospel.

That Paul had cause for concern in this respect is immediately signalled by his pursuant statement. He had come to Jerusalem to consult with and gain the cooperation of the Jerusalem apostles for the gospel which he preached among the Gentiles (Gal. 2.2b).[129] The gravity of the situation is further indicated by the fact that they met 'privately [κατ' ἰδίαν]'.[130] This phrase is used in 2 Maccabees in connection with a formal exchange between leaders.[131] Paul's expressed concern at Galatians 2.2c has nothing to do with the authenticity of his gospel and mission (which are beyond doubt), but rather indicates that his efforts are under threat and may be in vain.[132] Hence his desire that he receive the wholehearted endorsement of the Jerusalem apostles. The extent of his own commitment to the cause of Christ is implied in the foot-race metaphor τρέχειν δρόμον, which is analogous to τρέχειν ἀγῶνα.[133] It thus bears comparison to the ἀγών-motif evident elsewhere in Paul,[134] and which is so prominent in 2 and 4 Maccabees in reference to the Jewish

[128] So Howard, *Paul: Crisis in Galatia*, pp. 38ff., whose causative estimation of κατὰ ἀποκάλυψιν (viz., 'on account of') functions in support of a wide-ranging reconstruction which is *prima facie* highly improbable and greatly at variance with the Galatian evidence as reconstructed here.

[129] The force of ἀνατίθημι as 'consult with a view to cooperation' (cf. 2 Macc. 3.9; Acts 25.14) counts against the 'apologetic' interpretation, and the manifest stress upon 'the *gospel* which I preach' (rather than upon 'among the Gentiles') points in favour of a paradigmatic reading.

[130] This need not exclude an initial, more broadly based contact with the Jerusalem church (note εἰς Ἱεροσόλυμα, αὐτοῖς). However, the adversative δέ, the denotation of 'those of repute' (Gal. 2.2, 6, 9), and κατ' ἰδίαν itself, all suggest that the significant discussions and decision-making took place amongst the leading figures of the church.

[131] 2 Macc. 4.5; 9.26; 14.21.

[132] Burton, *Galatians*, pp. 73–4, rightly takes Gal. 2.2c as an object clause after an implied verb of fearing; cf. Gal. 4.11; 1 Thess. 3.5.

[133] On the wider ancient usage of this motif, see especially Pfitzner, *Paul and the Agon Motif*.

[134] See especially Rom. 15.30–1; 1 Cor. 9.24–7; Phil. 1.27–30 (cf. 3.12–15); 1 Thess. 2.2ff. (cf. 2.13–16; Acts 17.1–6); Col. 1.24–2.1; also 1 Cor. 4.8–13.

athlete-martyr.[135] In essence, Paul visited Jerusalem in order that his fellow apostles might vindicate his much afflicted ministry in service of the martyred and exalted Jesus, the Son of God.

Paul thus again appears as something of a martyr figure, and this becomes all the more evident from his ensuing account of the opposition he met while in Jerusalem (Gal. 2.3–5).[136] Certain 'false brethren' apparently infiltrated the private meeting, 'spied out' the freedom which those in Christ shared together, and demanded that Titus be circumcised. Paul construes this action as an attack on the truth of the gospel and an attempt to enslave. Though capable of association with a range of circumstances, Paul's depiction of this contentious situation could readily be construed as a Christian version of a typical Maccabean crisis, with the roles radically reversed.

Thus Paul, ardent apostle to the Gentiles, zealously defends the truth of the gospel – that is, God's covenant faithfulness in Christ which is now under threat – and resists all attempts to enslave those whom he represents.[137] However, his Jewish(-Christian) opponents, who may have seen themselves in the tradition of Judas Maccabeus and those who 'secretly entered' enemy territory to enlist any who remain in Judaism (2 Macc. 8.1),[138] are aligning themselves with all that is opposed to God in Christ. Their attempt to compel the Gentile Christian Titus to be circumcised is reminiscent of both Antiochus IV Epiphanes' efforts to compel the Maccabean martyrs to forsake their Torah food laws, and the Maccabees' enforced circumcision of apostate Jews. Paul now regards both forms of coercion as equally antipathetic to the gospel of Christ. In essence, Paul's stance – in which he was apparently supported by the Jerusalem apostles – was that God's covenant faithfulness (truth) was now manifest not via a Jewish way of life (as lived and died for during the Maccabean period), but through a new way of life ἐν Χριστῷ Ἰησοῦ: conformity to the martyred and risen Messiah Jesus.

---

[135] For example, 2 Macc. 14.18, 43; 15.9, 18R; 4 Macc. 11.20; 13.15; 14.5; 16.16; 17.10ff.

[136] These structurally awkward verses are best taken as an extended parenthesis on a Titus-focused 'test-case' scenario in Jerusalem. This majority view is much more cogent than attempts to sever Gal. 2.4–5 from 2.3, and then argue (variously) that it has a Galatian or Antiochene scenario in view (see Orchard, 'The Ellipsis'; Bruce, *Galatians*, pp. 115–17; Watson, *Paul, Judaism and the Gentiles*, pp. 50–1).

[137] Note the reference to the 'truth [being] cast down to the ground' in Dan. 8.12 as an assault upon God's covenant faithfulness and creation-wide purposes. Cf. our later discussion of 'the truth of the gospel' at Gal. 2.14 in chapter five.

[138] Cf. 1 Macc. 5.38 which, as Gal. 2.4, also evokes Josh. 2.1–3.

Paul readily acknowledges that he and the Jerusalem apostles arrived at an agreement concerning their respective missionary tasks. Indeed, far from imposing any requirements upon Paul,[139] his Jerusalem counterparts showed considerable theological discernment and conviction – note ἰδόντες and γνόντες (Gal. 2.7, 9) – in recognizing that God's grace was operative in his Gentile mission in a manner analogous to its outworking through Peter's work among the Jews. Thus, it is within the context of their fundamental common commitment to God's grace in Christ (and his people) – a cause which radically differentiated them from their fellow unbelieving Jews – that any understanding of the specifics of the agreement must be located. Indeed, the often narrowly focused and highly polarized debate as to whether the agreement was territorial or ethnic,[140] must first recognize the breadth and depth of the common ground between the two parties involved, and then a more viable estimation of its outworking in each case may be ventured.

Towards this end, we may focus briefly on the fact that the reciprocal recognition of the outworking of divine grace found formal expression in the form of 'the right hand of fellowship, that [Paul and Barnabas] should go to the Gentiles and [the Jerusalem apostles] to the circumcised' (Gal. 2.9). The expression διδόναι δεξιάν (or δεξιάς), though by no means of strict Jewish provenance, figures prominently in 1 and 2 Maccabees as that which betokens an official compact involving the giving and receiving of pledges of friendship and/or terms of peace.[141] Within the Maccabean framework, this was bound up with their efforts to live according to the Torah-based way of life, and thereby attain the truly lasting peace of the covenant. Here, however, this compact is defined as one of 'fellowship [κοινωνία]'. For Paul, fellowship is itself defined most fundamentally in terms of a common life conformed to the crucified and risen Christ, and common cause in the outworking of divine reconciliation thus effected.[142]

---

[139] The likely weight of προσανατίθημι at Gal. 2.6c; see Burton, *Galatians*, pp. 89–91; Rohde, *Der Brief des Paulus an die Galater,* pp. 83–4.

[140] Represented by Burton, *Galatians*, pp. 97–8, and Betz, *Galatians*, p. 100, respectively.

[141] 1 Macc. 6.58; 11.50, 62, 66; 2 Macc. 4.34; 11.26, 30; 12.11, 12; 13.22; 14.19. Cf. *J.W.* 6.318–20, 345, 356, 378; *Ant.* 8.387; 18.328; 20.62.

[142] 1 Cor. 1.9; 10.16; Phil. 1.5; 3.10; Phlm. 6; cf. Eph. 2.11–22. This matter will be pursued more fully in chapter five in connection with our estimation of the Antiochene table-fellowship.

Nonetheless, both parties no doubt encouraged one another to conform themselves to their common cause in Christ precisely in and through its outworking in the given situation(s) within which they lived and ministered, all the while remaining sensitive to the circumstances confronting their counterparts. So, for example, for Paul this would require discernment in ministering within a mixed (Jew + Gentile) Diaspora environment (such as Antioch); for the Jerusalem apostles it would involve a keen awareness of Israel-specific issues that bore upon a largely Jewish Christian community. But underlying and undergirding both these and all other specific concerns was the fundamental need to remain faithful to the God-in-Christ-in-believer shape of divine redemption and reconciliation for Jew and Gentile alike.

The Jerusalem apostles are successively referred to as οἱ δοκοῦντες, οἱ δοκοῦντες εἶναί τι, and οἱ δοκοῦντες στῦλοι εἶναι (Gal 2.2, 6, 9).[143] Together, these designations have been variously interpreted as (a) honorific,[144] (b) dismissive,[145] (c) rhetorically nuanced,[146] or (d) simply a way of indicating that one must judge not according to appearance but reality.[147] However, when it is realized that Paul's estimation of the apostles is fundamentally determined by the degree to which they conformed to Christ – to a κατὰ ἀποκάλυψιν Ἰησοῦ Χριστοῦ rather than a κατὰ ἄνθρωπον way of life – then the subtlety and significance of the designations may be understood. In emulating God-in-Christ the apostles are (a) worthy of their esteem; but to the degree that they ever become misaligned with that which is 'of man' rather than 'of God in Christ', then (b) their repute is undermined accordingly. It is this which accounts for (c) the rhetorical variability of the designations, and (d) provides the wider frame of reference within which to differentiate correctly between what is 'false' and what is 'real'.

That the ambiguous and multifaceted function of these desig-

[143] It is possible that the στῦλοι constitute a more closely circumscribed group within the wider category of οἱ δοκοῦντες.
[144] E.g., Burton, *Galatians*, p. 71; Bruce, *Galatians*, p. 109; Mußner, *Der Galaterbrief*, pp. 104–5.
[145] R. N. Longenecker, *Galatians*, p. 48.
[146] Betz, *Galatians*, pp. 86–7, suggests that they allow Paul to recognize the Jerusalem apostles' status but without compromising God and Christ as the authority underlying the gospel. Dunn, *Jesus, Paul and the Law*, pp. 92–3 straddles (b) and (c).
[147] So Hay, 'Paul's Indifference to Authority' (followed by Cousar, *Galatians*, pp. 40–1), arguing that Paul wants the Galatians to be able to adjudicate between the apostles' rank and their conformity to the gospel.

nations attests to some (recent) concern that the apostles' example – or at least that of Peter – may not be completely conformed to their leading role as servants of Christ may be indicated by reference to certain details. For example, their status is not to be measured in terms of 'what they were formerly',[148] but rather their ongoing life and work for the gospel: in short, what sort of Christians they currently are.[149] This is underscored by the present tense of δοκοῦντες and λαμβάνει, both implying that their reputable standing requires continued validation. Likewise the pointed expression 'God shows no partiality' – its Old Testament antecedents admonishing Israel against presuming upon her covenant status[150] – functions in the New Testament to warn both Jews and Jewish Christians that God judges according to no other criteria than conformity to Christ.[151]

Furthermore, the designation στῦλοι ('pillars') indicates something of the full measure of the standard Paul expects from the apostles. Richard Bauckham has recently demonstrated that underlying this designation is the Jerusalem Temple imagery deployed at Isaiah 54.11–12 in the course of an oracle assuring Israel of God's Zion-focused everlasting covenant with his righteous people (Isa. 54.9–17).[152] Such imagery could also have accrued associations with the steadfastness of the Maccabean martyrs (4 Macc. 17.3; cf. Rev. 3.12).[153] Indeed both Peter and Paul are later remembered as 'most righteous pillars [στῦλοι] of the church [who] were persecuted and contended unto death' (*1 Clem.* 5.2).[154] In sum, Paul recognizes the esteem of the Jerusalem apostles, and readily acknowledges their

[148] Most probably an oblique reference to their former privileged relationship with the earthly Jesus and/or their roles as founding members of the early church; and possibly also to their support for Paul at this earlier meeting.

[149] Cf. 1 Cor. 3.13; 1 Thess. 1.5; Acts 26.29.

[150] Deut. 10.16–17; Jer. 4.4; Amos 9.7.

[151] Cf. Rom. 2.11; Eph. 6.9; Col. 3.25; Acts 10.34; Jas. 2.1.

[152] Indeed, the reference to 'righteousness' at Isa. 54.14 may well have provided scriptural warrant for the church's later designation of James as 'just/righteous': his person and position marked him out as one who played a prominent role in upholding the Messiah Jesus-focused eschatological people of God. See Bauckham, 'James and the Jerusalem Church', pp. 441–50; note also his 'For What Offence', p. 207ff.

[153] Later rabbinic tradition attests to some debate whether the 'three pillars' upon whom God set the world were (a) Abraham, Isaac and Jacob; or (b) Hananiah, Mishael and Azariah (*Cant. Rab.* 7.8, on which see Agus, *The Binding of Isaac and Messiah*, p. 42).

[154] So van Henten, 'The Martyrs as Heroes of the Christian People', discusses the analogies between *1 Clem.* 5.2 and 4 Macc. 17.3 within their respective wider contexts, making particular reference to Peter and Paul as representative of Christian martyrs in the tradition of Jewish *exempla* who sacrificed themselves for their new 'nation [πολιτεία]'.

endorsement of his mission (despite considerable pressure upon them to do otherwise). Yet his equivocal language also intimates recent cause for concern, with the ensuing Antioch incident looming large as the major contributing factor.

A final possible indication of this is Paul's pivotal and polemical reference to the fact that he readily acceded to the Jerusalem apostles' specific request that he remember 'the poor [οἱ πτωχοί]' (Gal. 2.10).[155] If a partitive (rather than an epexegetic) reading of οἱ πτωχοὶ τῶν ἁγίων τῶν ἐν Ἰερουσαλήμ at Romans 15.26 is any indication, then 'the poor' constituted a materially deprived subsection of the Jerusalem church as a whole. Furthermore, there is some evidence to suggest that their deprivation (and designation) was a direct function of their exemplary '*anawim* piety' and the suffering which this engendered.[156] It is usually held that Paul's eager remembrance of 'the poor' either had already found expression in the now completed task of bringing famine relief, or subsequently did so in his Jerusalem collection.[157] However, it is at least as plausible that it was expressed in some unstated but tangible way immediately upon request: that is, Paul was zealous in identifying himself then and there with those who (like himself) were suffering for the cause of Christ.[158] As such, his conduct then was in marked contrast to that of Peter later: Paul stood firm with the afflicted Jewish Christians in Jerusalem; Peter withdrew from the afflicted Gentile Christians in Antioch.

4. Conclusion

Formerly conformed to Christ in their readiness to share in Paul's own afflictions, the Galatian brethren have since come under the

---

[155] The request is a function of the agreement itself, not an additional element or a concession thereto (contra Betz, *Galatians*, p. 101; Dunn, *Galatians*, p. 113).

[156] See especially the Jewish data surveyed by E. Bammel, 'Πτωχός', pp. 894–9. In *Pss. Sol.* 5.2, 13 πτωχός is synonymous with εὐσεβής ('pious') which, together with its cognate εὐσέβεια ('piety') is thematic for 4 Maccabees and its characterization of the martyrs. Note also the context of conflict and persecution within which Paul uses the term at 2 Cor. 6.10 (cf. 8.9).

[157] The minority and majority positions represented by Bruce, *Galatians*, p. 126; and Betz, *Galatians*, pp. 102–3, respectively.

[158] This offers a better account of the aorist ἐσπούδασα than efforts to construe it as a pluperfect or as denoting a determination only fulfilled much later. Of course both the earlier famine relief and later Jerusalem collection may still be viewed as variant expressions of the same sentiment acted upon by Paul at the time of agreement.

influence of certain Agitators who are now pressing them to observe Torah and practise circumcision. In both broad outline and certain of its details, this contentious scenario represents a remarkable inversion of that which obtained during the archetypal Maccabean crisis: the people of God under threat are the largely Gentile Christians (rather than Torah-obedient Jews), and their antagonists are certain Jewish(-Christian) 'apostates' (rather than Gentile overseers and their Jewish sympathizers). Paul's response to the Galatian crisis is to indicate the enormity of what is at stake in this movement towards a Jewish way of life (a 'non-gospel') by reference to the conceptual framework governing his own gospel and mission. The gospel which he lives and proclaims is not 'of men' but 'of God in Jesus Christ'. That is, it is not bound up with the old age/sphere, but with the now revealed eschatological messianic redeemer who gave himself to deliver Jew and Gentile alike from that very condition. Thus Paul's mission is no longer to persuade/please men or God of that which is 'of men' (in this instance, matters Jewish), but to serve the selfless Messiah who did not please himself.

All this is explicated by means of an autobiography whose fundamental intent is to counter the negative impact of the Agitators and any aligned therewith – whether the Galatian believers or even someone such as the apostle Peter – by setting forth Paul's apostolic ministry as a paradigmatic example of one who has been faithful to Christ in the face of opposition. Indeed, it is Paul's dramatic encounter with, and subsequent conformity to, the martyred and now exalted Son of God which governs his recollections throughout. Paul thus emerges as one who stands in ironic relation to the tradition of the Maccabees: the former zealous Jew who now expends himself in the service of Christ and his people. This is evident at every stage of his account: in the fact that the persecutor has turned proclaimer; in his defence of God's truth now manifest in Christ versus the demands of the 'false brethren'; in his ready identification with the afflicted 'poor' in Jerusalem. Furthermore, it is this which also governs the entirety of his relationship with the Jerusalem apostles – not least with Peter, who, though he commendably endorsed Paul's Gentile mission, has apparently since caused concern that his conformity to Christ may not have been as exemplary as that of Paul himself.

The ensuing Antioch incident which climaxes Paul's autobiography offers itself as the most likely immediate cause of such concern and, as will be seen, it too may be viewed in terms of an ardent apostle Paul who stands to defend the truth of the gospel of Christ against compulsion towards Judaism. However, before we pursue Paul's own argument in this direction, it will prove worth while to consider first the available external evidence concerning the Jewish and Christian communities in Antioch.

4

JEWS AND CHRISTIANS IN ANTIOCH

Having established in chapters one and two Maccabean martyrdom as a frame of reference for the analysis of Galatians 1–2 as a whole, here I consider the available external evidence in providing a related but more Antioch-specific framework for the ensuing detailed discussion of the Antioch incident in Galatians 2.11–21. The primary aim is to indicate how there would have been much tension and conflict between the Jewish and Christian communities in Antioch, especially insofar as this involved competing claims as to what it meant to be the faithful people of God. Whereas the Jewish community could readily have invoked the Torah-obedient Maccabeans as their ideal in this respect, the Christians would have laid claim to the martyred and exalted Messiah Jesus as their exemplar.

In what follows I shall examine in turn two different but complementary sources and observe the portraits which emerge therefrom. First, I offer a reconstruction of the history and self-identity of the Antiochene Jewish community as (largely) suggested by Josephus. This will be followed by an outline of the emerging Antiochene Christian community according to the narrative in Acts, with particular reference to its leadership and common life. From this broad standpoint I shall then be in a position to undertake the final stage of this enterprise: a detailed consideration of Paul's account of the Antioch incident, with its radical reworking of Maccabean themes and issues in service of a thoroughly Messiah Jesus understanding of God and his people.

1. The history and self-identity of the Jewish community in Antioch

By the first century AD Antioch was the third most important city in the Roman Empire (*J.W.* 3.29) and a key commercial, administrative and political centre.¹ Amongst its diverse populace was a significant Jewish community.² Indeed, the Jews had been among the original settlers when the city was founded by Seleucus I Nicator (312–281/280 BC) (*Ant.* 12.119; *Ag. Ap.* 2.39). In the following brief account of this community two main features will be highlighted: first, that periodically throughout its history it came under attack in ways that would have evoked notable precedents, not least Antiochus IV Epiphanes' archetypal assault upon the Jewish way of life; second, certain (albeit limited) indicators of its Torah-based common life suggest that its most zealous members would have been determined to uphold the Maccabean ideal of an undivided commitment to Torah/Israel/God, not least in the face of the competing claims of the rival Christian community.

A historical overview

The little information available to us suggests that during the Hellenistic period Antiochene Jews conducted their own affairs relatively unhindered, with the notable exception of Antiochus IV Epiphanes' rule (175–163 BC). While Antiochus' persecutions were focused mainly upon Jerusalem, it is likely that the Jewish community in his capital city did not emerge unscathed. Their citizenship rights seem to have been curtailed (*J.W.* 7.44); it is intrinsically probable that at least some Jewish captives were brought to Antioch; and, as noted in the excursus in chapter two, there is the traditional (if late) association of the Maccabean martyrs with the city.

The situation is likely to have been similar during Roman rule. That is, as in other cities throughout the empire, the Jewish community would have been free to pursue its own common life, but this could and did come under threat during periods of instability. A

---

[1] The standard study of ancient Antioch is still that of Downey, *A History of Antioch in Syria*. Additional important studies are referenced in Hengel and Schwemer, *Paul Between Damascus and Antioch*, pp. 178ff. (see especially p. 183 n. 949); to these may be added Levinskaya, *The Book of Acts in Its Diaspora Setting*, pp. 127–35; Barclay, *Jews in the Mediterranean Diaspora*, pp. 242–5, 249–58; Kolb, 'Antiochia in der frühen Kaiserzeit'; and Bockmuehl, *Jewish Law in Gentile Churches*, pp. 49–83.

[2] The primary sources concerning this community are discussed in Downey, *A History of Antioch*, pp. 24–45. In addition to the pertinent sections of the sources cited in n. 1, notable secondary studies on the Antiochene Jewish community include Kraeling, 'The Jewish Community at Antioch'; Smallwood, *The Jews Under Roman Rule*, pp. 358–64; Hann, 'Judaism and Jewish Christianity in Antioch'; and Kasher, *The Jews in Hellenistic and Roman Egypt*, pp. 297–309.

notable case in point, already discussed in some detail in chapter two is the Caligula Temple edict (AD 39–40). First transmitted to the Syrian governor Petronius in Antioch, it would have increased tension between outraged local Jews and Gentile citizens anxious not to offend Rome. Some evidence in this direction is Malalas' report that in AD 40 Gentile mobs attacked the Antiochene Jews, killing many and burning their synagogues.[3] Indeed, the ensuing attempts by the Jews in Ptolemais and Tiberias to dissuade Petronius from carrying out Caligula's command – offering themselves up as martyrs towards this end – might be seen 'as the continuation of a protest begun in Antioch'.[4] As such, this event, with its evocations of the Maccabean crisis, would have been fresh in the memories of the Antiochene Jews during the period in which the early church began to emerge within their city.

Josephus also attests to two further disturbances affecting the Jews of Antioch at the time of the Jewish War.[5] Initially, the Jews in Antioch were spared much of the trauma experienced by Syrian Jews during the early stages of the War (*J.W.* 2.457–79).[6] However, with Vespasian's arrival in Antioch in AD 67, an apostate Jew aptly named Antiochus – a son of the ἄρχων of the local Jewish community – incited the populace with a story that Jews were intending to burn the city.[7] This precipitated a series of actions which included – as during the Maccabean crisis – 'compelling [ἀναγκάζω]' the Jews to transgress the sabbath and to offer pagan sacrifices on pain of

---

[3] Dindorf (ed.), *Ioannis Malalae Chronographia*, 244.15–245.1; E. Jeffreys, M. Jeffreys and R. Scott, *The Chronicle of John Malalas*, pp. 129ff. Various studies connect Malalas' report of these local disturbances with the general impact of Caligula's action; see Kraeling, 'The Jewish Community at Antioch', pp. 148–9; Downey, *A History of Antioch*, pp. 192–5; Hengel and Schwemer, *Paul Between Damascus and Antioch*, pp. 184ff. More broadly, see esp. N. H. Taylor's 'Caligula'.

[4] So Kraeling, 'The Jewish Community at Antioch', p. 149.

[5] Downey, *A History of Antioch*, pp. 586–7, effectively dismisses the argument of Kraeling, 'The Jewish Community at Antioch', pp. 150–2, that we are dealing with two accounts of the same event.

[6] This was probably due less to local sympathy towards those Jews not aligned with the insurrectionists (so Josephus), and more to the restraint imposed by the presence of the Roman legate Cestius Gallus and his army (so Smallwood, *The Jews Under Roman Rule*, p. 361).

[7] This accusation is reminiscent of Nero's charge against the Roman Christians three years earlier in AD 64 (Tacitus, *Ann.* 15.44). Following Kasher, *The Jews in Hellenistic and Roman Egypt*, p. 305, we may note that this Antiochus differentiated between Jews resident in Antioch – describing himself as 'one of their own number', even though he 'domineered [them] with severity' (cf. *J.W.* 7.47, 52) – and those 'foreign Jews' (*J.W.* 7.47) whom he accused of plotting to burn the city, viz., non-residents who (Kasher speculates) were Jewish 'Zealots' from Palestine.

death (*J.W.* 7.46–53). The fact that antagonism continued thereafter may be inferred from the Greek citizens' (unsuccessful) attempt to have the Roman legate Mucianus revoke the Jews' oil-tax rebate (*Ant.* 12.120).[8] A second trauma four years later, involving Antiochus' incrimination of his fellow Jews following an actual fire in the city, was only averted through the intervention of the deputy governor, Gnaeus Collega. That the Jews nonetheless remained under considerable threat is evident from the subsequent (albeit vain) attempt of some of the populace to persuade Titus to expel them – and, upon his refusal, to have their political rights revoked (*J.W.* 7.100–3, 108–11; *Ant.* 12.121–4). Malalas reports that Titus did however erect several figures seized from the ruined Jerusalem Temple in proximity to the Jewish quarter, this being a reminder of the ignominious outcome of the War.[9] In sum, incidents such as these indicate that, on occasion, the Antiochene Jewish community could and did come under considerable threat, and in a manner which would have reminded them of similar traumas in their past, not least the archetypal Maccabean crisis.

The common life of the Jewish community

Although the details are limited and in certain respects unclear, it is possible to accrue some sense of the constitution and common life of the Jewish community in Antioch.[10] Perhaps one of our most important indicators is that it possessed its own πολιτεία. Unfortunately, the origin and precise significance of this fact remains much disputed, and thus requires some attention.

Josephus reports that on founding the city Seleucus I Nicator granted the Jews their πολιτεία – thereby affording them equal rights with their non-Jewish counterparts – and that this privilege remained intact even in his own day, notwithstanding (as noted above) attempts to have it revoked (cf. *Ant.* 12.199; *Ag. Ap.* 2.29). Yet several scholars have doubted that this πολιτεία originated

---

[8] This concession provided them with monies with which to purchase their own (undefiled) oil.

[9] See further Downey, *A History of Antioch*, pp. 206–7.

[10] Although estimates vary considerably, Bockmuehl, *Jewish Law In Gentile Churches*, p. 54, suggests that in the first century the Jews may have accounted for as many as thirty to fifty thousand of a total city population of around three hundred thousand; similarly Hengel and Schwemer, *Paul Between Damascus and Antioch*, pp. 186, 196.

as early as Seleucus (312–281/280 BC). They variously argue that Josephus' claim to this effect is (i) feebly supported by weak evidence (*Ant.* 12.120), (ii) without independent corroboration, (iii) undermined by his own earlier testimony in *J.W.* 7.43–44,[11] and (iv) intrinsically unlikely given the very modest size of the original Jewish settlement.[12] However, such arguments are not simply summoned against a claim for the early *origin* of the πολιτεία, itself perhaps still defensible.[13] They are usually cited in simultaneously rejecting a particular view of its *significance*, namely, that it refers to the Jewish community being granted citizenship in the Greek πολίς of Antioch. Indeed, contrary to Josephus' testimony, it has been suggested that this πολιτεία may have simply denoted the right of individual Jews to obtain citizenship on demand.[14] Alternatively, many scholars now think it likely that the πολιτεία pertained to the Antiochene Jews' citizenship in their own πολίτευμα; that is, membership in the Jewish community constituted as a quasi-autonomous socio-political body within the city as a whole.[15] Yet the latter view may itself be suspect, presupposing a definition of πολίτευμα whose application to Jewish communities – in any locale, let alone in Antioch – has recently been challenged.[16] Perhaps, then, the precise significance of Josephus' use of πολιτεία in reference to the Antiochene Jews will have to remain an open question.

[11] Here, it is suggested, Josephus appears to be under the impression that rights were not granted the Jews until some one hundred and fifty years later under the successors of Antiochus IV Epiphanes.
[12] Cf. Tcherikover, *Hellenistic Civilization and the Jews*, pp. 328–9; Smallwood, *The Jews Under Roman Rule*, pp. 359–60; Trebilco, *Jewish Communities in Asia Minor*, p. 168; Barclay, *Jews in the Mediterranean Diaspora*, pp. 244–6.
[13] For example, Kasher, *The Jews in Hellenistic and Roman Egypt*, pp. 298–9, argues that *J.W.* 7.43–4 must be read within its wider literary context, which comprises a litany of the many threats to the Antiochene Jews during the Jewish War (this account patterning the ancient tragedy of Antiochus IV Epiphanes' persecutions). So viewed, the specific reference to their rights establishes not the point of inception, but the fact that since the time of Antiochus there had been no legal warrant for their abrogation. Thus Josephus' remarks concerning origin are consistent, and it may be allowed that the Antiochene Jewish community and its πολιτεία are indeed traceable to Seleucus I Nicator.
[14] So Smallwood, *The Jews Under Roman Rule*, p. 359.
[15] So, for example, Tcherikover, *Hellenistic Civilization and the Jews*, pp. 299–305; Smallwood, *The Jews Under Roman Rule*, pp. 225–6, 359–60; Kasher, *The Jews in Hellenistic and Roman Egypt*, pp. 305–9; Trebilco, *Jewish Communities in Asia Minor*, p. 171.
[16] See especially Lüderitz, 'What is the Politeuma?', whose detailed study concludes that the purported evidence for Jewish πολιτεύματα is much more circumstantial and uncertain than has normally been recognized.

Nonetheless, before leaving this matter, it is worth at least registering certain further considerations. It is widely acknowledged that the semantic range of πολιτεία extended well beyond 'citizenship' to embrace 'constitution', 'state' and 'way of life', with this usage quite prominent in Jewish authors such as Philo and Josephus.[17] Indeed, πολιτεία was one of the principal categories used by Hellenistic Judaism to convey something of the content of life 'in Judaism [ἐν τῷ 'Ιουδαϊσμῷ]'.[18] This is consonant with the use of the term in the LXX. Found only in the Maccabean literature, it usually refers to attempts to defend (even via martyrdom) or destroy that which is constitutive of the Jewish (v. the Greek) way of life.[19] Hence, it might still be suggested that Josephus' use of πολιτεία has in view the fact that the Antiochene Jews had been allowed – and, in his day, still retained – the privilege of operating as a community according to their own ancestral laws and customs, to live 'in Judaism'.

The correlation of certain disparate evidence might further point in this direction. (i) 4 Maccabees also alludes to the recognition of the Jewish πολιτεία by Seleucus I Nicator, the context indicating that this author employs the term to denote the Jewish way of life (4 Macc. 3.20).[20] (ii) According to Josephus, Strabo observed that the Alexandrian Jewish community had been allocated its own settlement under an ethnarch who governed 'just as if he were the head of a sovereign state [ὡς ἂν πολιτείας ἄρχων αὐτοτελοῦς]' (Ant. 14.117). (iii) Both Josephus and Libanius indicate that the Antiochene Jews also had their own ἄρχων;[21] and Chrysostom, who likewise knew of this post,[22] also employs the term πολιτεία in reference to the Jewish community.[23]

On analogy with other Diaspora communities, the Antiochene Jews' πολιτεία would probably have meant that they possessed the 'right to build synagogues, to maintain independent courts of

---

[17] See Kasher, *The Jews in Hellenistic and Roman Egypt*, pp. 358–64.

[18] See Amir, 'The Term *Ioudaismos*'. After surveying the limited written sources for 'Ιουδαϊσμός – 2 Macc. 2.21; 8.1; 14.38; 4 Macc. 4.26; Gal 1.13–14 – Amir also notes a third-century BC dedicatory inscription from a synagogue in Stobi (former Yugoslavia) in which its donor claims that 'in all his public life he acted according to Judaism [πολιτευσάμενος πᾶσαν πολιτείαν κατὰ τὸν 'Ιουδαϊσμόν]', p. 35.

[19] 2 Macc. 4.11; 6.23A; 8.17; 13.14; 4 Macc. 8.7; 17.9.

[20] Although it would appear that the author has confused Seleucus I Nicator with the later Seleucus IV Philopater (187–175 BC).

[21] *J.W.* 7.45; *Ep.* 1251 (ET in Meeks and Wilken, *Jews and Christians in Antioch*, p. 60).

[22] Cited together with that of the προστάτης (*Adversus Judaeos* 5.3).

[23] *Adversus Judaeos* 1.3.

justice, to educate the youth in the spirit of the Torah, to set up communal institutions and to elect officials, and the like'.[24] It may be that the aforementioned office of the ἄρχων was related to the γερουσίαρχος, head of the council of elders, an organization composed of representatives from the city's synagogues.[25] Certainly it is likely that by the mid first century there was more than one synagogue in Antioch and its environs. Kraeling argues for at least three sites of concentrated Jewish settlement in the immediate area, with synagogues in the southern Jewish quarter (the Kerateion),[26] the suburb of Daphne, and perhaps also just north of the city on the plain of Antioch.[27] The intrinsic probability that they had regular contact with Jerusalem might find support in a possible reference by Josephus to the dispatch of votive offerings to the Temple (*J.W.* 7.45),[28] and in rabbinic sources recording the story of a regular visit of rabbis to collect money for Eretz Israel.[29] Indeed, for these and other reasons, Antioch 'was of very considerable socio-economic importance for Jews in the Land of Israel'.[30] Moreover, Gentiles were drawn to various aspects of the Antiochene Jewish community's common life, a fact that is attested by 'multitudes of Greeks' – men who became God-fearers or proselytes – being attracted to the synagogue (*J.W.* 7.45); one of these Greeks may well have been Nicolaus who subsequently joined the Christian movement (Acts 6.5).[31]

Throughout their long history the Jews of Antioch endeavoured

[24] Tcherikover, *Hellenistic Civilization and the Jews*, pp. 301–2. Of course, this does not preclude the likelihood that members of the Jewish community were variously involved in the wider aspects of civic life, though nonetheless *as Jews* (see Trebilco, *Jewish Communities in Asia Minor*, pp. 186ff.).

[25] So Meeks and Wilken, *Jews and Christians in Antioch*, p. 7. Kasher, *The Jews in Hellenistic and Roman Egypt*, pp. 306–7, notes the term in arguing that the community had its own magistrature; he cites Talmudic references to 'courts in Syria' and to 'two people who had a trial in Antioch'.

[26] The synagogue which some surmise held the relics of the Maccabean martyrs; see the excursus in chapter two.

[27] Kraeling, 'The Jewish Community at Antioch', pp. 140–3; cf. Meeks and Wilken, *Jews and Christians in Antioch*, pp. 8–9, who query the third location.

[28] Although ἱερόν could be a designation for their own synagogue (this nonetheless presupposing reverence for the Jerusalem Temple, the local site of worship functioning in lieu thereof).

[29] *Deut. Rab.* 4.8; *Lev. Rab.* 4.3.

[30] So Bockmuehl, *Jewish Law in Gentile Churches*, p. 56; see also pp. 61–70, concerning the idea of Antioch as part of the Holy Land.

[31] The Jewish way of life would continue to prove attractive even to Antiochene Christian converts, if the evidence of Ignatius and (in the fourth century AD) Chrysostom is any indication.

to maintain their distinctive way of life. Even in times of crisis – whether under Antiochus IV Epiphanes, Caligula or Titus – they strove to emulate the faithfulness of their ancestors by remaining the Torah-obedient Israel of God in Antioch. However, at some point within the fourth decade of the first century they (like their Maccabean forebears) found themselves under threat from both without and within. In an unprecedented and highly complex scenario, their very history and identity were now being radically reconfigured by a particularly potent force: the Jews and Gentiles who together claimed to comprise the Israel of God now conformed to the martyred and exalted Messiah Jesus.

2. The messianic community in Antioch

Any evaluation of the Antiochene Christian community is almost wholly dependent upon Acts.[32] While many details are disputed, at least three observations are now generally allowed: Antioch was the starting point for a self-conscious mission to the Gentiles; the disciples there were called 'Christians'; and amongst their number were prophets and teachers.[33] The following analysis of Luke's portrayal of the church in Antioch will pursue these and related considerations, doing so in two stages. First, some consideration is given to certain key narratives concerning three protagonists – Stephen, Paul and Peter – each of whom, to varying degrees, functions as a prophet-martyr figure, and subsequently proves to be influential in the emergence and development of the Antioch church. Second, there follows an examination of the main features of Luke's

---

[32] With respect to the vexed question of Acts' historical reliability, the position adopted here is that Acts is at least as viable an external source as Josephus, and that its portrait of the Antiochene church may be taken as generally complementing the brief glimpse given in Paul's remarks at Galatians 2.11–21. (Recent broadly based support for the general reliability of Acts is offered in the multi-volume series edited by Winter, *The Book of Acts in its First Century Setting*; see also Breytenbach, *Paulus und Barnabas*.) Here 'Luke' designates the author of Acts, whether or not he is to be identified with the Luke known to Paul (cf. Col. 4.14; Phlm. 24). The use of Matthew as a possible window upon the Antiochene church c. AD 70–100 (so Zumstein, 'Antioche sur l'Oronte', pp. 131–8; Brown and Maier, *Antioch and Rome*, pp. 15–27, 45–72, and others) is too conjectural to be employed with any confidence.

[33] Meeks and Wilken, *Jews and Christians in Antioch*, p. 15. In addition to the relevant sections of the many commentaries on Acts and Galatians, other notable recent reconstructions of the church in Antioch include Brown and Maier, *Antioch and Rome*, pp. 11–86; N. H. Taylor, *Paul, Antioch and Jerusalem*; and Hengel and Schwemer, *Paul Between Damascus and Antioch*, pp. 178–310.

Antioch-related narratives: for example, the community's inception and the designation of its members as 'Christians'; its common life and leadership; and the important role of the Jerusalem conference and decree. Throughout I shall be alert to the manner in which various themes and issues so prominent during the Maccabean period – and, as has been noted, of ongoing concern to Jews in Antioch (and elsewhere) – are clearly and contentiously addressed from the radical new standpoint of Messiah Jesus.

From Jerusalem to Antioch: Stephen, Paul and Peter as prophet-martyr figures

According to Luke, 'those who were scattered because of the persecution that arose over Stephen travelled as far as ... Antioch' (Acts 11.19a). With this comment the reader is immediately alerted to the fact that Luke's intermittent account of the origins and development of the church in Antioch is firmly plotted along the trajectory of his overall narrative concerning the remarkable expansion of the early church from Jerusalem to Rome and beyond. As such, the significance of the earlier Jerusalem-focused narrative carries forward and bears upon any estimation of the emerging situation in Antioch. In what follows our particular interest is in three narratives concerning Stephen's martyrdom, Paul's conversion and Peter's encounter with Cornelius. Each account focuses upon a protagonist who (albeit in different ways) emerges as a prophet-martyr figure, and who will later prove to be of influence in the formation of the Antiochene Christian community.[34]

Stephen: the vindicated prophet-martyr

Stephen's prophetic witness plays a pivotal role in Luke's narrative (Acts 6.8–8.1a), the long shadow of his martyrdom stretching to Antioch and beyond.[35] He is characterized from the outset as a man

---

[34] On the wider matter of the Jewish prophet-martyr model, see especially Fischel, 'Martyr and Prophet'; Pobee, *Persecution and Martyrdom*, pp. 27–9.

[35] Craig C. Hill, *Hellenists and Hebrews*, pp. 41–101, thoroughly addresses the various critical issues at hand. While sceptical as to what can be known about Stephen, Hill does accept that he suffered a martyr's death. On the martyr motif in this account, see Mundle, 'Die Stephanusrede Apg. 7'; Boismard, 'Le martyre d'Etienne'; and Moessner, 'The Christ Must Suffer'.

of faith and grace contesting for his convictions (Acts 6.8).[36] Thus he incurs the antagonism of certain Diaspora Jews who – despite the fact that they are unable '[to] withstand [ἀντιστῆναι] the wisdom and Spirit with which he spoke' (Acts 6.10) – nonetheless manage to orchestrate his appearance before the Sanhedrin. There, like Jesus before him and Paul soon thereafter,[37] he is charged by false witnesses in connection with 'speaking words' against the Temple and the customs of Moses (Acts 6.11–14), phraseology which suggests that censorious analogies are being drawn between Antiochus IV Epiphanes, Jesus and Stephen.[38] However, Luke's depiction of Stephen's face as like that of an angel readily indicates that he is not only innocent of the charges but, like the afflicted saints of Israel, will be vindicated even if only in and through a martyr's death (Acts 6.15).[39]

His ensuing lengthy discourse retells Israel's story, and is clearly designed to demonstrate how this bears witness to and is fulfilled in Jesus and the apostles.[40] It concludes with Stephen turning the tables on his accusers: the Sanhedrin (not he) is aligned with those who persecuted and killed God's faithful prophets, in virtue of their betrayal and murder of the Righteous One, Jesus.[41] The climactic final scene is variously evocative of Daniel 7. The soon-to-be-martyred Stephen gazes into heaven (cf. 4 Macc. 6.6, 26) and sees a vision of the divine glory and the exalted Son of Man, thereby again attesting to his own forthcoming vindication/exaltation (Acts 7.54–6). In essence, Stephen stands in ironic relation to the tradition of the Maccabean martyrs: in virtue of his revelation of and conformity to the crucified and now exalted Righteous One/Son of Man, it is he (not his Jewish detractors) who stands as the faithful saint who will live with God. As we shall see, some of Stephen's persecuted associates will find their way to Antioch and continue his faithful witness in that city.

---

[36] Similarly it is said of the martyr Polycarp, that 'his face was full of grace' (*Mart. Pol.* 12.1).

[37] Cf. Mark 14.57ff. and Acts 21.28; 28.17.

[38] Rightly Craig C. Hill, *Hellenists and Hebrews*, p. 64 (following Räisänen, *Torah and Christ*, p. 264), citing Dan. 7.25 and 1 Macc. 1.49.

[39] Cf. Dan.LXX/Th. 3.92; *1 Enoch* 46.1; Gal. 4.14; *Mart. Pol.* 2.3, and further observations in Goddard and Cummins, 'Ill or Ill-treated?', pp. 107–10.

[40] Such recitals may have been used in exhortatory preaching (παράκλησις) both within the Jewish synagogue and the early Christian communities; see the discussion below.

[41] Acts 7.51–3; cf. Matt. 23.29–37; Luke 11.47–51; 13.33–5; 1 Thess. 2.15–16.

Paul: the transformed prophet-martyr

Amongst those 'approving' Stephen's execution is Paul (Acts 8.1a).[42] Indeed, consonant with the earlier analysis of Paul's own testimony in Galatians 1.13–14, Luke's depiction of his role in the persecutions which ensued on Stephen's martyrdom (Acts 8.1b,c) is reminiscent of Antiochus IV Epiphanes' oppressive actions.[43] That is, from Luke's Christian perspective, the zealous Jew is now cast as the tormentor, and the supposedly apostate Jewish Christians are in fact the afflicted faithful. However, Paul the Jewish zealot is himself about to be transformed into Paul the Jewish Christian prophet-martyr. Furthermore, as we shall see, Luke's portrayal of this transformation is itself a radical reworking of a Maccabean literary motif.

Here we are not so much concerned with any discrepancies in the details of Luke's three lengthy accounts of Paul's conversion,[44] nor to approach the event from a rigorously historiographical or even psychological standpoint. Rather our primary interest is to observe the significance of the fact that these narratives, taken together, have their nearest literary analogue in the account of Apollonius' ill-fated attempt to plunder the Jerusalem Temple (4 Macc. 4.1–14), itself a development of the earlier account of Heliodorus' Temple assault (2 Macc. 3.7–40), and thus attesting to a living tradition which would have been available as a basis of comparison to Luke.[45] The various correspondences (and divergences) may be itemized as follows:

(1a) The Gentile Apollonius, 'uttering threats [ἀπειλῶν]' (4 Macc. 4.8), is dispatched by King Seleucus IV to Jerusalem with orders to return the contents of the Temple treasury to Syria.

(1b) Paul, 'breathing threats [ἐμπνέων ἀπειλῆς]' (Acts 9.1), is

---

[42] The verb 'approve, consent [συνευδοκέω]' occurs in the LXX only in reference to those martyred Jews who 'adhere' to Torah (1 Macc. 1.57) and thus refuse to 'consent' to Antiochus IV Epiphanes' introduction of Greek customs (2 Macc. 11.24).

[43] On 'dragged out [σύρω]', see 4 Macc. 6.1 (also Acts 17.6); on 'devastate, ruin [λυμαίνομαι]', see 4 Macc. 18.8.

[44] Johnson, *The Acts of the Apostles*, p. 166, rightly notes that any such discrepancies are much less consequential than the common underlying significance which is clearly attached to this dramatic event.

[45] Johnson, ibid., pp. 167–8, argues that *Joseph and Aseneth* also offers an impressive set of parallels. Also of significance is the Old Testament theophanic tradition; see Windisch, 'Die Christusepiphanie vor Damaskus'.

commissioned by the High Priest to go to Damascus with authority to return the followers of the Way to Jerusalem for punishment (Acts 9.2; 22.5; 26.9–12).

(2a) As Apollonius approaches Jerusalem he is challenged by a heavenly host of 'angels on horseback with lightning flashing [περιαστράπτοντες] from their weapons', and falls down half dead in the Temple precincts (4 Macc. 4.10–11).

(2b) En route to Damascus Paul encounters the risen Christ manifest in the midst of 'a light from heaven [which] flashed about [περιήστραψεν] him', and falls to the ground (Acts 9.3–4; 22.6–7; 26.13–14).[46]

(3a) The repentant Apollonius acknowledges Israel's God, receives atonement and deliverance from divine judgement, and returns to Antioch to report to the King all that had transpired (4 Macc. 4.11–14).

(3b) Paul is transformed by the one he had formerly persecuted (Acts 9.4–6; 22.7–10; 26.14–15), is baptized and 'immediately [εὐθέως]' proclaims in the synagogues and to the disciples in Damascus that Jesus is the Messiah, the Son of God (Acts 9.15, 18–22; 22.15; 26.16–18; cf. Gal 1.16).[47]

Thus, rather than the Gentile embracing the Maccabees' God, here we have the zealous Jew transformed by God in virtue of his encounter with one whom he now recognizes as the representative and redeemer of those he had being persecuting: the martyred but now exalted Messiah/Son of God. No longer a Maccabean-inspired servant of Judaism, Paul now embarks upon a prophetic ministry to Jew and Gentile alike, ready to suffer and die for Messiah Jesus and his people. Immediate confirmation of his transformation and its effect is provided by the plots[48] against him by antagonistic Jews both in Damascus and then Jerusalem (Acts 9.23–30).[49] Such opposition will continue throughout his ministry, not least in Antioch.

---

[46] These are the only biblical occurrences of the verb περιαστράπτω. Cf. also Daniel's alarmed response to his visions (e.g., Dan. 8.17).

[47] Further correspondences with the earlier account of Heliodorus in 2 Macc. 3.7–40 include (4) both protagonists being overcome by darkness/blindness and rendered speechless (2 Macc. 3.27–9; Acts 9.7–8 et par.); and (5) the whole event as constituting the divine scourging/disciplining of one who opposed God and persecuted his people (2 Macc. 3.12, 24–30, 34; Acts 9.4–5, 13–16; cf. Gal. 1.13–14, 23). Note also the scourging of Antiochus IV Epiphanes (2 Macc. 9.5–12).

[48] On ἐπιβουλή, see especially 2 Macc. 5.7; 8.7; 4 Macc. 4.13.

[49] Cf. 2 Cor. 11.32–3 (and Dan. 11.33–5).

Peter: the enlightened prophet figure

A third narrative in which the prophet-martyr motif is more latent but still discernible, and which focuses on a matter fundamentally constitutive of both the Maccabean crisis and the Antioch incident, is Peter's encounter with Cornelius.[50] A divine disclosure so convinces an initially reticent Peter that Jews and Gentiles in Christ are to share in table-fellowship together, that he then prophetically proclaims his new-found conviction in the face of those who think otherwise.

The contrast between the narrative's two protagonists is apparent from the outset: while the pious and God-fearing Gentile Cornelius is unequivocal in his obedience to the directive received in his vision (Acts 10.1–8), Peter remains perplexed and at odds with the implications of the *three* visions he has seen (Acts 10.9–17a). However, initial protest gives way to enlightenment, his dramatic shift in perspective well demonstrated in his remark to Cornelius: 'You understand how it is unlawful [ἀθέμιτόν] for a Jew to associate with or to visit someone of another race [ἀλλοφύλῳ]; but God has shown me not to call any person common [κοινόν] or unclean.'[51] Peter now understands that *God* has determined that neither food nor people are to be categorized as unclean.

In a speech often taken as an example of the apostolic kerygma in brief (Acts 10.34–43), Peter gives full prophetic voice to the outworking of God's covenant purposes through Jesus, who was first sent to the sons of Israel and yet is Lord of all, Jew and Gentile alike (Acts 10.36). Indeed, in their testimony to Jesus' life, death and resurrection, the apostles proclaim that to which the prophets themselves bore witness concerning Jesus, namely, that 'every one who believes in him [πάντα τὸν πιστεύοντα εἰς αὐτόν] receives forgiveness of sins through his name' (Acts 10.43; cf. Gal 2.16).

Yet Peter's mixed table-fellowship attracts opposition from 'those believers from the circumcision [οἱ ἐκ περιτομῆς πιστοί]' (Acts 10.45–7) and occasions a 'trial scene' in which he must give further account of his momentous experience to the Jerusalem Christian community

---

[50] It comprises an initial telling, a retelling and a final recapitulation (cf. Acts 10.1–48; 11.1–48; 15.6–11).

[51] Acts 10.28. On the terminology: ἀθέμιτος ('unlawful'), cf. especially 2 Macc. 6.5 and 7.1; while ἀλλόφυλος in the LXX normally renders the Hebrew פלשת ('Philistine'), this is extended to denote 'foreigners' in general (1 Macc. 4.12, 26; 5.15; 11.68, 74; 2 Macc. 10.2, 5).

(Acts 11.1–18). Though the issue for Peter is unambiguous – who is he 'to hinder God'? – not even his exhortations suffice to forestall further contention (see Acts 15.6–11). Indeed, that not even he himself is immune to pressure on this most fundamental of issues will become all too apparent from the incident in Antioch.[52]

The Acts narratives concerning Stephen, Paul and Peter suggest that these important Jewish-Christian leaders played an exemplary role within the early (and oft-afflicted) church as prophet-martyr figures. This was a source of inspiration to their fellow believers, but a cause of consternation to certain Jewish(-Christian) detractors. In part, this was due to the fact that the Jewish (not least Maccabean) conception of the prophet-martyr as one ready to suffer and die for Judaism had now been radically reconfigured in the form of one willing to be crucified with the martyred but now exalted Jesus. Given the influence of these (and other) Christian prophet-martyrs upon the emergence and development of the church in Antioch, together with our earlier estimation of the history and identity of the Jewish community there, it was inevitable that there would (as we shall see) be Jewish–Christian conflict over competing claims as to what it meant to be the faithful people of God.

The common life of the Antiochene Christian community

This section focuses upon three key stages in Luke's Antioch-related narratives. First, by reference to the inception of the Christian mission in the city, and to the designation of the community as Χριστιανοί, we shall observe how the emerging Christian community would have inevitably given rise to conflict with its Jewish counterpart. Then, in endeavouring to bring the nature of such conflict into sharper focus, it will be noted how two particular features of the church's common life – its prophet-martyr leadership and mode of instruction – would have represented a provocative reworking of elements of significance in the Maccabean period. Finally, consideration is given to Jewish Christian opposition to the Gentile mission, and to its resolution in the Jerusalem conference and decree. Again the nature and significance of both is highlighted by reference to certain important Maccabean issues and themes.

---

[52] Of course, it is because Peter's conduct in Antioch, according to Gal. 2.11ff., represents such a departure from his portrayal here in Acts that many commentators find the Acts account historically implausible.

The Antioch mission and the messianic community

It is historically probable that some of the Hellenistic Jewish Christians who were dispersed during the persecutions associated with Stephen's martyrdom found their way to Antioch, an important city with a significant Jewish community.[53] That their proclamation of the gospel was initially directed at the Jews is also entirely plausible, inasmuch as fellow Jews would have been a natural point of departure for their missionary activity (Acts 11.19b). Among them were Cyprian and Cyrenian Jewish Christians, the latter perhaps including some of those converted to the gospel by witnessing the 'mighty deeds of God' at Pentecost and/or Stephen's martyrdom (cf. Acts 2.10–12; 6.9).[54] It is they who also preached the gospel to 'the Greeks'.[55] Indeed, if the later reference to Lucius of Cyrene is any indication (Acts 13.1), some of them assumed a leading role within the prophetic and teaching ministry of the church. That all this represented the outworking of God's grace was readily confirmed by Barnabas.[56] Cast in the same prophet-martyr mould as Stephen (cf. Acts 6.3, 9; 11.24a), Barnabas encouraged the community to remain steadfast, an action which implies that there was always a temptation to act otherwise. In fact, given what we know of the Antiochene Jewish community, a Jewish Christian mission to both Jews and Gentiles, led by prophet-martyr figures such as Barnabas and (later) Paul, must have led to a considerable degree of tension and conflict.

That this was the case may be inferred from Luke's remark that 'in Antioch the disciples were for the first time called Christians [χρηματίσαι τε πρώτως ἐν Ἀντιοχείᾳ τοὺς μαθητὰς Χριστιανούς]' (Acts 11.26c). With respect to the term Χριστιανοί, the suffix -ιανοι, derived from the Latin -iani, renders it likely that it was ascribed to the Christians by the Roman authorities. Indeed, if references to the

---

[53] This is not obviated by the obvious *narrative* linkage between Acts 11.19a and 8.1–3.

[54] Recall the impact of τὸ μεγαλεῖον τοῦ θεοῦ upon Heliodorus (2 Macc. 3.34); God's 'mighty power' is deployed to convict and even condemn those who oppress his faithful people (2 Macc. 7.17).

[55] Commentators generally agree that the context – the juxtaposition with 'Ἰουδαῖοι (Acts 11.19) and the increasingly Gentile-mission-orientated narrative – favours Ἕλληνας over Ἑλληνιστάς (at Acts 11.20b). So, for example, Haenchen, *The Acts of the Apostles*, p. 365 n. 5.

[56] Acts 11.23; cf. 15.11; 20.24, 32. That Barnabas was dispatched by the Jerusalem church attests to the close communication between the Antiochene and Jerusalem believers.

'Chrestiani' (Χρηστιανοί) and 'Christus' (Χρηστός) in Tacitus and Suetonius are any indication,[57] the ascription may well have come about in the context of conflict involving Jews, Christians and their Gentile neighbours, and may reflect the Romans' perception of the Christians as a distinct, political entity allied under the name of the leader whom they followed.

Further weight and precision has recently been given such an interpretation by Justin Taylor who argues that the Roman designation Χριστιανοί (or *Christiani*), and the title Χριστός it presupposed, had its ultimate origin in the messianic preaching among the Antiochene Jews (Acts 11.19b). Such activity would have engendered conflict which the Romans interpreted politically as involving the seditious activity of the followers of Christus (Paul's οἱ τοῦ Χριστοῦ, Gal. 5.24).[58] Indeed, Taylor argues that a probable immediate context for such a conflict was the Jewish–Gentile disorder in AD 39–40 as recorded by Malalas, which was itself to be located against the wider backdrop of the Jewish–Gentile tensions associated with the Alexandrian pogrom in AD 38 and Caligula's Temple edict in 39–40.[59] With this context in view, Taylor stresses that the conflict aroused by the proclamation of the Messiah consisted of a 'nationalistic and revolutionary commotion' amongst restive Jews, and *not* a 'violent disagreement' between advocates and opponents of Jesus' messiahship.[60]

We may readily concur with Taylor that messianic preaching, especially within the context of Caligula-directed Jewish nationalist fervour (with its Maccabean overtones), could well have engendered conflict between Christians and Jews which then gave rise to the Romans' politically construed designation Χριστιανοί. However, the inextricable interrelationship between the religious and political within Judaism, and the critique of Judaism necessarily implicit in

---

[57] Tacitus, *Ann.* 15.44; Suetonius, *Claud.* 25.4. Reference to Chrestus/Χρηστός in lieu of Χριστός is not without parallel in Christian documents; see G. H. R. Horsley (ed.), *New Documents*, p. 102 (1977), p. 98 (1978).

[58] Justin Taylor, 'Why Were the Disciples First Called "Christians" at Antioch? (Acts 11,26)'; see especially Bickerman(n), 'The Name of Christians', who, though also pressing the fundamentally messianic aspect of the term, argues that it was a *self-*designation of the Christians (see Taylor, pp. 81–3).

[59] See Hengel and Schwemer, *Paul Between Damascus and Antioch*, pp. 225–30, who suggest that the name '*could* be the consequence of contacts between the new sect and the civic authorities, who in the tense situation of 39–41 also handed on their information to the Roman provincial administration', p. 229.

[60] Justin Taylor, 'Why Were the Disciples First Called "Christians" at Antioch? (Acts 11,26)', pp. 86–91.

the early Christians' proclamation of a crucified Messiah Jesus, suggests (contra Taylor) that there was indeed a highly contentious religio-political conflict between the advocates and opponents of Jesus' messiahship.[61] Three specific observations may be offered in support of this. (i) There may be a close logical connection between Luke's reference to the teaching of Barnabas and Paul – which no doubt centred upon Jesus as Messiah and Lord – and his immediately ensuing remark about the designation Χριστιανοί (Acts 11.26b,c; note the connective τε, 'and so'). (ii) Certainly a similar correlation between teaching/preaching Christ and willingness to be named after the one to whom one's life is conformed, seems to be in view in the Lukan Paul's use of the term Χριστιανός at Acts 26.28. There the apostle's account of his own transformation and subsequent proclamation that 'the Messiah must suffer ... [and] rise from the dead' (Acts 26.23), is such that even the Jewish King Herod Agrippa II is almost persuaded to become a Χριστιανός.[62] (iii) That such persuasion was still a (contentious) task pursued in Antioch some three or four generations later might be inferred from the concern of its bishop, Ignatius, that his faithfulness (πιστός) even to the point of martyrdom should demonstrate him to be not only named 'a Christian [Χριστιανός]' but also 'found [εὑρίσκω] to be one' (Ign., *Rom.* 3.2).[63] In essence, though perhaps coined by the Roman authorities, the designation Χριστιανός would have been understood by the Antiochene Jews and Christians alike as a term demarcating those who – not least in the midst of conflict and suffering – together conformed their lives to the crucified and risen Jesus, their Messiah and Lord. As such they rivalled the Jewish community as claimants to being the messianic people of God.

The Antiochene believers also understood that fellowship in Christ's sufferings entailed solidarity with his afflicted people, as is immediately illustrated in Acts by their decision to send Barnabas and Paul with material relief for their famine-struck brethren in Judaea (Acts 11.27–30). At this point there is an interlude in the

---

[61] The evidence of Acts as a whole suggests as much, not least the Christian call for Jews to conform their lives to a Messiah in whose death they were implicated: cf. Acts 2.36; 3.18, 20; 4.10, 26 (Ps. 2.2); 5.42; 10.36; 17.3; 18.5; 20.21; 24.24.

[62] This reading follows the rendering of Acts 26.28 by Johnson, *The Acts of the Apostles*, p. 431: 'You are persuading [πείθεις] me to play the Christian a little.' Note the virtually normative correlation between sharing in the suffering of the Messiah and being reviled 'as a Christian [Χριστιανός]' at 1 Pet. 4.12–16.

[63] Cf. Ign., *Eph.* 11.2; *Pol.* 7.1; the term also occurs at *Did.* 12.4.

Antioch-focused story-line as Luke shifts the scene to Jerusalem, providing an account of the persecutions of Herod Agrippa I (Acts 12.1–23) which exhibits three notable features. First, James the son of Zebedee becomes Luke's second recorded martyr (cf. Mark 10.35–45).[64] Second, inasmuch as James' execution 'pleased the Jews', Agrippa then arrested and imprisoned Peter, who only escapes a similar fate because he (like Daniel and the Three) is miraculously rescued by an angel of God.[65] Third, less fortunate is the oppressor Agrippa whose delusions of divine grandeur and the manner of his ignominious death are both reminiscent of the demise of Antiochus IV Epiphanes.[66] No doubt we are to assume that Barnabas and Paul – presumably witnesses to such events – returned to Antioch and reported what Luke's summary remarks underscore: God is with his faithful people and their mission will bear fruit even in adversity (Acts 12.24–5).

The common life of the messianic community: their prophet-martyr leadership and messianic 'word of exhortation'

Luke goes on to offer a glimpse of the church in Antioch as it commissions and later celebrates the mission of Barnabas and Paul to Asia Minor (Acts 13.1–3; 14.26–8). By correlating some of the details given here with information supplied elsewhere, two pertinent observations concerning the church's common life may be ventured.

First, its leadership included those whose role(s) could be viewed in ironic relation to that of the Jewish prophet-martyr. This may be suggested by the following collocation of (admittedly) disparate traditions, some of which we have already had cause to note.

(i) Stephen was a prophet-martyr whose exemplary witness was influential within the nascent church (Acts 6.8–8.1).

(ii) Some associated with Stephen later arrived in Antioch, and these may have included Lucius of Cyrene (cf. Acts 11.19–20; 13.1).

(iii) Lucius is numbered together with Barnabas, Paul and others

---

[64] See Cullmann, 'Courants multiples'.
[65] Acts 12.6–11; cf. Dan. 3.28; 6.23[22]; also Tob. 5.4–16. Note the exclamation of the servant girl Rhoda, 'It is his angel' (Acts 12.15), with which compare the discussion concerning the possible martyr associations of the term ἄγγελος at Gal. 4.14 in Goddard and Cummins, 'Ill or Ill-treated?', pp. 107–10.
[66] Acts 12.20–4; cf. 2 Macc. 9.5ff.; also Jdt. 16.17; *Ant.* 17.168–70 and *J.W.* 1.656 (concerning the death of Herod the Great).

as prophets and teachers within the Antiochene church (Acts 13.1). And, as has been noted, Paul and Barnabas are characterized by Luke in a manner which places them within the prophet-martyr tradition.

(iv) Judas and Silas, 'leading men [ἄνδρες ἡγουμένοι]' within the Jerusalem church, are chosen to bear its decree to the Antioch church. Also being prophets, they remain to exhort/ encourage the Antiochene believers (Acts 15.22, 30–3).

(v) It is likely that the deceased 'leaders [ἡγουμένοι]' of the community to whom Hebrews is addressed were martyred for their faith.[67]

(vi) The broadly descriptive term ἡγουμένοι, is used typically throughout the LXX in reference to political and military leaders, notably Judas and Jonathan Maccabeus who battle on Israel's behalf (1 Macc. 9.30; 2 Macc. 14.16; *Ant.* 13.198–9).

(vii) In his account of the Last Supper Luke uses the term 'the leader [ὁ ἡγουμένος]' interchangeably with the self-sacrificial designation 'one who serves [ὁ διακονῶν]' (Luke 22.26).[68]

(viii) Such, as we shall later see, is Paul's role in Antioch as he conforms himself to Christ who is disparaged as a 'servant [διάκονος] of sin' but is (he argues) the servant of divine reconciliation (Gal. 2.17).

Such traditions corroborate our earlier estimation of Stephen, Paul and Peter, as prophet-martyrs, but also now locate this motif in direct relation to the church in Antioch. Various Christian leaders in Antioch – charged with instructing and exhorting the community to faithfulness even in the midst of affliction – stood firmly (but ironically) within the Jewish tradition of the prophet-martyr. That is, rather than being the servants of a Maccabean-like zeal for Judaism, they were servants of the crucified and risen Christ.

Second, this estimation of both the leadership and the community as a whole may be developed by considering the church's teaching. Here, one may reasonably assume that the prophets and teachers in

---

[67] Heb. 13.7, 17, 24 (cf. 1 Thess. 5.12–13 and 2 Macc. 11.27). See Lane, *Hebrews*, p. liv, who offers a viable reconstruction of the circumstances surrounding these martyrdoms.

[68] The implication is that the exemplary follower of Jesus will emulate his servanthood even at the cost of affliction (cf. Luke 22.28ff., with particular reference to Peter).

Antioch would have retained and transmitted oral traditions concerning Jesus' ministry and teaching. Such teaching would have been vital to its identity and growth. However, given our interests, particularly significant (though often less noticed) is the crucial role of 'the word of exhortation [ὁ λόγος παρακλήσεως]': apparently a scripture-based homily delivered in both synagogues and the early Christian communities, including those addressed by Paul (Acts 13.15ff.).[69]

The precise development of this form of address is uncertain.[70] However, a notable precedent is Judas Maccabeus rallying his men for battle by encouraging them from the law and the prophets 'with fine words of exhortation' (2 Macc. 15.9–11).[71] Judas' appeal invokes former occasions when God acted redemptively on behalf of his people. This is also a prominent feature of Paul's λόγος παρακλήσεως at Acts 13.15ff., though now in making the claim that the Jesus rejected by Israel is in fact its Messiah/Saviour and God's Son (Acts 13.23, 33).[72] That Paul and the other Christian prophets and teachers in Antioch would have reworked the Jewish λόγος παρακλήσεως in such a fashion contributes further to our understanding of their role and mission, the emerging self-identity of the messianic community, and the fraught nature of their relationship with the Antiochene Jews.

Jewish–Christian conflict in Antioch and the Jerusalem conference and decree

Finally, the complex and fluid nature of the emerging Antioch church is such that (like the Maccabees) they find themselves under attack both from without and within. Certain Jewish(-Christian) individuals, governed by a Jewish conception of the people of God,

---

[69] Cf. also Rom. 12.7–8 where the gifts of teaching and exhortation are set in close proximity. Note also the prominence of παράκλησις in Paul's letters: it is that which renders the community faithful in affliction (1 Thess. 3.2; cf. 2.3) so that they may receive God's full and final vindication (1 Thess. 2.18–19; 3.11–13). It also functions reciprocally and even vicariously as believers assist one another by participating together in the sufferings of Christ (2 Cor. 1.3–12); indeed, its ultimate basis is in the paradigmatic example of Christ himself (Phil. 2.1ff.).

[70] See the discussions in McDonald, *Kerygma and Didache*; Wills, 'The Form of the Sermon'; and C. C. Black II, 'The Rhetorical Form'.

[71] This and 1 Macc. 10.24 are the only instances of λόγος παρακλήσεως in the LXX.

[72] Similarly Stephen's speech at Acts 7.2–53; cf. 1 Macc. 2.49–64; and Heb. 11.4–40. (Hebrews as a whole is termed a λόγος παρακλήσεως, Heb. 13.22).

seek to impose their way of life upon both Jewish and Gentile Christian converts. As will be noted, such conduct could be construed as a replication of the Seleucids' imposition of Hellenism upon their Jewish forebears. So crucial is this matter that it must be addressed by the Jerusalem apostles, and in a way that both recognizes the sacrifices and sensitivities of the Jewish people, while nonetheless also encouraging Christians to remain faithful to God in Messiah Jesus even in the face of affliction.

The inclusive (Jew + Gentile) composition and mission of the Antiochene church incurred the opposition of 'certain men' from Judaea who insisted that Gentiles not circumcised in keeping with the customs of Moses could not be saved (Acts 15.1).[73] Such people would appear to be in close alignment with 'those of the circumcision' who had objected to Peter's fellowship with Cornelius. The resultant discord forced adjournment of the debate to Jerusalem, where it is exacerbated by similar claims for circumcision and Torah-observance pressed by some believing Pharisees (Acts 15.5).

While Luke does not disguise the fact that there was considerable debate among the Jerusalem apostles and elders on this matter (Acts 15.6–7a), we are left in no doubt as to the eventual outcome of the deliberations. Thus Peter recapitulates his encounter with Cornelius, concluding with a rebuke of those who resist the outworking of God's elect purposes by 'putting a yoke upon the neck of the disciples' (Acts 15.7–11). The distinctive term 'yoke [ζυγός]' is used figuratively in the LXX to denote the oppression of Israel, not least during the Maccabean period when the final removal of the 'yoke' of Seleucid rule and concomitant inception of the Hasmonean dynasty is the cause of national celebration (1 Macc. 13.41; cf 8.18). The implication is clear: the unnecessary imposition of circumcision and Torah-observance upon the Gentile converts denotes a Jewish nationalism which is itself a function of the same enslavement Israel itself had experienced at the hands of its enemies, freedom from which is to be found only through God in Messiah Jesus.

At issue, then, is whether these Gentiles must become Jews in order to be the eschatological people of God. James, on the basis of his exegesis of certain Old Testament prophetic texts which associate the conversion of the nations with the restoration of the Temple in the messianic age (Isa. 45.21; Amos 9.11–12, et al.), concludes

---

[73] See Johnson, *The Acts of the Apostles*, pp. 269–70 for a temperate assessment of the various issues attending any attempt to correlate this event with Galatians 2.

that the Gentiles *qua* Gentiles belong to YHWH: it is precisely as 'all the nations' that they are included in the Messiah Jesus-governed covenantal people of God.[74] He thus stipulates that Gentiles who have turned to God are not to be 'troubled [παρενοχλεῖν]' by the claims now being made upon them (Acts 15.19). (Here we might note Antiochus IV Epiphanes' letter to the Jewish Senate granting permission 'for the Jews to enjoy their own food and laws' and guaranteeing that none of them would be 'molested [παρενοχλεῖν] in any way'.[75]) However, James does include in his decree the fourfold proviso that they avoid 'things sacrificed to idols', 'blood', 'things strangled' and 'sexual immorality' (Acts 15.20, 29; cf. 21.25). The rationale for this is to be found in reference to Leviticus 17–18 which suggests that the Gentiles who join the eschatological people of God are those 'in the midst' of Israel, and that thus these (but only these) four commandments apply.

As noted above, those authorized to carry and communicate the decree, Judas and Silas, may be located within the prophet-martyr tradition, and thus deemed worthy to accompany Barnabas and Paul, themselves men who had 'handed their lives over' to the cause of Christ (Acts 15.26).[76] So characterized, they stand in marked contrast to those who instead had 'troubled [ἐτάραξαν]' the Antiochene community (cf. Acts 17.8, 13), and who did so without any authorization from the Jerusalem church's leadership.[77] Finally, apparently the letter-decree has the desired effect inasmuch as it is gladly received as an 'exhortation [παράκλησις]' by the Antiochene community (Acts 15.30–2). That is, consonant with the function of the λογός παρακλήσεως, and as undergirded by the verbal exhortations of the prophets Judas and Silas, it serves to equip the faithful community to act with conviction and discernment in the face of ongoing opposition.

---

[74] On this and the ensuing comments concerning the decree, see the definitive discussion of Bauckham, 'James and the Jerusalem Church', pp. 452–62; and also 'James and the Gentiles (Acts 15.13–21)'.

[75] 2 Macc. 11.30–1. Note also the edict of the Seleucid King Demetrius I that no one 'annoy' the Jews in matters pertaining to their religion (1 Macc. 10.35); cf. the fact that Daniel's three companions were not 'troubled' by their trial (Dan.LXX/Th. 3.50).

[76] The Western Text underscores the nature and extent of the commitment in view with the addition of εἰς πάντα πειρασμόν; cf. Acts 20.19; Gal. 4.13.

[77] Their conduct aligns them with 'those troubling [οἱ ταράσσοντες]' the Galatians (Gal. 1.7; 5.10), a designation which (as we have seen) has notable antecedents in the Maccabean literature in reference to those Gentile and Jewish apostates disturbing faithful Israel.

3. Conclusion

These final remarks on Luke's Antioch-focused narrative may also serve as concluding comments upon the overall nature of Jewish and Christian relations in Antioch. The Antiochene church emerged and developed in a manner that would have inevitably brought it into conflict with the Jewish community. It had been initiated by a *Jewish* Christian mission; it comprised those designated Χριστιανοί; its common life was guided by prophet-martyr figures whose λόγος παρακλήσεως concerned conformity to Christ (not Torah); and it was affirmed and supported by Jerusalem-based apostles. As such it rivalled and threatened its Jewish counterpart – which had always struggled to preserve its own way of life (πολιτεία) – in two fundamental, interrelated and contentious respects: the nature and significance of Jesus, and what it meant to be the eschatological people of God.

The Jewish community was constituted according to God in Torah, and its exemplars would have numbered the Torah-obedient Maccabean martyrs. The Christian community was constituted according to God in Christ, and its leading figures comprised those faithful to him. Indeed, to compound the complexity and controversy, the Antiochene Christians would have claimed that it was precisely in and through his martyred and exalted servant Christ – and their conformity thereto – that God had now fulfilled Torah, manifested his covenant faithfulness to Israel (not least to her martyrs), and inaugurated the long-awaited resurrection life of the kingdom. Indeed, this will prove to be the burden of Paul's theological reflection upon the Antioch incident, to which we now turn.

5

PAUL AND THE CRUCIFIED CHRIST IN ANTIOCH: GALATIANS 2.11-14

Paul's autobiography climaxes with an account of, and theological reflection upon, his dramatic confrontation with Peter in Antioch (Gal. 2.11-14, 15-21). It has already been contended that the apostle's autobiographical remarks to date (chapter three), and the external evidence on Jewish and Christian relations in Antioch (chapter four) are both greatly illuminated when seen as a christological reworking of the Maccabean martyr model of Judaism (chapters one and two). The same claim will now be advanced concerning the Antioch incident (chapters five and six). Here, Paul again emerges as one standing in ironic relation to the Maccabean tradition as he now responds to Peter's movement in the direction of a rigorous Judaism by faithfully defending the truth of the gospel, namely, the outworking of God's grace in the martyred and exalted Jesus, Messiah and Son of God, and in the eschatological people of God together conformed to him.

At the outset I provide a brief introductory overview of the storyline of Galatians 2.11-21 as a whole, illustrating how this represents a christological reworking of the Maccabean narrative as, for example, exemplified in the story of the martyr Eleazar. The chapter then focuses specifically upon the account of the Antioch confrontation itself (Gal. 2.11-14). Our point of departure is the much debated question of the precise nature of the Antiochene table-fellowship, which also considers the related (but often overlooked) matter of the Lord's Supper. From this it is concluded that, for Paul, fundamentally (table-)fellowship is not a question of adherence to Torah food laws, but of the inclusive (Jew + Gentile) community's commensality with their eschatological redeemer in the already inaugurated messianic kingdom of God.

Thus it is this which Peter is forsaking as he withdraws from mixed table-fellowship. The ensuing analysis of his action will comprise its cause, nature, motivation and impact. By capitulating to those pressing for strict adherence to a Jewish way of life (who may themselves have come under the constraints of a Maccabean-inspired zeal), Peter fails to remain faithful to his martyr-exemplar Christ, and indeed also undermines the faithfulness of others. Hence, Paul responds by defending the truth of the gospel. The nature and significance of Paul's action will come into view as we consider the judicial setting, the issue at stake, the charge levelled at Peter and the verdict which is reached. In this contest Paul stands Daniel-like, but now in the cause of Christ rather than Judaism, and again demonstrates himself faithful to the martyred and exalted Messiah disclosed in him.

1. The narrative substructure of Galatians 2.11-21

It may be helpful to anticipate the direction of the ensuing exegesis of Galatians 2.11–14 (and 2.15–21) by suggesting at the outset the nature of its narrative substructure, namely, that it represents a christological reworking of the story of the righteous Jew as, for example, typified by the faithful Maccabean martyr Eleazar (2 Macc. 6.18–31; 4 Macc. 5.1–7.23). The common constituent elements of the respective narratives, and something of the continuity and discontinuity between the two, may be illustrated in advance of their detailed consideration by means of the following diagram and ensuing concise commentary.

To elaborate briefly, the narrative substructure of Paul's argument at Galatians 2.11ff. is all about the eschatological people of God (Jews and Gentiles together in Christ rather than Torah-obedient Israel), who face opposition (in this instance, Jews and 'apostate' Jewish Christians,[1] rather than Antiochus IV Epiphanes and his Jewish sympathizers). In the face of their affliction (compulsion to Judaize, not Hellenize) they are exhorted by their exemplar (Paul instead of Eleazar) who urges conformity to his own self-sacrificial covenant faithfulness (to God/Christ/his people, not God/Torah/ Israel). In this way he (and they) participate in the outworking of God's messianic redemption in and through the Jewish and Gentile community of faith (rather than the rescue of nation Israel), assured

---

[1] Elsewhere of course Paul and his converts encountered opposition from Gentiles and 'apostate' Gentile Christians; indeed, no doubt this was the case on other occasions in Antioch itself.

	'The Maccabean narrative'	'The Antioch narrative'
The people of God	Torah-obedient Israel (those in Judaism)	Jews and Gentiles in Messiah Jesus
Their opponents	Gentiles and apostate Jews	Jews and 'apostate' Jewish Christians
Their affliction	Religio-political persecution: enforced Hellenization	Coercion to Judaize, synagogal discipline
Their exemplar	Eleazar (conformed to Torah)	Paul (conformed to Christ)
His witness and exhortation	Covenant faithfulness to God in Torah in Israel in the face of martyrdom	Covenant faithfulness to God in the Messiah (and his people) in the midst of persecution
Its outcome	Israel's atonement, and God's condemnation of its opponents	Participation in the Messiah's vicarious atonement of his people and God's condemnation of their opponents
Vindication and exaltation	Israel's redemption and vindication, the martyr's 'living to God'	The Antiochene church's present (and future) justification, Israel-in-Christ 'living to God'

that they are (and will be) justified, even as the Israel-in-Christ is now (and will be) found 'living to God'.

It need not, of course, be claimed that as he wrote on (or earlier spoke to) the situation in Antioch Paul was consciously engaging the Maccabean narrative in the highly systematic fashion as set forth above.[2] Indeed, it is the very nature of narrative substructure that it operates at a much more deep-seated level, even if it is nevertheless variously discernible in the issues, themes and terminology which appear in the surface structure of the text. It is precisely these surface features which we shall now attempt to 'unpack'. In this way it will become more evident how (and why) the nature and significance of Paul's account of the Antioch incident is the

---

[2] Although, as we have already argued in chapters two and four, the climate of first-century Jewish nationalism was such that the traditions (and possibly texts) of Maccabean martyrdom would have been ready to hand, not least in Antioch. Furthermore, both Rom. 3.21–6 (see chapter two) and our analysis of Galatians 1–2 to date indicate that Paul as zealous Jew and now Christian apostle had indeed actively engaged the Maccabean model of Judaism.

more fully understood as a function of a messianically reconfigured Maccabean martyr theology.

2. Peter's table-fellowship with the Antiochene Christians and the delegation from James (Gal. 2.12a)

The nature of the table-fellowship

Paul informs his readers that prior to the arrival of certain men from James, Peter regularly ate meals together with the Gentile Christians in Antioch (Gal. 2.12a).[3] Precisely what this table-fellowship entailed in relation to Torah dietary laws and Gentile association, and what modification thereof was demanded by James' representatives, has become the subject of much scholarly speculation. There is a range of nuanced interpretations currently on offer which, at risk of oversimplification, may be set forth as follows.

(1) Peter and the Jewish Christians did *not* eat with the Gentile Christians, but rather observed Torah dietary regulations in their own separate gatherings.[4] On this reading it is difficult to know what additional demands would have been made upon them.[5]

Alternatively, Peter and the other Jewish Christians *did* indeed eat with the Gentile Christians, although various conditions could have obtained, as follows.

(2) Both the Jewish and Gentile Christians in Antioch ignored Torah dietary regulations.[6] Hence, at least minimal observance was now being urged by James' men.

(3) Both observed the essential Torah dietary regulations. However, the Jerusalem church sought a much stricter observance of ritual purity and tithing.[7]

---

[3] The apparent force of the imperfect συνήσθιεν is that 'he did so repeatedly and almost habitually' (so Betz, *Galatians*, p. 107, citing Burton, Schlier, and Mußner). Precisely why and when Peter came to Antioch is unclear, although from the mildly adversative ὅτε δέ it might be inferred that it was a pastoral and mission-orientated visit which ensued not long after the Jerusalem encounter just related (Gal. 2.1–10).

[4] Downey, *A History of Antioch*, p. 277: they 'presumably met separately, at least in so far as the orthodox Jews observed the Law in the matter of eating with Gentiles'.

[5] Although see item (5) below.

[6] So many commentators; e.g., Bruce, *Galatians*, p. 129: 'unreserved table-fellowship'.

[7] Dunn, *Jesus, Paul and the Law*, especially pp. 154–8.

(4) Both probably followed the biblical laws. Nonetheless, James was concerned about too close an association with Gentiles leading to contact with idolatry or the violation of a dietary law – or perhaps he might simply have been generally averse to eating Gentile food and wanted due caution exercised.[8]

(5) Both observed Torah dietary laws and also halakhic elaborations on tithes and purity. In this case, the people from James were wanting the God-fearing Gentile believers to take the final step of becoming proselytes.[9]

(6) Initially Jews and Gentiles were able to eat together, whether because the God-fearing Gentiles observed basic dietary laws, individual believers brought their own meals, or the meals took place in Jewish homes. Later, however, greater Jewish Christian freedom towards the Gentiles created concern over idol meat, news of which incurred the censure of Jerusalem who insisted on Jewish legal observance for its own sake.[10]

My own view on this admittedly complex matter is that, in its assessment of the initial situation, option (6) is closest to the mark, that is, the Jewish Christians observed the Torah dietary laws, and an indeterminate number of their Gentile counterparts may well have done likewise. Moreover, the ensuing disruption of their table-fellowship together had less to do with the food being eaten than with the (Gentile) company being kept.[11]

In support of this position we may consider, insofar as it is possible, the likely perspective of Diaspora Jews in general and Antiochene Jews in particular on the matter of eating food with Gentiles. With respect to the former, on balance, a consideration of the limited Graeco-Roman and Jewish sources available seems to

---

[8] E. P. Sanders, 'Jewish Association with Gentiles', p. 186; in this article and *Jewish Law from Jesus to the Mishnah*, pp. 255–308, Sanders strenuously rejects Dunn's specific proposal – (3) above – that ritual purity and tithing were being demanded.

[9] A position outlined but rejected by Dunn, *Jesus, Paul and the Law*, pp. 153–4.

[10] The reconstruction of Craig C. Hill, *Hellenists and Hebrews*, pp. 140–1, suggesting that James' representatives would have protested along the following lines: 'You must know that this is not what we agreed to in Jerusalem. Just because Gentiles do not need to live like Jews does not mean that Jews are therefore free to live like Gentiles!'

[11] Note the discussion in Nanos, *Mystery*, pp. 347ff.: 'The issue entirely concerned those with *whom* he had been eating and then withdrawn', p. 348.

indicate that there was a certain range of positions available and adopted, depending upon the halakhic stance taken (and perhaps also one's particular geographic location). So, in a manner comparable to option (6) above, Markus Bockmuehl has recently suggested that observant Jews could have held one of four positions on the matter:

(1) refuse all table fellowship with Gentiles and refuse to enter a Gentile house,
(2) invite Gentiles to their house and prepare a Jewish meal,
(3) take their own food to a Gentile's house, or indeed
(4) dine with Gentiles on the explicit or implicit understanding that food they would eat was neither prohibited in the Torah nor tainted with idolatry.[12]

It has been argued that a strict position was in fact the norm amongst Diaspora Jews.[13] Esler, for example, notes the lasting influence of the Maccabean crisis in which (as we have seen) adherence to food laws figured so prominently;[14] purity as a crucial boundary marker within the Essene community; and sources which not only presuppose strict food-law practice but which might be construed as disallowing Gentile association *per se*. Such evidence cannot simply be dismissed as unrepresentative or the exceptions which prove the rule.[15] Nonetheless, it may still have been the case that Jews engaged in 'a broad range of social intercourse with Gentiles'.[16] Sanders is probably correct to argue that the extent of the Diaspora Jews' preoccupation with ritual purity has been overstated,

---

[12] Bockmuehl, *Jewish Law in Gentile Churches*, p. 58.

[13] Alon, *Jews, Judaism and the Classical World*, pp. 146–89; Esler, *Community and Gospel in Luke–Acts*, pp. 71–86; and *Galatians*, pp. 93–116. Note the circumspect estimation in Barclay, *Jews in the Mediterranean Diaspora*, pp. 434–7.

[14] Esler, *Community and Gospel in Luke–Acts*, p. 80; cf. Dunn, *Jesus, Paul and the Law*, p. 137: 'No one who cherished the memory of the Maccabees would even dream of eating unclean food.'

[15] So E. P. Sanders, 'Jewish Association with Gentiles', p. 177 (similarly Craig C. Hill, *Hellenists and Hebrews*, p. 120), with particular reference to statements at *Jub*. 22.16 and *Jos. Asen*. 7.1.

[16] See Dunn, *Jesus, Paul and the Law*, p. 147 (affirmed by E. P. Sanders, 'Jewish Association with Gentiles', p. 180), who nevertheless observes that the fluid situation admitted stricter positions, especially when Judaism was under threat. The compilation and analysis of sources in Esler, *Community and Gospel in Luke–Acts*, pp. 76–84, is critiqued by E. P. Sanders, 'Jewish Association with Gentiles', pp. 176–80, and Craig C. Hill, *Hellenists and Hebrews*, pp. 118–22; with a response from Esler, *Galatians*, pp. 98–104. Note also the rabbinic evidence discussed in Tomson, *Paul and the Jewish Law*, pp. 230–6.

and that our limited sources allow that careful observance of food laws (notably on meat and wine) in avoidance of idolatry did not necessarily preclude association or even eating with Gentiles under the right circumstances.[17] Thus it would seem best to concur with Tomson's moderate assessment that there was a lack of unanimity on this matter.[18] Whereas some Diaspora Jews followed a fairly strict pattern, others exercised greater latitude. Hence, as Bockmuehl suggests, options (2), (3) and (4) could have been available to and exercised by Jewish Christians engaged in table-fellowship with Gentile Christians.[19]

But what of the Antiochene Jews in particular on the matter of eating food with Gentiles? It would seem reasonable to surmise that Antioch followed the pattern of Diaspora Judaism at large, and that positions ranging from the strict to a more open stance were also represented there. Thus Bockmuehl's overall assessment of the situation is that among the Jews in Antioch 'there were a good many who showed a relative latitude in their halakhic observance'.[20] Nonetheless, it is still worth stressing that at least some of them could have taken a strict position on the matter. Josephus avers that in granting the Antiochene Jews their πολιτεία, King Seleucus I Nicator (312–281/280 BC) had ordered that they receive a fixed sum of money with which to buy their own (undefiled) oil. It will be recalled from our earlier discussion of the Antiochene Jewish community, Josephus adds that attempts *in his own day* to revoke this πολιτεία – and, presumably, such attendant privileges as those pertaining to the oil – were rejected by Vespasian and Titus (*Ant.* 12.120). This early attestation of Jewish abstention from Gentile oil (and other food products) received dramatic re-enforcement (probably) in the period immediately prior to the Jewish War,[21] in conjunction with the promulgation of the 'Decree of Eighteen Things', whose enactment was associated with a leading Shammaite named

---

[17] For example, if the Jews brought their own food or the meal complied with Jewish requirements (*Ep. Arist.* 181ff.).

[18] Tomson, *Paul and the Jewish Law*, pp. 233–4, in reference to early rabbinic sources: 'the Tannaim were not unanimous on this matter'; there could be 'two divergent views on relations with gentiles within the same pious tradition'.

[19] Bockmuehl, *Jewish Law in Gentile Churches*, pp. 58–9.

[20] Ibid., p. 61.

[21] According to Kasher, *The Jews in Hellenistic and Roman Egypt*, p. 304, there was a three-stage halakhic development towards greater latitude in the use of Gentile oil; however, in the first stage, from the early Second Temple period (Jdt. 10.5) to the time of Josephus (*Ant.* 12.120; cf. *J.W.* 2.591ff.; *Life* 74), its use was prohibited.

Eleazar who was also involved in the updating and re-issuing of the *Megillath Taanith*, with its celebration of the victories of the Maccabees. From this correlation of oil, the Eighteen Halakhoth and the *Megillath Taanith*[22] with the Jewish community in Antioch in the second half of the first century, it might be inferred that certain Antiochene Jews could have taken a more conservative approach to matters such as table-fellowship. This would be consonant with our wider estimation of the Antiochene Jewish community in chapter four: they were concerned to preserve the characteristic aspects of the Jewish way of life.

With this admittedly circuitous evidence for a conservative element within Antiochene Judaism duly noted, it nevertheless remains likely that sufficient latitude existed for Torah-observant Jews to be able to find ways to eat with Gentiles, in accordance with options (2) to (4) above. Consonant with this it is noteworthy that the extant evidence points to Jerusalem (rather than to Antioch) as the *initial* source of the disruption amongst the Antiochene Christians concerning their mixed table-fellowship.[23] It is likely that, from the perspective of James and his delegation, the fundamental issue to be directed at the *Jewish* Christians in Antioch was their need to obey the Torah.[24] As various commentators have noted, it is reasonable to infer that James is largely motivated by a genuine concern that failure in this respect could precipitate or exacerbate any religio-political conflict between Jewish Christians and their fellow Jews in Jerusalem (and perhaps, by extension, in Antioch).[25] However, there is no indication that James' appeal regarding Torah-observance was intended to be applied to the *Gentile* Christians, nor that he in any way opposed mixed table-fellowship.[26] Yet, from Paul's strong condemnation of Peter – significantly, without any

---

[22] Discussed in Tomson, *Paul and the Jewish Law*, pp. 173–6.
[23] Bockmuehl, *Jewish Law in Gentile Churches*, p. 57; on his ensuing estimation of the issue at hand from the standpoint of James and his delegation, see Bockmuehl, pp. 70–82.
[24] As such, James' concerns are to be carefully differentiated from those of the 'Judaizing' opponents of Paul's Gentile mission, in Jerusalem, Antioch, Galatia and elsewhere.
[25] Recall the analysis of Jewish nationalism with particular reference to the Caligula episode in chapter two. See Jewett, 'The Agitators'; Dunn, *Jesus, Paul and the Law*, pp. 130ff.; Hengel and Schwemer, *Paul Between Damascus and Antioch*, especially pp. 245–57.
[26] Indeed, to the contrary, the earlier estimation of James' crucial role in the Jerusalem meetings concerning Paul's Gentile mission recounted in Gal. 2.1–10 (chapter three) and Acts 15 (chapter four) strongly suggests that he endorsed it.

explicit criticism directed towards James – it would appear that Peter, and those influenced by his withdrawal, interpreted the appeal along such lines. Thus Paul regarded their response to James' otherwise reasonable request to be excessive and injurious in various crucial respects: it tended in the direction of those who would compel Gentile believers to adopt Torah-observance and circumcision; it thus undermined the Gentile mission;[27] and it fractured the Christ-centred common life of the eschatological people of God.

Table-fellowship and the Lord's Supper

Before further consideration is given to Paul's concerns with Peter's conduct, a subject conspicuous by its absence in the recent debates over the Antiochene table-fellowship merits attention: the Lord's Supper. While this takes us beyond the immediate context of Galatians 2.11–14, it will become apparent that the important bearing of this matter demands its careful consideration. Indeed, by reference to the Corinthian crisis over its eucharistic-focused common meal – and not least certain key terms and issues evocative of the Maccabean crisis – we shall arrive at a greater appreciation of Paul's perspective upon the nature and significance of the Antiochene table-fellowship and Peter's withdrawal therefrom.

The lack of an explicit reference to the Lord's Supper in Paul's account at Galatians 2.11ff. does not obviate *the fact that* it would have been celebrated within the mixed Antiochene community,[28] nor the likelihood that this would inevitably have had a bearing upon any conflict over their common table-fellowship.[29] That is, for Paul the manifestly socio-political and ethnic dimensions of the debate over what went on at *table* would have been but a function of the more deep-seated question as to what constituted *fellowship*,[30]

---

[27] Which, of course, Peter himself had earlier endorsed (Gal. 2.7–9).

[28] What is virtually beyond doubt on grounds of intrinsic probability receives external confirmation in Luke's testimony that they worshipped together (Acts 13.1–3).

[29] This remains true whether or not the Lord's Supper actually took place in connection with their common meals, as would seem likely from 1 Cor. 11.20–1 (however regularly and whatever the precise form); note also the 'breaking of bread' at Acts 2.42, 46; 20.7, 11; 1 Cor. 10.16; 11.24. Amongst those who do associate the two at Antioch are Schütz, *Paul and the Anatomy of Apostolic Authority*, p. 150; Lührmann, 'Abendmahlsgemeinschaft? Gal. 2,11ff'; Bruce, *Galatians*, p. 129; Martyn, *Galatians*, p. 232.

[30] Here we may recall our earlier discussion concerning the significance of the 'right hand of *fellowship*' at Gal. 2.9.

this ultimately devolving upon the matter of common fellowship in the (one) body and blood of Christ. Certainly this is the case in his sharp delineation of the discord within the Corinthian community over idol food in terms of the mutual exclusivity of idolatry (whether pagan or Jewish) and fellowship in the Lord's table (1 Cor. 10.16–17, 21). As such, it is worth pausing to note also Paul's ensuing response to the conflict generated by the Corinthians' abuse of the Lord's Supper.

Notwithstanding Paul's former instruction on the subject, the Corinthian community's recent divisive abuse of their common meal and the Lord's Supper had forced the apostle to reiterate its nature and significance (1 Cor. 11.17–33).[31] Immediately apparent are the potent – and, from a Jewish standpoint, highly polemical – aspects of the tradition (1 Cor. 11.23–6), the most noteworthy of which may be quickly itemized as follows. (i) The Passover setting of the Last Supper suggests that Jesus' death (and resurrection) was viewed as an act of divine deliverance superseding even that of the Exodus, with (ii) this underscored by reference to the cup of the *new* covenant 'in [his] blood'. Furthermore, (iii) the statement that Jesus was 'handed over [παραδίδωμι]' functions as a historical allusion which may implicate the Jews in his trial and death (cf. Gal. 2.20). And (iv) the paradox of Israel's complicity in the self-sacrifice of her Messiah is latent in its depiction in language evocative of the Maccabean martyrs: 'this is my body [handed over] for you [ὑπὲρ ὑμῶν]'.[32] No doubt such traditions and their cultic re-enactment (regularly 'proclaiming the Lord's death') were also an integral aspect of (Paul's) teaching and practice within the Antiochene Christian community,[33] and provided much of the theological foundation for its common life (not least its table-fellowship) and any Jewish–Christian debates which arose in relation thereto.[34]

---

[31] The precise ground of their discord is now usually attributed to a rich–poor divide, variously nuanced as the rich eating ahead of, apart from, or failing to share their food with the poor (see the summary assessment in Fee, *The First Epistle to the Corinthians*, pp. 540–2).

[32] See immediately below concerning the Jewish martyr Razi. On Maccabean martyrdom and the Lord's Supper traditions, see especially Heard, 'Maccabean Martyr Theology', pp. 396–460.

[33] On the very concrete sociological implications of the Lord's Supper, not least *vis-à-vis* Jewish and Christian relations, see especially Meeks, *The First Urban Christians*, pp. 157–62.

[34] Such debates would have received added impetus if a Maccabean martyr cult was indeed already operative in Antioch (see pp. 83–6), and was seen as being rivalled by the Christian cult of a crucified Messiah.

In drawing out the implications of the Corinthians' abuse of the Lord's Supper (1 Cor. 11.27–34), Paul first admonishes that anyone partaking 'unworthily [ἀναξίως] will be liable for the body and the blood of the Lord' (1 Cor. 11.27). It would appear that this 'unworthiness' resides in reprehensible conduct at the common meal (1 Cor. 11.20–1, 33–4) which reflects a decided lack of commitment to (and thus an undermining of) that which the meal represents: selfless participation in corporate conformity to the crucified Christ (cf. Gal. 2.19b). An instructive comparison, all the more apt given our interest in correspondences between the table-fellowship in Corinth and Antioch, involves the only other biblical occurrence of the term ἀναξίως used in reference to the exemplary Jew, Razi (2 Macc. 14.37–46).[35] 'For in former times, when there was no mingling with the Gentiles, [Razi] had been accused of Judaism, and for Judaism [ὑπὲρ τοῦ Ιουδαϊσμοῦ] he had with all zeal risked body and life' (2 Macc. 14.38). Pursued to the point of death by the Seleucid forces, Razi prefers to fall upon his own sword and die nobly rather than suffer outrages 'unworthy' of his (Jewish) birth. The account is clearly stylized after the earlier martyr story of Eleazar who himself was resolved to remain 'worthy [ἄξιος]' of his exemplary 'way of life' by refusing the 'pretence [ὑπόκρισις]' (cf. Gal. 2.13) involved in eating pork in order to avoid martyrdom (2 Macc. 6.23–7). Indeed the 'worthiness' of the martyrs is thematic.[36] And it is this kind of willing and worthy self-sacrifice on behalf of Judaism which Paul now wants replicated in the Corinthian (and Antiochene) believers' common commitment to Christ and his people.

In warning the Corinthians that their abuse of the Lord's Supper will render them 'liable [ἔνοχος]' for Christ's death, Paul employs a term which in the LXX pertains to judicial liability under Torah, especially in relation to bloodshed and the death penalty.[37] In the New Testament it is found (re)appropriated by Jesus in reference to liability for one's brother (Matt. 5.21–4), and applied to Jesus himself in virtue of his purportedly blasphemous claims as Messiah/Son of God/Son of Man for which he is deemed liable to the death penalty under Torah (Matt. 26.66/Mark 14.64).[38] It would appear

---

[35] For analysis of the account of Razi's self-sacrifice for the Jewish cause, above all see van Henten, *The Maccabean Martyrs*, pp. 85–124.
[36] 2 Macc. 7.19–20, 29; 15.21; 4 Macc. 5.11; 7.6; 11.6.
[37] Lev. 20.9–16, 27; Num. 35.27, 31; Deut. 19.10; Josh. 2.19.
[38] This bears upon διὰ νόμου and ὁ υἱὸς θεοῦ at Gal. 2.19a, 20d, on which see chapter six. Note also ἔνοχος at Mark 3.29; Jas. 2.10 (cf. Gal. 3.12); Heb. 2.15.

then that Paul is concerned that the Corinthian brethren's lack of accountability to one another, not least in relation to participation in the Lord's Supper, is a function of a lack of conformity to the Messiah/the Son of God which could render them as liable for his death as those complicit in his execution. In this they are also undermining their status as the sons of God (cf. Gal. 2.20).

Within this framework the full weight of Paul's censure of the Corinthians for 'not discerning the body' and thereby bringing judgement upon themselves becomes evident: in failing to see the inextricable interrelationship between conformity to the crucified Christ and incorporation into his people, they are accountable before God for their abuse of both (1 Cor. 11.29; cf. 10.16–17). Paul's solution to this situation is to exhort the believers to examine/ test themselves – that is, to ensure that they conform to Christ and thus merit God's approval[39] – so that they may thereby worthily participate in the Lord's Supper. In this way they will avoid the divine judgement which is already being manifest within the community, though this is mercifully in the form of divine discipline now rather than irrevocable condemnation at the final judgement (1 Cor. 11.30–2). Here Paul offers a striking Christian reworking of a central motif at 2 Maccabees 6.12–16: the suffering and even martyrdom of God's faithful (here Jews and Gentiles in Christ rather than Torah-obedient Jews) is understood as divine discipline upon the impiety of the whole community (the Corinthian community rather than nation Israel), in lieu of eschatological judgement upon the accumulated sins of those outside God's people (Gentile and Jewish unbelievers rather than the Gentile nations).[40] All this bears upon Paul's estimation of and response to Peter's withdrawal. The immediate impact of conflict and division demands the divine discipline of Paul's censure of Peter as 'condemned' – in order to prevent the accumulation of such sin leading to the ultimate condemnation of final judgement (cf. Heb. 10.26–31).

---

[39] Such is the force of δοκιμάζω at Gal. 6.4 (in relation to ὁ νόμος τοῦ Χριστοῦ, at Gal. 6.2) and 1 Thess. 2.4; cf. Rom. 12.2; 1 Cor. 3.13; Phil. 1.10.

[40] On this reading, it might be that those who 'are weak and ill and are dying [ἀσθενεῖς καὶ ἄρρωστοι καὶ κοιμῶνται]' (1 Cor. 11.30)' are Corinthian believers whose faith is being compromised (whether by themselves or their brethren) and as such are suffering even to the point of death. Compare Dan. 11.33–5; 1 Macc. 6.8; and 1 Cor. 15.29–31 (which, whatever the precise significance of 'baptism on behalf of the dead', may have its nearest biblical analogue in 2 Macc. 12.39–45).

For Paul, fundamentally the Antiochene table-*fellowship* was not a matter of adherence to Torah food laws and the Jewish way of life they represented, but of a common life in Christ and his people. This was given its most potent cultic expression in the form of the Lord's Supper which was undoubtedly celebrated within the community, probably in some regular relation to its common meal. The profound and inevitably polemical significance of this rite must not be overlooked: it commemorated the self-sacrifice of one rejected by Israel as but a messianic pretender, and testified to his now risen presence amongst those conformed to him. Indeed, we may recall how the *Parables of Enoch* anticipated that the focal point of the final destiny of Israel's oppressed 'righteous ones' would be their life together with their eschatological redeemer: 'they shall eat and rest and rise with that Son of Man for ever and ever' (*1 Enoch* 62.14). For Paul, the Lord's Supper and related table-fellowship was a living witness to the fact that the martyred and exalted Jesus, the Messiah and Son of God, was indeed Israel's (and the world's) eschatological redeemer, and that his afflicted but already vindicated people even now enjoyed commensality with him in the inaugurated kingdom of God. Ultimately, it was all this which was being undermined by Peter's withdrawal from table-fellowship in Antioch (cf. Gal. 2.21).

3. Peter's withdrawal: its nature and significance (Gal. 2.11, 12–13)

At this point we may examine further Paul's estimation of Peter's withdrawal. Three aspects of Paul's perspective upon this dramatic event are considered, each illuminated by reference to the Maccabean crisis. First, a notable non-Pauline parallel is employed as a means of scrutinizing the significance of the fact that Peter 'withdrew' (and 'separated') himself, and it is concluded that in Paul's view this action inclined in the direction of forsaking the Righteous One/Son of God. Second, it is surmised that the primary motivation for the withdrawal was a fear of reprisal from 'those of the circumcision', and that for Paul this constituted a failure to remain faithful in the face of affliction. Finally, it is determined from Paul's assessment of Peter as being engaged in a 'pretence' that he regards his fellow apostle's conduct as tending towards Torah-obedience instead of greater conformity to Christ.

Peter's withdrawal as a failure of faithfulness

Paul states tersely that Peter 'withdrew and set himself apart [ὑπέστελλεν καὶ ἀφώριζεν ἑαυτόν]' (Gal. 2.12b). The imperfect verb tenses may indicate that this was a gradual process, though to what degree this is attributable to Peter's reluctance under duress, deliberation or discomfort must remain uncertain. What may be recoverable is Paul's estimation of the action on the basis of the significance of the verb 'withdraw [ὑποστέλλω]' elsewhere in the New Testament. Two of the three occurrences of the verb are found in Luke's account of Paul's speech to the Ephesian elders attesting that he did not '*shrink back*' in fear from proclaiming the gospel even in the face of 'trials ... through the plots of the Jews' (Acts 20.19–20, 27). The third is in Hebrews, and climaxes an exhortation (Heb. 10.19–39) which likewise speaks of fortitude in the face of affliction, certain aspects of which are worthy of note in that they are both redolent of themes (and even terminology) prominent in the Maccabean literature and bear upon Peter's action in Antioch.

First, the recipients of Hebrews are instructed to remain 'unwavering [ἀκλινής]' in their confession of the Christian hope (Heb. 10.23), a term found elsewhere in biblical literature only in reference to Eleazar and the martyred mother who remained unwavering in the midst of their torment (4 Macc. 6.7; 17.3a). Second, they are warned that wilful sin upon receiving knowledge of the truth forfeits Christ's sacrifice and incurs the judgement of God (Heb. 10.26–8). Indeed, inasmuch as anyone who 'violates' Torah may incur the death penalty,[41] then all the more worthy of divine punishment is the one who has 'trampled upon the Son of God [ὁ τὸν υἱὸν τοῦ θεοῦ καταπατήσας]' (Heb. 10.28–29a). While the verb καταπατέω occurs throughout the LXX, the Temple-cult aspect of the argument in Hebrews 10.19–39 especially invites comparison with the Temple-focused Maccabean crisis and the notable use of the verb in relation to the 'trampling' of the saints/host of heaven by the Fourth Beast (Dan.LXX 7.7, 19; 8.10) and the 'trampling' of the Temple sanctuary and 'oppression' of the people of God by the Gentile forces (1 Macc. 3.45, 51; 4.60; 2 Macc. 8.2). Third, the faltering Christian community is urged to recall how they formerly endured a great struggle, including public revilement and affliction, even as they

---

[41] Cf. Num. 35.30; Deut. 17.6; 19.15.

continued to show compassion to their imprisoned brethren (Heb. 10.32–4). Whatever the precise scenario in view here,[42] it is depicted in terms comparable to the account of the Jewish and Christian athlete-martyrs in 4 Maccabees 17.11–17 and *1 Clement* 5, the latter specifying both Peter and Paul as the most noble examples thereof. Finally, the believers are exhorted from scripture to be mindful that:

> My righteous one from faith will live,
> and if he draws back,
> my soul does not delight in him.
>
> ὁ δὲ δίκαιός μου ἐκ πίστεως ζήσεται,
> καὶ ἐὰν ὑποστείληται,
> οὐκ εὐδοκεῖ ἡ ψυχή μου ἐν αὐτῷ.
> (Heb. 10.38/Hab. 2.4).[43]

A concluding admonition reinforces the point: they are not of those who 'shrink back' (ὑποστολή) unto destruction, but those 'of faith [πίστεως] unto the possession of life' (Heb. 10.39). The overall argument is then underscored by a recapitulation of Israel's men and women of faith – from Abel to the Maccabean martyrs (Heb. 11.1–40) – which leads to another athlete-martyr metaphor urging that they complete with perseverance the contest before them, their eyes always fixed on their exemplar, Jesus (Heb. 12.1–2). In short, the author (as Paul) is urging the believers not to draw back under duress but rather to replicate the faith of their spiritual forebears, this climaxing in the faithfulness of the Righteous One/Messiah/Son of God.

However, it is Peter's deficiency in this respect which is a focus of Paul's concern in Antioch. At its worst, his withdrawal under pressure constitutes a failure to remain unwavering in his commitment to the truth of the gospel, and as such could be construed as 'trampling' upon the saints and the Son of God. That this necessarily entails dissociation from both is implied in Paul's somewhat ironical

---

[42] Lane, *Hebrews*, p. liv, postulates that it involved Claudius' expulsion of Jews from Rome.

[43] See Hays, '"The Righteous One" as Eschatological Deliverer', pp. 202–3, who concludes that although ὁ δίκαιος in Heb. 10.38 (Hab. 2.4) is not used as a messianic title, 'it does project a vision of faithfulness for which Jesus is the prototype'. Notably, however, Hays presses his case in relation to Paul, arguing that ὁ δίκαιος at Gal. 3.11 and Rom. 1.17 is indeed understood as a messianic designation (pp. 206–11; see also his *The Faith of Jesus Christ*, pp. 151–7, 206–9).

ensuing reference to the fact that Peter 'separated himself [ἀφώριζεν ἑαυτόν]'.[44] Paul conceived of his own life's work as being 'set apart' by the God who revealed his Son in him (Gal. 1.15–16; 2.20; cf. Rom. 1.1). He laboured to ensure that his converts remained unaffected by that which would undermine their nascent faith including those whose Torah-based conception of God's elect people caused them to insist that Gentile followers of Christ must adopt circumcision and strict Torah-observance. However, it is with such that Peter is now in danger of aligning himself in Antioch. Thus, whereas Peter may have conceived of his removal from mixed table-fellowship as a necessary act of separation/purity, Paul considers it to be a fundamental confusion of categories, and as a movement in the direction of *exclusion* from God's Son and his people.

Peter's motivation: a fear of reprisal

The stated motivation of Peter's conduct was 'fear of those of the circumcision'. Commentators have offered various nuanced proposals concerning the precise identity of οἱ ἐκ περιτομῆς and the nature of the fear they induced in Peter.[45] On the question of identity, it is likely that this group stood at some remove from the men from James.[46] That is, in a manner comparable to (if not identical with) 'those of the circumcision' already noted in connection with the Peter–Cornelius episode in Acts (Acts 11.2), they were those on the periphery of the Jerusalem Jewish Christian community (cf. Gal. 2.4–5),[47] who took an especially strict view concerning the maintenance of a Jewish way of life. In particular, as their name suggests, and like the Maccabees before them, they viewed circumcision as a non-negotiable demarcation of covenant loyalty.[48] As such, Paul

---

[44] Fundamentally concerned with 'separation', the semantic range of ἀφορίζω includes 'set apart, appoint, withdraw, purify, exclude'. In Judaism it focuses upon cultic separation from the 'unclean'.

[45] See R. N. Longenecker, *Galatians*, pp. 73–5; Craig C. Hill, *Hellenists and Hebrews*, pp. 128ff; Martyn, *Galatians*, pp. 236–40.

[46] Contra Burton, *Galatians*, p. 107, and many others; Martyn, *Galatians*, p. 239, speaks of them 'acting through James'.

[47] Although this need not exclude the possibility that they also had representation in Antioch.

[48] 1 Macc. 1.48, 60–1; 2 Macc. 6.10. On the correlation of covenant, Torah and circumcision within Second Temple Judaism, see Dunn, 'What Was the Real Issue Between Paul and "Those of the Circumcision"?'

would have been especially concerned that their commitment to matters Jewish not undermine their conformity to Christ.[49]

However, precisely such conduct seems to have been the case in Antioch where their strict position was brought to bear upon the matter of mixed table-fellowship (and perhaps other related but unstated issues such as circumcision). Furthermore, on analogy with Paul's remarks concerning the Agitators' rationale for their insistence on Torah-obedience and circumcision amongst the Galatian believers (Gal. 6.12–13; cf. 5.11),[50] it is possible that the stance of οἱ ἐκ περιτομῆς was at least in part attributable to the fact that they themselves were under threat from their fellow unbelieving Jews. Indeed, as observed earlier, this could have been an aspect of heightened tension in the period prior to the Jewish War, increasing pressure upon the Jerusalem church to conform to the Jewish cause.[51] This view would accord well with our earlier discussion of the continuity between the Maccabean movement and first-century Jewish nationalist aspirations.

In such circumstances it might be argued that Peter's fear consisted of a genuine concern for the well-being of beleaguered Jewish Christians and/or the Jewish mission (not least his own), both of which could have been adversely affected by Jewish reprisals ensuing upon his continued participation in a mixed table-fellowship.[52] That such factors could (and should) have comprised a legitimate aspect of his deliberations need not be doubted; that they constituted sufficient cause for his ensuing action and its negative impact upon the Antiochene community and the Gentile mission was another matter.

Both the complexity and the profundity of what is at stake in Peter's fear (φοβέομαι) of οἱ ἐκ περιτομῆς becomes the more apparent when it is recalled that the Maccabean martyrs were lauded

---

[49] In effect rendering them οἱ ἐκ νόμου rather than οἱ ἐκ πίστεως ['Ἀβραάμ, 'Ἰησοῦ], cf. Rom. 3.26; 4.12, 16; Gal. 3.7–10. This is consonant with Paul's use of περιτομή elsewhere in reference to unbelieving Jews (notably Gal. 2.7–9; cf. Rom. 3.30; 15.8; Eph. 2.11; Col. 3.11), and the fact that for him God had completely reconfigured the categories of Jew (circumcised) and Gentile (uncircumcised) in terms of faithful conformity to Christ rather than Torah-obedient Judaism – cf. Rom. 2.25–9; 3.27–31; 4.9–12; 1 Cor. 7.17–19; Phil. 3.2–3; Col. 2.11.
[50] Here taking οἱ περιτεμνόμενοι as denoting the Agitators; see chapter three, note 5.
[51] See note 25.
[52] So R. N. Longenecker, *Galatians*, pp. 74–5.

for their fear of God which enabled them to overcome the fear of torture and death – so that, for example, Antiochus IV Epiphanes was completely unable 'to persuade them out of fear to eat the defiling food' (4 Macc. 8.12).[53] It is precisely this level of fearlessness, though now transposed into an unerring commitment to God in Christ, which Paul expects Peter to exhibit by refusing to violate the Antiochene Christ-centred table-fellowship. What is required is that he pattern Christ's self-sacrificial faithfulness (cf. Gal. 5.6), as a fearless son of God ready to suffer with Christ and his people in order that he may be fully and finally vindicated and glorified with him (cf. Rom. 8.12–17).

The impact of Peter's withdrawal

The nature of Peter's conduct is further implied in Paul's ensuing brief but clearly aggrieved account of its unfolding impact: 'the rest of the Jews joined [Peter] in hypocrisy, so that even Barnabas was carried away by their pretence' (Gal. 2.13). Following classical usage, the biblical *hapax legomenon* συνυποκρίνομαι ('join in hypocrisy'), is often reasonably translated as 'play-acting'.[54] But such a rendering does not itself convey the full import of the act within a Jewish and/or Jewish Christian framework. In Jewish literature the cognate verb ὑποκρίνομαι can be found in condemning the conduct of the hypocritical 'devout' who fail to fear God, stumble over his law, and thus incur his judgement.[55] Most significant, however, is its use in the martyr narratives of 2 and 4 Maccabees. As already noted, Eleazar endured torment and death rather than 'pretend' to consume idol food, deeming it unworthy of his lifelong Torah-obedience, and a negative influence upon those who might be led astray by his 'pretence [ὑπόκρισις]' to an alien religion (2 Macc. 6.21–8; 4 Macc. 6.12–23).

When this understanding of 'hypocrisy' is transposed into Paul's Messiah Jesus-grounded assessment of the scenario in Antioch, once again the complexity and full significance of the situation becomes

---

[53] Cf. 2 Macc. 6.30; 4 Macc. 8.15–27; 14.8; 15.8.
[54] See especially Betz, *Galatians*, pp. 109–10, noting Epictetus, *Diss.* 2.9.19–20: 'why do you act the part of a Jew, when you are a Greek [τί ὑποκρίνῃ 'Ιουδαῖον ὤν ῞Ελλην]? ... whenever we see a man halting between two faiths, we are in the habit of saying, "He is not a Jew, he is only acting the part [οὐκ ἔστιν 'Ιουδαῖος, ἀλλ' ὑποκρίνεται]."' Cf. also *Ep. Arist.* 219, 267.
[55] Sir. 1.27–30; 32.15; 33.2; *Pss. Sol.* 4.

the more evident. Peter's hypocrisy consists in his unwillingness to risk reprisal by adopting a table-fellowship governed by Torah (rather than by Messiah Jesus). He is thus realigning himself with a life 'in Judaism' and in so doing he has had a detrimental effect upon those influenced by such pretence. The latter included not only 'the rest of the Jews', but even Barnabas. Paul's obvious pain at the involvement of his former advocate and mentor (Acts 9.26-8; 11.25-30) is only marginally mitigated by the fact that Barnabas' hypocrisy was derivative.[56]

The antidote to this hypocrisy is its exact antithesis: a self-sacrificial 'unhypocritical love [ἀγάπη ἀνυπόκριτος]' (Rom. 12.9a; cf. 2 Cor. 6.6) which issues in Christ-like 'love [for] one another with brotherly affection' (Rom. 12.10a).[57] And such 'unhypocritical love of the brethren' is to be evoked by obedience to the truth of God in Christ (1 Pet. 1.22). However, it is precisely Peter's deficiency in regard to the truth of the gospel which constrains Paul to confront him.

4. Paul's response: a defence of the truth of the gospel (Gal. 2.14)

Paul had already safeguarded the truth of the gospel against the incursion of certain 'false brethren' in Jerusalem (Gal. 2.3-5). Now, however, he must rise to defend it against those whose number includes one of the leading apostles. Our consideration of Paul's estimation of this matter comprises four elements. First, note is taken of the judicial setting. The Daniel-like Paul rises to confront Peter 'face to face', an analogous expression and scenario recounted in 2 Corinthians 10 suggesting that it is his conformity to the power-in-weakness of Christ which compels his martyr-like resistance of Peter's movement towards Judaism. Second, consideration is given to the full nature and significance of what is at stake, namely, the truth of the gospel; that is, the outworking of God's covenant faithfulness in Jesus the Messiah, and those conformed to him.

---

[56] See Bauckham, 'Barnabas in Galatians', for a shrewd estimation of how Barnabas' conspicuously minor role in Galatians is attributable to Paul's dismay at his role in the Antioch incident.

[57] The key terms 'brotherly love [φιλαδελφία]' and 'affection [φιλόστοργος]' are used in the LXX in reference to the selfless disposition of the martyred brothers towards one another (4 Macc. 13.23-14.1) and to the tender love of their mother for her sons (4 Macc. 15.13; cf. the cognate φιλοστοργία at 15.6-9) respectively.

Third, by reference to Paul's direct accusation, it is concluded that Peter's action – and its impact upon others – involves a profound confusion of categories, a shift from a messianic to a Jewish constituency and way of life. Finally, there is Paul's verdict, in which he somewhat ironically draws upon what may be the language of the synagogue law court in pronouncing Peter as 'condemned'. Indeed, once again, it is a Paul who stands in ironic relation to the tradition of Maccabees who proves faithful to the cause of the martyred Messiah.

The judicial setting

The precise outworking of the confrontation is not entirely clear. However, it may be suggested that Paul's opening statement at Galatians 2.11 *that* he opposed Peter is then subsequently elaborated upon by a summary statement as to *why* and *how* he did so at Galatians 2.14. That is, the confrontation was a single, public and climactic act which, as we shall now see, had judicial overtones. Indeed, that Paul's initial programmatic statement concerning his confrontation with Peter – 'I withstood him to his face [κατὰ πρόσωπον αὐτῷ ἀντέστην]' – possesses something akin to a judicial aspect may be adduced on the basis of certain disparate evidence.

First, it may be recalled that Daniel's third and final vision climaxes with a brief dramatic scene in which Michael 'stands, rises' (Dan. 12.2) as the representative judicial (and military) defendant of faithful Israel during the final 'time of trouble'. Indeed, the Hebrew verb here employed (עמד) occurs in judicial and military contexts throughout the MT and is often rendered in the LXX (and/or Th.) by ἵστημι and its cognates, including ἀν[θ]ίστημι.[58] Notably, ἀν[θ]ίστημι is found in reference to the Gentile nations which 'rise, stand' over and against each other and oppress Israel;[59] and, conversely, to Israel's faithful representative Daniel who is commanded to 'stand upright', assured that in so doing he will 'stand' (have his

---

[58] Cf., for example, in reference to both parties in a dispute 'standing before' the tribunal (Deut. 19.15–21); the manslayer who stands 'before the congregation [κατὰ πρόσωπον τῆς συναγωγῆς]' (Josh. 20.6); the Servant, confident that 'he who vindicates [ὁ δικαιώσας]' is near, asking 'Who will contend with me? Let us stand up together [ἀντιστήτω μοι ἅμα]' (Isa. 50.8).

[59] Cf. variously Dan.LXX/Th. 8.22–3; 10.13; 11.2, 3, 4, 7, 14–16, 20–1, 31.

rightful place) at the end.⁶⁰ Thus, Paul might be characterized in the tradition of Daniel as he 'withstands' his adversary Peter.⁶¹

Second, such an interpretation is consonant with certain New Testament cases where ἀνθίστημι likewise has a judicial context in view. Thus, for example, Jesus assures his disciples that in facing punishment in synagogues and witnessing before governors and kings, they will be given a wisdom which their adversaries 'will not be able to withstand [ἀντιστῆναι] or contradict [ἀντειπεῖν]' (Luke 21.15).⁶² A case in point, already examined earlier, concerns those synagogue-based Jews who disputed with the martyr Stephen and could not 'withstand' the Daniel-like wisdom and spirit with which he spoke (Acts 6.10).⁶³

Third, the judicial usage of the phrase κατὰ πρόσωπον can be found in the New Testament in connection with the trials of Jesus and Paul respectively (cf. Acts 3.13; 25.16).⁶⁴ Indeed, another notable instance of this expression, evoking a forensic (and perhaps military) background, is Paul's recollection of his detractors' dismissal of his bearing among the Corinthians as 'humble/demeaned when face to face' but bold when absent (2 Cor. 10.1). For Paul, the ironical truth of the matter is that his disposition amongst them κατὰ πρόσωπον was that of the meekness and forbearance of the Messiah.⁶⁵ Furthermore, he fears that their failure to recognize this may require him to be as bold with them as he is with 'certain men' who erroneously reckon him to be walking κατὰ σάρκα (2 Cor. 10.2). On the contrary, Paul's engagement in the world (ἐν σαρκί) is not that of one who battles κατὰ σάρκα, because his weapons of war are not fleshly (σαρκικός) but those which are powerful for God in tearing down fortresses (2 Cor. 10.4).

The fortresses include false 'reasonings [λογισμοί]' erected against

---

⁶⁰ Dan. 10.11; 12.13; cf. 12.2.

⁶¹ The verb is also used in connection with the Maccabees' strong resistance of Israel's enemies via their military exploits (1 Macc. 14.19, 32) and martyrdom (4 Macc. 6.30; 16.23).

⁶² See further Lampe, 'Martyrdom and Inspiration', pp. 129-31.

⁶³ Cf. ἀνθίστημι at Matt. 5.39; Rom. 13.2; Eph. 6.13; 2 Tim. 3.8; Jas. 4.7; 1 Pet. 5.9.

⁶⁴ Its employment, in conjunction with ἀνθίστημι and within a military context, may be attested in the LXX at Deut. 7.24; 9.2; 11.25; Josh. 1.5.

⁶⁵ Furnish, *II Corinthians*, p. 460, deems it likely that 'Paul is thinking of the pre-existent Lord who, in the gracious condescension of his incarnate life, became lowly, weak, and poor'; cf. Rom. 15.3; Phil. 2.8; 2 Cor. 8.9.

knowledge of God, with their defeated defenders ('every thought/ design') taken captive into the obedience of the Messiah. The wider context of 2 Corinthians 10–13, with certain Jewish(-Christian) opponents in view, and the elaborate military metaphor in which the main antagonist is false λογισμός[66] together suggest that Paul is battling against a Jewish(-Christian) line of thought significantly indebted to a Maccabean frame of reference. He must counter arguments in favour of complementing Christ with the 'rationalism' of a Torah-based Jewish nationalism, by urging the exclusive claims of a humiliated (but now exalted) Messiah – not least as lived out in his own 'demeaned' κατὰ πρόσωπον existence amongst his converts. Hence his injunction to the Corinthians to 'Look at what is before your eyes [Τὰ κατὰ πρόσωπον βλέπετε]': the claims of the afflicted apostle and his beleaguered converts to be 'of the Messiah' are second to none (2 Cor. 10.7a; cf. Gal. 3.1).[67] The broad comparison with the situation in Antioch is instructive: Paul's conformity to the power-in-weakness of Christ compels him to contend for the gospel and his converts now under attack due to Peter's movement towards Jewish(-Christian) superiority, and to do so κατὰ πρόσωπον even if this entails his own Christ-like public humiliation. For the martyr-like Paul, such is the setting of his confrontation with Peter.

The issue at stake: God's covenantal faithfulness in Messiah Jesus

Paul intervened and publicly accused Peter when it became clear that the manner and direction of his conduct – and that of those under his influence – was at variance with the truth of the gospel. The biblical *hapax legomenon* ὀρθοποδέω has been variously taken as indicating that Peter's action was not straightforward, upright, orthodox or advancing him in the direction of the truth of the gospel.[68] However, further precision may be obtained when it is noted that in the LXX the cognate adjective ὀρθός can refer to wise persons

---

[66] A term thematic for 4 Maccabees as noted in our discussion of this text in chapter two.

[67] Paul is resolved to abase himself on behalf of his converts, this being the outworking of the 'truth of Christ in [him]' (2 Cor. 11.7, 10), so that he might 'cut off' (ἐκκόπτω) opportunity for the competing but inequitable claims of others (cf. Gal. 5.7, 13).

[68] Cf. BAGD, p. 580; *TDNT* 5, pp. 449–51; Mußner, *Galatians*, pp. 143–4.

who, by their words and/or actions, are '(up)right' or 'righteous', even when hindered by those who act in a converse manner.[69] A significant case in point is the martyr Eleazar who, even under torture, 'kept his reason upright [ὀρθός] and unswerving' (4 Macc. 6.7). From this it may be inferred that Peter's failure to 'walk-ὀρθός' further attests to his failure to remain wise and righteous in the face of pressure to do otherwise.

Peter ought to have been conducting himself according to 'the truth of the gospel'.[70] Betz remarks that this expression 'is peculiar' and itemizes various definitions offered by commentators: the 'true gospel' versus the 'false gospel' (Bultmann); 'the real consequences of the gospel' (Schlier); 'the logic of the gospel' (Mußner); or, Betz's own preference, the 'integrity of the gospel' (Lightfoot, Burton).[71] However, all of these interpretations fail to take sufficient account of the Jewish conception of 'truth' which is here messianically recast by Paul. With respect to the Jewish background, the LXX regularly employs ἀλήθεια to render the Hebrew antecedent אמת, meaning 'truth, faithfulness', not least in relation to God's own faithfulness and the reciprocal faithfulness of those in covenant relation with him.[72] It is this which was catastrophically overthrown by Antiochus IV Epiphanes' attack upon Israel's Temple-focused and Torah-based way of life, its devastating impact described as 'truth [אמת, δικαιοσύνη]' being 'cast down to the ground' (Dan. 8.12). This situation could only be rectified by errant Israel returning to God's 'truth' – אמת (MT), δικαιοσύνη (LXX), ἀλήθεια (Th.); that is, by reciprocating the love and faithfulness so characteristic of God himself and of his covenant relationship with his people (Dan. 9.13).[73]

For Paul the truth of gospel centres upon God's love and faithfulness as now manifested in Messiah Jesus and his followers. Thus, for example, his statement that 'the truth of Christ is in me [ἔστιν ἀλήθεια Χριστοῦ ἐν ἐμοί]' attests to the fact that the faithful self-sacrifice of Christ is replicated in his own self-abasement on behalf of others (cf. 2 Cor. 11.7, 10a). Similarly, his ensuing claim that he

---

[69] Especially in Proverbs, e.g., 4.11, 25–7; 11.6; 12.6; 21.8.
[70] See Martyn, *Galatians*, p. 234 n. 95.
[71] Betz, *Galatians*, p. 92.
[72] Cf. *TDOT* 1.309–16; *TDNT* 1.241–7.
[73] Note also the discussion at pp. 80–3 concerning the contests between the martyrs and Antiochus IV Epiphanes in 4 Maccabees as a creation-wide battle for the truth that is the Jewish way of life.

and his companions 'cannot do anything against the truth, but only for the truth' has in view the 'power-in-weakness' of Christ selflessly and faithfully lived out in his own life and ministry amongst his converts (2 Cor. 13.3–4, 8). It is this 'truth of the gospel' which Peter's conduct has undermined. In his regression towards matters Jewish he has completely misconstrued the advantages of being a Jew by failing to conform his life to the outworking of God's truth – his covenant faithfulness – in Jesus the Messiah and his people.[74]

Paul's accusation

In Paul's estimation, Peter's withdrawal from table-fellowship has entailed a confusion of categories, a reversion to an erroneous understanding of God's people as being demarcated by Torah-obedience rather than Christ-like faithfulness. This comes to the fore in his climactic and public accusation at Galatians 2.14c,d:

> If you, a Jew, live as a Gentile and not as a Jew, how can you compel the Gentiles to Judaize?
>
> Εἰ σὺ Ἰουδαῖος ὑπάρχων ἐθνικῶς καὶ οὐχὶ Ἰουδαϊκῶς ζῇς, πῶς τὰ ἔθνη ἀναγκάζεις Ἰουδαΐζειν;

Combining some very difficult terminology[75] this highly rhetorical question, both in part and as a whole, must be interpreted with due attention to the immediate context.[76] Thus, for example, while Ἰουδαῖος itself regularly denotes a Jew by birth, upbringing and practice, in virtue of its linear qualification by ὑπάρχων ἐθνικῶς καὶ οὐχὶ Ἰουδαϊκῶς ζῇς, here it seems to refer to Peter's status as a Jew by birth and upbringing only. That is, at least until recently, Peter's current practice had in fact been to live ἐθνικῶς, clearly not as a pagan *per se*, but rather as one now participating in table-fellowship with Gentile Christians.[77] Thus he did not live Ἰουδαϊκῶς; not as

---

[74] Gal. 5.6–12; cf. Rom. 3.1–8. Note also Eph. 1.3–12; 2 Thess. 2.13–14; Col. 1.3–8.

[75] Including three New Testament *hapax legomena*: ἐθνικῶς, Ἰουδαϊκῶς and Ἰουδαΐζειν.

[76] Paul may well be appropriating the rhetoric of '*intra*-Jewish polemic, of Jewish factionalism' traceable throughout the Maccabean and post-Maccabean period (so Dunn, 'Echoes of Intra-Jewish Polemic', p. 128), as is the more apparent at Gal. 2.15.

[77] Again, while ἐθνικῶς may echo a Jewish(-Christian) charge of paganism against Peter, Paul's accusation appropriates the term in reference to his (former) association with Gentile *Christians* (this being consonant with τὰ ἔθνη which denotes not simply Gentiles but the Antiochene Gentile Christians).

one denying his Jewish heritage, but rather as a Jewish Christian whose table-fellowship practices did not preclude association with Gentile Christians.

It is therefore evident that Paul's unstated lowest common denominator throughout is not 'Jew' or 'Gentile' – the categories still employed by his Jewish(-Christian) opponents – but rather 'Christian'. His fundamental concern is that Peter is engaged in a category shift from 'Christian' (one conformed to Messiah Jesus and his people, both Jew and Gentile) to 'Jew' (one conformed to Torah and Israel). It suggests a reversion towards the life 'in Judaism' once so zealously pursued by Paul himself (Gal. 1.13–14; cf. 2 Macc. 8.2), but since superseded by God's revelation of the Son of God in him.

Furthermore, such is Peter's status that his action so impinges upon the Antiochene Gentile Christians that they are effectively now being compelled to Judaize, that is, to move in the direction of a Jewish way of life.[78] That this may have included a demand (at least from certain quarters) for circumcision, seems possible on the cumulative weight of the available evidence: the use of Ἰουδαΐζειν and its cognates elsewhere;[79] the fact that Peter's conduct was motivated by fear of οἱ ἐκ περιτομῆς (cf. EstherLXX 8.17); and the terms of the analogous coercion in Jerusalem (Gal. 2.3–5) and Galatia (Gal. 6.12).

In any event, both the complexity and significance of the Judaizing within the Antiochene community is the more clearly seen when Peter's 'compelling' is viewed in relation to the thematic usage of the verb ἀναγκάζω in 2 and 4 Maccabees in connection with the enforced Hellenization of the Jews. Jewish martyrs suffered torment and death from the Gentiles rather than be compelled to eat defiling foods and thereby forsake their Jewish way of life.[80] Peter, however, fearing reprisal from fellow Jews, instead withdraws from mixed table-fellowship, and so undermines Christ and his people. The

---

[78] Like Paul, Ignatius of Antioch would later regard judaizing as incompatible with conformity to Jesus Christ, inasmuch as Judaism (Ἰουδαϊσμός) and Christianity (Χριστιανισμός) were mutually exclusive (Ign., *Magn.* 10.3).

[79] Dunn, *Jesus, Paul and the Law*, pp. 149–50, 154 (see also *Galatians*, p. 129), may overstate any latitude inherent in the Jewish usage of Ἰουδαΐζειν as denoting 'the range of possible degrees of assimilation to Jewish customs, with circumcision as the [optional] endpoint'. He stresses *J.W.* 2.454 and 462–3, while depreciating EstherLXX 8.17 (where Judaizing and circumcision could be mutually reinforcing), and ignoring the significant usage of the cognate Ἰουδαϊσμός in 2 and 4 Maccabees (especially 4 Macc. 4.23–6) where martyrdom for Judaism and circumcision are one and the same.

[80] 2 Macc. 6.1, 7, 18; 7.1; 4 Macc. 4.26; 5.2, 27; 18.5.

irony is compounded in that while Peter may have been compelled towards his action by appeals to the zeal of the Maccabean martyrs, from Paul's standpoint he thus risks taking on the role of the (Jewish) oppressor (of Gentiles) rather than the (Christian) martyr figure – a part played by the Jerusalem false brethren and Galatian Agitators.

Paul's verdict

This being the case, Paul's verdict that Peter 'stood condemned' must be allowed its full breadth and depth. It is not simply condemnation – whether by himself and/or others – which arises out of the inconsistency of his actions.[81] Rather it concerns his condemnation before God (and thereby God's people),[82] and this demands repentance and reconciliation in order to avert eschatological judgement. Indeed the full force and function of Paul's pronouncement comes in view as we now consider both the judicial aspect of the term itself and the theological (and christological) framework within which Paul assesses the incident in question.

Some indication of the judicial aspect of the verb καταγιγνώσκω as applied within the context of the Antioch incident may be suggested by reference to its nearest LXX analogue at Deuteronomy 25.1–3:

> If there is a dispute between [two] men, and they come into court, and the judges decide between them, acquitting the innocent and condemning the guilty [δικαιώσωσιν τὸν δίκαιον καὶ καταγνῶσιν τοῦ ἀσεβοῦς], then if the guilty man deserves [ἄξιος] to be beaten, the judge shall cause him to lie down and be beaten in his presence with a number of stripes in proportion to his offence. Forty stripes may be given him, but not more; lest, if one should go on to beat him with more stripes than these, your brother be degraded in your sight.[83]

---

[81] So Lightfoot, *Saint Paul's Epistle to the Galatians*, p. 111; Burton, *Galatians*, p. 103; Bruce, *Galatians*, p. 129, et al.; cf. 1 John 3.20.
[82] Cf. Mußner, *Der Galaterbrief*, p. 135 n. 11; R. N. Longenecker, *Galatians*, p. 72.
[83] Paul regularly draws upon Deuteronomy, especially chapters 27–32, and invokes the verse immediately following this citation at 1 Cor. 9.9. Note the verb elsewhere in the LXX only at Prov. 28.11; Sir. 14.2; 19.5. On its judicial use in Josephus in relation to condemnation before God and/or a tribunal, see *J.W.* 1.635; 7.154, 327.

This text provided part of the legal justification for the synagogue-based corporal punishment of the thirty-nine stripes which was administered in cases of blasphemy and/or serious offences against Jewish customs (including those connected with food and purity).[84] Paul himself was subject to this punishment on several occasions (2 Cor. 11.23–4). Given the earlier discussion of the competing claims of the Jewish and Christian communities in Antioch (chapter four), it would seem highly likely that Jewish Christian participation in mixed table-fellowship would have involved a strained relationship with – if not a complete break from – their local synagogue(s). It is thus conceivable that Peter's withdrawal under fear of adversity included a concern that he (like Paul) could have been charged with Torah violation, condemned as guilty before God, and punished (disciplined) with the thirty-nine stripes.[85] Certainly Peter's fellow Jews could have added force to their castigation of his unworthy mixed table-fellowship by citing the worthy Eleazar. This exemplary Jew endured scourging and even martyrdom rather than eat defiling foods, bearing the weight of divine discipline upon Israel (2 Macc. 6.12–7.31).[86]

Paul, however, appropriates the language of the synagogue law court within a decidedly God-in-Christ rather than God-in-Torah/Israel frame of reference. By not remaining faithful to the Righteous One and his people – even if under the threat of adversity – Peter is guilty and subject to the condemnation of God. Indeed, his unworthy withdrawal from table-fellowship constituted a fundamental failure to 'discern the body' – to conform to the cruciform outworking of God's will for his people, Jew and Gentile alike – and in this way he stands under God's condemnation (cf. 1 Cor. 11.27–9). This takes the immediate form of Paul's public critique, which may also have been an attempt to address and (if possible) redress the debilitating impact of Peter's conduct upon the Christian community and the cause of Christ in Antioch. Whether or not this was successful, from the standpoint of his conformity to Christ, Paul would have seen himself as the faithful prophet-martyr whose ultimate vindication would ensue.

---

[84] See Pobee, *Persecution and Martyrdom*, p. 8; Harvey, 'Forty Strokes Save One', p. 84.
[85] So Harvey, 'Forty Strokes Save One', p. 85.
[86] Note the use of ἄξιος and the combination of μαστιγόω and πληγή (2 Macc. 6.23–7, 29–30). See also the divine 'scourging/disciplining' of Heliodorus (2 Macc. 3.26, 34, 38) and Antiochus IV Epiphanes (2 Macc. 9.5).

5. Conclusion

In part and in whole, the nature and significance of the Antioch incident gains clarity and force when viewed in relation to a Maccabean martyr tradition which, as understood by Paul, had since been superseded by conformity to Christ. From a Jewish and, in certain instances, Jewish Christian standpoint, the entire adversarial context would have evoked memories of the Maccabean martyrs' contest against the Gentile enemy who threatened the Jewish way of life. Thus Peter's withdrawal from mixed table-fellowship could have been construed as being loyal to all that the martyrs exemplified and for which they died.

However, Paul's Christ-governed perspective viewed matters differently. Peter's withdrawal represented a failure of faith which threatened the truth of the gospel and so had to be countered by Paul's own martyr-like stance. Its immediate consequence was already evident: Gentiles were being persuaded to displace Christ with an unnecessary, divisive and potentially apostate commitment to a Judaism which Paul himself had left behind. Indeed, at risk was inclusive commensality with the now exalted eschatological redeemer within the already inaugurated kingdom of God. In essence, this was an assault on the grace of God as revealed in the crucified and risen Jesus, and in those living in him. It is this matter which Paul now addresses in his theological reflections upon the Antioch incident in Galatians 2.15–21.

6

PAUL AND THE CRUCIFIED CHRIST IN ANTIOCH: GALATIANS 2.15–21

While it must remain an open question as to precisely where Paul's citation of his accusation against Peter in Galatians 2.14 ends, it is generally agreed that his pursuant remarks at Galatians 2.15–21 at least reflect the substance of the issues addressed during their Antioch confrontation.[1] This will be borne out in the following estimation of Paul's complex and much disputed line of argumentation which, both in terms of its underlying theological framework and key constituent features, may also be the more clearly comprehended when viewed as a dramatic reworking of a Maccabean martyr model of Judaism. It is not feasible to itemize at the outset every aspect of what will prove to be an intricate summoning of various lines of evidence. However, it will prove useful if the overall shape and substance of the ensuing interpretation is briefly set forth in advance.

Paul continues to remonstrate against the position taken by Peter in Antioch by ironically appropriating a piece of intra-Jewish polemic espousing Jewish superiority over Gentiles (Gal. 2.15), which he immediately relativizes by locating it within his decidedly christological understanding of the people of God (Gal. 2.16). That is, he reminds Peter of what he already knows: a person's covenant membership – and hence vindication before God – is not a function of adherence to 'the works of the law' and the way of life they represent, but of conformity to the faithfulness of Jesus the Messiah. Paul then echoes the objection of those in Antioch (and elsewhere) who hold an antithetical position, namely, that those who seek to be God's covenant people in virtue of their incorporation into Messiah

---

[1] Among those variously espousing this majority position, see Bruce, *Galatians*, p. 136; Mußner, *Der Galaterbrief*, p. 135. Such a view does not prejudice the obvious applicability of Gal. 2.15–21 to the current, and broadly analogous, situation in Galatia to which Paul returns directly at Gal. 3.1: 'O foolish Galatians!' (see Martyn, *Galatians*, pp. 229–30).

Jesus are in fact sinners; indeed the Messiah (Jesus) is himself a servant of sin. Paul immediately and emphatically denies any such claim (Gal. 2.17).

At this point Paul proceeds to offer both a negative and a more positive explanation for his denial. First, he counter-claims that in fact anyone (even Peter in Antioch) who rebuilds a dismantled Judaism proves to be a transgressor, that is, one who is found to be in an 'Israel-in-Adam' condition and thus a servant of sin (Gal. 2.18). Such a regression is all the more unconscionable in that, through Israel's conformity to the Messiah's διὰ νόμου death to that very condition, Israel-in-Adam may become Israel-in-Christ, and thereby even now live within the already inaugurated reign of God (Gal. 2.19; cf. Rom. 7.1–8.11). Indeed, Paul's own transformation and conformity to God's love and faithfulness in the (now exalted) Son of God in him, offers an exemplary case in point (Gal. 2.19–20). The implication is that far from being a servant of sin, the Messiah (and his people) is the servant of God's deliverance and reconciliation: the eschatological redeemer of Israel (and the world). That being the case, Paul does not set aside this gracious act of God (Gal. 2.21a). Indeed, if, as Peter's conduct implies, covenant life was a function of a διὰ νόμου existence, then the Messiah's death would have been in vain (Gal. 2.21b).

1. Paul's remonstration: an ironical use of intra-Jewish polemic (Gal. 2.15)

In keeping with the contentious issues raised by the mixed Antiochene table-fellowship, Paul's pursuant argument takes as its point of departure a piece of polemic often directed by Jews against Jewish apostates: 'We by nature Jews and not from Gentile sinners ['Ημεῖς φύσει 'Ιουδαῖοι καὶ οὐκ ἐξ ἐθνῶν ἁμαρτωλοί]' (Gal. 2.15). At least two notable aspects of this statement merit comment.

First, its initial stress is upon that which was of fundamental importance to devout Jews, namely, that they were Jews '*by nature* [φύσει]'. It has rightly been noted that this phrase refers to their privileged birth, heritage and upbringing as members of the nation of Israel.[2] Indeed, the analysis of 4 Maccabees in chapter two also

---

[2] BAGD, p. 869, mg.1, refers to 'natural endowment or condition, inherited [from] one's ancestors'; cf. *TDNT* 9, p. 272. Its apposition with ἐξ ἐθνῶν ἁμαρτωλοί suggests that φύσει 'Ιουδαῖοι is tantamount to οἱ ἐξ 'Ισραήλ (Rom. 9.6b).

observed a belief in what might be termed a nature/Torah-nurture fusion. That is, Israel's Creator God had ensured that instruction in Torah (not least the food laws) conformed both (i) to the very being of the Jewish people, enabling such virtues as courage, justice and piety (4 Macc. 5.22–6; cf. 5.8–9),[3] and (ii) to their natural lineage from Abraham, this effecting a brotherly love willing to endure suffering and even martyrdom (4 Macc. 13.19–27).[4] Thus, the assertion 'we, by nature Jews' lays claim to membership within an Israel in whom God's creational and covenantal purposes are ideally brought together, with Torah-obedience in affliction a major index of one's inclusion amongst the children of Abraham.[5]

Second, conversely, 'Jews by nature' are not 'from among Gentile sinners'. The Jews readily viewed Gentiles as *de facto* 'sinners' in virtue of their lawless standing outside God's covenant people Israel.[6] By definition 'Gentiles [were] those not pursuing the righteousness effected by Torah-obedience' (Rom. 9.30b). Additionally, however, Torah-faithful Jews could also (as here) apply this designation to fellow Jews whom they deemed to be apostate. A notable case in point is the castigation of the Jewish Hellenizers during the Maccabean crisis as 'lawless' and 'sinners' (1 Macc. 1.34; 2.44, 48).[7] It is likely, then, that Paul is echoing the language of his Jewish(-Christian) detractors, possibly οἱ ἐκ περιτομῆς. They regarded the mixed Antiochene table-fellowship as rendering its Jewish Christian participants tantamount to 'Gentile sinners' (cf. Gal. 2.17a). Hence they required withdrawal therefrom and, further, that any Gentiles who wished to remain in association with their Jewish Christian brethren must 'Judaize'.[8]

---

[3] Such is the exemplary conduct of the martyred brothers that they are lauded as the very embodiment of Torah-generated 'reason' (4 Macc. 14.2).

[4] Note the Maccabean mother's 'natural' (parental) love of her seven sons (4 Macc. 15.13, 25; 16.3), and how this undergirded rather than undermined her fortitude in the face of their deaths, indicating that she too was 'of the same mind as Abraham' (4 Macc. 14.20).

[5] Recall the use of the designation οἱ Ἀβραμιαῖοι παῖδες at 4 Macc. 18.23.

[6] 1 Sam. 15.18; Ps. 9.18[17]; *Jub.* 23.23–4; 24.28 (Barclay, *Obeying the Truth*, p. 77 n. 7, notes the corollary at 22.16, 'do not eat with them'); *Pss. Sol.* 2.1–2; 4 Ezra 4.23; Matt. 5.47/Luke 6.33.

[7] For evidence of an increasingly intra-Jewish usage of the term in the post-Maccabean period, see Dunn, 'What Was the Real Issue Between Paul and "Those of the Circumcision"?', pp. 74–7; *The Partings of the Ways*, pp. 102–7; and 'Echoes of Intra-Jewish Polemic', pp. 462–3.

[8] This reading renders unnecessary and unfounded the syntactical arrangements of Gal. 2.15 proposed by Neitzel, 'Zur Interpretation von Galater 2.11–21', p. 18 ('we Jews by birth and not Gentiles, sinners') and Suhl, 'Der Galaterbrief-Situation',

That being the case, Paul is clearly appropriating this claim somewhat ironically and dismissively, *not* as a conciliatory means of establishing certain common ground between himself and advocates of such a position.[9] Indeed, as was readily apparent from the earlier estimation of the conceptual framework governing Galatians, and is especially clear at Romans 1–3, for Paul any privileged Jewish claim to the mutually exclusive categories of 'Jew' and 'Gentile [sinner]' is completely relativized by the fact that both are in need of rescue from Adamic sin by God-in-Christ. So, for example, whenever Gentiles who do not have Torah φύσει,[10] nevertheless do what Torah seeks to evoke, they are Torah (Rom. 2.14).[11] Conversely, the falsehood of the Jew, notwithstanding the fact that it (paradoxically) attests to God's truth/faithfulness, renders him as much a 'sinner' outside the covenant people of God as any Gentile (Rom. 3.7).[12]

Therefore, Paul's echo of this Jewish(-Christian) polemic at Galatians 2.15 is itself polemical. As Galatians 2.16 will confirm, in remonstrating with Peter and those Jewish Christians who have withdrawn from the mixed Antiochene table-fellowship, he acknowledges only to dismiss the exclusivist claims of his fellow Jews. From this standpoint, the initial 'we' may be seen as functioning somewhat ambiguously as a reference both (i) to Paul's Jewish(-Christian) detractors as the authors of the self-claim being made, and (ii) to Paul, Peter and other Jewish Christians in Antioch who, as Jews-become-Christians, ought to be able to recognize and

---

p. 3103, ('we, Jews by birth and not Gentiles, sinners'). However, as will be seen below, the common conviction motivating their similar proposals – that *Paul* the Jewish *Christian* would never say that Jews could not be numbered amongst sinful humanity – remains valid.

[9] Contra Dunn, *Galatians*, p. 133.

[10] Taking φύσει with the antecedent ἔθνη τὰ μὴ νόμον ἔχοντα (with Cranfield, *Romans*, pp. 156–7, contra Dunn, *Romans*, pp. 98–9), thereby avoiding any suggestion of naturally good people which would undermine the whole argument of Romans 1–3.

[11] The Gentile's conscience is capable of arbitrating the relative merits of his own 'reasoning [λογισμός]' (Rom. 2.14–15; cf. 4 Macc. 14.2; Jas. 2.8, 12). Note also Rom. 2.27: the uncircumcised φύσει who nevertheless fulfil Torah, thereby condemn the circumcised who transgress Torah.

[12] The discontented Jewish interlocutor's ensuing *reductio ad absurdum* – 'why not do evil that good may come?' (Rom. 3.8) – may echo charges of blasphemy levelled by Jews against Paul himself for his ready acceptance of Gentiles in Christ without insisting on their adherence to matters Jewish.

reject any such claim as erroneous, knowing that they have instead since conformed themselves to Jesus Christ.[13]

2. Paul's remonstration. The vindication of the righteous: the 'works of the law' versus the faithfulness of the Messiah (Gal. 2.16)

Paul now presses this matter by relativizing all Jewish(-Christian) claims to privileged status as God's covenant people by immediately locating this within a christological frame of reference: justification is effected not by 'works of the law' but by Jesus Christ (Gal. 2.16). Before offering a detailed exegesis of the complex statements comprising this verse, it is first necessary to outline briefly something of the wider theological framework which it presupposes. Here, drawing especially (but not exclusively) upon evidence summoned in the course of the earlier evaluation of the conceptual frameworks governing (a) the Maccabean model of Judaism, particularly that of Daniel 7–12 and related texts (see chapter one), and (b) Galatians as a whole (see chapter three), I shall briefly set forth the evidence for an overall understanding of Paul's remark in terms of its main constituents: (i) the verb δικαιόω; (ii) the expression 'works of the law [ἔργα νόμου]'; and (iii) the phrase πίστις Ἰησοῦ Χριστοῦ. It will be seen that Paul is contending that justification, God's righteous declaration that a person (Jew or Gentile)[14] is a member of his true covenant people, is determined and demarcated not by adherence to Torah requirements and a Jewish way of life, but by conformity to the faithfulness of Messiah Jesus.

Justification, the 'works of the law', and πίστις Ἰησοῦ Χριστοῦ

The threefold use of the verb δικαιόω at Galatians 2.16 is a function of the δικ- terminology now widely recognized as fundamentally constitutive of Pauline theology in general and the arguments of

---

[13] It is thus possible that the textually uncertain [δέ] at the beginning of Gal. 2.16 has been added to render (ii) the more apparent.

[14] Without discounting their applicability to Gentiles, Paul's remarks are directed specifically at *Jewish* Christians (not least Peter); this is already evident from his line of argument thus far (especially Gal. 2.14–15) and will be become increasingly apparent from what follows.

Galatians and Romans in particular,[15] and whose determinative over-arching concept is δικαιοσύνη θεοῦ: 'the righteousness of God'.[16] This expression has itself of course been the subject of much debate with, at risk of oversimplification, three main interpretative options currently available.[17] (i) Bultmann held that δικαιοσύνη θεοῦ referred to the status of righteousness reckoned to human beings by a gracious God.[18] However, this view has justifiably been criticized for its highly anthropocentric and individualistic (as compared to a theocentric and apocalyptic) perspective, attributable in large part to its failure to take full account of Paul's Jewish (especially OT) background.[19] (ii) Conversely, Käsemann maintained that the phrase denoted God's dynamic and relational 'salvation-creating power'.[20] While rightly emphasizing the important bearing of Jewish apocalyptic, Käsemann also dubiously insisted that δικαιοσύνη θεοῦ was a technical term which had left behind its Jewish covenantal context. (iii) It is precisely this element which has been stressed by N. T. Wright, who has argued that δικαιοσύνη θεοῦ concerns God's own righteousness, the covenant faithfulness of (Israel's) God.[21]

The last-noted interpretation finds support in biblical and Second

[15] In Galatians, cf. the verb δικαιόω (Gal. 2.16, 17; 3.8, 11, 24); the noun δικαιοσύνη (Gal. 2.21; 3.6, 21; 5.5); and the adjective δίκαιος (Gal. 3.11). Key clusters of δικ- terminology in Romans include 1.17; 3.21–31; 4.3–13; 6.13–20; 9.30–10.10, with this letter also containing other significant cognates. The ever-expanding bibliography on this subject is well represented in Seifrid, *Justification by Faith*; note also Dunn, *The Theology of Paul the Apostle*, pp. 334–5.

[16] Rom. 1.17; 3.21–6; 10.3; cf. 2 Cor. 5.21; Phil. 3.9.

[17] Cf. especially the surveys in Müller, *Gottes Gerechtigkeit und Gottes Volk*, pp. 5–27; Stuhlmacher, *Gerechtigkeit Gottes bei Paulus*, pp. 11–73; Brauch, 'Perspectives on "God's Righteousness"', pp. 523–42; and Campbell, *The Rhetoric of Righteousness*, pp. 139–56.

[18] Here θεοῦ is taken as a genitive of origin, and δικαιοσύνη as that received by humanity as a gift from God. See Bultmann, *Theology*, vol. I, pp. 270–85; Conzelmann, *Theology*, pp. 218–20; Bornkamm, *Paul*, pp. 135–56; and Cranfield, *Romans*, pp. 92–9.

[19] The seminal critique of Bultmann's position is Käsemann's 1961 paper published in *New Testament Questions of Today*, pp. 168–82; note the response of Bultmann, 'ΔΙΚΑΙΟΣΥΝΗ ΘΕΟΥ'.

[20] Thus θεοῦ is taken as a subjective genitive, and δικαιοσύνη as God's saving activity in the world. See Käsemann, *New Testament Questions of Today*, pp. 168–82; Stuhlmacher, *Gerechtigkeit Gottes bei Paulus*, pp. 74–101.

[21] This takes θεοῦ as a possessive genitive, and δικαιουσύνη as God's faithfulness to his covenant with Israel. See N. T. Wright, 'The Messiah and the People of God', pp. 57–85; 'Romans and the Theology of Paul'; 'On Becoming the Righteousness of God'. Cf. Dunn, *Romans*, pp. 40–2; *The Theology of Paul the Apostle*, pp. 340–6.

Temple Judaism where the ever-present concern of God's faithfulness (צדק/צדקה, 'righteousness') to his covenant promises to Israel is a dominant motif.[22] This is particularly true in reference to times of crisis such as the tensions attending the return from the Babylonian exile, the Maccabean revolt and the Roman destruction of Jerusalem. A recurrent theme is that despite all appearances God will not forsake Israel but, after disciplining and delaying to allow time for repentance, he will act to inaugurate a glorious new Israel-centred kingdom. In the interim his people must themselves be 'righteous [δίκαιος]'; that is, even in the midst of suffering, they must remain faithful members of the covenant community – retain their 'righteousness [δικαιοσύνη]' – by remaining obedient to Torah and all that comprises the Jewish way of life, assured that their divine vindication will ensue.

Just such an understanding was evident at various junctures in the earlier reconstruction of Maccabean martyrdom. Thus, it was God's sovereign rule and covenantal faithfulness which came under attack when 'truth [אמת, δικαιοσύνη] was cast down to the ground' during the Maccabean crisis (Dan.MT/LXX 8.12). God's truth could only be restored when Israel reciprocated his covenant love and faithfulness, even if this entailed suffering and martyrdom. In this way the nation would atone for sin, experience divine deliverance and enjoy lasting vindication – the most potent symbol of this ultimate end being the Danielic vision of the exalted 'one like a son of man'. Indeed, the eschatological realization of God's righteousness/truth also figured prominently in those texts and traditions variously indebted to Daniel's human-like figure. Thus, God would rescue his afflicted people and initiate a kingdom characterized by peace and truth (so 4Q246); and, notwithstanding Israel's devastation by those devoid of truth/righteousness, God's covenant faithfulness would eventually be realized through Israel's eschatological redeemer (so 4 Ezra 6.55–9; 11–13). Likewise, first-century texts in the Maccabean tradition also shared this vision, notably 4 Maccabees with its martyr figures who lived in accordance 'with the truth', and thus gained the 'immortal victory' whereby they 'lived to God' (4 Macc. 6.16–18; 7.3, 19; 16.25).

---

[22] See the discussion in N. T. Wright, *The New Testament and the People of God*, pp. 271–2, citing *inter alia* Ezra 9.6–15; Neh. 9.6–38; Dan. 7; 9.3–19; Tob. 3.1–6, 13–14; *2 Apoc. Bar.*; and 4 Ezra.

As one in the tradition of the Maccabees the zealous Pharisee Paul had also vigorously upheld this ideal until God's dramatic disclosure of the risen Jesus, the exalted Son of God revealed 'in him' (Gal. 1.13–16). Thereafter, at the very heart of his conceptual framework was the conviction that God's righteousness had been finally manifested through Jesus Christ. Perhaps Paul's most compelling single statement of this view is to be found in Romans 3.21–6, a text having a traditio-historical background in Maccabean martyr texts (see chapter two). The eschatological outworking of God's covenant faithfulness and Israel's ultimate vindication (her justification) could not be brought about through martyr-like adherence to a Torah-based Jewish way of life, but only through the martyrdom and exaltation of her (unexpected) eschatological redeemer, Messiah Jesus. This is the 'truth of the gospel' which Paul proclaimed throughout his much afflicted apostolic ministry, whether in Jerusalem, Galatia or, as here, in Antioch (cf. Gal. 2.4, 14; 4.16; 5.7).

It is the incapacity of Torah-based Judaism to realize justification which underlies Paul's dismissal of the 'works of the law [ἔργα νόμου]'.[23] As is well known, the long-standing and variously articulated interpretation of this expression is that it denoted 'the way in which Jews attempted to earn salvation', and that Paul soundly rejected this because of its intrinsically legalistic outlook and/or the incapacity of sinful human beings to fulfil Torah.[24] However, this view has been challenged by reference to the Jewish covenantal context that has just been outlined, on which basis it is argued that the expression instead denotes 'the way in which Jews demonstrate themselves to be Jews'. That is, in virtue of Torah-obedience as lived out in the observance of such essential requirements as strict table-fellowship, circumcision, sabbath, and so forth,

---

[23] This expression occurs in Paul only at Gal. 2.16; 3.2, 5, 10; Rom. 3.20, 28; cf. τὸ ἔργον τοῦ νόμου (singular) at Rom. 2.15, probably denoting that which the law seeks to evoke.

[24] See the succinct summary of this position and its representative proponents in Schreiner, 'Works of the Law in Paul', pp. 218–20; see also his *The Law and Its Fulfillment*, pp. 41–71. On the vast and ever expanding literature concerning Paul and the law, see the bibliography in Dunn (ed.), *Paul and the Mosaic Law*, pp. 335–41; Westerholm's earlier *Israel's Law and the Church's Faith*; and the recent brief engagement with a limited but representative range of studies in Witherington, *Grace in Galatia*, pp. 341–57.

Jews both attest to and maintain their status as worthy members of the covenant people of God.[25]

This evaluation clearly fits well with the estimation of Maccabean martyrdom, the Galatian crisis and the immediate scenario in view in Antioch on offer here. Thus, the Maccabean martyrs' steadfast adherence to food laws, circumcision, sabbath observance, and suchlike, was regarded as both a witness to and assurance of their eventual vindication as God's true people. In Galatia, the Jewish(-Christian) Agitators were seeking to persuade Paul's converts to adopt circumcision and Jewish calendric practices, indeed, all 'works of the law' which represented a move towards a Jewish pattern of life (cf. Gal. 3.2, 5; 4.9–10; 5.3). Similarly, in Antioch, recourse to a strict Jewish table-fellowship (and possibly circumcision) entailed 'works of the law' tantamount to 'living Jewishly' (Gal. 2.11–14).

As will become increasingly evident from the ensuing exegesis of Galatians 2.17–20, Paul's (implicit) critique of the 'works of the law' was *not* that the Torah was bad, nor that the desire to obey it was misguided, nor even that a lifestyle of Torah-obedience (if and when properly executed) was necessarily without any value. Nor, as some proponents of the 'new perspective' have suggested, was it simply the fact that such practices raised a barrier between Jews and Gentiles and/or exhibited a debilitating Israel-focused 'nationalist righteousness'. Although these last two considerations do indeed represent part of Paul's concern, they were but symptomatic of, and only served to perpetuate, a much more deep-seated problem. For Paul, the (re)adoption of the 'works of the law', and of a life 'in Judaism', involved putting oneself 'under the law'. From its usage in Galatians and Romans it is clear that this phrase is shorthand for more than simply Israel's Torah-based way of life. Rather, in virtue of its conceptual alignment with cognate expressions such as 'under a curse' (Gal. 3.10), 'under the elemental spirits of the universe' (Gal. 4.3), and 'under sin' (Rom. 3.9; 7.14), and its direct contrast with

---

[25] For this so-called 'new perspective' upon Paul's view of the 'works of the law', note especially the several studies by Dunn, including *Jesus, Paul and the Law*, pp. 183–214; *The Partings of the Ways*, pp. 117–39; '4QMMT and Galatians'; and *The Theology of Paul the Apostle*, pp. 354–66. See also Abegg, 'Paul, "Works of the Law" and MMT'. For various objections raised against this position, see Cranfield, 'The Works of the Law' (and Dunn's, 'Yet Once More'); Schreiner, 'Works of the Law in Paul'; *The Law and Its Fulfillment*, pp. 41–71.

'under grace' (Rom. 6.14, 15), it takes on much darker overtones. That is, from Paul's God-in-Christ standpoint, life 'under [the curse of] the law' meant that Israel was both bound by but unable to obey Torah and thus incurred its condemnation rather than its blessing, and this was attributable to the fact that Israel (no less than the Gentiles) was given over to the old age/sphere of Adamic sin. Thus, to pursue the 'works of the law' was to exacerbate this most fundamental problem – and, indeed, to undermine its only solution: justification διὰ πίστεως Ἰησοῦ Χριστοῦ.

The precise and paradoxical means whereby justification came about διὰ πίστεως Ἰησοῦ Χριστοῦ will likewise only emerge from the pursuant exegesis of Galatians 2.17–20. At this stage I shall focus upon two important and related considerations: the meaning of 'Jesus *Christ* [Χριστός]', and the significance attached thereto when predicated by 'faith [πίστις]'. First, with respect to Χριστός, contrary to the current (but perhaps now changing) consensus, it may be argued that for Paul this term (a) retains the titular sense of Israel's 'Messiah' and (b) that much of its import resides in its representative and incorporative aspects.[26] Evidence in support of the existence of these inextricably interrelated features may be briefly itemized by drawing upon the most salient of the earlier conclusions concerning the Danielic 'one like a son of man' and related traditions (chapter one), and Paul's christological conceptual framework (chapter three), together with his use of the term Χριστός in Galatians and additional Antioch-specific considerations.

(i) Although still the subject of much debate, a strong case can be made that Daniel's 'one like a son of man' has in view Israel's Messiah, one fulfilling the Davidic promises.

(ii) Certainly there is evidence of a trajectory of Jewish exegesis spanning the period from the Maccabean crisis to the fall of Jerusalem and beyond which attests to a messianic understanding of the Danielic figure.

(iii) Through divine disclosure Paul recognized that the risen Jesus whose church he had been persecuting was in fact Israel's long-awaited (but unexpected) eschatological redeemer. Moreover, he now understood his own identity and

---

[26] The consensus position is well represented by Hengel, 'Christos in Paul', in his *Between Jesus and Paul*, pp. 65–77, 179–88, who concludes that Χριστός is not a title, but nevertheless (rightly) avers that it expresses 'the fact that the crucified Jesus and no other is the eschatological bringer of salvation', p. 77.

destiny to have been incorporated into that of the martyred and exalted Messiah/Son of God, and those likewise conformed to him. In view of this dramatic reconfiguration of Paul's former zealous life in Judaism, it would be most remarkable if his understanding and use of Χριστός in Galatians and elsewhere were not titular, representative and incorporative.

(iv) Indeed, the titular use of Χριστός is indicated by the employment of the definite article – '*the* Messiah' – at Galatians 5.24; 6.2 (cf. also Rom. 9.5; 15.3, 7; 1 Cor. 1.13; 10.4; 12.12).

(v) The representative and incorporative aspect is indicated by: (a) the possessive genitive – 'those of Christ' – at Galatians 3.29; 5.24; (b) the expression 'into Christ [εἰς Χριστόν]' at Galatians 2.16; 3.27; and (c) the phrase 'in Christ [ἐν Χριστῷ]' at Galatians 1.22; 2.4, 17; 3.14, 26, 28.[27] Much of this evidence is taken up in our ensuing analysis of εἰς Χριστόν and ἐν Χριστῷ at Galatians 2.16 and 2.17 respectively.

(vi) Additional evidence of this incorporative element in Galatians is found in the fact that its central argument (at Gal. 3–4) is that the beneficiaries of the Abrahamic promises are those 'of Christ', the sons of God whose destiny is realized through conformity to their Son of God (see especially Gal. 3.26–9; 4.1–7).

(vii) Finally, we may recall other Antioch-specific complementary evidence (from chapters four and five) which further suggests that Χριστός at Galatians 2.15–21 in particular is titular and incorporative. (a) Paul regarded the table-fellowship dispute as undermining the (mixed) Antiochene Christians' commensality with their now exalted eschatological redeemer. (b) Also at issue was who, in the midst of adversity, remained 'righteous [δίκαιος]', noteworthy in that it is possible that Paul's use of δίκαιος at Galatians 3.11 (cf. Rom. 1.17) embraces both Messiah and believer. (c) The designation Χριστιανός (Acts 11.26) may have arisen in the context of Jewish and Christian conflict over the identity of Messiah Jesus and the claims of those conformed to him that they now constituted the true people of God.

---

[27] On this estimation of these and other pertinent prepositional phrases, see N. T. Wright, *The Climax of the Covenant*, pp. 41–55; cf. 18–40; 157–74.

In sum, there is considerable reason to think that when Paul asserts that justification is διὰ πίστεως Ἰησοῦ Χριστοῦ, he is claiming that vindication as a member of God's people is in virtue of the incorporation of one's identity and destiny into *Messiah* Jesus.

All this makes it the more likely that the predicate 'faith [πίστις]' has in view the exemplary and representative role of Messiah Jesus. Indeed, the usual interpretation of the phrase πίστις Ἰησοῦ Χριστοῦ as 'faith in Jesus Christ' (an objective genitive) has recently been strongly challenged by those who would render it 'faith(fulness) of Jesus Christ' (a subjective genitive).[28] Certainly the latter position corresponds well with an estimation of Galatians 1–2 against a Maccabean background. The Maccabean martyrs were characterized by their ideal faithfulness to the point of death for Torah and Judaism, seen as a pivotal event in precipitating the outworking of God's righteousness in the form of Israel's deliverance and vindication. For Paul, however, the faithfulness (and efficacy) of the Maccabean martyr has been eclipsed by that of God in Messiah Jesus, Israel's (unexpected) eschatological redeemer (again, see especially Rom. 3.21–6).

It is, however, important to note that even the faithfulness of the martyred and exalted Jesus is but a function of the full scope of divine grace, God's overall unfolding purposes for his people. As the earlier evaluation of δικαιοσύνη θεοῦ indicates, and a later assessment of Galatians 2.20 will confirm, πίστις Ἰησοῦ Χριστοῦ is one (albeit the pivotal) element in the outworking of (a) God's covenant faithfulness (b) in Messiah Jesus' faithfulness (c) in the faithfulness of those believers conformed to him. Hence, it is likely that one or more of these elements is variously in play in Paul's use of πίστις Ἰησοῦ Χριστοῦ (and cognate phrases), with the immediate context determining the degree to which this may be the case.[29] In this par-

---

[28] Here too the literature is now considerable, with Hays (e.g., *The Faith of Jesus Christ*, 'ΠΙΣΤΙΣ and Pauline Christology') and Dunn (e.g., 'Once More ΠΙΣΤΙΣ ΧΡΙΣΤΟΥ'; *The Theology of Paul the Apostle*, pp. 371–85) and their lively interaction representative of the subjective and objective genitive readings respectively.

[29] This is consonant with the earlier suggestions concerning (i) an inclusive estimation of ἐξ ἀκοῆς πίστεως at Gal. 3.2, 5; (ii) 'the faith [πίστις]' as an elastic term; and (iii) ἐκ πίστεως at Gal. 3.11 as having both Messiah Jesus and the believer in view. Furthermore, (iv) it allows a mutually interpretative correlation between the designations οἱ ἐκ πίστεως (Gal. 3.7, 9) and οἱ τοῦ Χριστοῦ (Gal. 5.24; 6.2): God's promises to (faithful) Abraham are ultimately fulfilled in those whose identity and destiny is faithfully conformed to Messiah Jesus (Gal 3.22, 24), who share in the faithfulness of Messiah Jesus.

ticular instance (Gal. 2.16a,d), the faithfulness of both Jesus and the believers conformed to him is in view.[30]

In order to appreciate the full import of Paul's compressed remarks in Galatians 2.16, I have here first attempted to reconstruct something of the wider theological framework which they presuppose. By drawing upon and developing the earlier assessment of Galatians 1–2 against a Maccabean model of Judaism, we have arrived at a conclusion concerning the nature, significance and interrelation of the verse's main constituent elements. In essence, with the broad scope of divine grace in mind, Paul is asserting that a person is not deemed a member of God's vindicated covenant people (i.e., justified) through 'works of the law' and a life in Judaism which is bound up with the old age/sphere, but by means of a pattern of existence which conforms to the eschatological outworking of God's righteousness in the faithfulness of the martyred and exalted Messiah Jesus.

Paul's argument in Galatians 2.16: the vindication of the people of God

Having reconstructed its wider frame of reference, it is now possible to trace Paul's sequence of thought in Galatians 2.16 by attending in turn to each of its four key statements. In the first and second of these Paul reminds errant Jewish Christians (such as Peter) of certain fundamental facts that they already ought to know: (i) inasmuch as a person (Jew or Gentile) is not justified 'from works of the law' but only 'through the faithfulness of Jesus Christ', (ii) 'even we [Jewish Christians] believed in Christ Jesus' (Gal. 2.16a,b). Unpacking the full significance of this remonstration will demand careful attention to detail and to analogous lines of thought elsewhere in Paul (and, on occasion, other pertinent parallels).

With respect to the first statement, it may be inferred from the notable use of 'human [ἄνθρωπος]' (namely, Jew *or* Gentile) – rather than, for example, Ἰουδαῖος – that Paul has his eye upon the Antioch conflict. In particular he is noting the Jewish(-Christian) attempt to compel the Gentile Christians to Judaize on the grounds that they (like Jews) can only be justified 'from works of the law'.

---

[30] This is yet another indication of the representative and incorporative aspect of Χριστός.

Paul, however, counters that justification (now and always)[31] is only through the faithfulness of Jesus Christ, the outworking of God's covenant faithfulness for Jews and Gentiles alike through (διά) the faithfulness of the martyred and exalted Messiah Jesus – this calling forth Christ-like faithfulness in the lives of his followers.[32] There can be no middle ground on this most fundamental of issues.[33]

That this is the case is further attested in the second statement that even Jews (καὶ ἡμεῖς) such as Peter and Paul believed in Messiah Jesus. As already noted, this remark is regularly cited in support of an objective genitive rendering of πίστις Ἰησοῦ Χριστοῦ ('faith in Jesus Christ'). However, due consideration of the key expression '*into* Messiah Jesus [εἰς Χριστὸν Ἰησοῦν]' suggests that Paul has in view Jewish incorporation into and conformity to the outworking of God's righteousness in Messiah Jesus, an interpretation consonant with the covenantally contextualized subjective genitive reading of πίστις Ἰησοῦ Χριστοῦ offered above. Two classes of (interrelated) evidence may be noted by way of illustrating something of the full dimension of what is in view in Paul's statement: references in Paul and elsewhere to those who have (A) 'believed in/to' and (B) been 'baptized into' Messiah Jesus.

(A) 'Belief in/to ...'
(i) The combination of πιστεύω + εἰς Χριστόν/αὐτόν is otherwise attested in Paul's letters only in his exhortation to the Philippians that, even in the face of opposition, they live worthily of the gospel of the Messiah. 'For', he says, 'it has been granted to you on behalf of the Messiah [τὸ ὑπὲρ Χριστοῦ], not only *to believe into him* but also to suffer on behalf of him [τὸ ὑπὲρ αὐτοῦ πάσχειν], engaged in the same conflict [ἀγῶνα] which you saw in me and now hear to be in me [ἐν ἐμοί]' (Phil. 1.27–30; cf. Gal. 2.20).
(ii) Paul's polemical citation of Isaiah 53.1 at Romans 10.16b in reference to Jewish intransigence in the face of the gospel – 'Lord, who has believed what he has heard from us

---

[31] This the likely double significance of the present tense δικαιοῦται.

[32] Consonant with the use of the inclusive ἄνθρωπος, it is possible that διά indicates the breadth of the soteriological trajectory in view (Jew *and* Gentile), whereas ἐκ [πίστεως Χριστοῦ] denotes its Jewish-specific point of departure (see further the comments on Gal. 2.16c below).

[33] Clearly our whole exegesis thus far runs counter to that of Dunn, *Jesus, Paul and the Law*, p. 212; *Galatians*, pp. 134–41, which leans heavily on an exceptive (rather than adversative) reading of ἐὰν μή.

[Κύριε, τίς ἐπίστευσεν τῇ ἀκοῇ ἡμῶν]' - bears close comparison with the fact that, conversely, the Galatians *did* respond to the gospel of the crucified Messiah and received the Spirit, not 'from works of the law' but rather ἐξ ἀκοῆς πίστεως (Gal. 3.1–5).

(iii) It is noteworthy that Ignatius of Antioch later remarks, 'It is monstrous to talk of Jesus Christ and to practise Judaism ['Ιουδαΐζειν]. For Christianity did not base its faith on Judaism, but Judaism on Christianity [ὁ γὰρ Χριστιανισμὸς οὐκ εἰς Ἰουδαϊσμὸν ἐπίστευσεν, ἀλλ' Ἰουδαϊσμὸς εἰς Χριστιανισμόν] ...' (Ign., *Mag.* 10.3).[34] His fellow martyr Polycarp can exhort imitation of Christ who endured the cross that 'we might live in him [ἵνα ζήσωμεν ἐν αὐτῷ]', Christ's example being that which 'we have believed [ἡμεῖς ... ἐπιστεύσαμεν]' (Pol., *Phil.* 8.1–2).[35]

(B) 'Baptism [into]'
  (i) The correlation between believing in/to Christ, and baptism as the sign of one's incorporation into Christ and the one body thereby demarcated, may be illustrated by the following linguistically and conceptually parallel statements from Paul:

ἡμεῖς εἰς Χριστὸν Ἰησοῦν ἐπιστεύσαμεν (Gal. 2.16b)
εἰς Χριστὸν ἐβαπτίσθητε (Gal. 3.27a)
εἰς ἓν σῶμα ἐβαπτίσθημεν (1 Cor. 12.13)

This belief/baptism into Christ erases all Jew–Gentile distinctions between those who are now together heirs of the covenant promises to Abraham, justified as Sons of God through their incorporation into the faithfulness of Messiah Jesus (Gal. 3.26–9). The one body that is 'the Messiah [ὁ Χριστός]', Jew and Greek, have all been caused to drink of one Spirit, and are to be worthy participants in the body and blood of the Lord (1 Cor. 12.12–13; cf. 11.23–33).

(ii) The point just noted – that belief/baptism into Christ also involves baptism into his death (and resurrection) – receives

---

[34] Note also that Ignatius, like Paul, can refer to Jesus as the Davidic Messiah (ὁ Χριστός), as in *Eph.* 18.2 (cf. 20.2); *Trall.* 9.1; *Rom.* 7.3 – not least with regular reference to his exemplary faith, love, suffering (crucifixion) and resurrection.

[35] Indeed, Polycarp immediately illustrates this by reference to the exemplary endurance of Paul and the other apostles who '"ran not in vain", but in faith and righteousness [οὐκ εἰς κενὸν ἔδραμον, ἀλλ' ἐν πίστει καὶ δικαιοσύνῃ] ...' (Pol., *Phil.* 9.2; cf. Gal. 2.2, 20–1).

its most sustained treatment by Paul at Romans 6.1–11:

ἡμεῖς εἰς Χριστὸν Ἰησοῦν ἐπιστεύσαμεν
(Gal. 2.16b)

ἐβαπτίσθημεν εἰς Χριστὸν Ἰησοῦν
εἰς τὸν θάνατον αὐτοῦ ἐβαπτίσθημεν
(Rom. 6.3)

The most fundamental aspect of this compressed and highly complex passage is that of dying and rising with Christ: (a) through baptism into Christ's death 'our old self has been crucified'; and (b) just as Christ was raised and now 'lives to God', so we too, justified rather than enslaved to sin, are now alive to God in Messiah Jesus (cf. Gal. 2.19–20).

(iii) That belief/baptism into the death and resurrection of Christ – not least as proclaimed in the Lord's Supper – constitutes a (paradoxical) reworking of Jewish corporate identity and destiny is further implied by Paul's warning in 1 Corinthians 10. He admonishes the Corinthians not to replicate the idolatry of Israel – those who 'were baptized into Moses [εἰς τὸν Μωϋσῆν ἐβαπτίσθησαν]' (1 Cor. 10.2) – by themselves engaging in idolatrous conduct entirely incompatible with their participation in the body and blood of Christ.[36]

From such analogous lines of thought elsewhere, the full import of Paul's remark at Galatians 2.16b becomes the more apparent. In echoing what appears to be baptismal language, Paul reminds errant Jewish Christians – in Antioch, Galatia and elsewhere – that their belief/baptism into Christ entails dying and rising with him, an often afflicted life ever more conformed to the outworking of God's righteousness in Messiah Jesus and his followers, the heirs of Abraham.[37] Vindication is now a function of covenant faithfulness to God-in-Christ not God-in-Israel, and the Jew–Gentile divide has given way to sons of God demarcated by their common life in the Messiah. Far from 'Judaizing', they (like Paul) must replicate the

---

[36] Indeed, Paul seems to presuppose something of an analogy/typology between (a) Israel's paradigmatic Exodus deliverance focused upon its (Torah) representative figure Moses, and (b) the Corinthian believers' ever-formative experience of the Lord's Supper centred upon their representative Messiah – even going so far as to say that the Rock which had accompanied Israel in its wilderness wanderings was the Messiah.

[37] Note especially Gal. 3.16, on which see N. T. Wright, *The Climax of the Covenant*, pp. 157–74.

sufferings of Christ by withstanding the opposition of their fellow Jews, this martyred-Messiah disposition being a redemptive means whereby fellow believers may remain resolute and unbelievers come to faith in Jesus.

Having reiterated these known facts, by means of two further statements Paul notes their underlying rationale: Jews such as Peter and Paul believed into Messiah Jesus (iii) that they may be justified 'from the faithfulness of the Messiah' and not 'from works of the law' (Gal. 2.16c), (iv) because 'no flesh' will be justified 'from works of the law'. The former statement starkly juxtaposes the mutually exclusive Jewish and Jewish *Christian* conceptions of the means by which one will be declared to have been faithful members of God's covenant people: in virtue of a Torah-focused way of life in Judaism, or a Messiah-focused way of life in the new covenant community. Once again, the wider covenantal context here presupposed demands recognition of the full nature and scope of what is envisaged by the phrase ἐκ πίστεως Χριστοῦ. Paul has in view the outworking of God's covenant faithfulness via Messiah Jesus' faithfulness in the lives of the Jewish Christian believers, with the preposition ἐκ perhaps attesting to the Israel-specific context of origin 'out of' which this has taken place (cf. Rom. 3.30).

A further rationale for their incorporation into Messiah Jesus is provided by a final reference to the inadequacy of that which they have left behind: 'from works of the law "no [flesh] shall be justified"' (Gal. 2.16d). The initial 'because [ὅτι]' is clearly both causative and recitative, as Paul provides support for his antecedent statement by means of a modified citation from Psalm 142[143].2. It is likely that the use of 'all flesh [πᾶσα σάρξ]' – instead of the Psalmist's 'every living being [πᾶς ζῶν]' – is deliberate and polemical. That is, the expression is not just a neutral reference to 'every human', but is also intended to evoke the negative and often Jewish-specific (though not Jewish-exclusive) evocations of the term σάρξ as employed elsewhere in Galatians. The 'works of the law', not least circumcision, bind the Jew (and Judaizers) to Judaism and the old age/sphere, rather than bring about justification.

Paul's remonstration in Galatians 2.15 is clearly raised by Peter's withdrawal from mixed table-fellowship in Antioch. As was argued earlier, it involved a profound confusion of categories concerning what it meant to be the people of God: covenant membership, and vindication as such, is not a function of 'works of the law', but of conformity to Christ. Thus, even more fundamentally, conduct such as Peter's represented a failure to remain faithful to the outworking of God's grace in and through the faithfulness of the martyred and exalted Messiah Jesus. The root of this problem, as our consideration of Galatians 2.16 has already intimated, is that Jews – no less than the Gentiles – are subject to sin. That this is the case now becomes the more evident from Paul's pursuant line of argumentation.

3. An objection and its denial: servant(s) of sin versus servant(s) of God (Gal. 2.17)

At this point Paul entertains an objection only to deny it categorically: 'if in seeking to be justified in Messiah Jesus, we [Jewish Christians] are found to be sinners, then is the Messiah a servant of sin? In no way!' (Gal. 2.17). On the face of it, this seems a relatively straightforward rhetorical question and denial.[38] However, it has managed to attract a bewildering array of interpretations, these largely a function of significantly variant readings of Paul's overall argument. Here the main interpretations may be conveniently and briefly noted in terms of two broad camps, with the second of these further subdivided into two. The way will then be clear to offer a more nuanced interpretation of this verse by reference to three key elements: what it means to be justified '*in Christ*'; the significance of the accusation that those seeking justification in this way are '*found*' to be sinners; and why it is that Paul denies that the Messiah (and his people) is a servant of sin.

There is little doubt that the initial premise – that justification is being sought in Christ – is indeed correct. However, commentators become divided as to whether the second premise – that those seeking justification in Christ are thus found to be sinners – is to be taken as (a) *false*, and followed by an equally false conclusion (Christ is a servant of sin) or (b) *true*, but followed by a false deduction therefrom (Christ is a servant of sin).

Proponents of the former so-called *irrealis* position have offered various highly nuanced reasons as to why it must be false: any *bona fide* attempt to become justified in Christ cannot be regarded as

---

[38] Whether textually ἆρα (interrogative particle) or, more probably, ἄρα (inferential particle) is to be preferred at Gal. 2.17b, Paul's regular use of the immediately ensuing rejoinder μὴ γένοιτο renders it virtually certain that we are dealing with a question.

sinful;[39] the fact that justification can only be found in respect to Christ precludes any suggestion that those in Christ can be sinners;[40] Paul could not have conceived of (Gentile) Christians seeking justification as sinners still outside God's grace;[41] inasmuch as being 'in Christ' presupposes conversion from a life of sin under the law, then one is no longer a sinner.[42] Common to all of these explanations is the assumption that Paul is employing ἁμαρτωλός in the absolute sense of 'sinner' from the standpoint of the gospel of Christ. On this view, the claim that anyone seeking justification in Christ, namely, to be rendered guiltless before God in virtue of their deliverance from sin by Christ, can only be false, as likewise the nonsensical conclusion that Christ himself is a servant of sin. However, as will become apparent, all such readings too quickly bypass the fundamentally *Jewish* perspective which governs the premise.

Proponents of the latter so-called *realis* position argue that the second premise is indeed true – those seeking to be justified in Christ *are* sinners – but offer two very different explanations of this. It is claimed either that (a) Paul is tacitly admitting his detractors' observation that Christians continue to fall victim to sin;[43] or that (b) from a Jewish standpoint, Jewish Christians are tantamount to Gentile sinners because they now live (together with Gentiles) outside the purview of the Torah.[44] The former shares the same drawback as those noted under the *irrealis* category, namely, the erroneous assumption that ἁμαρτωλός is only used absolutely. The latter, more cogent, interpretation takes account of the covenantal and Antioch-specific context of the argument, not least the fact that ἁμαρτωλός echoes the meaning of the term as used at Galatians 2.15. Jews seeking to be justified in Christ, in virtue of their common life with *Gentile* Christians, put themselves outside the covenant people of God, and are thus tantamount to Gentile sinners, but Paul denies that this renders Christ himself a servant of sin. However, certain considerations suggest that the full import of what is being

---

[39] Schmithals, *Paul and James*, p. 75; cf. Bultmann, 'Zur Auslegung von Gal. 2, 15–18', p. 396; Beyer and Althaus, 'Der Brief an die Galater', p. 20.
[40] Kieffer, *Foi et justification à Antioche*, pp. 55–9; Mußner, *Der Galaterbrief*, pp. 176–8.
[41] Betz, *Galatians*, pp. 119–20.
[42] Böttger, 'Paulus und Petrus in Antiochien', p. 91.
[43] R. N. Longenecker, *Galatians*, p. 90.
[44] Barclay, *Obeying the Truth*, pp. 78–9; Dunn, *Galatians*, p. 141.

said at Galatians 2.17 runs deeper than even this last explanation allows.

First, as argued above, that Jews such as Peter and Paul seek to be justified '*in Christ*' (rather than 'in Torah') means that they have incorporated themselves into the destiny of Messiah Jesus and his people (rather than Torah-focused Israel). As the Antioch situation readily indicates, this finds expression in a redrawing of the boundary-markers and behavioural patterns of the people of God.[45] However, this radical reworking necessarily implies a departure from that which it has left behind: life in Judaism. Furthermore, as we shall see, it does so on the grounds that the Jewish way of life is (as implied earlier) equally complicit in Adamic sin, and thus in need of divine deliverance in the form of conformity to Christ and his people.[46]

Second, from its usage elsewhere in Paul it is clear that the verb 'found [εὑρίσκω]' can carry covenantal (perhaps even judicial) overtones within both Jewish and Christian frameworks. Thus, for example, Paul claims that through God's righteousness manifested in the faithfulness of Christ (Rom. 3.21–6), the covenant has been so fulfilled that Abraham is now 'found' to be the forefather of those who share in Jesus' faithfulness. He is *not* the forefather 'according to the flesh'; that is, of those living 'from works of the law'.[47] Indeed, the Abrahamic covenant is realised not διὰ νόμου, but διὰ δικαιοσύνης, because otherwise 'faith' would be in vain and the promise void, and election a matter of race rather than grace (Rom. 4.13–16; cf. Gal. 2.19–21). Thus a clear line is drawn in Paul's thought:

(a) *from* Abraham, whom the Maccabees revered as the prototypical devout Jew because he 'was *found* faithful when tested';[48]

(b) *via* Messiah Jesus, himself 'found' a servant, a human being

---

[45] Barclay, *Obeying the Truth*, pp. 76–83.

[46] It is noteworthy that three of the most clearly incorporative instances of the phrase 'in Christ' in Paul occur within the wider context of an Adam–Christ argument in which Israel is increasingly implicated as also in need of God's deliverance in Messiah Jesus (Rom. 5–8; cf. 5.11; 8.1–3).

[47] For the reading of Romans 4.1 presupposed here, see N. T. Wright, 'Romans and the Theology of Paul', p. 191, modifying Hays, 'Have We Found Abraham?'

[48] Mattathias' testamentary speech begins with the rhetorical question: 'Was not Abraham found faithful when tested, and it was reckoned to him as righteousness? [Αβρααμ οὐχὶ ἐν πειρασμῷ εὑρέθη πιστός, καὶ ἐλογίσθη αὐτῷ εἰς δικαιοσύνην;]' (1 Macc. 2.52); cf. also the characterization of Daniel (Dan.LXX 1.17–20; 6.5[4]).

who humbled himself upon the cross, his death a paradoxical reworking of Maccabean precedent;[49]
(c) *to* those Jews and Gentiles together in Christ who are likewise 'found' faithful,[50] even in the face of martyrdom;[51]
(d) this *bypassing* unbelieving Jews who remain zealously committed to 'works of the law' (emulating their Maccabean forebears), opposed to Christ, and thus regard Jewish Christians to be 'found' in violation of Torah – the scenario in Antioch being a notable case in point (Gal. 2.17).

In fact, as we shall see, the root cause of the problem of such Jewish intransigence is that sin's abuse of Torah in nation Israel – replicating its abuse of the Edenic commandment in Adam – was such that the very commandment which promised life was itself 'found' to bring death (Rom. 7.9–10; cf. 7.20). From the standpoint of Paul the Jew-become-Christian, the very basis upon which he and other Jewish Christians in Antioch were found to be sinners was itself found to be a function of the outworking of sin in the form of a self-serving and self-destructive Jewish nomism and nationalism. Therefore, it is true that in seeking to be justified in Christ they – and, as is next implied, Christ himself – are found to be sinners according to the Jewish 'works of the law'. However, the greater (unstated) truth is that it is also precisely in this way that they are found faithful to the Messiah who has rescued them from the 'works of the law' and all that goes with it: a Judaism given over to the old age/sphere of Adamic sin.

Third, these two antithetical perspectives also come into play in the ensuing inference (ἄρα) which Paul immediately and categorically denies: 'is Christ a servant of sin? In no way!' (Gal. 2.17c). Two preliminary observations concerning the premise will facilitate an estimation of its adamant denial by Paul. (i) Given the wider covenantal context and the incorporative aspect of Χριστός, it must

---

[49] Phil. 2.6–8, cf. Rom. 3.21–6; the paradox resides not least in the fact that this is *divine* self-sacrificial humility at work: *God*-in-Messiah Jesus (cf. the discussion of Gal. 2.20 below).

[50] Paul is prepared to suffer loss that he may 'be found' in Christ, not having his righteousness (covenant membership) ἐκ νόμου ἀλλὰ τὴν διὰ πίστεως Χριστοῦ (Phil. 3.9a). He thus regards apostolic ministry as that of 'servants of Christ' who must 'be found faithful' (1 Cor. 4.1–2).

[51] Note Ignatius of Antioch's request for prayer that 'I may not only be called a Christian, but may also be found to be one', explicated as being 'deemed faithful' in virtue of his martyrdom (Ign., *Rom.* 3.2).

be allowed that the usage of Χριστός here can embrace both the Messiah himself and those who are together conformed to him as his people. (ii) Commentators are too quick to move to the otherwise valid conclusion that ἁμαρτία is here used in an absolute, typically Pauline sense as that power which holds sway over the whole of humanity.[52] Rather, as has already been noted, there is a *Jewish*-specific aspect to ἁμαρτωλός at Galatians 2.17b (and 2.15), expressing the claim that Jewish Christians are tantamount to (Gentile) sinners in virtue of seeking justification outside the parameters of Torah. From such a perspective it could be inferred that Christ himself was also a servant of sin (outside the covenant people) – and, indeed, was no Messiah at all.

The nature and significance of this claim and its denial emerges more clearly by reference to Paul's use of 'servant [διάκονος]' and the cognate 'service/ministry [διακονία]' elsewhere – both as applied to Christ and to his people (not least Paul himself).

(A) The Messiah as servant
   (i) In what might be taken as a summary statement of the theology of Romans, Paul remarks that 'the Messiah became a servant of the circumcision on behalf of the truth/ righteousness of God', (a) to fulfil the covenant promises to the Patriarchs, and (b) that the Gentiles might glorify God for his mercy to them (Rom. 15.7–9). The immediate corollary is that Jewish and Gentile Christians in Rome (as Antioch) ought to welcome one another rather than dispute over such matters as idol food.
   (ii) Undergirding all this is the archetypal role of Jesus the Messiah who did not exploit his divine equality but took this as a vocation to become a 'servant [δοῦλος]',[53] found to be a human being humiliated to the point of death on the cross, exalted by God to share in divine glory (Phil. 2.5–11).[54] Christians are called to imitate this exemplary self-sacrifice, assured that they too will be vindicated (Phil. 2.1–4; 12–18).

---

[52] So, for example, Dunn, *Galatians*, p. 141.

[53] That δοῦλος ('servant, slave') and διάκονος ('servant') can overlap conceptually in reference to apostolic ministry – replicating the faithfulness of Christ himself – is attested in Col. 1.3–7. This is consonant with the synoptic tradition at Matt. 20.25–8/ Mark 10.42–5, where διάκονος and δοῦλος are used interchangeably of those who would emulate the servanthood of the Son of Man.

[54] See N. T. Wright, *Climax of the Covenant*, pp. 56–98.

(B) *The Messiah's people as servants*
  (i) Paul refers to himself and his fellow apostles in 2 Corinthians 3 as 'servants [διάκονοι] of [God's] *new* covenant'. Here he details two antithetical types of 'ministry [διακονία]': that of (a) 'death' or 'condemnation' – as seen in life under Torah in Israel – eclipsed by that of (b) 'the Spirit/righteousness' whereby God's glory is reflected in those whose lives together pattern the suffering and vindication of Christ.
  (ii) Paul pursues the latter aspect by arguing that God's reconciliation in Christ is operative through those who no longer regard the Messiah from a κατὰ σάρκα standpoint but rather have been given 'the ministry of reconciliation'. Indeed, 'on behalf of us, God made [Christ] – who did not know sin – a sin offering [ἁμαρτία], that in him we may become God's righteousness'.[55] That is, the Messiah's self-sacrificial and atoning death, now replicated in the lives of those in him, is the means whereby God's covenant faithfulness is at work in the world (2 Cor. 5.16–21).
  (iii) Conversely, Paul later dismisses certain rival 'super apostles' – preaching another Jesus, spirit, gospel – as 'false apostles' who, though disguising themselves as apostles of Christ and 'servants of righteousness', are in fact 'servants of Satan' (2 Cor. 11.1–15).

The magnitude of Paul's emphatic denial now becomes evident. Far from being a servant of sin, the Messiah, whose divine equality with God was expressed through becoming a servant until death, is in fact the startling means whereby God has manifested his covenant faithfulness to Israel and thence to the whole world. Furthermore, those who are conformed to the Messiah are likewise servants of that which God has accomplished through him.

However, all this was being undercut in Antioch by a Jewish (-Christian) return to 'works of the law', from which standpoint those seeking justification in Christ – and Christ himself – were found to be servants of sin.[56] From his Jewish *Christian* standpoint

---

[55] See N. T. Wright, 'On Becoming the Righteousness of God'; also *The Climax of the Covenant*, pp. 220–5, on περὶ ἁμαρτίας at Rom. 8.3 as 'sin offering'. Obviously Rom. 3.21–6 again looms large here: God manifesting his righteousness by putting forward Messiah Jesus as a ἱλαστήριον.

[56] To offer an expanded paraphrase of Gal. 2.17: 'If in seeking to be justified in Messiah Jesus (as we are), we Jewish Christians are ourselves found to be sinners

Paul categorically denies all that is entailed in this position. He then proceeds to offer both a negative (Gal. 2.18) and a more positive (if paradoxical) explanation (Gal. 2.19–20) for so doing. In the course of this the full enormity of what God has done in Israel's Messiah Jesus, already implied in his denial, will become more explicit.

4. Paul's counter-claim: Israel-in-Adam as a servant of sin (Gal. 2.18)

Paul initially follows his strong denial (μὴ γένοιτο) with an explanation in the form of a counter-claim:[57] 'For if those things which I have torn down I again build up, I demonstrate myself to be a transgressor [εἰ γὰρ ἃ κατέλυσα ταῦτα πάλιν οἰκοδομῶ, παραβάτην ἐμαυτὸν συνιστάνω]' (Gal. 2.18). The nature and function of this statement is still much disputed.[58] Modern commentators generally – and, given the context, rightly – agree that 'those things [ταῦτα]' refers in *some* sense to the Torah, even if they variously focus upon the Torah-obedient way of life as a whole, the 'works of the law' in particular, or the specific attempt to be justified via Torah.[59] However, they then differ considerably as to how they regard the rebuilding of 'those things' formerly destroyed as serving to make one a transgressor, and precisely what that transgression entails.

Some argue that it is the act and/or outcome of the *rebuilding* itself which renders one a transgressor, but offer various accounts of why this is so. (i) Rebuilding Torah in virtue of one's withdrawal from table-fellowship with Gentile Christians in Antioch makes one a trangressor of no mere legal ordinance, but of the very gospel of God's grace in Christ.[60] (ii) To reinstate Torah as though it were

---

(which, from a Jewish standpoint, we are), then may it be inferred that Christ (and those in him) is a servant of sin (as, from a Jewish standpoint, is being claimed)? In no way!'.

[57] The connective γάρ, introducing a condition of fact, is not simply continuitive (Lambrecht, 'The Line of Thought in Gal. 2.14b–21', p. 493), but explanatory and asseverative.

[58] The ensuing synopsis of interpretations is indebted to Neitzel, 'Zur Interpretation von Galater 2.11–21', pp. 132–5; Wechsler, *Geschichtsbild und Apostelstreit*, pp. 384–95, and an unpublished paper by Goddard, 'Galatians 2.17–21'.

[59] Recent representatives of this spectrum are Betz, *Galatians*, p. 21; Mußner, *Der Galaterbrief*, p. 178; and R. N. Longenecker, *Galatians*, pp. 90–1.

[60] Cousar, *Galatians*, p. 51, following Ziesler, *The Meaning of Righteousness in Paul*, pp. 172–4 (cf. Lambrecht, 'Transgressor by Nullifying God's Grace', for a variation on this position). However, this requires παραβάτης to carry an explicitly Christian rather than its normal Jewish meaning.

still valid is to transgress its divine intent, which is (albeit paradoxically) that it lead one to die to it in Christ.⁶¹ (iii) Inasmuch as justification is to be found only in Christ, to re-establish Torah is to render oneself once more unjustified, still in sin, a transgressor.⁶² (iv) Since the Torah itself engenders transgression, its rebuilding necessarily results in its wilful violation, whether as in the past or inevitably so in the future.⁶³ Others argue that the stress is upon that which the rebuilding serves to reveal (and retract), namely, an earlier transgression involving a *tearing down*. Here two possibilities are suggested: to rebuild Torah is an admission (v) that one's original conversion to Christ was a transgression resulting in the destruction of Torah and its way of life;⁶⁴ or (vi) that the relaxation of Torah-demands with a view to table-fellowship with Gentile Christians in Antioch renders one a transgressor of Torah.⁶⁵

In an attempt to draw upon the strengths while avoiding the weaknesses of such a daunting array of interpretations, we may first note the subtle but discernible shift from the first person plural (Gal. 2.15–17a) to the first person singular (Gal. 2.18) which both personalizes and universalizes the scenario in view.⁶⁶ This suggests that, on the one hand, Paul is asserting that the actual conduct of Peter and other Jewish Christians in Antioch constitutes a rebuilding of the Torah-based way of life in Judaism⁶⁷ which had been

---

⁶¹ Burton, *Galatians*, pp. 130–1; R. N. Longenecker, *Galatians*, p. 91. This also requires παραβάτης to depart from its usual meaning, though it does rightly anticipate the paradox about to be stated in Gal. 2.19.

⁶² Bruce, *Galatians*, p. 142. This focuses too narrowly upon justification, itself too narrowly conceived of from a pre-'new perspective' standpoint.

⁶³ A common interpretation represented by Bultmann, 'Zur Auslegung von Gal. 2, 15–18', p. 398; Böttger, 'Paulus und Petrus in Antiochien', p. 92; and Bachmann, *Sünder oder Übertreter*, pp. 46–7, 74–5. However, as will be seen from Gal. 2.19, Torah itself is more of a victim than a perpetrator of sin in Israel.

⁶⁴ Lightfoot, *Galatians*, p. 117; Bring, *Commentary on Galatians*, p. 91. Against this it is claimed that there is little contextual support for any allusion to conversion, and that such a reading fails to address the more immediate matter of the Antioch incident.

⁶⁵ Borse, *Der Brief an die Galater*, p. 116; Mußner, *Der Galaterbrief*, pp. 178–9; Barclay, *Obeying the Truth*, p. 80 n. 13. While obviously relevant to the immediate Antioch scenario, it is not clear that such relaxation does full justice to the force and scope of καταλύω, and that the connection is explained.

⁶⁶ However, as throughout, the primary subjects remain Jewish Christians, without this precluding the bearing of the argument upon Gentile Judaizers (in Antioch, Galatia or elsewhere).

⁶⁷ While the neuter plural ἃ ... ταῦτα might well have immediate reference to 'the works of the law [τὰ ἔργα τοῦ νόμου]' so prominent at Gal. 2.16, the latter is itself clearly a subset of an entire Torah-focused Jewish way of life (recall Ἰουδαϊκῶς ζῇς at Gal. 2.14c).

destroyed when they believed in Messiah Jesus.[68] At the same time he is asserting that the same would have been (and always will be) true of himself and any other Jewish Christian who did not (and does not) remain faithful to his belief/baptism into God in Messiah Jesus (cf. Gal. 2.20–1).

It is important to note the interrelated personal, corporate and even cosmic dimensions of what is at stake in this destroying and rebuilding of the Jewish way of life. From a Jewish standpoint, God's building up of Israel found expression in the destruction of its enemies.[69] Conversely, as notably in the Maccabean period, all efforts to destroy Israel's Torah and Temple-based way of life (πολιτεία) were to be resisted, as exemplified by the martyrs whose courage and endurance in turn served to destroy/nullify Jewish apostasy and Gentile tyranny over the nation.[70] Indeed, as was noted in chapter four, the Jewish community in Antioch stood firmly in this tradition in their concern to preserve their Jewish identity and common life. Likewise in the tradition of his Maccabean forbears, as a zealous Pharisee Paul had himself attempted to advance (in) Judaism, not least by destroying (πορθέω) the Christian church (Gal. 1.13–14). However, his encounter with the risen Christ had overturned all this, and inaugurated an apostolic ministry in which he now sought to build up the church,[71] not least by adopting as his own disposition that of the power-in-weakness of Christ (cf. 2 Cor. 13.3–4, 10).

The net result of any Jewish Christian such as Peter – or, if he were to act likewise, Paul – rebuilding a hitherto dismantled Judaism is that he thereby demonstrates himself to be a 'transgressor [παραβάτης]'. That παραβάτης is a Jewish-specific term denoting Torah or covenant violation is readily discernible from the use of its cognate verb παραβαίνω in the LXX, most graphically in reference to the Maccabean martyrs who preferred death rather than trans-

---

[68] Note the parallel aorists ἐπιστεύσαμεν (Gal. 2.16b) and κατέλυσα (Gal. 2.18a).

[69] Note καταλύω especially at Jer.LXX 1.10; 12.16–17.

[70] In the LXX καταλύω finds theological and thematic significance in 2 Maccabees (2.22; 4.11) and especially 4 Maccabees (1.11; 4.16–24; 5.33; 7.9; 8.15; 11.24; 14.8; 17.2, 9).

[71] As his use of οἰκοδομέω and cognate noun οἰκοδομή readily indicate: e.g., Rom. 15.20; 1 Cor. 3.9; 14.3–12; 2 Cor. 10.8; 12.19; 13.10; 1 Thess. 5.11; cf. Eph. 2.21; 4.12, 16, 29. Note also the synoptic tradition concerning Jesus' destruction of the Temple and rebuilding of another not made with hands (Matt. 26.61/Mark 14.58; Matt. 17.40/Mark 15.29).

gress their ancestral laws (not least, the food laws).[72] However, παραβάτης is here used by a Jewish *Christian* concerning Jewish Christians who reinstate their former Jewish way of life, which affords it a certain ambiguity that must be allowed to ring.[73] Thus, from a *Jewish* standpoint, in putting himself back under Torah, Peter shows himself to have been a transgressor of Torah during the period in which he was a faithful follower of Messiah Jesus and thus at odds with Judaism.[74] From Paul's Jewish-*Christian* standpoint, however, the problem is more profound: Peter is in danger of returning to an Israel whose constant Torah transgression attests to the fact that Israel serves, rather than solves, the worldwide problem of Adamic sin, which has in fact now been dealt with in Messiah Jesus.

This problem, and something of its solution, already seen in the previous discussion of the 'works of the law' at Galatians 2.16, again emerges from a consideration of Paul's other references to παραβάτης and its cognate παραβάσις ('transgression'). Jews boasting in their status 'in Torah' nevertheless continue to transgress Torah. Thus they render their privileges void, stand condemned before those Gentiles who in principle keep Torah, and dishonour God (Rom. 2.23, 25, 27). Indeed, rather than keep Torah, the nation abuses it through preoccupation with 'works of the law', with national privilege under the guise of covenant obedience (cf. Rom. 9.30–2). In this way Israel replicates the trespass of Adam (cf. Rom. 5.14; 7.9–10). Torah was added because of transgressions (Gal. 3.19), and stands over and condemns/curses errant Israel for not keeping it (Gal. 3.10; Deut. 27–30). However, by itself Torah is incapable of rectifying Israel's predicament – a condition under which any Jewish Christian who rebuilds their former Jewish way of life again becomes subject (Gal. 2.18). Hence, while no longer, in Jewish estimation, 'Gentile sinners', they again become Jewish transgressors – an Israel-specific function of the underlying problem of Adamic sin.[75]

---

[72] 2 Macc. 7.2; 4 Macc. 9.1; 13.15; 16.24; cf. Dan. 7.24–5. Παραβάτης itself is not found in the LXX.

[73] One must resist the temptation to qualify παραβάτης with νόμου in the way that Paul does at Rom. 2.25, 26, but conspicuously fails to do so here.

[74] Not simply because certain Torah prescriptions were being violated (the nature and extent of this varying somewhat from one Jewish Christian to another), but in the same fundamental way that Paul as a Pharisee had deemed Jewish Christians as antithetical to Judaism.

[75] Cf. the condition in view at Rom. 7.1–8.11 as discussed below.

In the case of Peter in Antioch, this finds expression in a withdrawal which dangerously aligns him with the false arguments implied in Galatians 2.15-17. Its immediate impact is evident in a fractured Christian community in Antioch, and it has the potential to undermine the Gentile mission elsewhere. Indeed, Peter's conduct fails to remain completely faithful to the Messiah Jesus-focused fulfilment of the Abrahamic covenant which is now issuing in an inclusive and worldwide eschatological people of God. Indeed, it is to this Israel/Messiah-shaped outworking of God's redemptive purposes – variously attested elsewhere in his letters – that Paul now turns in Galatians 2.19-20. In so doing he offers a more constructive response to the erroneous claim that Messiah Jesus (and those 'in him') is a servant of sin.

5. Paul's positive explanation: Israel-in-Adam and Israel-in-Christ (Gal. 2.19-20)

Like its immediate antecedent, Galatians 2.19-20 has given rise to a wide range of interpretations, each focusing upon the programmatic but puzzling initial statement 'For I through the law died to the law ... [ἐγὼ γὰρ διὰ νόμου νόμῳ ἀπέθανον]' and its relationship to the ensuing 'I have been crucified with Christ [Χριστῷ συνεσταύρωμαι]'. Here two fundamental and inextricably interrelated issues are raised: (a) the identity of the subject 'I', and (b) what it means to say that this 'I' has died to the law through the law itself, such that a new Christ-centred life in God is made possible (Gal. 2.20). After briefly reviewing and responding to the current range of scholarly positions on these matters, I shall offer a necessarily succinct evaluation of Paul's profound and paradoxical remarks. This analysis will again draw upon various aspects of the earlier estimation of Galatians 1-2 in relation to Maccabean martyrdom, with particular reference to Paul's line of argument in Galatians 2.15ff. to date. Furthermore, this is complemented by (but not wholly contingent upon) a somewhat tendentious reading of Romans 7.1-8.11 which, it is suggested, gives greater account of the problem and solution which is so cryptically asserted at Galatians 2.19-20. In essence, it will be argued that here in view is a transformation involving and encompassing the death of Paul-in-Israel-in-Adam and the resurrection of Paul-in-Israel-in-Christ, this effected by conformity to the grace of God in the διὰ νόμου martyrdom and exaltation of Jesus, the Messiah and Son of God.

With respect to the identity of the subject 'I', most commentators agree that Paul himself is intended, and many also recognize the generalized and even paradigmatic aspect which suggests that he is also representative of a wider class.[76] The argument of both Galatians 1–2 as a whole and Galatians 2.15ff in particular leads one to concur with this assessment and, further, to stress its Jewish Christian and Israel-specific aspect. It has already been contended at some length that Paul's autobiography is essentially paradigmatic, and that it urges his Galatian converts to reject matters Jewish by recalling his own dramatic shift *away* from Judaism and by emulating his present conformity to Christ. More immediately compelling is the fact that Paul's Antioch-focused argument at Galatians 2.15ff. has been critiquing Jewish Christians in general and Peter in particular concerning their regression from a Christ-focused to a Torah/Israel-focused understanding of the justification of the people of God. Indeed, as noted above, the immediately antecedent remark at Galatians 2.18 involved a subtle shift from the first person plural to the singular, thereby simultaneously personalizing and universalizing this critique. Hence, it is highly likely that the ensuing emphatic 'I' is also paradigmatic and incorporative. While Paul himself is in near view, also included are all Jewish Christians (not least Peter), whose reversion towards their former Israel-focused Adamic existence Paul seeks to counteract by recalling his (and their) transformation through conformity to the crucified Christ.

This brings us to the more difficult question as to what is entailed in the fact that the 'I' has died to the law through the law itself, this issuing in a new Christ-centred life in God. Before offering a particular solution to this difficult problem, the main answers currently on offer may be briefly itemized as follows:

(i) The word νόμος is being used in two different senses: the subject has died to the law of Moses through the law of faith/Christ.[77]

---

[76] See, for example, Betz, *Galatians*, p. 122; R. N. Longenecker, *Galatians*, p. 91; Dunn, *Galatians*, p. 143, equivocates as to how generalized the 'I' may be.

[77] Lagrange, *Saint Paul, Epître aux Galates*, p. 51; Neitzel, 'Zur Interpretation von Galater 2.11–21', pp. 138–42. That Paul can and does redefine the law in terms of faith/Christ is not insignificant here. However, in the evidence usually cited for this (Rom. 3.27; 8.2; Gal. 6.2; 1 Cor. 9.21), νόμος is explicitly qualified in a manner conspicuously absent in this case (e.g., ὁ νόμος τοῦ Χριστοῦ, Gal. 6.2). This supports what is here intrinsically probable: a consistent use of νόμος at Gal. 2.19 and of διὰ νόμου in Gal. 2.19, 21, all in reference to the Mosaic Torah.

(ii) The law had a provisional role in preparing for and pointing towards the advent of Christ (this being concomitant with its own demise), whether in virtue of (a) its manifest incapacity to deal with sin such that it had to be abandoned; (b) condemnation of the 'I' as dead in sin, such that it must look to Christ for deliverance; or (c) its simply confining the subject under sin until Christ's arrival.[78]

(iii) Inasmuch as the law was instrumental in the death of Christ (however precisely understood), those who are crucified with him likewise die through the law (Gal. 3.13; Rom. 7.4).[79]

(iv) Paul is depicting his own personal experience of dying through the law to the law, in terms of either (a) his recognition and rejection of it as in some way deficient,[80] or (b) his zeal for the law which led him to, and ended with, his encounter with the risen Christ.[81]

In attempting to draw upon the insights while avoiding the deficiencies of these interpretations, and consonant with an inclusive estimation of the identity of the 'I', it may be proposed that Paul's remarks can be more clearly understood in terms of three elements which are inextricably interrelated to – indeed, 'superimposed upon' – one another. They comprise the following: (i) *Paul's* pre-Christian διὰ νόμου way of life which both required and led to his deliverance therefrom by the risen Christ (Gal. 1.13–16); (ii) *Israel's* διὰ νόμου

---

[78] Represented by Burton, *Galatians*, p. 133; Mußner, *Der Galaterbrief*, p. 180; and Betz, *Galatians*, p. 122, respectively. That the law had *a* preparatory role has already been suggested above; but none of these suggestions do justice to the demands of the immediate context of the argument by explaining its Israel-specific and paradoxical outworking in terms of Christ.

[79] This increasingly popular view is represented by Tannehill, *Dying and Rising with Christ*, pp. 58–9; Kieffer, *Foi et justification à Antioche*, p. 69; and Barclay, *Obeying the Truth*, p. 81 n. 14. While not without merit (after all, Χριστῷ συνεσταύρωμαι appears to have *some* bearing on the matter), this position requires greater precision in determining the respective roles of the law, 'the curse of the law', and 'through the law' in relation to the death of Christ and those Jewish Christians (here in view) who are conformed thereto.

[80] So Duncan, *Galatians*, p. 70 (the law 'revealed to him [its] ineffectiveness'). Older views of Paul as frustrated with Judaism have been particularly discredited in post-Sanders scholarship (cf. Phil. 3.4–5). However, Paul's zealous commitment to 'covenantal nomism' need not preclude entirely his recognition and critique of the extent to which Israel was continually deficient in this respect.

[81] Dunn, *Galatians*, p. 143. This too has merit (cf. above concerning ἃ κατέλυσα ταῦτα at Gal. 2.18 in reference to Paul's encounter with Christ); however, the significance of ἐγώ, and of the statement as a whole, is not exhausted by reference to Paul alone.

existence from which deliverance was required by its eschatological redeemer, Jesus Christ (Rom. 7.1–8.11; cf. Gal. 3.19–25); (iii) the Messiah Jesus' own διὰ νόμου experience in virtue of which (paradoxically) the rescue of Paul, Israel and the whole world was accomplished (e.g., Gal. 3.13; 4.4–5; Rom. 3.21–6), such that the resurrection life of God's reign could now be enjoyed by his people.

I begin with and quickly pass over the first of these – Paul's own transformation (Gal. 1.13–16) – because (a) it is readily recognized as being in view (in some form) at Galatians 2.19–20;[82] (b) it has already been given significant consideration (in chapter three); and (c) its corroboration and further illumination will require consideration of the second and third elements. Briefly put, it was Paul's zealous life in Judaism, issuing in his persecution of the church, which precipitated his dramatic transformation via God's disclosure of the risen Christ, the Son of God, in him. Invoking the earlier evaluations of Paul's Jew-become-Christian conceptual framework, his christological reconfiguration at Galatians 1.13–16 and the implied Torah/Israel critique at Galatians 2.15ff., the following 'Paul-specific' interpretation of Galatians 2.19–20 may be ventured. The individual 'I' (Paul-in-Israel-in-Adam), through his abuse of Torah in service of persecuting the Messiah and his people (διὰ νόμου), became confronted with and was transformed by the crucified and risen Messiah (Χριστῷ συνεσταύρωμαι). He thus died to his former way of life (νόμῳ ἀπέθανον), in order that 'I' (Paul-in-Israel-in-Christ) might live to God.

However, given the (above) arguments in favour of an incorporative and paradigmatic estimation of the subject 'I' at Galatians 2.19–20, it is virtually certain that Paul's own transformation was but a particular instance of a prior and more wide-ranging problem/solution pertaining to Jews in general. I shall attempt to corroborate this, and thereby cast further light upon Paul's terse assertion, by means of an excursus offering a necessarily attenuated exegesis of Paul's argument at Romans 7.1–8.11.

An excursus: the Messiah's deliverance of Israel-in-Adam (Rom. 7.1–8.11)

That what is so cryptically alluded to at Galatians 2.19–20 receives greater consideration at Romans 7.1–8.11 appears *prima facie* likely

---

[82] Thus, for example, Dunn, ibid., remarks concerning Gal. 2.19: 'this can hardly be other than a reference once again to the contrast already described in i.13–16 ...'

on the basis of certain common ground: the emphatic ἐγώ, a concentrated use of διὰ νόμου (and διὰ τῆς ἐντολῆς), and common key issues or themes (Torah, sin, death, deliverance through Jesus Christ/God's Son).[83] Of course, this text, especially Romans 7.1–25, is an exegetical minefield. Here we can but briefly canvass and critique two dominant lines of interpretation, and then quickly outline what is admittedly a rather tendentious reading.

Broadly speaking, there are two main approaches to Romans 7 itself, each focusing upon the identity and predicament of the emphatic ἐγώ.[84] First, some argue that the ἐγώ denotes Paul the Pharisee, representative of every Jew's struggle to fulfil Torah, typifying humanity's attempt to earn life by establishing a claim over and against God (so Bultmann et al.). However, the subject matter and scope of Romans 7 is not offering a general analysis of the plight of mankind, but rather is concerned with those under Torah (cf. Rom. 3.19–20). Second, others, focusing upon Romans 7.13–25, maintain that we have Paul the representative Christian, still struggling with the constant threat of sin (so Cranfield, Dunn, etc.). But there are several factors which count against this position. (i) The scenario involving Torah/sin/death is one from which the Christian is said to have been removed (Rom. 6.14; 7.4–6). (ii) That this condition can be described as enslavement to indwelling sin (Rom. 7.14b) requiring deliverance (Rom. 7.24) is incompatible with Christian life as one of liberation from sin (Rom. 6.12–23; 7.6; 8.9–11, 15). (iii) Romans 8.2 is best taken as both summarizing the problematic situation just depicted at Romans 7.15ff. and claiming that its solution is found in Christ. This brings us to a third interpretation which will be pursued here:[85] it may be suggested that the ἐγώ is Paul the Jew-become-Christian, now viewing retrospectively the problem of the outworking of sin's abuse of Torah within Israel, this being a Jewish-specific function of the wider problem of Adamic sin. The solution to this problem is Israel's deliverance through Messiah Jesus (Rom. 7.4–6, 24a; 8.1–11). The viability of this

---

[83] It has also often been noted that Paul's argument at Gal. 3.19–26 bears close comparison with that of Rom. 7 (even if the former is set against the wider backdrop of the Abrahamic covenant).

[84] Among the many surveys and assessments of a more nuanced range of positions and proponents, cf. Cranfield, *Romans*, pp. 340–7; Ziesler, *Romans*, pp. 181–4, 190–5; Moo, *Romans*, pp. 424–31, 442–51; Schreiner, *Romans*, pp. 359–65, 379–92.

[85] On this appoach, see N. T. Wright, *The Climax of the Covenant*, 196–200, 217–19; cf. Moo, *Romans*, pp. 406–67; and also Nanos, *Mystery*, 337–71, whose comparative analysis of Gal. 2.11–21 and Rom. 7 bears comparison at certain points to that on offer here.

interpretation may be considered in relation to the brief exegesis of Romans 7.1–8.11 which now follows.

By means of a programmatic marriage analogy (Rom. 7.1–6) Paul reminds *those who know the law* (Rom. 7.1a)[86] that according to its teaching a wife is bound to her husband while he lives, but free to marry another without being named an adulteress when he dies (Rom. 7.1b–3; cf. Deut. 24.1ff.). In this illustration the husband does not (as is commonly held) denote the Torah, which actually functions to govern the marriage relationship. Rather, as the ensuing application suggests, the husband and wife perform a double role. (i) First, they together represent Israel inextricably bound up in a debilitating relationship with its 'old Adamic self', such that in this condition even the Torah, which rightly stands over and condemns it, is itself used by the outworking of sin (διὰ τοῦ νόμου) which bears fruit leading to death (Rom. 7.5).[87] (ii) Second, they together represent Israel freed from this crippling existence in virtue of the death of its 'old Adamic self'. This release is described as (a) being put to death to the sphere of the Torah (τῷ νόμῳ) through the body of the Messiah (Rom. 7.4a);[88] and (b) being discharged from the Torah in virtue of being 'dead in that to which we were confined' (Rom. 7.6a,b).[89] In essence, Adamic sin's abuse of Israel's Torah-governed life no longer obtains. The outcome is that Israel is now free to belong to its risen Messiah, with the Spirit (not Torah) governing a relationship which bears fruit to God (Rom. 7.4b, 6c).

At this point Paul draws back to allow a broader perspective upon the nature of the problem which is detailed by reference to two

---

[86] That is, whether or not *Jewish* Christians are primarily in view at this point, Paul is at least presupposing that his addressees are capable of identifying fully with the Israel-specific nature of the situation and argument he is about to unfold (cf. Rom. 3.19a). See εἰδότες at Gal. 2.16, and the Jewish Christian specific argument throughout Gal. 2.15–21.

[87] Cf. Rom. 5.20–1; 6.14; and 7.23.

[88] The use of divine passive ἐθανατώθητε – in contrast to the different and active verb ἀπέθανον at Gal. 2.19 – may indicate that the 'intra-Jewish' aspect of the outworking of God's purposes is here in view: Jews who 'have been put to death by/from within Israel' through their conformity to their Messiah who was likewise put to death 'in Israel' (thereby dying to the Torah governed sphere of life). Cf. the ensuing note on Rom. 7.6b. That this necessarily entailed incorporation into a new sphere – the new resurrection life of those in Christ – suggests that an ecclesiological element cannot be excluded from τὸ σῶμα τοῦ Χριστοῦ.

[89] The difficult and perhaps ambiguous phrase ἀποθανόντες ἐν ᾧ κατειχόμεθα (Rom. 7.6b) is suggestive of both the condition 'in which' one was once found – viz., the 'living death' of Adamic sin abusing Torah in Israel (Rom. 7.5, διὰ τοῦ νόμου; this condition is about to be detailed in Rom. 7.7–25; cf. 8.10) – and also the site 'in which' death thereto was effected (by Messiah Jesus, cf. Rom. 7.4, 25).

interrelated rhetorical questions at Romans 7.7a and 7.13a, both answered and then drawn to a conclusion at Romans 7.21–5. In the first question, Paul asks 'is the Torah *sin*?', only to dismiss the idea with an unequivocal 'in no way' (Rom. 7.7a; cf. Gal. 2.17). However, he also immediately adds (note ἀλλά) that 'I' did not know sin except 'through the Torah [διὰ νόμου]', explicating this by saying that 'I' had not known 'desire [ἐπιθυμία]' but for the Torah prohibition 'you shall not covet' (Rom. 7.7b). That is, even as Torah stood over the 'I' to check and condemn its transgression, sin took the opportunity 'through the commandment [διὰ τῆς ἐντολῆς]' itself to effect 'in me [ἐν ἐμοί]' every desire (Rom. 7.8a).[90] In fact, without Torah and its commandments, sin would have had no base of operation (Rom. 7.8b; cf. 5.13) and would be as good as dead. Thus, far from Torah being able to control 'desire' – a claim central to the thesis of 4 Maccabees,[91] and which it seeks to establish by reference to the lauded Maccabean martyrs – Torah itself is so victimized by sin that it engenders covetousness.

That this is an Israel-specific aspect of the underlying and worldwide problem of Adamic sin becomes evident with a discernible shift to the emphatic ἐγώ at Romans 7.9–11, serving to indicate a stress upon Israel insofar as it is in Adam. Formerly 'I' (Israel-in-Adam) was alive apart from Torah (as Adam). However, at the arrival of the commandment (at Sinai, as in Eden), sin revived and 'I' died; the very commandment intended to bring life was in fact found to bring death 'to me', because sin seized the opportunity through the commandment to deceive 'me' and through it to kill 'me' – recapitulating and filling out Adamic sin (cf. Rom. 5.20; 7.13). Thus it can still be affirmed that the Torah *qua* Torah is holy, and that the commandment is holy, just and good (Rom. 7.12). However, both are nevertheless exploited to ill-effect within Israel by the enemy sin.

The second question Paul likewise raises only to reject is the inference that the good Torah (and its commandments) itself effects death (Rom. 7.13a).[92] Rather the true nature of the problem is sin

---

[90] As will be seen, the interaction between the Torah (νόμος) and this quintessential Torah commandment (ἐντολή) facilitates a subtle interplay between the Mosaic and Edenic commandments.

[91] 4 Maccabees also makes direct reference to the Torah prohibition of covetousness (4 Macc. 2.5–6).

[92] Typical of the various Deuteronomic summary comments concerning Israel's covenant blessing (versus curse) is that 'the Lord will make you abound in prosperity/ good [ἀγαθά]' (Deut.LXX 28.11; cf. 28.12, 47; 30.9; 31.20, 21).

working death 'in me' through the commandment in order that sin be shown for what it is by becoming sinful 'beyond measure [καθ' ὑπερβολήν]' (Rom. 7.13).[93] Comparison of καθ' ὑπερβολήν with its use at Galatians 1.13 corroborates what was earlier surmised in connection with the 'Paul-specific' estimation of the ἐγώ at Galatians 2.19–20, namely, that one of the ways in which sin's abuse of Torah in Israel is manifest is in the form of a misguided and self-defeating nationalism, with Paul's pre-Christian zeal a notable case in point. So, while the Torah itself is spiritual and good, 'I' am fleshly in virtue of having been 'sold under sin [πεπραμένος ὑπὸ τὴν ἁμαρτίαν]' (Rom. 7.14).[94] In the Maccabean literature, this image is employed both figuratively of apostate Jews going over to the Gentiles and, conversely, literally of faithful defenders of the Jewish nation who are captured and sold into slavery.[95] Here Paul has relativized this aspect; Israel *as a whole* is sold over to sin.[96] This is graphically portrayed at Romans 7.15–20. In essence, the 'I' (Israel-in-Adam) finds itself struggling in vain to obey Torah, with evil rather than good being effected, this due to the root problem of indwelling sin. Thus the 'I' can only lament 'I know that there does not dwell in me [ἐν ἐμοί] – that is, in my flesh [ἐν τῇ σαρκί μου] – good' (Rom. 7.18). There is no covenant life, but only the cursedness of what is tantamount to a living death.

The depiction of this scenario climaxes at Romans 7.21–5. What the 'I' finds in respect to Torah is that even in wanting to obey it, evil is immediately at hand (Rom. 7.21). For even as the ἐγώ delights in God's Torah 'according to the inner man' (namely, even as Israel strives to fulfil Torah in spite of being in Adam), it recognizes that 'another Torah' (the Torah taken over by sin) is at war against 'the Torah of my mind' (once again, the 'inner' Israel that would fulfil Torah), and indeed is taking the ἐγώ captive within its very self: 'in the Torah of sin that is in my constituent members'

---

[93] At this stage Paul is not concerned to detail *why* sin is operating in this way (a matter later taken up at Rom. 9–11), but only to depict something of its devastating impact upon Israel.

[94] The movement from the past to present tense suggests that Paul's focus has shifted from an account of the problem of Adamic sin as it *was* manifest in Israel (Rom. 7.7–12), to a depiction of the *ongoing* problem of Israel's condition in Adam (Rom. 7.12ff.).

[95] 1 Macc. 1.15; 2 Macc. 5.14; 8.14; cf. 10.21.

[96] As in the LXX where figurative usage can denote the consequences of sin: God 'sells' errant Israel (Isa. 48.10; 50.1) or an individual 'sells' himself in doing evil (1 Kings 20[21].20, 25; 2 Kings 17.17).

(Rom. 7.22–3; cf. 7.5–6).[97] As the re-emerging military imagery implies,[98] the divided ἐγώ denotes a Torah-grounded (and Temple-focused) nation Israel as vulnerable from within as without – because the common (but unrecognized) enemy is sin – such that Israel has become both prisoner and prison. It is not simply, as the Maccabean crisis was understood, a question of the Gentile enemy without and/or the apostate Jew within, but of sinful Israel *qua* Israel – as a subset of humanity *qua* humanity – which is the root of the problem. Hence, Israel is in dire need of rescue, from itself as much as from its equally sinful Gentile enemies, before it collapses completely. The 'wretched' ἐγώ's climactic cry for release from this 'body of death'[99] is answered by a parenthetical exclamation of thanksgiving from Paul the Jew-become-Christian regarding God's deliverance through the Lord Jesus Christ (Rom. 7.24–25a).[100]

Additional information on Israel's problem and especially the nature of the solution is given in Romans 8.1–11. Those in Messiah Jesus are excluded from God's condemnation of sin (Rom. 8.1) because 'the Torah of the Spirit of life in Messiah Jesus' has set them free from 'the Torah of sin and death' (Rom. 8.2).[101] That is, they have been liberated from the Torah as taken over by sin such that it could only engender death, and the Torah is now fulfilled in Jesus and the Spirit who effect covenant life. This is further explicated with the claim that what Torah could not do in that (condition wherein) it was weakened through the flesh,[102] God has done by sending his Son who identifies himself with sinful humanity and indeed becomes a 'sin offering [περὶ ἁμαρτίας]' on their behalf. He thus condemns sin and enables the covenant decree (cf. Deut. 30.6–

[97] At an individual level, the 'inner man'/'the Torah of my mind' is the would-be Torah-obedient Jew still bound up in Adam. It is by means of his deliverance through Christ, such that he fulfils Torah in virtue of having the mind of Christ (Rom. 12.2; 1 Cor. 2.16), that he may become the 'inner man' who is daily renewed, even though in the form of his 'outer nature' he is still under attack from those opposed to his transformation (2 Cor. 4.16). See further on Gal. 2.20 below.

[98] Cf. Rom. 6.12–14, 23; 7.14b.

[99] Contrast the depiction of the Maccabean martyrs' mother as one who could have lamented (but did not) her condition as one of 'wretchedness' (4 Macc. 16.7); cf. ταλαίπωρος in reference to the victimized faithful among Israel (2 Macc. 4.47; 3 Macc. 5.5, 22, 47).

[100] This is immediately and starkly juxtaposed by a summary recapitulation of Israel's anguished predicament from which he is now released (Rom. 7.25b).

[101] The reading σε is to be preferred over με, and it is likely that Paul has in view 'those knowing the law' (Rom. 7.1) who are able to identify themselves fully with the now released ἐγώ.

[102] Viz., the body of death; cf. above on ἐν ᾧ at Rom. 7.6 and ἐν at Rom. 7.23.

20) to be fulfilled by those living according to the Spirit (Rom. 8.3–4). In essence, God takes sin upon himself in the person of his Son, Israel's Messiah, and thereby effects for Israel (and the world) what Israel could not: death to the Adamic problem of sin manifest within Israel (and the world) and its entail (condemnation).

The Messiah's deliverance of Israel-in-Adam (Gal. 2.19–20)

At Romans 8.3 (and context) we are once again at one of the nerve centres of Paul's atonement theology and of its outworking within the lives of those identified with God in Christ. It is this which also underlies Paul's cryptic assertion at Galatians 2.19–20 which, as stated earlier, may be explicated in terms of three interrelated (superimposed) levels. The first two of these may be recapitulated and the third added. First, the individual 'I' (Paul-in-Israel-in-Adam), through his abuse of Torah in service of persecuting the Messiah and his people (διὰ νόμου) became confronted with and was transformed by the crucified and risen Messiah (Χριστῷ συνεσταύρωμαι). He thus died to his former way of life (νόμῳ ἀπέθανον) in order that 'I' (Paul-in-Israel-in-Christ) might live to God. Second, Paul's own experience represents a particular instance of the transformation of the corporate 'I' (Israel-in-Adam) who was subject to the outworking of sin's abuse of Torah within Israel (διὰ νόμου). But, in a paradoxical way to be noted momentarily, this enabled conformity to Israel's crucified Messiah (Χριστῷ συνεσταύρωμαι), and thereby death to the condition it was in (νόμῳ ἀπέθανον) – in order that the now transformed 'I' (Israel-in-Christ) may live to God.

Third, from this account of the transformation of the ἐγώ (individual and corporate) it becomes evident that at its heart is the Messiah's own prior experience of sin's abuse of Torah in Israel which culminated in his crucifixion (διὰ νόμου). Paradoxically, this was the very means whereby God fully dealt with Israel's (and Adam's) condition, as authenticated in the Messiah's resurrection and exalted life with God. Ancillary arguments which provide a consonant but broader perspective upon this are close at hand in Paul's later remarks at Galatians 3.13 and 4.5–6.[103] Paul can speak

---

[103] These texts were noted in chapter three in connection with the discussion of the conceptual framework governing Galatians.

of Jesus' divine equality being expressed precisely in his servanthood as a human being to the point of death on the cross (so Phil. 2.5–11). Similarly, in his more Israel-focused remarks at Galatians 3.13 and 4.5–6, he speaks of God sending his Son, residing with Israel in its condition 'under the law', and redeeming Israel from the curse of the law by becoming a curse on Israel's behalf. (This is in order that the Abrahamic blessing might reach all – Jew *and* Gentile – in Messiah Jesus, those who are God's sons in virtue of him sending the Spirit of his Son into their hearts.) Moreover, this account of God's redemptive activity through his Son is cognate with Paul's claims elsewhere (pre-eminently at Romans 3.21–6), that God's covenant faithfulness has been manifest in the faithfulness of the Messiah – the one whom God put forward as a ἱλαστήριον διὰ [τῆς] πίστεως.

Hence, the enormity and paradoxical aspect of Paul's response at Galatians 2.19–20 to Jewish(-Christian) claims for justification through 'works of the law' (Gal. 2.16) and the charge that the Messiah was a servant of sin (Gal. 2.17) now becomes fully evident. God's covenant faithfulness, and the justification of his faithful people, took the form of his own Son, Jesus the Messiah, who far from being a servant of sin, died through the law to the law in order to reconcile sinful Israel (and the world) to himself. This involved a dramatic reworking of Israel's understanding of God and his people, not least as this had been given sharp expression in the form of its Maccabean martyr theology and the emergent expectations concerning an eschatological redeemer. Astonishingly, (a) the one rejected was in fact Israel's Messiah who, in and through his suffering and martyrdom, became exalted as the Son of God with a share in divine glory; and (b) the atonement and vindication thereby made possible, pertained not to the nation of Israel alone, but to those whom Jesus represented, Jews and Gentiles alike conformed to him.

Thus the transformed 'I' no longer experiences the 'living death' of sin's abuse of Torah in Israel as typified in Jewish nomism and nationalism, but rather can now 'live to God'.[104] In virtue of dying and rising with the Messiah who himself now 'lives to God' (Rom. 6.10; 14.8–9), the subject experiences even here and now the inaugurated resurrection life – the very reign of God – which the Maccabean martyrs could only hope to share in with their faithful

---

[104] The subject 'I' continues to evoke a dual (individual and corporate) aspect throughout the remainder of Gal. 2.20–1.

forebears beyond death.[105] All this is because 'I [Israel-in-Christ] live, but no longer I [Israel-in-Adam]';[106] rather 'Christ lives in me [ἐν ἐμοί]' (Gal. 2.20a). That is, instead of Adamic sin being operative within the ἐγώ – ἐν ἐμοί, in accordance with Romans 7.15–20 – now it is the Son of God who is alive within those who are his (not least Paul himself).[107] Indeed, it may be said that the ἐγώ has been transformed by, and its destiny now taken up into, that of its eschatological redeemer who, contrary to Israel's expectations and estimation, is the martyred but now exalted Messiah Jesus/the Son of God.

The transformed existence of the subject in whom the Messiah lives is further explicated by Paul: 'and the life I now live in the flesh, I live in the faithfulness of the Son of God who loved me and gave himself for me' (Gal. 2.20b). Here 'in the flesh [ἐν σαρκί]' is not used pejoratively, as in Paul's use of ἐν τῇ σαρκί in reference to Israel-in-Adam (Rom. 7.5), a condition replicated in the Galatian Agitators' preoccupation with that which is ἐν σαρκί (Gal. 6.12–13). Rather, in stark contrast, it denotes the new (νῦν) locus and mode of the subject's existence (wherein the risen Messiah is operative) which – encompassing the cosmic, corporate and individual spheres – may be glossed as 'on this earth, within the Israel of God, in my very person'. The exalted Son of God is with his oft-afflicted saints on earth who, even in and through their suffering, manifest and advance the kingdom of God which is to be fully and finally theirs.

Indeed, such Messiah-like suffering is further implied in the fact that the faithful subject's life is indwelt, empowered by, and so emulates the faithfulness of the Son of God,[108] itself a function of the outworking of God's covenant faithfulness.[109] This Son-of-God-faithfulness is characterized as that of 'the one who loved me' and who 'gave himself for me'. The latter is evocative both of the deaths of the Maccabean martyrs on behalf of (ὑπέρ) Torah and Israel[110]

---

[105] 4 Macc. 7.19; 16.25; cf. Luke 20.38.
[106] Alternatively, taking ἐγώ as the subject of ζῶ, simply 'I [Israel-in-Adam] no longer live'.
[107] Recall the discussion of God's revelation of his Son in Paul (ἐν ἐμοί) at Gal. 1.16a in chapter three.
[108] This is the significance of the deferred article τῇ, prominently positioned prior to τοῦ υἱοῦ θεοῦ rather than πίστει. Cf. 2 Cor. 13.5.
[109] This is implicit in the pursuant reference to the grace of God (Gal. 2.21a; cf. Rom. 3.24) and δικαιοσύνη (Gal. 2.21b), and explicit in the well-attested and more difficult variant reading θεοῦ καὶ Χριστοῦ.
[110] 2 Macc. 7.9; 8.21; 4 Macc. 1.8, 10.

and, of course, of Jesus handing himself over to his destiny on the cross on behalf of Adamic humanity.[111] Together these mutually reinforcing phrases indicate that the obedient life and death of the Son of God give expression to God's own selfless love.

6. Paul's concluding statement: the grace of God in the death of the Messiah (Gal. 2.21)

Paul's final remark is a succinct summary refutation and condemnation of those claiming that Christ is a servant of sin. First, he disavows that he 'nullifies [ἀθετέω]' the grace of God (Gal. 2.21a). The verb has legal overtones. Notably, it is employed within the context of the Maccabean revolt in connection with treaty violations.[112] Indeed, we may recall that in determining that Simon Maccabeus should be empowered as Israel's leader and High Priest 'until a trustworthy prophet should arise', Israel also declared that anyone who nullified (ἀθετέω) his decisions would be held liable to the death penalty (1 Macc. 14.41–5). There is some suggestion that Jewish expectation concerning this prophet-Messiah figure who would arise to aid Israel,[113] was brought to bear upon Jesus' own ministry.[114] Such a claim would have been readily interpreted as an attempt to nullify the then High Priest's authority and the Jewish way of life which he represented, and thus be a contributing factor in Jesus' eventual sentence of death.

Likewise, in his own claims for and conformity to Jesus as the Messiah, with its concomitant rejection of a life in Judaism, Paul was also open to such charges – and just as likely to have turned them back against his detractors. Given this, and in view of the immediate context of the argument at Galatians 2.15–21, it is likely that Paul is here redeploying a charge directed at himself (that he nullifies God's covenant with Torah-centred Israel) against his accusers (that they nullify God's covenant with the Messiah-centred people of God). At the heart of Paul's countercharge is that Jewish Christians – such as Peter and his followers in Antioch – who move in the direction of a Jewish way of life on the strength of the erro-

---

[111] Note (i) παραδίδωμι at Rom. 4.25; 8.32; 1 Cor. 11.23–4; cf. Gal. 1.4; and (ii) ὑπέρ at Rom. 14.15; 1 Cor. 1.13; 11.24; 15.3; Gal. 1.4; 3.13, etc.

[112] R. N. Longenecker, *Galatians*, p. 94, rightly notes 1 Macc. 11.36; 2 Macc. 13.25.

[113] Deut. 18.15ff.; 1QS 9.11; 4 Ezra 2.17; cf. 2 Macc. 15.15.

[114] John 1.21; 6.14–15; 7.40; cf. Acts 3.22.

neous argument that this constitutes them as the people of God, not only risk putting themselves back into an Israel-in-Adam condition (the problem), but are thereby also nullifying God's ultimate manifestation of his grace in Israel's martyred and exalted Messiah, Jesus (the solution). Paul, however, does not nullify God's grace. On the contrary, he had been so transformed by the risen Messiah that his oft-afflicted apostolic ministry was itself a testimony to God's grace in Christ in him (cf. 1 Cor. 15.9–10; 2 Cor. 4.15; Gal. 2.9).

Paul drives home this point with a contrary to fact conditional statement (thus implying that the premise is that of his detractors) and a *reductio ad absurdum* (which highlights the wholly untenable nature of their premise). If covenant life were attainable διὰ νόμου, then the logical consequence of this would be that the Messiah died in vain (Gal. 2.21b). Consonant with its notable usage at Galatians 2.19a, διὰ νόμου here denotes the outworking of sin through its abuse of Torah within Israel, a condition which instead of bringing about covenant life (δικαιοσύνη) actually results in the covenant curse. Indeed, it is all the more insidious in that it perpetuates the unconscionable idea that the Messiah, through whom Israel-in-Adam is in fact delivered from its condition, died to no avail. Such, then, is the potential scope of Peter's conduct and its wide-ranging implications for the gospel and the church in Antioch and elsewhere. Instead of withdrawing from the table-fellowship, he (like Paul) ought to have remained faithful to the martyred and exalted Messiah and to the inclusive (Jew + Gentile) community conformed thereto.

7. Conclusion

Paul's line of argumentation in Galatians 2.15–21 gives theological breadth and depth to what was at stake in his stance against Peter's withdrawal from table-fellowship in Antioch. He systematically subverts the position of those Jewish(-Christians) who, in the tradition of the Maccabees, equated life among the people of God with a Torah-focused Judaism. Remonstrating against such a view, Paul first polemicizes against that very Jewish polemic so characteristic of the Maccabean period: there is no longer a Jew–Gentile (sinner) divide because vindication as the (afflicted) covenant people of God is not a function of adherence to 'works of the law', but of corporate conformity to the faithful Messiah Jesus. In advocating this radical claim, Paul clearly comes under considerable opposition. Indeed, in the view of his adversaries, it means that he – and all other such Jewish Christians – are sinners, found to be outside the people of God. Indeed, a further and even more extreme inference is that the Messiah is a servant of sin.

Paul recoils at the very idea, and presses his counter-claim. Indeed, now the profound and paradoxical aspect to his role as one who stands in ironic relation to the Maccabean tradition emerges all the more clearly. He will not, as the Maccabees did, and Peter and others now risk doing, rebuild Judaism – a Judaism which was dismantled when he encountered, believed in, and became conformed to Christ. Paul's rationale is twofold. First, Israel's ultimate enemy is not found in the form of Gentile sinners or even Jewish apostates, but deeply within itself: no less than the Gentiles, Israel is in Adam. Hence, it is not Paul but rather his Jewish(-Christian) opponents who could be designated servants of sin. Second, this scenario is all the more incredible since it is precisely in and through Christ that they have been rescued from that very condition towards which they are in danger of returning. Here the paradox is at its most profound. It is the Jesus whom Israel rejected due to sin's abuse of Torah within the nation who, in taking Israel's sin upon himself, proved to be Israel's representative martyred and now exalted Messiah. He is the eschatological redeemer who rescued Israel from an affliction which lay within, and even now he enables Israel to live a risen and exalted life as the people of God. Such is the transformed existence of Paul himself who, with Christ in him, is now fully conformed to his faithfulness and so lives to God. Thus he will not nullify all that has been accomplished. A gracious God has ultimately manifested his love and covenant faithfulness in the self-sacrifice of his Son; through him, and those in him (Jew and Gentile), he has reconciled Israel and thence the whole world.

CONCLUSION

This monograph has attempted to forge a new interpretation of a text central to any estimation of both Pauline theology and the early Christian church. Inasmuch as this has arisen from the cumulative weight of converging lines of evidence – often novel and significant in their own right – we may conclude by briefly recapitulating the most important contributions made at each stage of our enterprise. In sum, it has been contended that:

(i) Constitutive of the Jewish response to the epic Maccabean crisis were two key interrelated themes: (a) the suffering and vindication of the people of God, especially as focused upon certain martyr figures; and (b) emerging from this, in relation to Daniel 7.13–14, ongoing messianic speculation concerning an eschatological redeemer who would deliver and restore afflicted Israel.

(ii) The ethos and religio-political aspirations of the Maccabees remained a living tradition in first-century Judaism, fuelling Jewish–Christian conflict – not least insofar as this involved Paul, whether as a zealous Pharisee or a Jewish Christian convert.

(iii) All this is of significant bearing upon the Galatian crisis, the conceptual framework governing Paul's response thereto, and his autobiographical narrative in Galatians 1 and 2. The Galatian scenario, attended by conflict and persecution, may be perceived as an inversion of the Maccabean crisis. Paul's conceptual framework may be understood as a Jewish apocalyptic (e.g., Danielic) schema now radically reconfigured through Jesus Christ, Israel's (unexpected) eschatological redeemer. From the essentially paradigmatic autobiography, Paul emerges as one in ironic relation to the Maccabean tradition, who – though afflicted by Jewish

(-Christian) opponents – remains conformed to the Son of God 'in him'.

(iv) The distinct but complementary impressions which emerge from Josephus and Acts on the Jewish and Christian communities in Antioch, suggest the inevitability of a Messiah Jesus-focused conflict over who comprised the faithful people of God.

(v) When seen in relation to Maccabean martyrdom, and also its more circumscribed (but consonant) literary and historical context(s), the account of the Antioch incident at Galatians 2.11–14 appears as a conflict between Peter the Jewish Christian at some risk of reverting to a life 'in Judaism' and Paul the 'ironic Maccabean' zealously committed to a life 'in Christ'. Paul regarded Peter's move towards Judaism as threatening the mixed Antiochene community's commensality with their now exalted eschatological redeemer – and, by extension, the gospel and the church's inclusive mission at large – and so he stood to defend the truth of the gospel.

(vi) From the pursuant theological argument at Galatians 2.15–21, it is evident that for Paul the truth of the gospel centred upon the outworking of God's grace in the death and resurrection of Christ. In contrast to his Jewish (-Christian) detractors, Paul discerned both the severity of the problem (the διὰ νόμου existence of Israel-in-Adam) and the profound nature of the solution (dying and rising as Israel-in-Christ). In sum, the Maccabean model of Judaism is radically reconfigured in a paradoxical and provocative fashion: the rejected Jesus turns out to be the martyred and exalted Messiah, the eschatological redeemer who rescued Israel (and the world) from the Adamic enemy within, so that together they might live to God.

By this route we have arrived at what was at stake in Antioch and, indeed, throughout Paul's life and ministry amongst the messianic people of God.

BIBLIOGRAPHY

Primary sources: texts and translations

Apocalypsis Henochi Graeci in *Pseudepigrapha Veteris Testamenti*, ed. M. Black, PVTG 3, Leiden, E. J. Brill, 1970.
The Apostolic Fathers, 2 vols., ed. and trans. K. Lake, LCL, Cambridge, Mass., Harvard University Press, 1913.
The Arabic Original of Ibn Shahin's Book of Comfort, ed. J. Obermann, Yale Oriental Series XVII, New Haven, Yale University Press, 1933.
Die Aramäischen Texte vom Toten Meer, ed. K. Beyer, Göttingen, Vanderhoeck & Ruprecht, 1984.
The Assumption of Moses, R. H. Charles, London, 1897.
The Assumption of Moses. A Critical Edition with Commentary, ed. Johannes Tromp, Leiden, E. J. Brill, 1993.
Biblia Hebraica Stuttgartensia, ed. K. Elliger and W. Rudolph, Stuttgart, Deutsche Bibelstiftung, 1977.
The Chronicle of John Malalas, trans. Elizabeth Jeffreys, Michael Jeffreys and Roger Scott, Australian Association for Byzantine Studies, Melbourne, Byzantina Australiensia, 1986.
The Dead Sea Scrolls Translated, ed. Florentino García Martínez, trans. Wilfred G. E. Watson, Leiden, E. J. Brill, 1994.
Diodorus Siculus, trans. Francis R. Walton, LCL, Cambridge, Mass., Harvard University Press, 1967.
Epictetus, 2 vols., trans. W. A. Oldfather, Cambridge, Mass., Harvard University Press, 1925, 1928.
Eusebius: The Ecclesiastical History, 2 vols., ed. and trans. K. Lake and J. C. L. Oulton, LCL, Cambridge, Mass., Harvard University Press, 1926–32.
The Fourth Book of Ezra. The Latin Version Edited from the MSS, ed. R. L. Bensly, TextS 3.2, Cambridge, 1895.
Die Geschichte von den Zehn Märtyrern. Synoptische Edition mit Übersetzung und Einleitung, ed. G. Reeg, TSAJ 10, Tübingen, J. C. B. Mohr (Paul Siebeck), 1985.
The Greek New Testament, ed. Kurt Aland, Matthew Black, Carlo M. Martini, Bruce M. Metzger and Allen Wikgren, 3rd edition, London, British and Foreign Bible Society, 1975.

The Greek New Testament, ed. Kurt Aland, Matthew Black, Carlo M. Martini, Bruce M. Metzger and Allen Wikgren, 3rd edition, United Bible Societies, 1975.
Hebrew–English Edition of the Babylonian Talmud, 20 vols., ed. I. Epstein, London, Soncino, 1972–84.
Ioannis Malalae Chronographia, ed. Wilhelm Dindorf, Bonn, Corpus Scriptorum Historiae Byzantinae, 1831.
Josephus: Works, 10 vols., ed. H. St. J. Thackeray, R. Marcus, A. Wikgren and L. H. Feldman, Cambridge, Mass., Harvard University Press, 1926–65.
Libanius, 'Antiochikos', trans. with commentary by G. Downey, *PAPS* 103 (1959) 652–86.
Livy, vol. XII, trans. Evan T. Sage and Alfred C. Schlesinger, LCL, Cambridge, Mass., Harvard University Press, 1938.
The Third and Fourth Books of Maccabees, ed. and trans. M. Hadas, Philadelphia, Dropsie College, 1953.
Midrash Rabbah, 10 vols., ed. H. Freedman and M. Simon, London, Soncino, 1961.
The Mishnah, trans. Herbert Danby, Oxford, Oxford University Press, 1933.
Mishnayoth, 7 vols., ed. P. Blackman, 2nd edition, New York, The Judaica Press, 1964.
New Documents Illustrating Early Christianity, ed. G. H. R. Horsley, Macquarie, The Ancient History Documentary Research Centre, 1977–8.
The New Oxford Annotated Bible with the Apocrypha. Revised Standard Version, ed. Herbert G. May and Bruce M. Metzger, 2nd edition, Oxford, Oxford University Press, 1977.
Novum Testamentum Graece, eds. Kurt Aland, Matthew Black, Carlo M. Martini, Bruce M. Metzger and Allen Wikgren, 26th edition, Stuttgart, Deutsche Bibelgesellschaft, 1979.
The Old Testament Pseudepigrapha, 2 vols., ed. J. H. Charlesworth, Garden City, Doubleday, 1983, 1985.
Philo: The Complete Works, 12 vols., ed. F. H. Colson, G. H. Whitaker, J. W. Earp and R. Marcus, LCL, Cambridge, Mass., Harvard University Press, 1929–53.
Polybius, Histories, vol. V, trans. W. R. Paton, LCL, Cambridge, Mass., Harvard University Press, 1927.
Pseudo-Philon, Les antiquités bibliques, ed. D. J. Harrington, J. Cazeaux, C. Bogaert, C. Perrot and P.-M. Bogaert, Paris, Sources Chrétiennes, 1976.
Saint John Chrysostom: Discourse Against Judaizing Christians, trans. P. W. Harkins, Washington, D.C., The Catholic University of America Press, 1979.
Septuaginta, ed. A. Rahlfs, Stuttgart, Deutsche Bibelstiftung, 1935.
Suetonius, vol. II, trans. J. C. Rolfe, LCL, Cambridge, Mass., Harvard University Press, 1938.
Tacitus: The Annals, trans. John Jackson, LCL, Cambridge, Mass., Harvard University Press, 1937.
Tacitus: The Histories, vol. I, trans. Clifford H. Moore, LCL, Cambridge, Mass., Harvard University Press, 1925.

Die Texte aus Qumran: Hebräisch und Deutsch, ed. E. Lohse, 3rd edition, Darmstadt, Wissenschaftliche Buchgesellschaft, 1981.
Theophilus of Antioch: Ad Autolycum, trans. R. M. Grant, Oxford Early Christian Texts, Oxford, Clarendon, 1970.

Secondary sources

Abegg, Martin. 'Paul, "Works of the Law" and MMT', *BAR* 20 (1994) 52–5.
Abel, F. M. *Les livres des Maccabées*, 2nd edition, Paris, Gabalda, 1949.
Agus, Aharon. *The Binding of Isaac and Messiah. Law, Martyrdom and Deliverance in Early Rabbinic Religiosity*, Albany, State University of New York Press, 1988.
Alon, G. 'Did the Nation and Its People Cause the Hasmoneans to be Forgotten?', in his *Jews, Judaism and the Classical World. Studies in Jewish History in the Times of the Second Temple and Talmud*, ET, Jerusalem, The Magnes Press, 1977, 1–17.
Amadi-Azuogu, C. A. *Paul and the Law in the Argument of Galatians: A Rhetorical and Exegetical Analysis of Galatians 2,14–6,2*, BBB 104, Weinheim, Beltz Athenäum, 1996.
Amir, Y. 'The Term *Ioudaismos*: A Study in Jewish-Hellenistic Self-identification', *Immanuel* 14 (1982) 34–41.
Auvray, P. 'Saint Jérôme et Saint Augustin. La controverse au sujet de l'incident d'Antioch', *RevScRel* 29 (1939) 594–610.
Baasland, E. 'Persecution: A Neglected Feature in the Letter to the Galatians', *ST* 38 (1984) 135–50.
Bachmann, Michael. *Sünder oder Übertreter. Studien zur Argumentation in Gal. 2,15ff*, WUNT 59, Tübingen, J. C. B. Mohr (Paul Siebeck), 1992.
Bacon, B. W. 'The Festival of Lives Given for the Nation in Jewish and Christian Faith', *HeyJ* 15 (1916–17) 256–78.
Balsdon, J. P. V. D. *The Emperor Gaius (Caligula)*, Oxford, Oxford University Press, 1934.
Bammel, C. P. Hammond. 'Ignatian Problems', *JTS* 33 (1982) 62–97.
Bammel, E. 'Zum jüdischen Märtyrercult', *TLZ* 78 (1953) 119–26.
  'Galater 1,23', *ZNW* 59 (1968) 108–12.
  'Πτωχός', *TDNT* 6 (1968) 888–915.
Barclay, John M. G. 'Paul and the Law: Observations on Some Recent Debates', *Themelios* 12 (1986) 5–15.
  'Mirror-Reading a Polemical Letter: Galatians as a Test Case,' *JSNT* 31 (1987) 73–93.
  Obeying the Truth: A Study of Paul's Ethics in Galatians, Edinburgh, T. & T. Clark, 1988.
  Jews in the Mediterranean Diaspora: From Alexander to Trajan (323 BCE–117 CE), Edinburgh, T. & T. Clark, 1996.
Bar-Kochva, Bezalel. *Judas Maccabaeus: The Jewish Struggle Against the Seleucids*, Cambridge, Cambridge University Press, 1989.
Barré, M. L. 'Paul as "Eschatologic Person"', *CBQ* 37 (1975) 508–19.
Barrett, C. K. 'Paul and the "pillar" Apostles', in *Studia Paulina, in Honorem Johannes de Zwaan Septugenerii*, ed. J. N. Sevenster and W. C. van Unnik, Haarlem, Bohn, 1953, 1–19.

Essays on Paul, London, SPCK, 1982.
Freedom and Obligation. A Study of the Epistle to the Galatians, Philadelphia, Westminster Press, 1985.
Bartlett, John R. *1 Maccabees*, Guides to Apocrypha and Pseudepigrapha, Sheffield, Sheffield Academic Press, 1998.
Bauckham, R. J. 'Barnabas in Galatians', *JSNT* 2 (1979) 61–70.
'James and the Jerusalem Church', in *The Book of Acts in Its First Century Setting*, volume 4: *The Book of Acts in Its Palestinian Setting*, ed. Richard Bauckham, Grand Rapids, Eerdmans, 1995, 415–80.
'James and the Gentiles (Acts 15.13–21)', in *History, Literature, and Society in the Book of Acts*, ed. B. Witherington, Cambridge, Cambridge University Press, 1996.
'For What Offence Was James Put to Death?', in *James the Just and Christian Origins*, ed. Bruce Chilton and Craig A. Evans, Leiden, E. J. Brill, 1999, 199–232.
Bauer, W., Arndt, W. F., Gingrich, F. W., and Danker, F. W. *A Greek–English Lexicon of the New Testament and Other Early Christian Literature*, 2nd edition, Chicago, University of Chicago Press, 1979.
Baumeister, Theofried. *Die Anfänge der Theologie des Martyriums*, MBT 45, Münster, Aschendorff, 1980.
Baumgarten, Albert I. *The Flourishing of Jewish Sects in the Maccabean Era: An Interpretation*, SJSJ, Leiden, E. J. Brill, 1997.
Baur, F. C. 'Die Christuspartei in der korinthischen Gemeinde, der Gegensatz des petrischen und paulinischen Christenthums in der ältesten Kirche, der Apostel Petrus in Rom', *TZT* 4 (1831) 61–206.
Beasley-Murray, G. R. 'The Interpretation of Daniel 7', *CBQ* 45 (1983) 44–58.
Becker, J. *Der Brief an die Galater*, 17th edition, NTD 8, Göttingen, Vanderhoeck & Ruprecht, 1990, 1–85.
Betz, H. D. *Galatians: A Commentary on Paul's Letter to the Churches in Galatia*, Hermeneia, Philadelphia, Fortress Press, 1979.
Beyer, H. W. and Althaus, P. 'Der Brief an die Galater', in *Die kleineren Briefe des Apostels Paulus*, NTD 8, Göttingen, Vandenhoeck & Ruprecht, 1965, 1–55.
Bickerman(n), E. J. 'The Name of Christians', *HTR* 42 (1949) 109–24.
'The Date of Fourth Maccabees', in his *Studies in Jewish and Christian History*, part I, Leiden, E. J. Brill, 1976, 276–81.
The God of the Maccabees: Studies on the Meaning and Origin of the Maccabean Revolt, ET, Leiden, E. J. Brill, 1979.
'Un document relatif à la persécution d'Antiochus IV Epiphane', in his *Studies in Jewish and Christian History*, part II, Leiden, E. J. Brill, 1980, 105–36.
'Les Maccabées de Malalas,' in his *Studies in Jewish and Christian History*, part II, Leiden, E. J. Brill, 1980, 192–201.
Bilde, P. 'The Roman Emperor Gaius (Caligula)'s Attempt to Erect His Statue in the Temple of Jerusalem,' *ST* 32 (1978) 67–93.
Bittner, W. 'Gott-Menschensohn-Davidsohn. Eine Untersuchung zur Traditionsgeschichte von Daniel 7,13f.', *Freiburger Zeitschrift für Philosophie und Theologie* 32 (1985) 343–72.

Black II, C. C. 'The Rhetorical Form of the Hellenistic Jewish and Early Christian Sermon: A Response to Lawrence Wills', *HTR* 81 (1988) 1–18.
Black, M. 'Die Apotheose Israels: Eine neue Interpretation des danielischen "Menschensohns"', in *Jesus und der Menschensohn. FS A. Vögtle*, ed. R. Pesche and R. Schnackenburg, Freiburg, Basel and Vienna, 1975, 92–9.
'The Throne-Theophany Prophetic Commission and the "Son of Man": A Study in Tradition-History', in *Jews, Greeks and Christians*, ed. R. Hamerton-Kelly and R. Scroggs, Leiden, E. J. Brill, 1976, 56–63.
The Book of Enoch or 1 Enoch, SVTP 7, Leiden, E. J. Brill, 1985.
'The Messianism of the Parables of Enoch. Their Date and Contribution to Christological Origins', in *The Messiah. Developments in Earliest Judaism and Christianity*, ed. J. H. Charlesworth, Minneapolis, Fortress Press, 1992, 145–68.
Blass, F., Debrunner, A. and Funk, R. W. *A Greek Grammar of the New Testament and Other Early Christian Literature*, Chicago, University of Chicago Press, 1961.
Bockmuehl, Markus N. A. *Jewish Law in Gentile Churches. Halakhah and the Beginning of Christian Public Ethics*, Edinburgh: T&T Clark, 2000.
Boismard, M.-E. 'Le martyre d'Etienne: Actes 6,8–8,2', *RSR* 69 (1981) 181–94.
Bonnard, Pierre. *L'Epitre de Saint Paul aux Galates*, 2nd edition, CNT 9, Paris, Delachaux et Niestlé, 1972.
Bornkamm, G. *Paul*, ET, San Francisco, Harper & Row, 1971.
Borse, Udo. *Der Brief an die Galater*, RNT, Regensburg, Pustet, 1984.
Botterweck, G. Johannes and Ringgren, Helmer, (eds.). *Theological Dictionary of the Old Testament*, trans. John T. Willis, David E. Green, Geoffrey W. Bromiley and Douglas W. Stott, Grand Rapids, Eerdmans, 1974–.
Böttger, Paul C. 'Paulus und Petrus in Antiochien. Zum Verständnis von Galater 2.11–21', *NTS* 37 (1991) 77–100.
Bouchier, E. S. *A Short History of Antioch, 300 B.C.–A.D. 1268*, Oxford, Basil Blackwell, 1921.
Bowersock, G. W. *Martyrdom and Rome*, Cambridge, Cambridge University Press, 1995.
Boyarin, Daniel. *A Radical Jew. Paul and the Politics of Identity*, Berkeley and Los Angeles: University of California Press, 1994.
Brauch, Manfred T. 'Perspectives on "God's Righteousness" in Recent German Discussion', in *Paul and Palestinian Judaism: A Comparison of Patterns of Religion*, by E. P. Sanders, Philadelphia, Fortress Press, 1977.
Breitenstein, U. *Beobachtungen zu Sprache, Stil und Gedankengut des Vierten Makkabäerbuchs*, Basel and Stuttgart, Schwabe & Co., 1976.
Breytenbach, C. *Versöhnung: Eine Studie zur paulinischen Soteriologie*, WMANT 60, Neukirchen-Vluyn, Neukirchener, 1989.
Paulus und Barnabas in der Provinz Galatien: Studien zu Apostelgeschichte 13f.; 16.6; 18.23 und den Adressaten des Galaterbriefes, AGJU, Leiden, E. J. Brill, 1996.

Bring, R. *Commentary on Galatians*, ET, Philadelphia, Muhlenberg Press, 1961.
Bringmann, K. 'Die Verfolgung der jüdischen Religion durch Antiochos IV: Ein Konflikt zwischen Judentum und Hellenismus', *Antike und Abendland* 26 (1980) 176–90.
Hellenistische Reform und Religionsverfolgung in Judäa. Eine Untersuchung zur jüdisch-hellenistischen Geschichte (175–163 v. Chr.), Göttingen, Vandenhoeck & Ruprecht, 1983.
Broshi, Magen and Eshel, Esther. 'The Greek King is Antiochus IV (4QHistorical Text = 4Q248)', *JJS* 48 (1997), 120–9.
Brown, Francis, Driver, S. R. and Briggs, Charles A. *A Hebrew and English Lexicon of the Old Testament*, Oxford, Clarendon, 1977.
Brown, R. E. 'Not Jewish Christianity and Gentile Christianity but Types of Jewish/Gentile Christianity', *CBQ* 45 (1983) 74–9.
Brown, R. E. and Meier, J. P. *Antioch and Rome: New Testament Cradles of Catholic Christianity*, London, Geoffrey Chapman, 1983.
Brox, Norbert. *Zeuge und Märtyrer. Untersuchungen zur frühchristlichen Zeugnis-Terminologie*, STANT 5, Munich, Kösel-Verlag, 1961.
Bruce, F. F. *The Epistle to the Galatians: A Commentary on the Greek Text*, NIGTC, Grand Rapids, Eerdmans, 1982.
1 & 2 Thessalonians, WBC, Waco, Word Publishing, 1982.
The Acts of the Apostles. The Greek Text with Introduction and Commentary, 3rd revised and enlarged edition, Grand Rapids, Eerdmans, 1990.
Bultmann, R. *Theology of the New Testament*, 2 vols., ET, London, SCM Press, 1952, 1955.
'Ignatius und Paulus', in *Studia Paulina, in Honorem Johannes de Zwaan Septugenerii*, ed. J. N. Sevenster and W. C. van Unnik, Haarlem, Bohn, 1953, 37–51.
'ΔΙΚΑΙΟΣΥΝΗ ΘΕΟΥ', *JBL* 83 (1964) 12–16.
'Zur Auslegung von Gal. 2, 15–18', in *Exegetica: Aufsätze zur Erforschung des Neuen Testaments*, ed. Erich Dinkler, Tübingen, J. C. B. Mohr (Paul Siebeck), 1967, 394–9.
Bunge, J. G. *Untersuchungen zum zweiten Makkabäerbuch: Quellenkritische, literarische, chronologische und historische Untersuchungen zum zweiten Makkabäerbuch als Quelle syrisch-palestinenischer Geschichte im 2. Jh. v. Chr.*, Bonn, Rheinischen Friedrich-Wilhelms Universität, 1971.
Burton, Ernest de Witt. *A Critical and Exegetical Commentary on the Epistle to the Galatians*, ICC, Edinburgh, T. & T. Clark, 1921.
Campbell, D. A. *The Rhetoric of Righteousness in Romans 3.21–26*, JSNTSup 65, Sheffield, JSOT Press, 1992.
Caquot, A. 'Le messianisme Qumrânien', in *Qumrân: sa piété, sa théologie et son milieu*, ed. M. Delcor, BETL 46, Paris, Leuven, 1978, 231–47.
Caragounis, Chrys C. *The Son of Man*, Tübingen, J. C. B. Mohr (Paul Siebeck), 1986.
Carrington, P. 'Peter in Antioch', *ATR* (1933) 15:1–15.
Casey, P. M. *The Son of Man: The Interpretation and Influence of Daniel 7*, London, SPCK, 1979.

From Jewish Prophet to Gentile God. The Origins and Development of New Testament Christology, Cambridge, James Clarke & Co., 1991.
'Method in Our Madness and Madness in Their Methods. Some Approaches to the Son of Man Problem in Recent Scholarship', *JSNT* 42 (1991) 17–43.
Catchpole, D. R. 'Paul, James and the Apostolic Decree', *NTS* 4 (1977) 428–45.
Charlesworth, J. H. (ed.). *The Messiah. Developments in Earliest Judaism and Christianity*, Minneapolis, Fortress Press, 1992.
Ciampa, Roy E. *The Presence and Function of Scripture in Galatians 1 and 2*, WUNT 2, Tübingen, J. C. B. Mohr (Paul Siebeck), 1998.
Cohen, S. J. D. *From the Maccabees to the Mishnah*, Philadelphia, Westminster Press, 1987.
'Religion, Ethnicity and "Hellenism" in the Emergence of Jewish Identity in Maccabean Palestine', in *Religion and Religious Practice in the Seleucid Kingdom*, ed. P. A. O. Bilde, Aarhus, Aarhus University Press, 1990.
Cohn-Sherbok, Dan. *The Jewish Messiah*, Edinburgh, T. & T. Clark, 1997.
Collins, J. J. *The Apocalyptic Vision of the Book of Daniel*, Missoula, Scholars Press, 1977.
'Messianism in the Maccabean Period', in *Judaisms and Their Messiahs at the Turn of the Christian Era*, ed. Jacob Neusner, Scott Green and Ernest S. Frerichs, Cambridge, Cambridge University Press, 1987, 97–110.
'The Son of Man in First Century Judaism', *NTS* 38 (1992) 448–66.
A Commentary on the Book of Daniel, Hermeneia, Minneapolis, Fortress Press, 1993.
'The Son of God Text from Qumran', in *From Jesus to John: Essays on Jesus and NT Christology in Honour of Marinus de Jonge*, ed. Martinus De Boer, JSNTSup 84, Sheffield, JSOT Press, 1993.
The Scepter and the Star: The Messiahs of the Dead Sea Scrolls and Other Ancient Literature, ABRL, New York, Doubleday, 1995.
'Jesus and the Messiahs of Israel', in *Geschichte – Tradition – Reflexion: Festschrift für Martin Hengel*, vol. I, ed. H. Cancik, H. Lichtenberger and P. Schäfer, Tübingen, J. C. B. Mohr (Paul Siebeck), 1996, 287–302.
'The Background of the "Son of God" Text', *BBR* 7 (1997) 51–62.
The Apocalyptic Imagination: An Introduction to Jewish Apocalyptic Literature, 2nd edition, Grand Rapids, Eerdmans, 1998.
Between Athens and Jerusalem. Jewish Identity in the Hellenistic Diaspora, 2nd edition, BRS, Grand Rapids, Eerdmans, 2000.
Conzelmann, H. *An Outline of the Theology of the New Testament*, ET, London, SCM Press, 1969.
Cook, Edward M. '4Q246', in *BBR* 5 (1995) 43–66.
Coppens, J. *La relève apocalyptique du messianisme royal*, volume II: *Le fils d'homme vétéro et intertestamentaire*, Leuven, Leuven University Press, 1983.
Corwin, Virginia. *St Ignatius and Christianity in Antioch*, Yale Publications in Religion 1, New Haven, Yale University Press, 1960.

Cousar, Charles B. *Galatians*, Interpretation, Atlanta, John Knox Press, 1982.
— *A Theology of the Cross. The Death of Jesus in the Pauline Letters*, Minneapolis, Fortress Press, 1990.
Cranfield, C. E. B. *A Critical and Exegetical Commentary on the Epistle to the Romans*, 2 vols., ICC, Edinburgh, T. & T. Clark, 1975, 1979.
— 'The Works of the Law', *JSNT* 43 (1991), 89–101.
Crossan, John Dominic. *The Historical Jesus: The Life of a Mediterranean Jewish Peasant*, Edinburgh, T. & T. Clark, 1991.
Crowe, J. *From Jerusalem to Antioch. The Gospel Across Cultures*. Collegeville, Liturgical Press, 1997.
Cullmann, O. *The Christology of the New Testament*, rev. edn., Philadelphia, Westminster Press, 1963.
— 'Courants multiples dans la communauté primitive: à propos du martyre de Jacques de Zebedée', *RevScRel* 60 (1972) 55–68.
Dahl, N. A. *Jesus the Christ. The Historical Origins of Christological Doctrine*, ed. Donald H. Juel, Minneapolis, Fortress Press, 1991.
Dauer, Anton. *Paulus und die christliche Gemeinde im syrischen Antiochia. Kritische Bestandsaufnahme der modernen Forschung mit einigen weiterführenden Überlegungen*, BBB 106, Weinheim, Beltz Athenäum, 1996.
Davies, P. E. 'Did Jesus die as a Martyr Prophet?', *BR* 2 (1957) 19–30.
Davies, Philip R. *Daniel*, Old Testament Guides, Sheffield, JSOT Press, 1985.
Davies, W. D. and Finkelstein, Louis. *The Cambridge History of Judaism*, volume II: *The Hellenistic Age*, Cambridge, Cambridge University Press, 1989.
De Boer, Martinus (ed.). *From Jesus to John. Essays on Jesus and New Testament Christology in Honour of Marinus de Jonge*, JSNTSup 84, Sheffield, JSOT Press, 1993.
Delcor, M. *Le livre de Daniel*, SB, Paris, Gabalda, 1971.
Dequeker, Luc. 'The Saints of the Most High in Qumran and Daniel', *OTS* 18 (1973) 133–62.
Derfler, Steven L. *The Hasmonean Revolt. Rebellion or Revolution*, Lewiston, Lampeter and Queenston, Edwin Mellen Press, 1989.
deSilva, David A. *4 Maccabees*, Guides to Apocrypha and Pseudepigrapha. Sheffield, Sheffield Academic Press, 1998.
Dodd, Brian J. 'Christ's Slave, People Pleasers and Galatians 1.10', *NTS* 42 (1996) 90–104.
Doeve, J. W. 'Paulus der Pharisäer und Galater 1:13–15', *NovT* 6 (1963) 170–81.
Donaldson, T. L. 'The "Curse of the Law" and the Inclusion of the Gentiles: Galatians 3.13–14', *NTS* 32 (1986) 94–112.
— 'Zealot and Convert: The Origin of Paul's Christ-Torah Antithesis', *CBQ* 51 (1989) 655–82.
— *Paul and the Gentiles: Remapping the Apostle's Convictional World*, Minneapolis, Fortress Press, 1997.
Doran, R. 'The Martyr: A Synoptic View of the Mother and Her Seven Sons', in *Ideal Figures in Ancient Judaism*, ed. J. J. Collins and G. W. E. Nickelsburg, Chico, Calif., Scholars Press, 1980.

Temple Propaganda: The Purpose and Character of 2 Maccabees, CBQMS 12, Washington, D.C., Catholic Biblical Association of America, 1981.
Dornseiff, F. 'Der Märtyrer: Name und Berwertung', *ARW* 22 (1923-4) 133-9.
Downey, G. 'The Political Status of Roman Antioch', *Berytus* 6 (1939-40) 1-6.
'Strabo on Antioch: Notes on His Method', *TAPA* 72 (1941) 85-95.
'Libanius' Oration in Praise of Antioch', *PAPS* 103 (1959) 652-86.
A History of Antioch in Syria from Seleucus to the Arab Conquest, Princeton, Princeton University Press, 1961.
Ancient Antioch, Princeton, Princeton University Press, 1963.
Downing, John. 'Jesus and Martyrdom', *JTS* 14 (1963) 279-93.
Duncan, G. S. *The Epistle of Paul to the Galatians*, MNTC, London, Hodder & Stoughton, 1934.
Dunn, James D. G. '"A Light to the Gentiles": The Significance of the Damascus Road Christology for Paul', in *The Glory of Christ in the New Testament: Studies in Christology in Memory of George Bradford Caird*, ed. L. D. Hurst and N. T. Wright, Oxford, Oxford University Press, 1987, 251-66.
Romans, 2 vols., WBC 38A,B, Dallas, Word Books, 1988.
Jesus, Paul and the Law. Studies in Mark and Galatians, London, SPCK, 1990.
'What Was the Real Issue Between Paul and "Those of the Circumcision"?', in *Paulus als Theologe und Missionar und antike Judentum*, ed. M. Hengel and U. Heckel, WUNT 58, Tübingen, J. C. B. Mohr (Paul Siebeck), 1990, 295-317.
The Partings of the Ways Between Christianity and Judaism and Their Significance for the Character of Christianity, London, SCM Press, 1991.
'The Justice of God: A Renewed Perspective on Justification by Faith', *JTS* 43 (1992) 1-22.
'Messianic Ideas and Their Influence on the Jesus of History', in *The Messiah. Developments in Earliest Judaism and Christianity*, ed. J. H. Charlesworth, Minneapolis, Fortress Press, 1992, 365-81.
Galatians, BNTC, London, A. & C. Black, 1993.
The Theology of Paul's Letter to the Galatians, Cambridge, Cambridge University Press, 1993.
'Echoes of Intra-Jewish Polemic in Paul's Letter to the Galatians', *JBL* 112 (1993) 459-77.
'Once More ΠΙΣΤΙΣ ΧΡΙΣΤΟΥ', *SBLSP* (1993) 730-44.
'Yet Once More – "The Works of the Law": A Response', *JSNT* 46 (1996) 99-117.
'Paul and Justification by Faith', in *The Road from Damascus: The Impact of Paul's Conversion on His Life, Thought, and Ministry*, ed. R. N. Longenecker, Grand Rapids, Eerdmans, 1997, 85-105.
'4QMMT and Galatians', *NTS* 43 (1997) 147-53.
The Theology of Paul the Apostle, Grand Rapids, Eerdmans, 1998.
'Who Did Paul Think He Was? A Study of Jewish-Christianity', *NTS* 45 (1999) 174-93.

Dunn, James D. G. (ed.). *Paul and the Mosaic Law. The Third Durham–Tübingen Research Symposium on Earliest Christianity and Judaism (Durham, September, 1994)*, WUNT 89, Tübingen, J. C. B. Mohr (Paul Siebeck), 1996.

Dupont, J. 'Pierre et Paul à Antioche et Jérusalem', in *Etudes sur les Acts des Apôtres*, LD 45, Paris, Cerf, 1967.

Dupont-Sommer, André. *Le quatrième livre des Machabées. Introduction, traduction et notes*, Paris, Librairie Ancienne Honoré Champion, 1939.

Eckert, J. *Die urchristliche Verkündigung im Streit zwischen Paulus und seinen Gegnern nach dem Galaterbrief*, BU 6, Regensburg, Friedrich Pustet, 1971.

Eckstein, H.-J. *Verheissung und Gesetz. Eine exegetische Untersuchung zu Galater 2,15–4.7*, WUNT 86, Tübingen, J. C. B. Mohr (Paul Siebeck), 1996.

Efron, Joshua. *Studies on the Hasmonean Period*, Leiden, E. J. Brill, 1987.

Ehrman, Bart D. 'Cephas and Peter', *JBL* 109 (1990) 463–74.

Ellicott, C. J. *St Paul's Epistle to the Galatians*, 3rd edition, London, Longman, 1863.

Eltester, W. 'Die Kirchen Antiochias im IV. Jahrhundert', *ZNW* 36 (1937) 251–86.

Emerton, J. A. 'The Origins of the Son of Man Imagery', *JTS* 9 (1958) 225–42.

Esler, Philip F. *Community and Gospel in Luke–Acts. The Social and Political Motivations of Lucan Theology*, SNTSMS 57, Cambridge, Cambridge University Press, 1987.

Galatians, New Testament Readings, London and New York, Routledge, 1998.

Fairchild, Mark R. 'Paul's Pre-Christian Zealot Associations: A Re-examination of Gal 1.14 and Acts 22.3', *NTS* 45 (1999) 514–32.

Farmer, W. R. *Maccabees, Zealots and Josephus*, New York, Columbia University Press, 1956.

Fee, Gordon D. *The First Epistle to the Corinthians*, NICNT, Grand Rapids, Eerdmans, 1987.

Feld, H. '"Christus, Diener der Sünde": Zum Ausgang des Streites zwischen Petrus und Paulus', *TQ* 153 (1973) 119–31.

Feldman, Louis H. *Jew and Gentile in the Ancient World: Attitudes and Interactions from Alexander to Justinian*, Princeton, Princeton University Press, 1993.

Feuillet, A. 'Le fils de l'homme de Daniel et la tradition biblique', *RB* 60 (1953) 170–202, 321–46.

Fischel, H. A. 'Martyr and Prophet: A Study in Jewish Literature', *JQR* 37 (1946–7) 265–80, 363–86.

Fischer, T. *Seleukiden und Makkabäer: Beiträge zur Seleukidengeschichte und zu den politischen Ereignissen in Judäa während der 1. Hälte des 2. Jahrhunderts v. Chr.*, Bochum, 1980.

Fitzmyer, Joseph A. '4Q246: The "Son of God" Document from Qumran', *Bib* 74 (1993) 153–74.

Flusser, D. 'Das jüdische Martyrium im Zeitalter des zweiten Tempels und die Christologie', *FrRu* 25 (1973) 187–94.

'The Hubris of the Antichrist in a Fragment from Qumran', *Immanuel* 10 (1980) 31–7.
'"Durch das Gesetz dem Gesetz gestorben" (Gal 2.19)', *Judaica* 43 (1987) 30–46.
Fossum, Jarl. 'Son of God', *ABD* 6 (1992) 128–37.
Fredriksen, Paula. 'Judaism, the Circumcision of Gentiles, and Apocalyptic Hope: Another Look at Galatians 1 and 2', *JTS* 42 (1991) 532–64.
Frend, W. H. C. *Martyrdom and Persecution in the Early Church. A Study of a Conflict from the Maccabees to Donatus*, Oxford, Basil Blackwell, 1965.
Friedrich, G. *Die Verkündigung des Todes Jesu im Neuen Testament*, BTS 6, Neukirchen, Neukirchen-Vluyn, 1982.
Fung, R. Y. K. *The Epistle to the Galatians*, NICNT, Grand Rapids, Eerdmans, 1988.
Furnish, Victor Paul. *II Corinthians*, AB 32A, New York, Doubleday, 1984.
Gaechter, P. 'Jerusalem und Antiochia: Ein Beitrag zur urkirchlichen Rechtsentwicklung', *ZKT* 70 (1948) 1–48.
'Petrus in Antiochia (Gal. 2.11–14)', *ZKT* 72 (1950) 177–212.
Gafni, Isayah M. 'The Historical Background', in *The Literature of the Sages. First Part: Oral Tora, Halakha, Mishna, Tosefta, Talmud, External Tractates*, ed. Shmuel Safrai, CRINT 2.3.1, Assen/Maastricht, Van Gorcum, 1987, 1–34.
García Martínez, Florentino. 'The Eschatological Figure of 4Q246', in *Qumran and Apocalyptic: Studies on the Aramaic Texts from Qumran*, Leiden, E. J. Brill, 1992, 162–79.
Garlington, Don B. *The Obedience of Faith. A Pauline Phrase in Historical Context*, WUNT 38, Tübingen, J. C. B. Mohr (Paul Siebeck), 1991.
Gaventa, B. R. *From Darkness to Light: Aspects of Conversion in the New Testament*, Philadelphia, Fortress Press, 1986.
'Galatians 1 and 2: Autobiography as a Paradigm', *NovT* 28 (1986) 309–26.
Geffcken, J. 'Die christlichen Martyrien', *Hermes* 45 (1910) 481–505.
Gelin, A. 'Les origines bibliques de l'idée de Martyre', *LumVie* 36 (1958) 123–9.
Gerdes, H. 'Luther und Augustin über den Streit zwischen Petrus und Paulus zu Antiochien (Galater 2, 11ff.)', *Luther-Jahrbuch* 29 (1962) 9–24.
Goddard, A. J. 'Galatians 2.17–21', an unpublished paper.
Goddard, A. J. and Cummins, S. A. 'Ill or Ill-treated? Conflict and Persecution as the Context of Paul's Original Ministry in Galatia (Galatians 4.12–20)', *JSNT* 52 (1993) 93–126.
Goldingay, John E. *Daniel*, WBC 30, Dallas, Word Books, 1989.
Goldstein, Jonathan A. *I Maccabees*, AB 41, New York, Doubleday, 1976.
II Maccabees, AB 41A, New York, Doubleday, 1983.
'How the Authors of 1 and 2 Maccabees Treated the "Messianic" Promises', in *Judaisms and Their Messiahs at the Turn of the Christian Era*, ed. Jacob Neusner, William Scott Green and Ernest S. Frerichs, Cambridge, Cambridge University Press, 1987, 69–96.

'The Hasmonean Revolt and the Hasmonean Dynasty', in *The Cambridge History of Judaism*, vol. II, ed. W. D. Davies and Louis Finkelstein, Cambridge, Cambridge University Press, 1989, 292–351.

Goodblatt, D. 'The Place of the Pharisees in First-century Judaism: The State of the Debate', *JSJ* 20 (1989) 12–30.

Goodman, Martin. *The Ruling Class of Judaea: The Origins of the Jewish Revolt Against Rome A.D. 66–70*, Cambridge, Cambridge University Press, 1987.

Grabbe, Lester L. *Judaism from Cyrus to Hadrian*, 2 vols., Minneapolis, Fortress Press, 1992.

Grappe, Christian. 'De l'interêt de 4 Maccabeés 17.18–22 (et 16.20–1) pour la christologie du NT', *NTS* 46 (2000) 342–57.

Greenfield, Jonas C. and Stone, Michael E. 'The Enochic Pentateuch and the Date of the Similitudes', *HTR* 70 (1977) 51–5.

Grimm, C. L. W. 'Das zweite, dritte, und vierte Buch der Maccabäer', in *Kurzgefasstes exegetisches Handbuch zu den Apokryphen des Alten Testaments*, Leipzig, S. Hirzel, 1857, 283–370.

Gruen, Erich S. 'Hellenism and Persecution: Antiochus IV and the Jews', in *Hellenistic History and Culture*, ed. and intro. Peter Green, Berkeley, University of California Press, 1993, 238–64.

Güttgemanns, Erhardt. *Der leidende Apostel und sein Herr: Studien zur Paulinischen Christologie*, FRLANT 90, Göttingen, Vandenhoeck & Ruprecht, 1966.

Haacker, K. 'Die Berufung des Verfolgers und die Rechtfertigung des Gottlosen', *TBei* 6 (1975) 1–19.

Habicht, C. *2 Makkabäerbuch*, JSHRZ 1/3, Gütersloh, G. Mohn, 1976.

'The Seleucids and Their Rivals', *CAH* 8 (1989) 324–87.

Haddad, G. 'Aspects of Social Life in Antioch in the Hellenistic-Roman Period', Ph.D. dissertation, Chicago, 1949.

Haenchen, Ernst. *The Acts of the Apostles. A Commentary*, trans. Bernard Noble and Gerald Shinn, revised by R. M. L. Wilson, Oxford, Basil Blackwell, 1971.

Haider, P. W., Hutter, M. and Kreuzer, S. (eds.). *Religionsgeschichte Syriens. Von der Frühzeit bis zur Gegenwart*, Stuttgart, Berlin and Cologne, Kohlhammer, 1996.

Hall, R .G. 'Historical Interference and Rhetorical Effect: Another Look at Galatians 1 and 2', in *Persuasive Artistry: Studies in New Testament Rhetoric in Honor of G. A. Kennedy,* ed. D. F. Watson, JSNTSS 50, Sheffield, JSOT Press, 1991.

Hann, Robert R. 'Judaism and Jewish Christianity in Antioch: Charisma and Conflict in the First Century', *JRH* 14 (1987) 341–60.

Hansen, G. Walter. *Abraham in Galatians. Epistolary and Rhetorical Contexts*, JSNTSup 29, Sheffield, JSOT Press, 1989.

Harrington, D. J. *The Maccabean Revolt: Anatomy of a Biblical Revolution*, Wilmington, Del., Michael Glazier, 1988.

'Did the Pharisees Eat Ordinary Food in a State of Ritual Purity?', *JSJ* 26 (1995) 42–54.

Hartman, Louis F. *Prophecy Interpreted: The Formation of Some Jewish Apocalyptic Texts and of the Eschatological Discourse Mark 13 par.*, Lund, Gleerup, 1966.

Hartman, Louis F. and Di Lella, Alexander A. *The Book of Daniel*, AB 23, Garden City, Doubleday, 1978.
Harvey A. E. 'Forty Strokes Save One: Social Aspects of Judaizing and Apostasy', in *Alternate Approaches to New Testament Study*, ed. A. E. Harvey, London, SPCK, 1985, 79–96.
Hatch, Edwin and Redpath, Henry A. *A Concordance to the Septuagint and the Other Greek Versions of the Old Testament (Including the Apocryphal Books) in Three Volumes*, Grand Rapids: Baker, 1983.
Hay, David M. 'Paul's Indifference to Authority', *JBL* 88 (1969) 36–44.
Hayes, John H. and Mandell, Sara R. *The Jewish People in Classical Antiquity: From Alexander to Bar Kochba*, Louisville, Westminster John Knox Press, 1998.
Hays, Richard B. *The Faith of Jesus Christ. An Investigation of the Narrative Substructure of Galatians 3:1–4:11*, SBLDS 56, Chico, Calif., Scholars Press, 1983.
  'Have We Found Abraham to Be Our Forefather According to the Flesh? A Reconsideration of Rom 4.1', *NovT* 27 (1985) 76–98.
  '"The Righteous One" as Eschatological Deliverer', in *Apocalyptic and the New Testament: Essays in Honor of J. Louis Martyn*, ed. Joel Marcus and Marion L. Soards, JSNTSup 24, Sheffield, JSOT Press, 1989.
  'ΠΙΣΤΙΣ and Pauline Christology: What is at Stake?', *SBLSP* (1993) 714–29.
Head, Peter M. *Christology and the Synoptic Problem: An Argument for Markan Priority*, Cambridge, Cambridge University Press, 1997.
Heard, W. J. 'Maccabean Martyr Theology: Its Genesis, Antecedents, and Significance for the Earliest Soteriological Interpretation of the Death of Jesus', Ph.D. dissertation, Aberdeen, 1987.
Heiligenthal, R. *Werke als Zeichen*, WUNT 2.9, Tübingen, J. C. B. Mohr (Paul Siebeck), 1983.
Hemer, C. *The Book of Acts in the Setting of Hellenistic History*, ed. Conrad H. Gempf, WUNT 49, Tübingen, J. C. B. Mohr (Paul Siebeck), 1989.
Hengel, Martin. *Judaism and Hellenism: Studies in Their Encounter in Palestine During the Early Hellenistic Period*, 2 vols., ET, London, SCM, 1974.
  Acts and the History of Earliest Christianity, ET, London, SCM Press, 1979.
  The Atonement. A Study of the Origins of the Doctrine in the New Testament, ET, London, SCM Press, 1981.
  Between Jesus and Paul. Studies in the Earliest History of Christianity, ET, London, SCM Press, 1983.
  The Cross and the Son of God, ET, London, SCM Press, 1986.
  The Zealots. Investigations Into the Jewish Freedom Movement in the Period from Herod Until 70 A.D., ET, Edinburgh, T. & T. Clark, 1989.
  The Pre-Christian Paul, ET, London, SCM Press, 1991.
Hengel, Martin and Deines, Roland. 'E. P. Sanders' "Common Judaism", Jesus, and the Pharisees', *JTS* 46 (1995) 1–10.
Hengel, Martin and Schwemer, Anna Maria. *Paul Between Damascus and Antioch: The Unknown Years*, ET, Louisville, Westminster John Knox Press, 1997.

Hill, Craig C. *Hellenists and Hebrews. Reappraising Division Within the Earliest Church*, Minneapolis, Fortress Press, 1992.
Hill, David. *Greek Words and Hebrew Meanings. Studies in the Semantics of Soteriological Terms*, SNTSMS 5, Cambridge, Cambridge University Press, 1967.
Hoenig, S. B. 'Oil and Pagan Defilement', *JQR* 61 (1970–1) 63–75.
Hofius, O. 'Gal.1.18: ἱστορῆσαι Κηφᾶν', *ZNW* 75 (1984) 73–85.
Holl, K. 'Die Vorstellung vom Märtyrer und die Märtyrerackte in Ihrer Geschichtlichen Entwicklung', *Neue Jahrbücher für Klassische Altertum* 33 (1914) 521–56.
Holmberg, Bengt. *Paul and Power. The Structure of Authority in the Primitive Church as Reflected in the Pauline Epistles*, Lund, CWK Gleerup, 1978.
'Jewish *Versus* Christian Identity in the Early Church?', *RB* 105 (1998) 397–425.
Hölscher, G. 'Der Ursprung der Apokalypse Mk 13', *ThBl* 12 (1933) 193–202.
Holtz, T. 'Zum Selbstverständnis des Apostels Paulus', *TLZ* 91 (1966) 322–30.
'Der antiochenische Zwischenfall (Galater 2.11–14)', *NTS* 32 (1986) 344–61.
Hooker, M .D. *The Son of Man in Mark*, London, SPCK, 1967.
Horbury, William. 'The Messianic Associations of "the Son of Man"', *JTS* 36 (1985) 34–55.
Jewish Messianism and the Cult of Christ, London, SCM Press, 1998.
'The Cult of Christ and the Cult of the Saints', *NTS* 44 (1998), 444–69.
Horbury, William and McNeill, Brian (eds.). *Suffering and Martyrdom in the New Testament. Studies Presented to G. M. Styler by the Cambridge New Testament Seminar*, Cambridge, Cambridge University Press, 1981.
Horsley, R. A. 'The Sicarii: Ancient Jewish "Terrorists"', *JR* 59 (1979) 435–58.
'Ancient Jewish Banditry and the Revolt Against Rome, A.D. 66', *CBQ* 43 (1981) 409–32.
'The Zealots: Their Origin, Relationships and Importance in the Jewish Revolt', *NovT* 28 (1986) 159–92.
'"Messianic" Figures and Movements in First Century Palestine', in *The Messiah. Developments in Earliest Judaism and Christianity*, ed. J. H. Charlesworth, Minneapolis, Fortress Press, 1992, 276–95.
Galilee: History, Politics, People, Valley Forge, Trinity Press International, 1995.
Horsley, Richard A. and Hanson, John S. *Bandits, Prophets and Messiahs: Popular Movements at the Time of Jesus*, Edinburgh, T. & T. Clark, 1985.
Howard, George. *Paul: Crisis in Galatia. A Study in Early Christian Theology*, SNTSMS 35, Cambridge, Cambridge University Press, 1979.
Hultgren, Arland. 'Paul's Pre-Christian Persecutions of the Church: Their Purpose, Locale, and Nature', *JBL* 95 (1976) 97–104.
Humphreys, W. Lee. 'A Life-style for Diaspora: A Study of the Tales of Esther and Daniel', *JBL* 92 (1973) 211–23.

Jeremias, J. 'Die Makkabäer-Kirche in Antiochia', *ZNW* 40 (1941) 254–5.
Heiligengräber in Jesu Umwelt (Mt. 23, 29; Lk. 11, 47). Eine Untersuchung zur Volksreligion der Zeit Jesu, Göttingen, Vandenhoeck & Ruprecht, 1958.
'Paulus als Hillelit', in *Neotestamentica et Semitica: Studies in Honour of M. Black*, ed. E. E. Ellis and M. Wilcox, Edinburgh, T. & T. Clark, 1969, 88–94.
Jewett, R. 'The Agitators and the Galatian Congregation', *NTS* 17 (1970–1) 198–212.
Johnson, L. T. *The Acts of the Apostles*, Sacra Pagina 5, Collegeville, Liturgical Press, 1992.
Christology in Context. The Earliest Christian Response to Jesus, Philadelphia, Westminster Press, 1988.
Jonge, Marinus de. 'Earliest Christian Use of Christos: Some Suggestions', *NTS* 32 (1986) 321–43.
'Jesus' Death for Others and the Death of the Maccabean Martyrs', in *Text and Testimony. Essays on New Testament Apocryphal Literature in Honour of A. F. J. Klijn*, ed. T. Baarda, A. Hilhorst, G. P. Luttikhuizen and A. van der Woude, Kampen, Netherlands, J. H. Kok, 1988, 14–31.
Jesus, the Servant-Messiah, New Haven, Yale University Press, 1991.
Kampen, John. *The Hasideans and the Origin of Pharisaism. A Study in 1 and 2 Maccabees*, Atlanta, Scholars Press, 1988.
Käsemann, E. *New Testament Questions of Today*, ET, London, SCM Press, 1969.
Kasher, Aryeh. *The Jews in Hellenistic and Roman Egypt. The Struggle for Equal Rights*, TSAJ 7, Tübingen, J. C. B. Mohr (Paul Siebeck), 1985.
Jews and Hellenistic Cities in Eretz-Israel: Relations of the Jews in Eretz-Israel with the Hellenistic Cities During the Second Temple Period (332 BCE–70 CE), TSAJ 21, Tübingen, J. C. B. Mohr (Paul Siebeck), 1990.
Kellermann, U. *Auferstanden in den Himmel. 2 Makkabäer 7 und die Auferstehung der Märtyrer*, SBS 95, Stuttgart, Katholisches Bibelwerk, 1979.
'Zum traditionsgeschichtlichen Problem des stellvertretenden Sühnetodes in 2 Makk 7, 37f', *BN* 13 (1980) 63–83.
'Das Danielbuch und die Märtyrertheologie der Auferstehung', in *Die Entstehung der Jüdischen Martyrologie*, ed. J. W. van Henten, Leiden, E. J. Brill, 1989, 51–75.
Kertelge, Karl. *'Rechtfertigung' bei Paulus: Studien zur Struktur und zum Bedeutungsgehalt des Paulinischen Rechtfertigungsbegriffs*, Münster, Aschendorff, 1967.
'Zur Deutung des Rechtfertigungsbegriffs im Galaterbrief', *BZ* 12 (1968) 211–22.
Kieffer, R. *Foi et justification à Antioche. Interprétation d'un conflit (Gal 2, 14–21)*, LD 111, Paris, Cerf, 1982.
Kilpatrick, G. D. 'Gal 2.14: ὀρθοποδοῦσιν', in *Neutestamentliche Studien für R. Bultmann*, ed. W. Eltester, BZNW 21, Berlin, Alfred Töpelmann, 1957, 269–74.
'Peter, Jerusalem and Galatians 1.13–2.14', *NovT* 25 (1983) 318–26.
Kim, S. *'The "Son of Man"' as the Son of God*, WUNT 30, Tübingen, J. C. B. Mohr (Paul Siebeck), 1983.

The Origin of Paul's Gospel, 2nd edition, WUNT II/4, Tübingen, J. C. B. Mohr, 1984.
Kittel, Gerhard and Friedrich, Gerhard (eds.). *Theological Dictionary of the New Testament*, 10 vols., trans. Geoffrey Bromiley, Grand Rapids, Eerdmanns, 1964-74.
Klauck, Hans-Josef. *4. Makkabäerbuch*, JSHRZ 3.6, Gütersloh, G. Mohn, 1989.
'Hellenistische Rhetoric im Diasporajudentum. Das Exordium des vierten Makkabäerbuchs (4 Makk 1. 1-12)', *NTS* 35 (1989) 451-65.
Klein, G. 'Individualgeschichte und Weltgeschichte bei Paulus – Eine Interpretation ihres Verhältnisses im Galaterbrief', *EvT* 24 (1964) 126-65.
Kleinknecht, K. Th. *Der leidende Gerechtfertigte. Die alttestamentlich-jüdische Tradition vom "leidenden Gerechten" und ihre Rezeption bei Paulus*, WUNT 2, Tübingen, J. C. B. Mohr (Paul Siebeck), 1984.
Knibb, Michael A. 'Messianism in the Pseudepigrapha in the Light of the Scrolls', *DSD* 2 (1995) 165-84.
Koch, Klaus. *Das Buch Daniel*, Darmstadt, Wissenschaftliche Buchgesellschaft, 1980.
Koester, Helmut. 'φύσις', *TDNT* 9 (1974) 251-77.
Kok, E. 'The Truth of the Gospel: A Study in Galatians 2.15-21', Ph.D. dissertation, Durham, 1993.
Kolb, Frank. 'Antiochia in der frühen Kaiserzeit', in *Geschichte – Tradition – Reflexion: Festscrift für Martin Hengel*, vol. II, ed. H. Cancik, H. Lichtenberger and P. Schäfer, Tübingen, J. C. B. Mohr (Paul Siebeck), 1996, 97-118.
Kraeling, Carl H. 'The Jewish Community at Antioch', *JBL* 51 (1932) 130-60.
Kramer, W. *Christ, Lord, Son of God*, ET, London, SCM Press, 1966.
Krauss, S. 'Antioche', *REJ* 45 (1902) 27-49.
Kruse, Colin G. *Paul, the Law, and Justification*, Leicester, Apollos, 1996.
Kümmel, W. G. *Introduction to the New Testament*, ET, from the 17th rev. edn, London, SCM, 1975.
'"Individualgeschichte" und "Weltgeschichte" im Gal. 2.15-21', in *Christ and the Spirit in the New Testament: Essays in Honour of C. F. D. Moule*, Cambridge, Cambridge University Press, 1975, 157-73.
Lacocque, André. *The Book of Daniel*, ET, Atlanta, John Knox Press, 1979.
Lagrange, M. *Saint Paul, Epître aux Galates*, 2nd edition, Paris, Gabalda, 1925.
Lambrecht, J. 'The Line of Thought in Gal. 2.14b-21', *NTS* 24 (1977-8) 484-95.
'Once Again Gal. 2,17-18 and 3,21', *ETL* 63 (1987) 148-53.
'Transgressor by Nullifying God's Grace. A Study of Gal. 2,19-21', *Bib* 72 (1991) 217-36.
'Paul's Reasoning in Galatians 2:11-21', in *Paul and the Mosaic Law*, ed. James D. G. Dunn, WUNT 89, Tübingen, J. C. B. Mohr (Paul Siebeck), 1996, 53-74.
Lampe, G. W. H. 'Martyrdom and Inspiration', in *Suffering and Martyrdom in the New Testament*, ed. William Horbury and Brian McNeill, Cambridge, Cambridge University Press, 1981, 118-35.

Lane, William L. *Hebrews*, vol. I, WBC 47A, Dallas, Word Books, 1991.
Larsson, Edvin. 'Die Hellenisten und die Urgemeinde', *NTS* 33 (1987) 205–25.
Lassus, J. 'La ville d'Antioche à l'époque Romain d'après l'archéologie', *ANRW* 8 (1977) 54–102.
Lategan, B. C. 'Is Paul Defending His Apostleship in Galatians? The Function of Galatians 1.11–12 and 2.19–20 in the Development of Paul's Argument', *NTS* 34 (1988) 411–30.
Lattey, C. J. 'The Messianic Expectation in "the Assumption of Moses"', *CBQ* 4 (1942) 9–21.
Lebram, J. C. H. 'Die literarische Form des vierten Makkabäerbuches', *VC* 28 (1974) 81–96.
Lenglet, A. 'La structure littéraire de Daniel 2–7', *Bib* 53 (1972) 169–90.
Lévi, I. 'Le martyre des sept Maccabées dans la Pesikta Rabbati', *REJ* 54 (1907) 138–41.
Levinskaya, Irina. *The Book of Acts in Its First Century Setting*, volume V: *The Book of Acts in Its Diaspora Setting*, Grand Rapids, Eerdmans, 1996.
Licht, J. 'Taxo, or the Apocalyptic Doctrine of Vengeance', *JJS* 12 (1961) 95–103.
Lichtenstein, Hans. 'Die Fastenrolle: Eine Untersuchung zur jüdischehellenistischen Geschichte', *HUCA* 8–9 (1931–2) 257–351.
Liddell, Henry George and Scott, Robert. *A Greek–English Lexicon*, Oxford, Clarendon Press, 1968.
Lietzmann, H. *An die Galater*, 4th edition, HNT 10, Tübingen, J. C. B. Mohr (Paul Siebeck), 1971.
Lightfoot, J. B. *Saint Paul's Epistle to the Galatians: A Revised Text with Introduction, Notes, and Dissertations*, New York, Macmillan and Co., 1890.
Lincoln, A. T. *Paradise Now and Not Yet: Studies in the Heavenly Dimension in Paul's Thought with Special Reference to His Eschatology*, SNTSMS 43, Cambridge, Cambridge University Press, 1981.
Loftus, F. 'The Martyrdom of the Galilean Troglodytes (B. J. i 312–3; A. xiv 429–30) a Suggested Traditionsgeschichte', *JQR* 66 (1976) 212–23.
Lohmeyer, E. 'Die Idee des Martyriums im Judentum und Urchristentum', *ZST* 5 (1928) 232–49.
  Märtyrer und Gottesknecht. Untersuchungen zur urchristlichen Verkündigung vom Sühntod Jesu Christ, 2nd edition, Göttingen, Vandenhoeck & Ruprecht, 1963.
Longenecker, Bruce W. 'Defining the Faithful Character of the Covenant Community', in *Paul and the Mosaic Law*, ed. James D. G. Dunn, WUNT 89, Tübingen, J. C. B. Mohr (Paul Siebeck), 1996, 75–97.
  The Triumph of Abraham's God: The Transformation of Identity in Galatians, Edinburgh, T. & T. Clark, 1998.
  '"Until Christ is Formed in You": Suprahuman Forces and Moral Character in Galatians', *CBQ* 61 (1999) 92–108.
Longenecker, R. N. *Galatians*, WBC 41, Dallas, Word, 1990.
Lönning, I. 'Paulus und Petrus. Gal. 2, 11ff als kontrovers-theologisches Fundamentalproblem', *ST* 24 (1970) 1–69.

Lüdemann, Gerd. *Opposition to Paul in Jewish Christianity*, ET, Philadelphia, Fortress Press, 1989.
Lüderitz, Gert. 'What is the Politeuma?', in *Studies in Early Jewish Epigraphy*, ed. J. W. van Henten and P. W. van der Horst, Leiden, E. J. Brill, 1994, 183–225.
Lührmann, D. 'Abendmahlsgemeinschaft? Gal. 2,11ff', in *Kirche. Festschrift für Günter Bornkamm zum 75 Geburtstag*, ed. D. Lührmann and G. Strecker, Tübingen, J. C. B. Mohr (Paul Siebeck), 1980.
Der Brief an die Galater, 2nd edition, ZBK 7, Zürich, Theologischer, 1988.
Luther, Martin. *A Commentary on St Paul's Epistle to the Galatians*, London, James Clark & Co. Ltd., 1953.
Lyons, G. *Pauline Autobiography: Toward a New Understanding*, SBLDS 73, Atlanta, Scholars Press, 1985.
Maas, M. 'Die Makkabäer als christliche Heilige', *MGWJ* 44 (1900) 145–56.
McDonald, James I. H. *Kerygma and Didache. The Articulation and Structure of the Earliest Christian Message*, SNTSMS 37, Cambridge, Cambridge University Press, 1980.
Manson, T. W. 'Martyrs and Martyrdom', *BJRL* 39 (1957) 463–84.
Mantel, H. 'Fastenrolle', *TRE* 11 (1983) 59–61.
Martin, Troy W. 'Whose Flesh? What Temptation? (Galatians 4.13–14)', *JSNT* 74 (1999) 65–91.
Martyn, J. L. 'Apocalyptic Antinomies in the Letter to the Galatians', *NTS* 31 (1985) 410–24.
'A Law-observant Mission to Gentiles: The Background of Galatians', *SJT* 38 (1985) 307–24.
Galatians: A New Translation with Introduction and Commentary, AB 33A, New York, Doubleday, 1997.
Marxsen, W. 'Sündige tapfer. Wer hat sich beim Streit in Antiochien richtigverhalten?', *EvK* 20 (1987) 81–54.
Mason, S. N. 'Josephus and Nicolaus on the Pharisees Reconsidered: A Critique of Smith/Neusner', *SR* 17 (1988) 455–67.
Flavius Josephus on the Pharisees: A Composition-critical Study, Studia Post-Biblica 39, Leiden, E. J. Brill, 1991.
Matera, F. J. *Galatians*, Sacra Pagina 9, Collegeville, Liturgical Press, 1992.
Mattila, Sharon Lea. 'Two Contrasting Eschatologies at Qumran (4Q246 vs 1 QM)', *Bib* 75 (1994) 518–38.
Mattingley, Harold B. 'The Origin of the Name Christiani', *JTS* 9 (1958) 26–37.
Meeks, Wayne A. *The First Urban Christians. The Social World of the Apostle Paul*, New Haven, Yale University Press, 1983.
Meeks, Wayne A. and Wilken, Robert L. *Jews and Christians in Antioch in the First Four Centuries of the Common Era*, SBLSBS 13, Missoula, Scholars Press, 1978.
Méhat, A. '"Quand Kèphas vint à Antioche ..." Que s'est-il passé entre Pierre et Paul?', *LumVie* 192 (1989) 29–43.
Mendels, D. *The Rise and Fall of Jewish Nationalism*, ABRL, New York, Doubleday, 1992.

'Pseudo-Philo's Biblical Antiquities, the "Fourth Philosophy" and the Political Messianism of the First Century A.D.', in *The Messiah. Developments in Earliest Judaism and Christianity*, ed. J. H. Charlesworth, Minneapolis, Fortress Press, 1992, 261–75.

Metzger, Bruce M. 'Antioch-on-the-Orontes', *BA* 11 (1949) 69–88.

A Textual Commentary on the Greek New Testament, Stuttgart, German Bible Society, 1971.

Michel, O. 'Prophet und Märtyrer', BFCT 37 (1932) 59–127.

Der Brief an die Römer, 14th edition, Göttingen, Vandenhoeck & Ruprecht, 1978.

Milik, J. T. 'Les modèles araméens du livre d'Esther dans la grotte 4 de Qumrân', *RevQ* 15 (1992) 321–99.

Millar, F. 'The Background of the Maccabean Revolution: Reflections on Martin Hengel's "Judaism and Hellenism"', *JTS* 29 (1978) 1–21.

Moessner, D. 'The Christ Must Suffer: New Light on the Jesus–Peter, Stephen, Paul Parallels in Luke–Acts', *NovT* 28 (1986) 220–56.

Montgomery, James A. *A Critical and Exegetical Commentary on the Book of Daniel*, ICC, Edinburgh, T. & T. Clark, 1927.

Moo, Douglas. *The Epistle to the Romans*, NICNT, Grand Rapids, Eerdmans, 1996.

Mørkholm, Otto. *Antiochus IV of Syria*. Classica et Medievalia Dissertationes 8, Copenhagen, Gyldendalske Boghandel, 1966.

'Antiochus IV', in *The Cambridge History of Judaism*, volume II: *The Hellenistic Age*, ed. W. D. Davies and Louis Finkelstein, 1989, 278–91.

Moule, C. F. D. 'A Note on Galatians 2.17, 18', *ExpT* 56 (1945) 223.

The Origin of Christology, Cambridge, Cambridge University Press, 1977.

The Birth of the New Testament, 3rd edition, BNTC, London: A. & C. Black, 1981.

Moulton, James Hope and Turner, Nigel. *A Grammar of New Testament Greek*, Edinburgh, T. & T. Clark, 1976.

Moulton, W. F. and Geden, A. S. (eds.). *A Concordance to the Greek Testament*, 5th edition, Edinburgh, T. & T. Clark, 1976.

Müller, C. *Gottes Gerechtigkeit und Gottes Volk: Eine Untersuchung zu Römer 9–11*, FRLANT 86, Göttingen, Vandenhoeck & Ruprecht, 1964.

Munck, J. *Paul and the Salvation of Mankind*, ET, Richmond, John Knox Press, 1959.

Mundle, Wilhelm. 'Die Stephanusrede Apg. 7: Eine Märtyrerapologie', *ZNW* 20 (1921) 133–47.

Murphy-O'Connor, Jerome. 'Paul in Arabia', *CBQ* 55 (1993) 732–37.

Paul: A Critical Life, Oxford, Clarendon Press, 1996.

Mußner, F. *Der Galaterbrief*, 5th edition, HTKNT 9, Freiburg, Herder, 1988.

Nanos, Mark D. *The Mystery of Romans: The Jewish Context of Paul's Letter*, Minneapolis, Fortress Press, 1996.

Neitzel, H. 'Zur Interpretation von Galater 2.11–21', *TQ* 163 (1983) 15–39, 131–49.

Neusner, Jacob. *The Rabbinic Traditions About the Pharisees Before 70*, 3 vols., Leiden, E. J. Brill, 1971.
From *Politics to Piety*, Englewood Cliffs, Prentice-Hall, 1973.
Neusner, Jacob, Green, William Scott and Frerichs, Ernest S. (eds.). *Judaisms and Their Messiahs at the Turn of the Christian Era*, Cambridge, Cambridge University Press, 1987.
Nickelsburg, George W. E. '1 and 2 Maccabees – Same Story, Different Meaning', *CTM* 42 (1971) 515–26.
Resurrection, Immortality and Eternal Life in Intertestamental Judaism, HTS 26, Cambridge, Mass., Harvard University Press, 1972.
'Apocalyptic and Myth in 2 Enoch 6–11', *JBL* 96 (1977) 383–405.
Jewish Literature Between the Bible and the Mishnah. A Historical and Literary Introduction, London, SCM Press, 1981.
'Salvation Without and With a Messiah: Developing Beliefs in Writings Ascribed to Enoch', in *Judaisms and Their Messiahs at the Turn of the Christian Era*, ed. Jacob Neusner, William Scott Green and Ernest S. Frerichs, Cambridge, Cambridge University Press, 1987, 49–68.
'Son of Man', *ABD* 6 (1992) 137–50.
Nickelsburg, George W. E. (ed.). *Studies on the Testament of Moses*, SBLSCS 4, Cambridge, Mass., Society of Biblical Literature, 1973.
Nickelsburg, George W. E. and Stone, Michael E. *Faith and Piety in Early Judaism*, Philadelphia, Fortress Press, 1978.
Niebuhr, K.-W. *Heidenapostel aus Israel. Eine jüdische Identität des Paulus nach ihrer Darstellung in seinen Briefen*, WUNT 62, Tübingen, J. C. B. Mohr (Paul Siebeck), 1992.
'"Judentum" und "Christentum" bei Paulus und Ignatius von Antiochien', *ZNW* 85 (1994) 218–233.
Nolland, J. 'Sib. Or. III, 265–94, an Early Maccabean Messianic Oracle', *JTS* 30 (1979) 158–67.
Norris, Fredrick W. 'Antioch of Syria', *ABD* 1 (1992) 265–69.
Noth, M. 'The Holy Ones of the Most High', in *The Laws in the Pentateuch and Other Essays*, Philadelphia, Fortress Press, 1967, 215–28.
Obermann, J. 'The Sepulchre of the Maccabean Martyrs', *JBL* 50 (1931) 230–65.
Oegema, Gerben S. *The Anointed and His People: Messianic Expectations from the Maccabees to BarKochba*, JSPSup 27, Sheffield, Sheffield Academic Press, 1998.
Oepke, A. *Der Brief des Paulus an die Galater*, ed. J. Rohde, 3rd edition, THKNT 9, Berlin, Evangelische, 1973.
O'Hagan, A. P. 'The Martyr in the Fourth Book of Maccabees', *SBFLA* 24 (1974) 94–120.
Orchard, B. 'The Ellipsis Between Galatians 2, 3 and 2, 4', *Bib* 54 (1973) 469–81.
Overbeck, Franz. *Über die Auffassung des Streits des Paulus mit Petrus in Antiochien (Gal. 2.11ff) bei den Kirchenvätern*, Basel [Darmstadt], 1968 [1877].
Perler, Othmar. 'Das vierte Makkabäerbuch, Ignatius von Antiochien und die ältesten Märtyrerberichte', *Rivista di archeologia cristiana* 25 (1949) 47–72.

Pfitzner, Victor C. *Paul and the Agon Motif. Traditional Athletic Imagery in the Pauline Literature*, Leiden, E. J. Brill, 1967.
Pieper, K. 'Antiochien am Orontes in apostolischen Zeitalter', *TGL* 22 (1930) 710–28.
Plöger, O. *Das Buch Daniel*, Gütersloh, G. Mohn, 1965.
Pobee, J. S. *Persecution and Martyrdom in the Theology of Paul*, JSNTSup 6, Sheffield, JSOT Press, 1985.
Pomykala, Kenneth E. *The Davidic Dynasty Tradition in Early Judaism: Its History and Significance for Messianism*, SBLEJL, Atlanta, Scholars Press, 1995.
Porteous, Norman W. *Daniel: A Commentary*, OTL, Philadelphia, Westminster, 1965.
Priest, J. 'Some Reflections on the Assumption of Moses', *Perspectives in Religious Studies* 4 (1977) 92–111.
'Testament of Moses', in *The Old Testament Pseudepigrapha*, vol. II, ed. J. H. Charlesworth, Garden City, Doubleday, 1985, 919–26.
Procksch, O. 'Die Berungsvision Hesekiels', in *Beiträge zur alttestamentlichen Wissenschaft, FS K. Budde*, ed. K. Marti, Berlin, de Gruyter, 1920, 141–9.
'Der Menschensohn als Gottessohn', *Christentum und Wissenschaft* 3 (1927) 425–43.
Puech, Emile. 'Fragment d'une apocalypse en Araméen (4Q246 = psDand) et le "Royaume de Dieu"', *RB* 99 (1992) 98–131.
'Notes sur le fragment d'apocalypse 4Q246 – "Le Fils de Dieu"', *RB* 101 (1994) 533–58.
Räisänen, Heikki. *The Torah and Christ: Essays in German and English on the Problem of the Law in Early Christianity*, Publications of the Finnish Exegetical Society 45, Helsinki, Kirjapaino Raamattutalo, 1986.
'Galatians 2, 16 and Paul's Break with Judaism', *NTS* 31 (1986) 543–53.
Rajak, Tessa. 'The Hasmoneans and the Uses of Hellenism', in *A Tribute to Geza Vermes: Essays on Jewish and Christian Literature and History*, ed. Philip R. Davies and Richard T. White, JSOTSup 100, Sheffield, Sheffield Academic Press, 1990, 261–80.
Rampolla, Card [y Tindaro]. 'Martyre et sepulture des Machabées', *Revue de l'art chrétien* 10 (1899) 290–305, 377–92, 457–65.
Ramsey, W. M. *A Historical Commentary on St Paul's Epistle to the Galatians*, 2nd edition, London, Hodder & Stoughton, 1900.
Rappaport, Uriel. 'Maccabean Revolt', *ABD* 4 (1992) 433–9.
Redditt, P. L. 'The Concept of Nomos in Fourth Maccabees', *CBQ* 45 (1983) 249–70.
Reicke, Bo. 'Der Geschichtliche Hintergrund des Apostelkonzils und der Antiochia Episode, Gal. 2, 1–14', in *Studia Paulina, in Honorem Johannes de Zwaan Septugenerii*, ed. J. N. Sevenster and W. C. van Unnik, Haarlem, Bohn, 1953.
Renehan, R. 'The Greek Philosophic Background of Fourth Maccabees', *RMP* 115 (1972) 223–38.
Rhoads, David M. *Israel in Revolution 6–74 C.E. A Political History Based on the Writings of Josephus*, Philadelphia, Fortress Press, 1976.

Richardson, P. *Israel in the Apostolic Church*, SNTSMS 10, Cambridge, Cambridge University Press, 1969.
'Pauline Inconsistency: 1 Corinthians 9.19-23 and Galatians 2.11-14', *NTS* 26 (1979-80) 347-62.
Ridderbos, Herman N. *The Epistle of Paul to the Churches of Galatia*, ET, NICNT, Grand Rapids, Eerdmans, 1953.
Riesner, Rainer. *Paul's Early Period: Chronology, Mission Strategy, Theology*, ET, Grand Rapids, Eerdmans, 1998.
Rohde, J. *Der Brief des Paulus an die Galater*, THKNT 9, Berlin, Evangelische, 1989.
Rordorf, Willy. 'Wie steht es um den jüdischen Einfluss auf den christlichen Märtyrerkult?', in *Juden und Christen in der Antike*, ed. J. van Amersfoort and J. van Oort, Kampen, Kok, 1990.
Rowland, Christopher C. 'The Visions of God in Apocalyptic Literature', *JSJ* 10 (1979) 137-54.
The Open Heaven. A Study of Apocalyptic in Judaism and Early Christianity, London, SPCK, 1982.
Christian Origins: From Messianic Movement to Christian Religion, London, SPCK, 1985.
Ruppert, L. *Der leidende Gerechte. Eine motivgeschichte Untersuchung zum Alten Testament und zwischen testamentlichen Judentum*, Forschung zur Bibel, Würzburg, 1972.
Safrai, Samuel. 'Martyrdom in the Teachings of the Tannaim', in *Sjaloom. Ter Hagedachtenis Van Mgr Dr A. C. Ramselaar*, ed. Th. C. de Kruijf and H. V. D. Sandt, Arnhem, 1983, 145-64.
Safrai, Samuel and Stern, Menachem (eds.). *The Jewish People in the First Century: Historical Geography, Political History, Social, Cultural and Religious Life and Institutions*, 2 vols., CRINT 1.1-2, Assen, Van Gorcum, 1974, 1976.
Sahlin, Harald. 'Antiochus IV Epiphanes und Judas Makkabäus', *ST* 23 (1969) 41-68.
Saldarini, Anthony J. 'Johanan Ben Zakkai's Escape from Jerusalem: Origin and Development of a Rabbinic Story', *JSJ* 6 (1975) 189-204.
Pharisees, Scribes and Sadducees in Palestinian Society. A Sociological Approach, Edinburgh, T. & T. Clark, 1988.
Sampley, J. P. '"Before God, I Do not Lie" (Gal. 1.20). Paul's Self-defence in the Light of Roman Legal Praxis', *NTS* 23 (1977) 477-82.
Sanders, E. P. *Paul and Palestinian Judaism. A Comparison of Patterns of Religion*, Philadelphia, Fortress Press, 1977.
Paul, the Law, and the Jewish People, Philadelphia, Fortress Press, 1983.
Jewish Law from Jesus to the Mishnah. Five Studies, London, SCM Press, 1990.
'Jewish Association with Gentiles and Galatians 2.11-14', in *Studies in Paul and John in Honour of J. Louis Martyn*, ed. R. T. Fortna and B. Gaventa, Nashville, Abingdon Press, 1990, 170-88.
Judaism: Practice and Belief, 63 BCE-66 CE, London, SCM Press, 1992.
Sanders, Jack T. 'Paul's "Autobiographical" Statements in Galatians 1-2', *JBL* 85 (1966) 335-43.

Schäfer, Peter. 'Der vorrabinische Pharisäismus', in *Paulus und das antike Judentum*, ed. Martin Hengel and Ulrich Heckel, WUNT 58, Tübingen, J. C. B. Mohr (Paul Siebeck), 1991, 125–72.
Schatkin, Margaret. 'The Maccabean Martyrs', *VC* 28 (1974) 98–108.
Schlier, H. *Der Brief an die Galater*, 15th edition, KEK 7, Göttingen, Vandenhoeck & Ruprecht, 1989.
Schmid, Herbert. 'Daniel der Menschensohn', *Judaica* 27 (1971) 192–221.
Schmidt, A. 'Das Missiondekret in Galater 2.7–8 als Vereinbarung vom ersten Besuch Pauli in Jerusalem', *NTS* 38 (1992) 149–52.
Schmidt, N. 'Was *bar nash* a Messianic Title?', *JBL* 15 (1896) 36–53.
'The "Son of Man" in The Book of Daniel', *JBL* 19 (1900) 22–8.
Schmithals, W. *Paul and James*, ET, SBT 46, London, SCM Press, 1965.
Schoedel, William. *Ignatius of Antioch. A Commentary on the Letters of Antioch*, Hermeneia, Philadelphia, Fortress Press, 1985.
Schreiner, T. R. 'Works of the Law in Paul', *NovT* 33 (1991) 217–44.
The Law and Its Fulfillment: A Pauline Theology of Law, Grand Rapids, Baker, 1993.
Romans, BECNT, Grand Rapids, Baker, 1998.
Schunck, K.-D. *Die Quellen des 1. und 11. Makkabäerbuches*, Halle, Neimeyer, 1954.
Schürer, E. *The History of the Jewish People in the Age of Jesus Christ (175 BC–AD 135)*, vols. I–III, revised and edited by G. Vermes, F. Millar, M. Goodman and P. Vermes, Edinburgh, T. & T. Clark, 1973–87.
Schütz John Howard. *Paul and the Anatomy of Apostolic Authority*, SNTSMS 26, Cambridge, Cambridge University Press, 1975.
Schwartz, Daniel R. *Studies in the Jewish Background of Christianity*, WUNT 60, Tübingen, J. C. B. Mohr (Paul Siebeck), 1992.
Schwartz, S. 'Israel and the Nations Roundabout: 1 Maccabees and the Hasmonean Expansion', *JJS* 42 (1991) 16–38.
Schwemer, Anna Maria. 'Prophet, Zeuge und Märtyrer: Zur Entstehung des Märtyrerbegriffs in frühesten Christentum', *ZTK* 96 (1999) 320–50.
Scott, R. B. Y. 'Behold He Cometh with Clouds', *NTS* 5 (1959) 127–32.
Scurlock, JoAnn. '167 BCE: Hellenism or Reform', *JSJ* 31 (2000) 125–61.
Seeley, David. *The Noble Death: Graeco-Roman Martyrology and Paul's Concept of Salvation*, JSNTSup 28, Sheffield, JSOT Press, 1990.
Segal, Alan F. *Paul the Convert. The Apostolate and Apostasy of Saul the Pharisee*, New Haven, Yale University Press, 1990.
Seifrid, M. A. *Justification by Faith: The Origin and Development of a Central Pauline Theme*, NovTSup 68, Leiden, E. J. Brill, 1992.
Sieffert, F. *Der Brief an die Galater*, KEK 7, Göttingen, Vandenhoeck & Ruprecht, 1899.
Sievers, Joseph. *The Hasmoneans and Their Supporters. From Mattathias to the Death of John Hyrcanus I*, South Florida Studies in the History of Judaism, Atlanta, Scholars Press, 1990.
Simon, M. 'Les saints d'Israël dans la dévotion de l'église ancienne', *RHPR* 34 (1954) 98–127.
Sjöberg, Erik. *Der Menschensohn im Äthiopischen Henochbuch*, Lund, Gleerup, 1946.

Slater, Thomas B. 'One Like a Son of Man in First-Century CE Judaism', *NTS* 41 (1995) 183–98.
Smallwood, E. Mary. *The Jews Under Roman Rule. From Pompey to Diocletian. A Study in Political Relations*, Leiden, E. J. Brill, 1981.
Stauffer, E. *New Testament Theology*, ET, London, SCM Press, 1955.
Steck, O. *Israel und das gewaltsame Geschick der Propheten. Untersuchungen zur Überlieferung des deuteronomistischen Geschichtsbildes im Alten Testament, Spätjudentum und Urchristentum*, WMANT 23, Neukirchen-Vluyn, Neukirchener, 1967.
Stein, S. 'The Liturgy of Hanukkah and the First Two Books of Maccabees', *JJS* 5 (1954) 100–6, 148–55.
Stemberger, G. 'The Maccabees in Rabbinic Tradition', in *The Scriptures and the Scrolls. Studies in Honour of A. S. Van der Woude on the Occasion of His 65th Birthday*, ed. F. García Martínez, A. Hilhorst and C. J. Labuschagne, Leiden, E. J. Brill, 1992.
Jewish Contemporaries of Jesus: Pharisees, Sadducees, Essenes, ET, Minneapolis, Fortress Press, 1995.
Stinespring, W. F. 'The Description of Antioch in Codex Vaticanus Arabicus 286', Ph.D. dissertation, Yale University, 1932.
Stone, Michael E. *Features of the Eschatology of 4 Ezra*, Atlanta, Scholars Press, 1989.
A Commentary on Fourth Ezra, Hermeneia, Minneapolis, Fortress Press, 1990.
Stowers, Stanley K. '4 Maccabees', in *Harper's Bible Commentary*, ed. James L. Mays, San Francisco, Harper & Row, 1988, 921–34.
Strobel, August. 'Lukas der Antiochener', *ZNW* 49 (1958) 131–4.
Stuhlmacher, P. *Gerechtigkeit Gottes bei Paulus*, FRLANT 87, Göttingen, Vandenhoeck & Ruprecht, 1966.
Suhl, Alfred. 'Der Galaterbrief-Situation und Argumentation', *ANRW* II 2.25.4 (1987) 3067–134.
Surkau, Hans-Werner. *Martyrien in jüdischer und frühchristlicher Zeit*, Göttingen, Vandenhoeck & Ruprecht, 1938.
Suter, D. W. 'Weighed in the Balance: The Similitudes of Enoch in Recent Discussion', *RelSRev* 7 (1981) 217–21.
Tannehill, R. C. *Dying and Rising with Christ: A Study in Pauline Theology*, BZNW 32, Berlin, Töpelmann, 1967.
Taylor, Justin. 'Why Were the Disciples First Called "Christians" at Antioch? (Acts 11, 26)', *RB* 101 (1994) 75–94.
Taylor, N. H. *Paul, Antioch and Jerusalem: A Study in Relationships and Authority in Earliest Christianity*, JSNTSup 66, Sheffield, JSOT Press, 1992.
'Palestinian Christianity and the Caligula Crisis. Part I. Social and Historical Reconstruction', *JSNT* 61 (1996) 101–24.
'Palestinian Christianity and the Caligula Crisis. Part II. The Markan Eschatological Discourse', *JSNT* 62 (1996) 13–41.
'Caligula, the Church of Antioch and the Gentile Mission', *Religion & Theology* 7/1 (2000) 1–23.
'Popular Opposition to Caligula in Jewish Palestine', *JSJ* 32 (2001) 54–69.

Tcherikover, V. *Hellenistic Civilization and the Jews*, Philadelphia, The Jewish Publication Society of America, 1959.
Theisöhn, Johannes. *Der auserwählte Richter: Untersuchungen zum traditionsgeschichtlichen Ort der Menschensohngestalt der Bilderreden des Äthiopischen Henoch*, SUNT 12, Göttingen, Vandenhoeck & Ruprecht, 1975.
Theissen, Gerd. *The Gospels in Context. Social and Political History in the Synoptic Tradition*, ET, Minneapolis, Fortress Press, 1991.
Thielman, Frank. *From Plight to Solution: A Jewish Framework for Understanding Paul's View of the Law in Galatians and Romans*, Leiden, E. J. Brill, 1989.
Tödt, H. E. *The Son of Man in the Synoptic Tradition*, ET, London, 1965.
Tomson, P. *Paul and the Jewish Law: Halakha in the Letters of the Apostle Paul to the Gentiles*, vol. I, CRINT III, Assen, Van Gorcum, 1990.
Tracey, Robyn. 'Syria', in *The Book of Acts in Its First Century Setting*, volume II: *The Book of Acts in Its Graeco-Roman Setting*, ed. D. W. J. Gill and C. Gempf, Carlisle, Paternoster Press, 1994, 223–78.
Trebilco, Paul. *Jewish Communities in Asia Minor*, SNTSMS 69, Cambridge, Cambridge University Press, 1991.
Trevett, Christine. *A Study of Ignatius of Antioch in Syria and Asia*, Studies in the Bible and Early Christianity 29, Lewiston, Queenston and Lampeter: The Edwin Mellen Press, 1992.
Tyson, J. B. 'Paul's Opponents in Galatia', *NovT* 10 (1968) 241–54.
VanderKam, J. C. 'Righteous One, Messiah, Chosen One, and Son of Man in 1 Enoch', in *The Messiah. Developments in Earliest Judaism and Christianity*, ed. J. H. Charlesworth, Minneapolis, Fortress Press, 1992, 169–91.
Enoch: A Man for All Generations, Columbia, University of South Carolina Press, 1995.
van Henten, J. W. 'Einige Prolegomena zum Studium der jüdischen Martyrologie', *Bijdragen* 46 (1985) 381–90.
'De Joodse martelaren als grondleggers van een nieuwe orde', Ph.D. dissertation, Leiden, 1986.
'Datierung und Herkunft des vierten Makkabäerbuches', in *Tradition and Re-interpretation in Jewish and Early Christian Literature*, Leiden, E. J. Brill, 1986.
'Das jüdische Selbstverständnis in den ältesten Martyrien', in *Die Entstehung Der jüdischen Martyrologie*, ed. J. W. van Henten, Leiden, E. J. Brill, 1989, 127–61.
'The Tradition-historical Background of Romans 3.25: A Search from Pagan and Jewish Parallels', in *From Jesus to John. Essays on Jesus and New Testament Christology in Honour of Marinus de Jonge*, ed. Martinus C. De Boer, JSNTSup 84, Sheffield, JSOT Press, 1993, 101–27.
'Zum Einfluss jüdischer Martyrien auf die Literatur des frühen Christentums, II. Die Apostolischen Väter,' *ANRW* II.27.1 (1993) 700–23.
'A Jewish Epitaph in a Literary Text: 4 Macc 17:8–1a', in *Studies in Early Jewish Epigraphy*, ed. J. W. van Henten and P. W. van der Horst, Leiden, E. J. Brill, 1994, 44–67.

'The Martyrs as Heroes of the Christian People: Some Remarks on the Continuity between Jewish and Christian Martyrology, with Pagan Analogies', in *Martyrium in Multidisciplinary Perspective: Memorial Louis Reekmans*, ed. M. Lamberigts and P. van Deun, BETL 117, Leuven, 1995, 303–22.

The Maccabean Martyrs as Saviours of the Jewish People: A Study of 2 and 4 Maccabees, SJSJ, Leiden, E. J. Brill, 1997.

van Henten, J. W., Dehandschutter, B. A. G. M. and van der Klaauw, H. J. W. (eds.). *Die Entstehung der jüdischen Martyrologie*, Leiden, E. J. Brill, 1989.

Verseput, D. J. 'Paul's Gentile Mission and the Jewish Christian Community. A Study of the Narrative in Galatians 1 and 2', *NTS* 39 (1993) 36–58.

von Campenhausen, H. *Die Idee des Martyriums in der alten Kirche*, Göttingen, Vandenhoeck & Ruprecht, 1936.

Wallace-Hadrill, D. S. *Christian Antioch: A Study of Early Christian Thought in the East*, Cambridge, Cambridge University Press, 1982.

Walter, N. 'Paulus und die urchristliche Jesustradition', *NTS* 31 (1985) 498–522.

Watson, Francis. *Paul, Judaism and the Gentiles: A Sociological Approach*, SNTSMS 56, Cambridge, Cambridge University Press, 1986.

Weber, Reinhard. 'Eusebeia und Logismos. Zum Philosophischen Hintergrund von 4. Makkabäer', *JSJ* 22 (1991) 212–34.

Wechsler, A. *Geschichtsbild und Apostelstreit: Eine forschungsgeschichtliche und exegetische Studie über den antiochenischen Zwischenfall (Gal 2,11–14)*, BZNW 62, Berlin, Walter de Gruyter, 1991.

Wenham, David. 'Paul and the Synoptic Apocalypse,' in *Gospel Perspectives*, volume II: *Studies of History and Tradition in the Four Gospels*, ed. R. T. France and David Wenham, Sheffield, JSOT Press, 1981, 345–75.

'Acts and the Pauline Corpus II. The Evidence of Parallels', in *The Book of Acts in Its First Century Setting*, volume I: *The Book of Acts in Its Ancient Literary Setting*, ed. Bruce W. Winter and Andrew D. Clark, Grand Rapids, Eerdmans, 1993, 215–58.

Westerholm, Stephen. *Israel's Law and the Church's Faith. Paul and His Recent Interpreters*, Grand Rapids, Eerdmans, 1988.

Wilckens, Ulrich. 'ὑποκρίνομαι', *TDNT* 8 (1972) 559–71.

Williams, S. K. *Jesus' Death as Saving Event. The Background and Origin of a Concept*, HDR 2, Missoula, Scholars Press, 1975.

'The "righteousness of God" in Romans', *JBL* 99 (1980) 214–90.

'Again Pistis Christou', *CBQ* 49 (1987) 431–47.

'The Hearing of Faith: ΑΚΟΗ ΠΙΣΤΕΩΣ in Galatians 3', *NTS* 35 (1989) 82–93.

Wills, Lawrence. 'The Form of the Sermon in Hellenistic Judaism and Early Christianity', *HTR* 77 (1984) 277–99.

Windisch, H. 'Die Christusepiphanie vor Damaskus (Acts 9, 22, und 26) und ihre Religionsgeschichte Parallelen', *ZNW* 31 (1932) 1–23.

Winslow, D. F. 'The Maccabean Martyrs: Early Christian Attitudes', *Judaism* 3 (1974) 78–86.

Winston, David. *Wisdom of Solomon*, AB 43, Garden City, Doubleday, 1979.
Winter, Bruce W. (series editor), *The Book of Acts in Its First Century Setting*, 6 vols., Grand Rapids, Eerdmans, 1993–98.
Witherington III, Ben. *The Christology of Jesus*, Minneapolis, Fortress Press, 1990.
  Grace in Galatia: A Commentary on Paul's Letter to the Galatians, Grand Rapids, Eerdmans, 1998.
Wright, N. T. 'The Messiah and the People of God: A Study in Pauline Theology with Particular Reference to the Argument of the Epistle to the Romans', D.Phil dissertation, Oxford, 1980.
  The Climax of the Covenant: Christ and the Law in Pauline Theology, Edinburgh, T. & T. Clark, 1991.
  The New Testament and the People of God, London, SPCK, 1992.
  'Romans and the Theology of Paul', *SBLSP* (1992) 184–213.
  'On Becoming the Righteousness of God', in *Pauline Theology*, volume II: *1 & 2 Corinthians*, ed. David M. Hay, Minneapolis, Fortress Press, 1993, 200–8.
  'Paul, Arabia, and Elijah (Galatians 1:17)', *JBL* 115 (1996) 683–92.
Wright, W. 'An Ancient Syrian Martyrology', *The Journal of Sacred Literature* 8 (1866) 44–57, 423–32.
Zahn, T. *Der Brief des Paulus an die Galater*, HKNT 9, Leipzig, Deichert, 1910.
Zeitlin, S. *Megillat Taanit as a Source for Jewish Chronology and History of the Hellenistic and Roman Periods*, Philadelphia, printed at the Oxford University Press, 1922.
  'Hanukkah. Its Origin and Its Significance', *JQR* 29 (1938) 1–36.
  'The Legend of the Ten Martyrs and Its Apocalyptic Origin', *JQR* 36 (1945) 1–16.
Zevit, Z. 'The Structure and Individual Elements of Daniel 7', *ZAW* 80 (1968) 385–96.
Ziesler, J. A. *The Meaning of Righteousness in Paul. A Linguistic and Theological Enquiry*, SNTSMS 20, Cambridge, Cambridge University Press, 1972.
  Paul's Letter to the Romans, London, SCM Press, 1989.
Zumstein, Jean. 'Antioche sur l'Oronte et l'évangile selon Matthieu', *SNTU* 15 (1980) 2–38.

INDEX OF PASSAGES

1. OLD TESTAMENT

Genesis
15.6	103
18.2	45
19.1	45
22	103
49.9–10	51

Exodus
15.15–16	32
23.27–8	32

Leviticus
16	87
17–18	159
20.9–16	171
20.27	171

Numbers
24.7	40
24.17	46
35.27	171
35.30	174
35.31	171

Deuteronomy
7.24	181
9.2	181
10.16–17	134
11.25	181
17.6	174
18.15ff.	228
19.10	71
19.15	174
19.15–21	180
24.1ff.	221
25.1–3	186
27–30	215
27–32	186
28.11	222
28.12	222
28.47	222
30.6–20	224–5
30.9	222
30.20	83
31.20	222
31.21	222
32.39	83
33.26	45

Joshua
1.5	181
2.1–3	131
2.19	171
5.13	45
6.18	101
7.25	101
20.6	180

Judges
11.35	101
13.6	45
13.8	45
13.16	45

1 Samuel
11.2	99
14.29	101
15.18	191
24.7[6]	39

2 Samuel
7.14	48
23.1	46

1 Kings
LXX 20[21].20	223
LXX 20[21].25	223
22.19–22	45

2 Kings		54.9–17	134
17.17	223	54.11–12	134
18.13–19.36	37, 58	54.14	134
Ezra		Jeremiah	
9.6–15	195	1.5	123
		1.10	214
Nehemiah		12.16–17	214
9.6–38	195		
		Ezekiel	
Esther		1.26–8	45
8.17	185	2.1ff.	45
		8.1–2	45
Psalms		8.2	45
2	46, 50, 51	9.11	45
2.2	154	10.1–4	45
2.7	48	36.12–15	105
9.18[17]	191	37.2–3	83
20–1	46		
45	46	Daniel	
68.5[4]	45	1–6	27, 28
72	46	1.4	28
80.18[17]	46	1.17–20	28, 208
82.6–7	49	2	28, 64
89.27–8[26–7]	48	2.1–45	61
104.3	45	2.11	28
110	46	2.34–5	28
110.1	52	2.44	29
LXX 142[143].2	205	3 and 6	13, 34
		3.12	29
Proverbs		3.13–15	29
4.11	183	3.17	29
4.25–7	183	3.25 [LXX/Th.	
11.6	183	3.92]	29, 147
12.6	183	3.28	155
21.8	183	3.33[4.3]	47
28.11	186	4.6[8]	29
		4	28, 29
Isaiah		4.24[27]	29
6.1–8	45	4.28–34[31–7]	29
11.1–5	50	4.31[34]	47
11.4	51	5	28, 29
14.12–19	36	5.1–4	29
42.6	123	5.6	47
45.21	158	5.13–16	29
48.10	223	5.20–1	29
49.1–6	123	6.5[4]	208
50.1	223	6.21–4[20–3]	29
50.8	180	6.21[20]	29
52–53	123	6.23[22]	29, 155
52.13–14	28	6.24[23]	29
53	40	7	40, 43, 46, 47, 49, 51, 105, 147, 195
53.1	202		
53.2–3	28		

Daniel (cont.)

Reference	Pages
7–12	32, 44, 60, 93, 106, 114, 193
7.7	174
7.8–27	70
7.9	50, 52
7.9–10	50
7.9–14	45
7.13	50, 52
7.13–14	10, 14, 19, 47, 61, 66, 71, 123, 231
7.14	45, 46, 47
7.17	44
7.18	44
7.19	174
7.22	45, 47
7.23	47, 101
7.24–5	215
7.25	44, 46, 47
7.27	45, 47
8.9–12	36, 44
8.9–26	70
8.10	174
8.12	74, 131, 183, 195
8.15	45
8.16–26	44
8.17	149
8.22–3	180
8.22–5	44
9	21, 88
9.3–19	195
9.13	24
9.21	45
9.21–7	44
9.24–7	44, 70
9.25	42
9.25–6	39, 42
9.26	42
9.27	24
10.5	45
10.5ff.	44
10.11	181
10.12	29
10.13	44, 46, 75, 180
10.19	29
10.20–1	46
10.21	44, 75
11	43
11.2	180
11.2–39	44
11.3	180
11.4	180
11.7	180
11.12	29, 101
11.14–16	180
11.20–1	180
11.21–12.13	70
11.22	42
11.28	23
11.29–30	23
11.30	21, 44
11.31	24, 180
11.31–5	74
11.33	122
11.33–5	27, 98, 104, 149, 172
11.36	71
11.39	23
11.40–5	44
11.44	101
12.1	44, 47, 60, 74, 75
12.1–3	82
12.2	181
12.3	27, 75, 122
12.5–7	45
12.11	24
12.13	181

Amos

Reference	Pages
9.7	134
9.11–12	158

Habakkuk

Reference	Pages
2.3	40
2.4	175

Zechariah

Reference	Pages
6.12	46
13.7	40

2. APOCRYPHA

Additions to Daniel (LXX/Th.)

Reference	Pages
3.24–45	87
3.28	88
3.32	88
3.34–6	88
3.38	88
3.39–40	87
3.39–41	88
3.40b	88
3.50	159

4 Ezra

Reference	Pages
2.17	228
4.23	191
6.55–9	51, 195

Index of passages 263

7.28	51	3.10–26	24
7.33	51	3.13	31
11–13	47, 195	3.19	32
11.1–12.51	51	3.24	122
12.11	51	3.27–37	24
12.32	51	3.34b–36	105
12.34	51	3.38–4.25	24
13	48, 51	3.45	31, 174
13.1–13	51	3.48	31
13.1–56	51	3.51	174
13.10–11	51	3.56	31
13.12–13	51	3.58–9	31
13.33–8	51	4.9	31
13.37	51	4.10	32
13.39–40	43	4.12	150
13.52	51	4.24	32
		4.26	150
Judith		4.26–35	24
10.5	167	4.30	31
16.17	155	4.36–59	24, 76
		4.59	76
1 Maccabees		4.60	174
1–7	33	5	24, 31
1.11	21	5.15	150
1.11–16	30	5.38	131
1.15	22, 223	5.62	30
1.16–28	23	6.1–17	25
1.29–32	23	6.8	172
1.33–40	23	6.18–27	24
1.34	191	6.55–63	25
1.41–3	21, 23	6.58	31, 132
1.44–64	23	7.1–4	25
1.48	176	7.12–16	25
1.49	147	7.12–23	30
1.54	24	7.21–4	105
1.57	31, 148	7.22	101
1.60–1	176	7.26–50	25
1.60–3	31	7.39–50	76
1.64	32, 74	7.49	76
2.15ff.	68, 70	8.1–9.22	25
2.23–6	31	8.18	158
2.42–8	24	9	25
2.44	191	9.19–21	32
2.45–6	31	9.23	31
2.47	122	9.30	156
2.48	191	10.18–20	25
2.49–60	31	10.24	157
2.49–64	157	10.35	159
2.52	98, 103, 208	10.59–66	25
2.57	43	11	26
2.70	32	11.36	228
3.1–9	105	11.50	132
3.5	30, 32, 101, 122	11.62	132
3.8	32, 74	11.66	132

Index of passages

1 Maccabees (*cont.*)

11.68	150
11.74	150
12.1–23	26, 31
12.6	31
12.7	31
12.9	31
12.11	31
12.15	31
12.25–30	32
12.30	32
12.39–53	26
12.53–13.6	105
13.3–6	31
13.20	105
13.23	26
13.41	26, 105, 158
13.51	76
13.51–2	26
14.16–24	26
14.19	181
14.27–47	26
14.32	181
14.35	32
14.41–5	32, 228
15.15–24	26
16.23–4	26

2 Maccabees

1.1–2.18	76
1.5	88
1.24–9	43
1.27	99
2.17–18	43
2.19–22	33
2.21	33, 121, 143
2.22	214
2.23–32	33
3	22, 33
3.1–3	20
3.7–21	58
3.7–40	148, 149
3.8	125
3.9	130
3.12	149
3.24–30	149
3.25–6	34
3.26	187
3.27–9	149
3.34	149, 152, 187
3.38	187
4	33
4.2	22
4.5	130
4.9–17	22
4.10	125
4.11	143, 214
4.13	33
4.14	22
4.16	121
4.16–17	34
4.18–20	22
4.33–5	23
4.34	42, 132
4.47	224
5.2–4	34
5.5–10	23
5.7	149
5.11	23
5.11–14	23
5.14	223
5.15–21	23
5.17–20	34
5.17–21	21
5.20	88
5.20b	34
5.22–3	23
5.24–6	23
5.27	24
6–7	73, 78
6.1	102, 122, 185
6.1–11	23
6.2	24
6.5	150
6.6	33
6.7	102, 185
6.8	121
6.9	21
6.9b	34
6.10	176
6.12–16	21, 172
6.12–17	34
6.12–7.31	187
6.18	102, 185
6.18–31	34, 162
6.18–7.40	77
6.21	34
6.21–8	178
6.23	121
6.23–7	171, 187
6.23A	143
6.24	34
6.28	34, 125
6.28b–31	34
6.29–30	187
6.30	34, 178
7	29, 35, 86
7.1	102, 150, 185
7.1–42	35
7.2	35, 122, 215

Index of passages

7.6	35	10.38	36
7.9	35, 227	11.6	36
7.11	35	11.6–15	24
7.14	35	11.8	34
7.16	35	11.8–9	36
7.17	35, 152	11.13	36, 37, 66, 104
7.18–19	35	11.24	21, 104, 121, 148
7.19	35	11.26	132
7.19–20	171	11.27	156
7.23	35	11.30	132
7.24	104, 122	11.30–1	159
7.28	35	12.11	132
7.29	35, 171	12.12	132
7.31	35, 36, 37, 66, 104	12.22	34
		12.39–45	172
7.32–3	35	13.3–8	21
7.33	35, 88	13.14	143
7.34–5	35	13.21	122
7.36	35	13.22	132
7.37	35, 88, 122	13.23–4	25
7.37–8	35, 89	13.25	228
7.37–8.5	87, 88	14.1–2	25
7.38	88, 124	14.12	125
7.40	88	14.12–15.36	25
7.41	82	14.16	125, 156
8.1	121, 122, 131, 143	14.18	131
		14.19	132
8.1ff.	88	14.19–25	36
8.1–5	35	14.21	130
8.2	174, 185	14.31–3	76
8.4	88	14.34–6	36
8.7	149	14.37–8	36
8.8	122	14.37–46	171
8.8–36	24	14.38	121, 143, 171
8.11	125	14.43	131
8.12–29	36	14.46	36
8.14	223	15.6–11	76
8.17	143	15.7–9	36
8.21	122, 227	15.9	131
8.28	35	15.9–11	157
8.29	88	15.10	127
8.30	35	15.12–16	37
8.36	36	15.15	228
9	25, 69	15.18R	131
9.1–10.9	36	15.20–7	37
9.5	187	15.21	171
9.5–12	149	15.22–36	76
9.26	130	15.27	34
10.1–8	24, 36	15.36	76
10.2	150	15.37	37, 66, 104
10.5	150		
10.8	76	3 Maccabees	
10.14–11.15	36	5.5	224
10.21	223	5.22	224
10.29–30	34, 36	5.47	224

4 Maccabees

1.1a	79	8.3	86
1.1–12	79	8.5	81
1.8	227	8.7	122, 143
1.10	78, 227	8.12	178
1.11	81, 214	8.15	214
1.13–3.18	79	8.15–27	178
1.33–5	79	9.1	122, 215
2.5–6	222	9.8	81
2.5–6b	79	9.22	81
3.19	78	9.24	81, 89
3.19–18.24	79	9.30–2	89
3.20	143	11.4	122
3.20–4.26	80	11.6	171
4.1–14	148	11.15	81
4.8	148	11.20	131
4.10–11	149	11.20–7	81
4.11–14	149	11.24	214
4.13	149	12.7	66
4.16–24	214	12.17	89
4.22–6	80	12.17–18	81
4.23	122	13.15	131, 215
4.23–6	185	13.19–27	191
4.26	102, 121, 143, 185	13.19–14.1	81
		13.23–14.1	179
5.1–7.23	162	14.2	124, 191, 192
5.2	102, 185	14.5	131
5.8–9	191	14.5–6	81
5.11	171	14.7–10	81
5.22–6	191	14.8	178, 214
5.25b–26	80	14.9	78
5.27	102, 185	14.11–20	82
5.29	127	14.11–17.6	82
5.29–30	99	14.20	191
5.33	214	15.6–9	179
6.1	148	15.8	178
6.6	147	15.13	179, 191
6.7	174, 183	15.17	99
6.10	81	15.24	82
6.11	81	15.25	191
6.12–23	178	15.28	82
6.15–18	81	16.3	191
6.16–18	195	16.7	224
6.18–7.40	77	16.15	66
6.26	147	16.16	122, 131
6.28–9	81, 87, 89	16.22	89
6.30	181	16.23	181
7.3	195	16.24	215
7.6	171	16.25	195, 227
7.9	214	17.2	89, 214
7.17–19	81	17.2–6	82
7.19	195, 227	17.2–24	87
7.21	89	17.3	134
7.41	82	17.3a	174
		17.7–10	86

17.7–18.24	82	Mark	
17.8–10	78	3.29	171
17.9	143, 214	9.12	99
17.9–10	82	10.35–45	155
17.10ff.	131	10.42–5	210
17.11	80	13	69
17.11–16	82	13.6	71
17.11–17	175	13.7	70
17.14	80	13.7–8	69
17.20–2	81, 89	13.9–13	69
17.20–4	89	13.12	69
17.20c–22	82	13.14	58, 70
18.1	104	13.14–16	69
18.1–4	82	13.21–2	71
18.4	81	13.26	71
18.5	102, 185	13.32	71
18.8	148	14.57ff.	147
18.9–19	82–3	14.58	214
18.16–19	83	14.62	52
18.23	82, 191	14.64	171
18.24	83	15.29	214
Sirach		Luke	
1.27–30	178	1.32	48
14.2	186	1.35	48
19.5	186	2.28ff.	156
32.15; 33.2	178	6.33	191
44.20	103	10.1	3
		11.47–51	147
Tobit		13.33–5	147
3.1–6	195	20.38	227
3.13–14	195	21.15	181
4.14	121	22.26	156
5.4–16	155	23.11	99
		24.25–6	104
Wisdom			
1–6	104	John	
2.13	51	1.21	228
2.16	51	1.42	39
4–5	123	1.45	52
		4.25	39
		6.14–15	228
3. NEW TESTAMENT		7.40	228
		10.33	76
Matthew		12.34	52
5.21–4	171		
5.39	181	Acts	
5.47	191	2–15	117
17.40	214	2.10–12	152
20.25–8	210	2.36	154
23.29–37	147	2.42	169
24.15	58	2.46	169
26.61	214	3.13	181
26.66	171	3.18	154

Index of passages

Acts (*cont.*)

3.20	154	11.24a	152
3.22	228	11.25–30	179
4.10	154	11.26	153, 199
4.11	99	11.26b,c	154
4.26	154	11.26c	152
5.42	154	11.27–30	154
6.1–8.4	4	11.28	129
6.3	152	12.1–23	155
6.5	144	12.6–11	155
6.8	147	12.15	155
6.8–8.1	155	12.20–4	155
6.8–8.1a	146	12.24–5	155
6.9	152	13.1	152, 155, 156
6.10	147, 181	13.1–3	155, 169
6.11–14	147	13.2	129
6.15	147	13.15ff.	157
7.2–53	157	13.23	157
7.51–3	147	13.33	157
7.54–6	147	14.26–8	155
8.1a	148	15	168
8.1–3	66, 152	15.1	158
8.1b,c	148	15.5	158
9.1	111, 148	15.6–7a	158
9.1–2	66	15.6–11	150, 151
9.2	149	15.7–11	158
9.3–4	149	15.11	152
9.4–5	149	15.13–21	159
9.4–6	149	15.19	159
9.7–8	149	15.20	159
9.13–16	149	15.22	156
9.15	149	15.26	98, 159
9.18–22	149	15.29	159
9.20	125	15.30–2	159
9.21	122	15.30–3	156
9.23–30	149	16.1–3	97
9.26–8	179	17.1–6	130
10.1–8	150	17.3	154
10.1–48	150	17.6	148
10.9–17a	150	17.8	159
10.28	150	17.13	159
10.34–43	150	18.5	154
10.36	150, 154	20.7	169
10.43	150	20.11	169
10.45–7	150	20.19	98, 159
11.1–18	151	20.19–20	174
11.1–48	150	20.21	154
11.2	176	20.24	152
11.19	152	20.27	174
11.19a	146, 152	20.32	152
11.19b	152, 153	21.25	159
11.19–20	155	21.28	147
11.20b	152	21.37–22.5	66
11.23	152	22.3	122
		22.5	149

22.6–7	149	4.3–13	194
22.7–10	149	4.9–12	177
22.15	149	4.12	177
23.6	66, 122	4.13–16	208
24.14	122	4.16	177
24.24	154	4.25	228
25.14	130	5–8	208
25.16	181	5.11	208
26.4–11	66	5.13	222
26.9–12	149	5.14	215
26.13–14	149	5.19	103
26.14–15	149	5.20	222
26.16–18	149	5.20–1	221
26.23	154	6.1–11	204
26.28	154	6.3	204
28.17	122, 147	6.10	226
		6.12–14	224
Romans		6.12–23	220
1–3	192	6.13–20	194
1.1	176	6.14	198, 220, 221
1.17	175, 194, 199	6.15	198
2.14	192	6.23	224
2.14–15	192	7	124, 220
2.15	196	7.1	224
2.23	215	7.1–6	221
2.25	215	7.1–25	220
2.25–9	177	7.1–8.11	80, 190, 215, 216, 219, 221
2.26	215		
2.27	192, 215	7.1a	221
3.1–8	184	7.1b–3	221
3.5	110	7.4	218, 221
3.7	192	7.4–6	220
3.8	192	7.4a	221
3.9	197	7.4b	221
3.19	121	7.5	221, 227
3.19–20	220	7.5–6	224
3.19a	221	7.6	220, 224
3.20	196	7.6a,b	221
3.21–6	54, 86, 87, 90, 163, 194, 196, 200, 208, 209, 211, 219, 226	7.6b	221
		7.6c	221
		7.7–12	223
		7.7–25	221
3.21–31	194	7.7a	222
3.24	227	7.7b	222
3.24–6	87	7.8a	222
3.25	87, 88, 89	7.8b	222
3.25a	87	7.9–10	209, 215
3.26	177	7.9–11	222
3.27	217	7.12	222
3.27–31	177	7.12ff.	223
3.28	196	7.13	222, 223
3.30	177, 205	7.13–25	124, 220
4.1	208	7.13a	222
4.1–3	103	7.14	197, 223

Index of passages

Romans (cont.)

7.14b	220, 224
7.15–20	223, 227
7.18	223
7.20	209
7.21	223
7.21–5	222, 223
7.22–3	223–4
7.23	221, 224
7.24	220
7.24–25a	224
7.24a	220
7.25	221
7.25b	224
8.1	224
8.1–3	208
8.1–11	220, 224
8.2	217, 220, 224
8.3	109, 211, 225
8.3–4	225
8.9–11	220
8.10	221
8.12–17	178
8.14–18	103
8.18ff.	105
8.32	228
9–11	223
9.3–5	66
9.5	199
9.6b	190
9.7	104
9.30b	191
9.30–2	215
9.30–10.10	194
10.3	194
10.16b	202
11.1	66, 104
11.36	83
12.2	172, 224
12.7–8	157
12.9a	179
12.10a	179
12.14	122
13.2	181
14.8–9	226
14.15	228
15.1–3	113
15.3	181, 199
15.7	199
15.7–9	210
15.8	177
15.19	103
15.20	214
15.26	135
15.30–1	130
16.27	83

1 Corinthians

1.9	132
1.12ff.	4
1.13	199, 228
1.28	99
2.6–8	106
2.16	224
3.3	110
3.9	214
3.13	172
4.1–2	209
4.8–13	130
4.12	122
7.17–19	177
7.18–19	97
8.6	109
9.1	123
9.9	186
9.21	217
9.24–7	130
10	204
10.2	204
10.4	199
10.16	132, 169
10.16–17	170, 172
10.21	170
10.31–3	113
11.2	117
11.17–33	170
11.20–1	169, 171
11.22–9	104
11.23–4	228
11.23–6	170
11.23–33	203
11.24	169, 228
11.27	171
11.27–9	187
11.27–34	171
11.29	172
11.30	172
11.30–2	172
11.33–4	171
12.10	103
12.12	199
12.12–13	203
12.13	203
12.26	103
12.28	103
14.3–12	214
14.6	129
14.26	129

Index of passages

15.1–11	117	12.19	214
15.3	117, 228	13.3–4	184, 214
15.8–10	123	13.5	227
15.9	122	13.8	184
15.9–10	229	13.10	214
15.29–31	172		
15.32	110	Galatians	
		1.1	115
2 Corinthians		1.1a	111
1.3–12	157	1.1b	111
1.6	103	1.4	106, 123, 228
3	211	1.5	83
4.4	106	1.6	96, 105, 125
4.4–6	123	1.6–7a	104
4.9	122	1.6–7	108
4.10	101	1.6–9	95, 111, 116
4.15	229	1.7	159
4.16	224	1.7b	101
5.9	113	1.8	107, 112
5.11	113	1.8–9	97, 98, 105
5.11b	127	1.9	112
5.16	113	1.10	110, 111, 114, 115, 122
5.16–21	211		
5.21	194	1.10–12	93, 106, 108, 109, 110, 114, 115
6.5	101		
6.6	179	1.11	118, 130
6.10	135	1.11b	110
8.9	135, 181	1.11–12	111, 115, 117
10	179	1.12	118
10–13	182	1.12a,b	111
10.1	181	1.12c	110, 130
10.2	181	1.13	100, 223
10.4	181	1.13a	121
10.7a	182	1.13b–14	121
10.8	214	1.13ff.	116
10.10	99	1.13–14	55, 66, 86, 122, 143, 148, 149, 185, 214
10.10–11	116		
11.1–15	211		
11.4–15	108	1.13–16	196, 218, 219
11.5–6	116	1.13–16a	112
11.7	182, 183	1.13–17	117, 120
11.10	182	1.13–2.10	11, 15, 94, 114, 115, 119
11.10a	183		
11.12–13	116	1.13–2.21	93
11.21b–22	66	1.15–16	176
11.21b–29	98	1.15–16a	123
11.22	66	1.16	88, 99, 110, 128, 149
11.23	101		
11.23–4	187	1.16a	130, 227
11.23–9	128	1.16b	124
11.27	101	1.16b–17	125
11.29	122	1.16c	124
11.32–3	125, 149	1.16–17	123
12.9–12	103	1.17	69

272 Index of passages

Galatians (*cont.*)		2.14–15	193
1.17–2.10	96	2.14b–21	212
1.17a	124	2.14c	213
1.17b,c	125	2.14c,d	184
1.18	117, 127	2.15	184, 189, 190, 191, 192, 205, 207, 210
1.18a	126		
1.18–24	126		
1.19	127	2.15–17	216
1.20	127	2.15–17a	213
1.22	121, 128, 199	2.15–18	207, 213
1.22–3	118	2.15–21	11, 15, 90, 108, 109, 161, 162, 188, 189, 199, 221, 228, 229, 232
1.23	66, 109, 122, 128, 149		
1.24	100, 128		
2	117		
2.1–2a	129	2.15ff.	216, 217, 219
2.1–2	129	2.16	4, 8, 9, 150, 189, 192, 193, 194, 196, 199, 201, 206, 213, 215, 221, 226
2.1–10	126, 129, 168		
2.2	118, 130, 133, 203		
2.2b	130		
2.2c	116, 130	2.16a	8
2.2–4	116	2.16a,b	201
2.3	97, 102, 131	2.16a,d	201
2.3–5	97, 129, 131, 179, 185	2.16b	203, 204, 214
		2.16b–d	8
2.4	121, 131, 196, 199	2.16c	202, 205
		2.16d	205
2.4–5	131, 176	2.17	121, 156, 190, 194, 199, 206, 208, 209, 211, 222, 226
2.5	2		
2.6	130, 133		
2.6c	132		
2.6–10	129	2.17a	191
2.7	132	2.17b	206, 210
2.7–9	116, 118, 169, 177	2.17c	209
		2.17–20	197, 198
2.8	116	2.17–21	212
2.9	130, 132, 133, 169, 229	2.18	190, 212, 213, 215, 217, 218
2.10	116, 135	2.18a	214
2.11	173, 180	2.19	80, 190, 213, 217, 219, 221
2.11–14	15, 97, 161, 162, 169, 197, 232		
		2.19a	171, 229
2.11–21	1, 16, 53, 93, 114, 138, 145, 161, 162, 191, 212, 217, 220	2.19b	171
		2.19b–20	102
		2.19–20	99, 107, 109, 190, 204, 212, 216, 217, 219, 223, 225, 226
2.11ff.	4, 5, 6, 151, 162, 169		
2.12a	164	2.19–21	97, 124, 208
2.12b	174	2.20	88, 110, 111, 123, 170, 172, 176, 200, 202, 209, 216, 224
2.12–13	173		
2.13	171, 178		
2.14	97, 102, 131, 180, 189, 196		
		2.20a	227

Index of passages

2.20b	227	4.11	130
2.20d	171	4.12a	98
2.20–1	203, 214, 226	4.12b	98
2.21	7, 173, 194, 217, 221, 228	4.12–20	95, 98, 99, 100, 112, 119, 124
2.21a	190, 227, 228	4.13	98, 159
2.21b	190, 227, 229	4.13–15	98
3–4	117, 199	4.14	104, 107, 124, 147, 155
3.1	96, 97, 102, 104, 182, 189	4.14a	98, 101
3.1–5	97, 98, 101, 102, 108, 203	4.14b,c	99
		4.15	99
3.1–6.18	100	4.15a	99
3.2	196, 197, 200	4.16	99, 196
3.3	104, 108	4.16–20	100
3.5	103, 196, 197, 200	4.17	101, 105
		4.19	97, 99
3.6	194	4.21	97, 109
3.6ff.	103	4.21–31	107
3.7	200	4.25–6	97
3.7–10	177	4.25bc–26	107
3.8	194	4.29	97, 101, 103, 108
3.9	200	4.29–30	105
3.10	196, 197, 215	4.30	101
3.11	105, 175, 194, 199, 200	5–6	117
		5.1	105
3.12	171	5.2–12	97
3.13	109, 218, 219, 225, 226	5.3	96, 97, 197
		5.4	105
3.14	199	5.5	104, 194
3.16	204	5.6	178
3.19	215	5.6–12	184
3.19–25	219	5.7	182, 196
3.19–26	220	5.7a	98, 104
3.21	194	5.7b–8	104
3.22	200	5.7–8	113
3.23–5	109	5.7–12	97
3.24	194, 200	5.10	96, 101, 159
3.26	199	5.10b	104, 105
3.26–9	199, 203	5.11	97, 104, 108, 112, 177
3.27	199		
3.27a	203	5.11a	97
3.28	199	5.11b	97
3.29	199	5.11c	104
4.1–7	199	5.12	101, 104
4.3	107, 197	5.13	182
4.4–5	219	5.15	105
4.4–6	109	5.17	101, 103, 108
4.5–6	225, 226	5.24	199, 200
4.6	97, 103, 123	6.2	172, 199, 200, 217
4.8–9	96		
4.8–11	105	6.4	172
4.9	107	6.7–8	105
4.9–10	197	6.8b	105
4.10	97	6.10	109

Index of passages

Galatians (*cont.*)
6.11–17	101	1.24–2.1	130
6.12	96, 97, 104, 185	1.29	103
6.12b	102	2.6	117
6.12c	102	2.8	110
6.12–13	97, 129, 177, 227	2.11	177
6.12–14	97	3.11	177
6.12–15	107	4.14	145
6.13	96, 108		
6.13a	97	1 Thessalonians	
6.15–16	105	2.2ff.	130
6.16	117, 123	2.3	157
6.17	97, 101, 102	2.4	113, 172
6.17b	98	2.13–16	130
		2.14	103
		2.14–16	128
Ephesians		2.15	122
1.3–12	184	2.15–16	147
2.11	177	2.18–19	157
2.11–22	132	3.2	157
2.21	214	3.5	130
4.12	214	3.11–13	157
4.16	214	4–5	71
4.20–4	110	4.1	117
4.29	214	5.11	214
6.13	181	5.12–13	156

Philippians		2 Thessalonians	
1.5	132	2	87
1.10	172	2.4	71
1.27–30	130, 202	2.1–12	71
1.29	103	2.13–14	184
1.30	124		
2.1ff	157	1 Timothy	
2.1–4	210	4.12	121
2.5–11	210, 226		
2.6–8	109, 209	2 Timothy	
2.8	181	3.8	181
2.12–18	210	4.18	83
3.2–3	177		
3.4–5	218	Philemon	
3.4–6	66	6	132
3.5	66	24	145
3.6	121, 122		
3.9	194	Hebrews	
3.9a	209	2.15	171
3.10	132	10.19–39	174
3.12–15	130	10.23	174
		10.26–8	174
Colossians		10.26–31	172
1.3–7	210	10.28–29a	174
1.3–8	184	10.32–4	175
1.15–19	109	10.38	175
1.21–4	121	10.39	175
1.24	98, 101	11.1–40	175

Index of passages 275

11.4–40	157	10.2	75
12.1–2	175	10.3–6	75
12.22	107	10.8–10	75
13.7	121, 156		
13.17	156	*1 Enoch*	
13.21	83	14.18	45
13.22	157	37–71	47, 104
13.24	156	38–44	49
		38.2	33
James		38.4	33
2.8	192	38.6	33
2.10	171	46.1	50, 147
2.12	192	46.1–3	50
4.7	181	47–57	49
		47.3	50
1 Peter		48.8–10	50
1.22	179	49.2–4	50
4.1–2	110	52.4	50
4.12–16	154	58–69	49
5.9	181	60.2	45
passim	121	62–3	123
		62.2	50
2 Peter		62.14	50, 173
passim	121	70–1	49, 50
		85–90	105
1 John		90.19	37
3.20	186	90.20	45
		90.34	37
Revelation			
3.12	107	*Epistles of Aristeas*	
21.2	107	181ff.	167
21.10	107	219	178
		267	178

4. PSEUDEPIGRAPHA

Ezekiel the Tragedian
passim 49

Apocalypse of Baruch/2 Baruch			
36–40	51	*Joseph and Aseneth*	
57.1–2	103	7.1	166
Assumption of Moses		*Jubilees*	
5–10	73	17.15–18	103
6–7	73	21.2	103
6.1–7.10	73	22.16	166, 191
6.2	74	23.13–14	191
6.8–9	74	24.28	191
7	74		
8	74	*Psalms of Solomon*	
8–9	73	2.1–2	191
8–10	73	4	178
8.1–9.7	73	5.2	135
8.1–5	70	5.13	135
9	24, 74	17.26	43, 51
9.1	75	17.42–4	43
10	75		

Index of passages

Sibylline Oracles	
5.108–109	52
5. 414–33	52

Testament of Benjamin	
9.3	99

Testament of Levi	
16.2	99

5. DEAD SEA SCROLLS

1QS 9.11	228
1QSa	48
4Q169	74
4Q246	
1.1–4	47
1.2	48
1.4–6	48
1.4–2.3	48
1.7–2.1	48
2.1	47, 49
2.1–3	49
2.2–3	47, 48
2.4	47
2.4–9	48
2.5	47
2.7a	47
2.7b	47
4Q369	48
4QFlor	48
4QpHab 7.10	74
11QMelch	49

6. PHILO

Legatio ad Gaium	
188	68
197–227	67
198	68
199–205	67
207	68
233	113
240	113
242	113
346	68
passim	67

In Flaccum	
passim	67

7. JOSEPHUS

Against Apion	
2.29	141
2.39	139

Antiquities	
8.387	132
10.203–10	28, 61
12	74
12.119	139
12.120	141, 142, 167
12.121 4	141
12.138–46	20
12.199	141
12.237–14.79	22
12.240	23
12.251–54	23
12.252	23
12.253	24
12.290–92	31
12.316–25	24
12.319	76
12.324–25	76
12.383–5	25
12.385	21
12.412	76
13.163	62
13.171–73	63
13.198–99	31, 156
13.212	32
13.288–98	63
13.297	122
13.372–3	63
13.399–404	63
13.408	122
13.408–18	63
14.117	143
14.172–76	63
15.1–4	63
15.365	69
15.370	64
16.149	59
17.41–5	64
17.149	64
17.149–67	64
17.152	64
17.168–70	155
17.273–84	61
18.4–10	65
18.90	69
18.111–12	69
18.256–309	67
18.256ff.	68
18.262	68
18.263–72	58
18.287	68
18.302	68
18.328	132
19.278–91	67
19.332–4	65

20.62	132	132–5	116
20.200–2	65	149	102
		189–90	116
Jewish War		189–98	65
1.31–58	22	197	63
1.88–9	63	270	63
1.110–14	63	424–6	116
1.185–7	68		
1.425	57		
1.571–73	64	## 8. RABBINIC TEXTS	
1.635	186		
1.648–55	64	Mishnah	
1.656	155	*m. Bik.* 1.6	76
2.57–98	61	*m. Shab.* 1.4	65
2.118	65	*m. Rosh HaSh.* 1.3	76
2.184	68	*m. Taan.* 2.10	76
2.184–98	58	*m. Meg.* 3.4, 6	76
2.184–203	67	*m. Moed Q.* 3.9	76
2.185	68	*m. B. Qam.* 6.6	76
2.185–7	68		
2.186	68	Babylonian Talmud	
2.201	69	*b. Shab.* 13b	65, 76
2.409–10	68	*b. Hag.* 14a	52
2.433	65	*b. Sanh.* 38b	52
2.433–9	61		
2.451	63	Palestinian Talmud	
2.454	185	*y. Shab.* 1,3c	65
2.457–79	140	*y. Sanh.* 29c	86
2.462–3	185		
2.591ff.	167	Tosefta	
3.29	138	*t. Shab.* 1.16–20	65
4.159	65		
5–6	61	Midrash	
6.312–15	61	*Lev. Rab.* 4.3	144
6.316	58	*Deut. Rab.* 4.8	144
6.318–20	132	*Lam. Rab.* 2.9	86
6.345	132	*Cant. Rab.* 7.8	134
6.356	132		
6.378	132	## 9. GREEK AND ROMAN AUTHORS	
7.25–36	61		
7.43–4	142		
7.44	139		
7.45	143, 144	Epictetus	
7.46–53	141	*Disc.* 2.9.19–20	178
7.47	140		
7.52	140	Livy	
7.100–3	141	41.20.1–4	21
7.108–11	141		
7.153–4	61	Malalas	
7.154	186	43.10	69
7.327	186	44.15–245.1	140
Life		Polybius	
74	167	26.1	21
113	102		

Suetonius
    Claud. 25.4   153

Tacitus
    Ann. 15.44   140, 153
    Hist. 5.8   21
    Hist. 5.9   67, 68

10. EARLY CHRISTIAN TEXTS

Augustine
    In solemnitate
        martyrum
        Machabaeorum
        (*PL* 38.1379) 84

Chrysostom
    Adversus Judaeos
        1.3   143
    Adversus Judaeos
        5.3   143
    Adversus Judaeos
        5.4   86
    Adversus Judaeos
        5.7   86
    Adversus Judaeos
        6.2   86
    De sanctis
        martyribus
        sermo 1 (*PG* 50.
        647)   85
    In santos
        Maccabaeos
        homilia 1,1 (*PG*
        50.617)   85

Clement of Rome
    1 Clem. 5   175
    1 Clem. 5–6   3
    1 Clem. 5.2   134

Didache
    12.4   154

Eusebius
    HE 3.5.4   58

Ignatius
    Eph. 11.2   154
    Eph. 18.2   203
    Eph. 20.2   203
    Mag. 10.3   185, 203
    Pol. 7.1   154
    Rom. 3.2   154, 209
    Rom. 7.3   203
    Trall. 9.1   203

Gregory of Nazianzus
    In laudem
        Machabaeorum
        (Oration 15)
        (*PG* 35.911–34) 85

Justin Martyr
    Dial. 32.1   52

Libanius
    Ep. 1251   143

Martyrdom of Polycarp
    7.3   147
    12.1   147

Polycarp
    Phil. 8.1–2   203
    Phil. 9.2   203

SELECT INDEX OF GREEK WORDS AND PHRASES

αἷμα, 87, 89
ἀλήθεια, 81, 183–4
ἁμαρτία, 210, 211, 223, 224
ἁμαρτωλός, 190, 207, 210
ἀναγκάζω, 34, 80, 97, 102, 140, 184, 185
ἀναστατόω, 101
   see οἱ ἀναστατοῦντες
βαπτίζω, 203–4
διάκονος, 156, 210–11
διδόναι δεξιάν, 31, 36, 132
δίκαιος, 175, 186, 194, 195, 199
δικαιοσύνη, 29, 32, 183, 194–5, 203, 208, 227, 229
   δικαιοσύνη θεοῦ, 194, 200
δικαιόω, 186, 193, 194, 202
ἐγώ, 216, 218, 220, 222–4, 225–7
ἐθνικῶς, 184, 185
ἐν ἐμοί, 29, 88, 123–4, 128, 183, 222, 227
εὑρίσκω, 29, 154, 208–9
ἱλαστήριον, 82, 87, 89, 211, 226
Ἰουδαΐζειν, 184, 185, 203
Ἰουδαϊκῶς, 184
Ἰουδαϊσμός, 33, 36, 80, 121, 143, 171
   ἐν τῷ Ἰουδαϊσμῷ, 35, 121, 122, 143
ἱστορῆσαι Κηφᾶν, 126–7
κατὰ ἄνθρωπον, 110, 111, 118, 125, 130, 133
κατὰ ἀποκάλυψιν, 118, 129–30
κατὰ πρόσωπον, 180–2
κατὰ σάρκα/σάρκα, 113, 125, 181
καταλύω, 36, 80, 82, 212–14, 218
λογισμός, 79, 181–2, 192
λόγος παρακλήσεως, 157, 159, 160
   παράκλησις, 147, 157, 159
μετατίθημι, 35, 104
νόμος, 172, 217, 222
   διὰ νόμου, 171, 190, 208, 216, 217, 218–22, 225, 229, 232
   διὰ τῆς ἐντολῆς, 220, 222

   see οἱ ἐκ νόμου
   τὰ ἔργα τοῦ νόμου, 193, 196–8
οἱ ἀναστατοῦντες, 101
οἱ δοκοῦντες, 133–4
οἱ ἐκ νόμου, 177
οἱ ἐκ περιτομῆς, 150, 176–8, 185, 191
οἱ ἐκ πίστεως, 177, 200
οἱ περιτεμνόμενοι, 96, 177
οἱ πτωχοί, 135
οἱ ταράσσοντες, 30, 32, 101, 159
   ὁ ταράσσων, 96
οἱ τοῦ Χριστοῦ, 153, 200
παραβαίνω, 35, 214–15
παραβάτης, 212–15
πείθω, 35, 112–13, 122
περὶ ἁμαρτίας, 211, 224
πιστεύω, 202–4, 214
πίστις, 32, 89, 175, 198, 200, 203, 227
   διὰ τῆς πίστεως, 87, 89
   ἐκ πίστεως, 175
   ἐξ ἀκοῆς πίστεως, 103, 200, 203
   see also οἱ ἐκ πίστεως
πίστις Ἰησοῦ Χριστοῦ, 10, 103, 193, 198–200, 205, 209
   διὰ πίστεως Ἰησοῦ Χριστοῦ, 198, 200
   διὰ πίστεως Χριστοῦ, 209
   ἐκ πίστεως Χριστοῦ, 205
πολιτεία, 22, 36, 82, 134, 141–3, 160, 167, 214
πολίτευμα, 22, 142
πορθέω, 80, 122, 214
στῦλοι, 82, 133, 134
τὰ ἔργα τοῦ νόμου, *see* νόμος
ὑποκρίνομαι, 34, 81, 178
συνυποκρίνομαι, 178
ὑπόκρισις, 34, 171, 178
Χριστιανισμός, 203
Χριστιανός/Χριστιανοί, 151, 152–4
Χριστός, 110–11, 121, 131, 133, 153, 172, 183, 193, 198–200, 202–4, 209–10, 217, 221, 227

Χριστός (cont.)
  εἰς Χριστόν ['Ιησοῦν], 202–4
  ἐν Χριστῷ ['Ιησοῦ], 121, 128, 131, 199
  see also οἱ τοῦ Χριστοῦ; πίστις 'Ιησοῦ
    Χριστοῦ and subentries
  Χριστῷ συνεσταύρωμαι, 102, 216,
    218, 225

INDEX OF MODERN AUTHORS

Abegg, Martin, 197
Abel, F. M., 30, 33
Agus, Aharon, 27, 134
Alon, G., 61, 76, 166
Althaus, P., 207
Amir, Y., 121, 143
Auvray, P., 3

Baasland, E., 99, 100
Bachmann, Michael, 213
Balsdon, J. P. V. D., 67
Bammel, E., 83, 85, 86, 128, 135
Barclay, John M. G., 7, 55, 78, 95, 97, 105, 108, 115, 117, 118, 119, 139, 142, 166, 191, 213, 218
Bar-Kochva, Bezalel, 24, 30, 33
Barré, M. L., 98
Barrett, C. K., 96, 107
Bartlett, John R., 30
Bauckham, R. J., 134, 159, 179
Baumeister, Theofried, 13
Baur, F. C., 4–5, 6
Beasley-Murray, G. R., 46
Betz, H. D., 96, 102, 105, 107, 127, 132, 135, 164, 178, 183, 212, 217, 218
Beyer, H. W., 207
Beyer, K., 75
Bickerman(n), E. J., 22, 78, 84, 85, 153
Bilde, P., 67, 68
Bittner, W., 45
Black II, C. C., 157
Black, M., 44, 45, 50
Bockmuehl, Markus N. A., 139, 141, 144, 166, 167, 168
Boismard, M.-E., 146
Bornkamm, G., 194
Böttger, Paul C., 213
Boyarin, Daniel, 7
Brauch, Manfred T., 194
Breitenstein, U., 78

Breytenbach, C., 145
Bring, R., 213
Bringmann, K., 22, 23
Brown, R. E., 94
Bruce, F. F., 145
Bultmann, R., 183, 194, 207, 213, 220
Burton, Ernest de Witt, 105, 107, 111, 112, 125, 132, 133, 164, 176, 183, 186, 218

Campbell, D. A., 78, 194
Caragounis, Chrys, 45
Casey, P. M., 44
Catchpole, D. R., 129
Charles, R. H., 73
Charlesworth, J. H., 38
Ciampa, Roy E., 101, 114, 121
Cohn-Sherbok, Dan, 38
Collins, J. J., 27, 38, 40, 43, 44, 45, 46, 47, 48, 49, 50, 52, 55
Conzelmann, H., 194
Cook, Edward, 47, 48
Coppens, J., 49
Cousar, Charles B., 133
Cranfield, C. E. B., 192, 194, 197, 220
Crossan, John Dominic, 68
Cullmann, O., 47, 155
Cummins, S. A., 98, 99, 100, 147, 155

Davies, Philip R., 28
Deines, Roland, 61
Delcor, M., 27
deSilva, David A., 77
Di Lella, Alexander A., 27, 44
Dindorf, Wilhelm, 69, 84, 140
Dodd, Brian J., 114
Donaldson, T. L., 7, 109, 122
Doran, R., 53
Downey, G., 139, 140, 141
Duncan, G. S., 129

Dunn, James D. G., 1, 2, 7–10, 96, 102, 103, 109, 120, 121, 122, 127, 133, 135, 164, 165, 166, 168, 176, 184, 191, 192, 194, 196, 197, 200, 202, 207, 210, 217, 219, 220
Dupont-Sommer, André, 78

Efron, Joshua, 28, 76
Ehrman, Bart D., 3
Emerton, J. A., 45
Esler, Philip F., 166

Fairchild, Mark R., 122
Farmer, W. R., 54, 56, 57–9, 61, 76, 122
Fee, Gordon D., 170
Feldman, Louis H., 20, 55
Feuillet, A., 45
Fischel, H. A., 13, 146
Fischer, T., 20
Fitzmyer, Joseph A., 47
Flusser, D., 47, 48, 49
Frend, W. H. C., 13
Fung, R. Y. K., 126, 127

Gafni, Isayah, 65
Gaventa, B. R., 115, 116, 117–18, 119
Goddard, A. J., 98, 99, 100, 147, 155, 212
Goldingay, John, 27, 28, 29, 44
Goldstein, Jonathan A., 22, 30, 33, 35
Goodblatt, D., 62
Goodman, Martin, 56, 64
Grabbe, Lester L., 20, 22, 23, 24, 25, 55
Greenfield, Jonas C., 49
Gruen, Erich S., 21

Haacker, K., 66
Habicht, C., 21, 33
Hadas, M., 83
Haenchen, Ernst, 152
Hall, R. G., 117
Hann, Robert R., 139
Hansen, G. Walter, 96, 103
Hanson, John S., 56
Hartman, Louis F., 27, 44, 70
Harvey, A. E., 187
Hay, David M., 133
Hayes, John H., 55
Hays, Richard B., 103, 175, 200, 208
Head, Peter, 52
Heard, W. J., 12, 87, 170
Hengel, Martin, 20, 21, 54, 56, 57, 59–61, 62, 66, 86, 87, 122, 126, 127, 139, 140, 141, 145, 153, 168, 198

Hill, Craig C., 4, 94, 146, 147, 165, 166, 176
Hill, David, 87
Hofius, O., 127
Holmberg, Bengt, 124
Hooker, M. D., 44
Horbury, William, 39–42, 43, 46, 49, 52, 83
Horsley, G. H. R., 153
Horsley, R. A., 56, 61
Howard, George, 96, 130
Humphreys, W. Lee, 28

Jeffreys, E., 140
Jeffreys, M., 140
Jeremias, J., 66
Jewett, R., 168
Johnson, L. T., 154, 158

Kampen, John, 24
Käsemann, E., 194
Kasher, Aryeh, 139, 140, 142, 143, 144, 167
Kellermann, U., 35
Kieffer, R., 2, 3, 218
Kim, S., 45, 47
Klauck, Hans-Josef, 77, 78, 79, 86
Kleinknecht, K. Th., 13
Knibb, Michael, 47, 50
Koch, Klaus, 46
Kolb, Frank, 139
Kraeling, Carl H., 84, 139, 140, 144
Kruse, Colin G., 7

Lambrecht, J., 212
Lampe, G. W. H., 103, 124, 128, 181
Lane, William, 156
Lategan, B. C., 110, 119
Levinskaya, Irina, 139
Licht, J., 73
Lichtenstein, Hans, 75, 76
Lightfoot, J. B., 96, 183, 186
Lincoln, A. T., 107
Lohmeyer, E., 12
Longenecker, Bruce W., 99, 106
Longenecker, R. N., 96, 103, 105, 107, 109, 124, 128, 133, 176, 177, 186, 207, 212, 213, 217, 228
Lüderitz, Gert., 142
Lührmann, D., 169
Lyons, G., 115, 116, 118, 119

McDonald, James I. H., 157

Index of modern authors

Maier, J. P., 145
Mandell, Sara R., 55
Mantel, H., 75
Martin, Troy W., 99
Martyn, J. L., 102, 106, 107, 169, 176, 183, 189
Mason, S. N., 62
Matera, F. J., 102, 109
Meeks, Wayne A., 143, 144, 145, 170
Mendels, D., 56, 61, 65
Michel, O., 12
Milik, J. T., 47, 48
Millar, F., 20
Moessner, D., 146
Montgomery, James A., 27
Moo, Douglas, 220
Mørkholm, Otto, 21
Moule, C. F. D., 44, 71
Müller, C., 194
Munck, J., 96
Mundle, Wilhelm, 146
Murphy-O'Connor, Jerome, 66
Mußner, F., 2, 95, 96, 101, 105, 107, 123, 133, 164, 182, 183, 186, 189, 207, 212, 213, 218

Nanos, Mark D., 165, 220
Neitzel, H., 191, 212, 217
Neusner, Jacob, 38, 61, 62
Nickelsburg, George W. E., 49, 52, 71, 73
Niebuhr, K.-W., 121

Obermann, J., 84, 85
Oegema, Gerben S., 38
Oepke, A., 105
Orchard, B., 131

Pfitzner, Victor C., 130
Plöger, O., 27
Pobee, J. S., 13, 27, 101, 103, 146, 187
Pomykala, Kenneth E., 38
Porteous, Norman W., 27, 44
Priest, J., 73
Procksch, O., 45
Puech, Emile, 47, 48

Räisänen, Heikki, 147
Rajak, Tessa, 20
Rampolla, Card [y Tindaro], 83, 84
Renehan, R., 79
Rhoads, David M., 62
Richardson, P., 96
Rohde, J., 129, 132

Rowland, Christopher C., 44, 45
Ruppert, L., 13

Safrai, Samuel, 55
Saldarini, Anthony J., 61, 62, 64
Sanders, E. P., 6–7, 55, 61, 165, 166, 218
Sanders, Jack T., 117
Schäfer, Peter, 61
Schatkin, Margaret, 83, 84, 85
Schlier, H., 105, 121, 164, 183
Schmidt, N., 44
Schreiner, T. R., 7, 196, 197, 220
Schunck, K.-D., 30
Schürer, E., 20, 22, 30, 51, 55, 61, 65, 67, 75
Schütz, John Howard, 117, 169
Schwartz, Daniel R., 68
Schwemer, Anna Maria, 86, 87, 126, 127, 139, 140, 141, 145, 153, 168
Scott, R., 140
Scott, R. B. Y., 45
Seifrid, M. A., 194
Sievers, Joseph, 22, 24, 26, 30, 33, 62
Slater, Thomas B., 44, 45
Smallwood, E. Mary, 67, 139, 140, 142
Steck, O., 13
Stein, S., 76
Stemberger, G., 61–2
Stern, Menachem, 55
Stinespring, W. F., 84
Stone, Michael E., 49, 51
Stuhlmacher, P., 194
Suhl, Alfred, 191–2
Surkau, Hans-Werner, 12
Suter, D. W., 49

Tannehill, R. C., 218
Taylor, Justin, 153–4
Taylor, N. H., 67, 68, 69, 71, 72, 120, 140, 145
Tcherikover, V., 20, 22, 23, 142
Theisöhn, Johannes, 50
Theissen, Gerd, 67, 68, 69–70
Thielman, Frank, 7
Tödt, H. E., 47
Tomson, P., 166, 167, 168
Trebilco, Paul, 142, 144
Tromp, Johannes, 73, 74, 75

VanderKam, J. C., 49, 50
van Henten, J. W., 1, 12–14, 33, 35, 77, 78, 79, 80, 81, 82, 87–90, 134, 171
Verseput, D. J., 118

von Campenhausen, H., 13

Walter, N., 127
Watson, Francis, 7, 96, 117, 131
Weber, Reinhard, 79
Wechsler, A., 2, 5, 212
Wenham, David, 71, 126
Westerholm, Stephen, 7, 196
Wilken, Robert L., 143, 144, 145
Williams, S. K., 13, 83, 85, 87, 103
Wills, Lawrence, 157

Windisch, H., 148
Winter, Bruce W., 145
Witherington III, Ben, 46, 95, 196
Wright, N. T., 54, 55, 56, 61–5, 122, 194, 195, 199, 204, 208, 210, 211, 220
Wright, W., 84

Zeitlin, S., 75, 76
Ziesler, J. A., 212, 220
Zumstein, Jean, 145

SELECT INDEX OF NAMES AND SUBJECTS

Abraham, and
  Galatian Agitators, 97
  Galatian brethren, 103–4, 199, 200, 203, 204, 208, 216, 226
  Maccabean martyrs, 82, 191
Adam, see Israel-in-Adam
Agitators, the Galatian, 95–8, 100–2, 104–6, 108–14
Antioch, city of, 138ff.
  Christian community, 145–59
    called 'Christians', 152–5
    Jerusalem meeting/decree, 157–9
    prophet-martyr figures/leaders, 146–51, 155–7
  Jewish community, 139–45
    history, 139–41
    life and politeia, 141–5, 167–8
  see Maccabean martyrdom (martyr cult and Antioch)
Antioch incident, interpretations of
  exegesis and apologetics, 5–6
  Luther and Baur, 4–5
  'new perspective' on, 6–9, 196–7
  patristic period, 2–3
Antiochus IV Epiphanes, and Daniel/*Daniel*, 28–9, 43–4, 183
  first-century Jewish nationalism, 58, 59
  the Jewish community in Antioch, 139, 142, 145
  Paul's Jewish(-Christian) detractors, 94, 131
  pre-Christian Paul, 122, 148, 149
  Stephen, 147, 148
  see Maccabean crisis/revolt,
apocalyptic discourse, Marcan, 67, 69–71
Apollonius, 148–9
Assumption of Moses, 73–5
atonement
  Maccabean martyrs, 35, 81, 87ff., 163

Paul, 87ff., 225–6
autobiography, Paul's
  'apologetic' and 'paradigm', 114–20
  Galatians 1.13–2.10, 120–35

baptism [into], 203–4, 214
Barnabas, 129, 152, 154–5, 178–9

Caligula Temple episode, 66–72, 76, 113, 126, 140, 153, 168
'Christians' in Antioch, 152–4
circumcision
  Agitators on, 96, 97, 102, 104, 108, 111, 112, 114
  Maccabean period, 23, 30, 31, 74, 131, 197
  'those of the circumcision', 150, 176–8, 185, 191
  Titus, 131
  see works of the law
conceptual framework, Paul's, 106–14

Daniel (figure) as exemplar
  martyrs of *4 Maccabees*, 79, 80, 82
  Paul, 104, 162, 179, 180–2
  Stephen, 104, 147, 181
Daniel (text)
  apocalyptic discourse, 70–1
  stories of contest/conflict, 27–30
  see Son of Man

Eleazar, the martyr, 34–5
eschatological redeemer
  table-fellowship, 173, 199
  see Jesus Christ

faith/faithfulness
  Galatian believers, 102–4
  Jesus' faithfulness, 198, 200–1
  Maccabees, 29, 32, 35, 81, 86–90
  Paul's 'logic of faith', 8–10

285

faith/faithfulness (cont.)
  Paul's paradigmatic example, 98–100
  Peter's failure of, 173–6
  Romans 3.21–6, 86–90
  see πίστις and related phrases*, righteousness (God's)

Galatian church and Paul, 95–106
  Galatian crisis, 95–8
  Paul's original ministry, 98–100
  Paul's current ministry, 100–6
gospel (Paul's), and
  autobiography, 114–20
  Galatians' reception of, 98–106
  Jerusalem apostles, 126–35
  mission, 109–14
  truth of, 94, 99, 104, 179–87
  versus the Agitators' 'non-gospel', 95ff., 108

Hanukkah, 24, 76, 78
Hasmoneans
  rule/dynasty, 22–6, 37, 48–9
  and Pharisees, 59, 62–4
Heliodorus, 22, 33, 58, 148–9, 152, 187

Israel-in-Adam and Israel-in-Christ, 109, 162–3, 190, 212–28

James, brother of Jesus, 65, 127, 134, 158–9, 164ff.
Jerusalem and/or its Temple
  attacked in the Maccabean period, 20–4, 29, 33, 43, 148–9, 183, 214
  and Jews in Antioch, 140, 141, 144
  Maccabean and first-century zeal for, 24, 36–7, 57–8
  within Paul's conceptual framework, 107
  'pillar' apostles, 184
  and the Pharisees, 64–5
  see Caligula Temple episode
Jerusalem apostles and/or church
  conference and decree, 157–9
  and the Galatian Agitators, 96–7, 109–10, 115ff.
  Paul's perspective on/relations with, 94, 109–10, 114ff., 124–35
  as 'pillars', 134
Jesus Christ, and
  belief/baptism in[to], 202–4
  'Christians' in Antioch, 152–4
  eschatological redeemer within Paul's conceptual framework, 99, 106–14, 119, 198–9
  faithfulness of, 198, 200–1, 225–8
  Lord's Supper, 169–73
  narrative substructure of Galatians 2.11–21, 162–4
  Paul's conformity to, 94–137
    in Galatia, 95–106
    in Jerusalem, 126–37
  Paul's transformation by, 120–6
  servant(s) of sin? 206–12
  title Χριστός, 198–200
  see Israel-in-Christ, and Χριστός*
Jewish(-Christian) opponents of Paul, 11, 229–30, 232
  in Jerusalem, 131
  and Maccabean opponents and apostates, 119–20, 129, 131
  their polemic, 190–3, 206ff.
  their rationale, 97
  see Agitators
Jewish nationalism, 40, 55–72
  Antioch incident, 7ff., 168, 176ff.
  Jewish War, 56, 60, 140–1, 167–8, 177
  Maccabean martyrdom, 55, 72
    Farmer and Hengel on, 56–61
    Pharisees (Wright), 61–5
    Paul, 66, 86
  see Caligula's Temple episode, Israel-in-Adam, messianism, Ἰουδαϊσμός and cognate terms*
justification
  Luther, 4–6
  Paul (esp. Gal 2.16ff.), 193–206, 206ff.

Lord's Supper (in Corinth), 169–73

Maccabean crisis/revolt, 20–6
Maccabean martyrdom
  in 2 Maccabees, 33–8
  in 4 Maccabees, 77–83
  martyr cult and Antioch, 83–6
  methodological considerations, 12–6
  Romans 3.21–6, 86–90
Maccabees, the
  Judas, 24–5
  Jonathan and Simon, 25–6
  saviours of Israel, 30–2
Megillath Taanith, 65, 67, 75–6, 168
messianism, Jewish
  development of, 39–42

Maccabean period, 42–6
messianic community in Antioch, esp.
    152–5
  see Israel-in-Christ, Jesus Christ,
    Jewish nationalism, Son of Man

persecution, conflict and
  in Antioch, 153–5, 162–4
  in Paul's Galatian ministry, 98–106
  pre-Christian Paul, 121–2, 126, 128
  see Antiochus IV Epiphanes, suffering
    and vindication
Peter
  initial meeting with Paul, 126–7
  Jerusalem agreement, 132–5
  prophet figure, 150–1
  table-fellowship in Antioch
    initial arrangement, 164–9
    withdrawal, 173–9
    confrontation by Paul, 179–87
  see Jerusalem apostles
Petronius, 58, 67, 68, 69, 71, 113, 140
Pharisees, 61–6
politeia, Jewish,
  and the Maccabees, 22, 35–6, 82, 134,
    214
  see Antioch, πολιτεία*
Prophet-martyr figures/leaders, see
    Antioch

Razi, 36, 171
righteousness
  Abraham, 103–4, 208–9
  God's righteousness (faithfulness), 37,
    90, 182–4, 193–6, 200–2, 204,
    208ff.
    see δικαιοσύνη θεοῦ*
  Maccabean period, 29, 31, 194–5
  'new perspective' on, 6ff.
  'righteous pillars', 134
  'servants of ...', 108, 211
Romans
  tradition-history of 3.21–6, 86–90
  excursus on 7.1–8.11, 219–25

servants of sin/God, 108, 128–9, 206–12
  Messiah Jesus as servant, 210–12
son of man, Daniel's
  as heavenly being, 44–5
  as Israel, 44
  as Israel's Messiah, 45–6

messianic interpretations of, 47–52
  4 Ezra, 51
  Parables of Enoch, 49–50
  4Q246, 47–9
Stephen, 146–7, 151, 152, 155, 157, 181
suffering and vindication, 10, 19
  early church/Galatians, 135, 147, 189,
    193–206, 226–8
  1 and 2 Maccabees, 26–38
  texts c. first century, 73–83, 88–9
  see Maccabean martyrdom,
    persecution

Table-fellowship in Antioch
  nature and significance, 164–9
  Lord's Supper, 169–73
  Peter's withdrawal, 173–9
  Paul's response, 179–87
Temple, see Jerusalem and/or its
    Temple
Torah
  'new perspective on', 6–8
  observance/obedience
    Agitators, 97–8, 102, 108–9, 111
    church in Antioch, 157–9, 184–7,
      190–3
    4 Maccabees, 79–81, 124, 190–1
  transgression, 32, 35, 37, 64, 74–5,
    80–1, 192, 212–6, 221–2
  see νόμος*, works of the law

vindication, see suffering and
    vindication

word of exhortation, 156–7
works of the law, 6–8, 193, 196–8, 205–
    6, 208–9
  see Israel-in-Adam

zeal
  Agitators, 100, 113
  first-century zealots/Zealots, 57–61
  Maccabean army and martyrs, 31–8,
    171
  Paul, 66, 95, 120–3, 125, 156, 223
  Pharisees, 61–5
  Phineas, 24, 59, 82

* see Index of Greek words and phrases